River
Plants

DATE DUE	DATE DUE	DATE DUE

5/08 K:/Proj/Acc&Pres/CIRC/DateDue.indd

River
Plants

The macrophytic vegetation of watercourses

SECOND REVISED EDITION

S.M. HASLAM M.A., Sc.D.

DEPARTMENT OF PLANT SCIENCES, UNIVERSITY OF CAMBRIDGE

ILLUSTRATED BY

P.A. WOLSELEY

FORREST

XXVI

Published by
FORREST TEXT
Sŵn y Nant, Tresaith, Cardigan, Ceredigion SA43 2JG, UK

© S.M. Haslam 1978, 2006

First published in Great Britain in 1978 by Cambridge University Press
This revised second edition published in Great Britain in 2006 by Forrest Text

ISBN   0-9550740-4-5

The designations of geographical entities in this book, and the presentation
of the material, do not imply the expressions of any opinion whatsoever on
the part of the publisher, the editors, or any other participating organisations
concerning the legal status of any country, territory, or area, or of its
authorities, or concerning the delimitation of its frontiers or boundaries.

British Library Cataloguing in Publication Data
Data available

Cover photographs
© Mark Everard

Printed & bound in Great Britain by
CPI Antony Rowe, Eastbourne

Paper produced from wood grown in sustainable forests

TO THE LATE DR A.S. WATT, FRS

Contents

Preface to the first edition

Water plants have received much less attention from botanists than have land plants, and the plants of steams have had the least attention. Arber's (1920) *Water plants* was the pioneer book on the larger aquatic plants, and describes how plants' structures are adapted to life in the water. Sculthorpe (1967) drew together much information in *The biology of aquatic vascular plants*. The early research on ecology, on how and why plants grow in some places and not in others, is summarised in Tansley's (1949) *The British Islands and their vegetation*. Since then, the water plants of lakes have received considerable attention, e.g. by Spence (1964) , who pointed out the importance of nutrients and water movement in controlling plant distribution. Butcher's (1927, 1933) classic papers on river plants described different types of stream vegetation, and the importance of currents, soil, shading, etc. in forming plant communities. Careful surveys of river vegetation have been carried out by Whitton and his colleagues, while Westlake and his colleagues have studied the physiology and productivity of chalk stream plants (see Bibliography).

This book describes the hitherto unpublished research of the author, except where the contrary is specifically stated. The parts of Chapter 8 relating plants to the nutrient status of streams are taken from the unpublished work of Mrs M.P. Everitt. It would not have been possible to write this book without the unfailing helpfulness of the Engineering, Fisheries and Pollution Prevention Departments of the River Authorities (now Water Authorities) of England and Wales, the River Purification Boards of Scotland and the Drainage Boards of England. The River Authorities, in particular, have provided what must have seemed to them endless information on plant distribution, channel maintenance, control of excessive plant growth, water analyses, effluents and pollution. To all, I express my sincerest thanks.

To make this book more easily understood by those who are not professional botanists:

(1) The contents of each chapter (except for Chapter 1) are summarised at the start of each.
(2) Towards the end of Chapter 1 is a section listing the most important river plants, classifying them according to their characteristic habitats, and illustrating them to show their typical appearance in streams.

(3) Small symbols are used, wherever possible, to represent the commonest species. They show some characteristic feature or habit of the plant, and should help to relate unfamiliar plant names to the relevant river plants.

(4) Figures have been provided wherever practical.

(5) A glossary is provided at the end of the text.

Streams are complex and diverse, a book of this type cannot include all possible variations in vegetation, so plants can be found away from the habitats which are described here as characteristic. The term 'plant' is used for the larger plants of watercourse, the flowering plants (angiosperms), horsetails and water fern (pteridophytes), mosses (byrophytes) and two groups of large algae occurring in watercourses — the stoneworts (Characeae) and *Enteromorpha*. The mosses are not otherwise named or distinguished. The smaller algae are usually excluded from the general text, but the microscopic floating algae, the phytoplankton, are referred to as causing turbidity in water and as forming part of the living entity of stream vegetation. In the illustrations of the vegetation along whole rivers, in Chapters 11 and 22, two other categories of algae are used, namely blanket weed (for filamentous algae sufficiently long and dense to be easily seen from above the water) and benthic algae (here defined as algae growing on the channel bed in sufficient quantity to be easily seen as green areas from above the water but not trailing away from the bed as does blanket weed). Only especially relevant references are cited in the text, but a list of additional references is given in the Bibliography.

I am much indebted to Mr F.G. Charlton, Mr W.H. Palmer and Mrs P.A. Wolseley for their careful reviews of the typescript; to Mr P.F. Barret, Dr F.H. Dawson, Dr P.J. Grubb, Dr N.T.H. Holmes, Mr T.O. Robson, Professor S.G. Smith and Dr B.A. Whitton for use of an unpublished manuscript. I am very grateful for the technical assistance of Mrs M. Ellis, Mrs J. Hayes, Mrs S.M. Hornsy, Miss M. Steiner, Miss J.S. Whiteside and Mr R.W. Worland, and for the carefull typing of Mrs A. Hill.

The research described in this book was financed by the Natural Environment Research Council, the Commission of the European Communities (under Contract 079-74-1 ENV UK) and the Phyllis and Eileen Gibbs Travelling Fellowship of Newnham College, Cambridge to whom I express my appreciation.

July 1976   S.M. Haslam

Preface to the second edition

Much water has flowed under the bridge, figuratively as well as literally, since the first edition of this book was prepared for Press, nearly thirty years ago.

Plants are living organisms, evolved in their own right, with habit and habitat requirements quite independent of the 'requirements' of people. (These, though, have an immense impact on the plants, by altering habitats and therefore which plant species can grow where.) That independence of plants means that their 'behaviour' in relation to habitat remains unchanged whatever the impact, and consequently few changes have been made to the chapters. Where later research has advanced understanding, some new text has been inserted (into Chapters 8, 10).

The community chapters (Chapters 12–14) gave and give one possible way of describing and classifying some British vegetation types. It is not the method later used by either this or other authors, but has its own validity, and provides interpretation to help the understanding of other methods. (These, being already published elsewhere, are listed in the Bibliography but not described in the text.)

In the first edition there were three chapters on North American river plant communities. Their academic level, being based on only a six-week survey, is no longer satisfactory (even though no better research has been published to take its place), and they are omitted.

The final section on human impacts and management now has a chapter on Restoration, not a subject in fashion, or even much practised, in the 1970s! This chapter looks at rivers and catchments as a whole, and follows the chapters describing the effect on river plants of the impacts of flood control, dredging, pollution, etc. Those chapters remain: the plants still respond in the same way to the same factors. (Though some new text, particularly in Chapter 19, includes later study and practise.)

This is still a British book. Most of the principles and much of the practice also apply in Europe and indeed elsewhere. But, for instance, snow-melt in the north, and, even more, the summer drought in the south of Europe, are among the extra habitat factors not found in Britain, and not included. Geographic variation both in species and within species (see Haslam, 1987) preclude some of the detail being correct elsewhere (e.g., the difference in habitat and occurrence of *Apium nodiflorum* and *Berula erecta* does not apply when only one species is present). There has been an explosion of research since the first edition.

References in the new text are the current ones. Those in the first edition have not been updated when updating is hardly more than adding more publications without appreciably expanding the text. The Bibliography has been divided into two parts, the first being publications used for the first edition.

To ensure readers have access to recent literature, and in particular continental literature not specifically discussed in the text, the second part of the Bibliography lists a selection which should enable any reader to get into and find this recent work. **This should be read as part of the text.** I am much obliged to those colleagues who have most kindly contributed to this.

Finally, I would like to give more thanks. Firstly to Mrs P.A. Wolseley, who has permitted her beautiful illustrations for the first edition to be used again in this one, and to Dr M. Everard and Dr T. Langford for helping me into Restoration (on which, I having recently been studying riverscape/landscape/ecology and wetlands, was far too ignorant).

Mrs Y. Bower gave permission for the use of (an intentionally ugly) figure. Mrs Tina Bone, Desktop Publisher, Illustrator and Designer once more produced my script with her usual efficiency.

And to all who helped with the first edition, my sincere appreciation.

Spring 2006   S.M. Haslam

1

Introduction

Plants and animals, large and small, live in, on and beside streams and man-made channels. This book describes the larger plants, mainly the angiosperms (flowering plants). Streams are complex habitats, ranging from mountain torrents to quiet, still lowland waters, and may be deep or shallow, large or small. These differences and many more, affect the vegetation. The first part of this book describes the effect of different physical features of the river on the plants. These features are often associated: for instance a swiftly flowing stream will also have a stony substrate, be sited in the hills and be liable to frequent fierce storm flows from heavy rainfall. In order to understand and interpret the plant community, however, it is necessary to have a basic understanding of all these features and so the early chapters separate out single factors or simple combinations of factors, such as channel width and channel width plus slope. Inevitably, there is some overlap between these chapters, since the vegetation of, for example, a large slow-flowing river is controlled by the slow water movement, silty bed, deep water and wide channel, and so is described in relation to each of these facets of the habitat.

The most important physical variables are:
1. the water movement, the quantity of water, or **flow**;
2. the soil or **substrate** on the bed of the watercourse;
3. the **width** of the channel;
4. the **depth** of the channel;
5. the general position of the channel in the river system, its **drainage order**;
6. the downwards **slope** or gradient of the channel.

Acting through these are:
7. **channel shape**; and
8. horizontal **pattern** of the watercourse.

In Chapter 2 flow and substrate are considered (as independent factors), with types of flow and substrate being described and then linked to the plants characteristic of those types. Chapter 3 considers how flow and substrate, singly and in combination, affect plants: the effects of erosion, battering, etc. and the responses of different plant species to these. In Chapter 4 three more factors — width, depth and drainage order — are, as in Chapter 2, described and linked to plants characteristic of different degrees of these. Chapter 5 takes up the wider aspects of flow, and considers the effects of storm damage in different streams, and the different streams and different annual patterns of flow that occur in Britain. The last chapter in this group, Chapter 6, again widens the picture by discussing the integration of the flow and substrate characters in the combination of width and slope known as the **width–slope pattern**. The habit and distribution of the different common river plants are closely linked to these width–slope patterns, and much of the interpretation of plant behaviour in relation to physical factors is given here.

The next two chapters consider habitat factors not here linked to the earlier ones: Chapter 7 describes the effect of **light**, since trees, etc., may reduce the light reaching the water, and deep or turbid water may prevent light reaching the channel bed; and Chapter 8 discusses the plant **nutrients**, the substances in the soil and water which are needed for plants to grow well, including the **dissolved gases** in the water (oxygen and carbon dioxide) needed for metabolism.

Chapter 9 is independent, as it describes **plant production** in rivers, that is, how much vegetation is produced in different streams.

The emphasis then moves to the **plant communities**. First, in Chapter 10, **small-scale plant patterns** are described. These are often due to variations in the factors discussed in Chapters 2 to 8, and are linked back to these. Chapter 11 increases the scale of the plant pattern by dealing with the **downstream variation** found between the source of a stream and its mouth; i.e. the changes with increasing size and decreasing water movement.

Once all these natural reasons for plant and vegetation behaviour are understood, a picture can be given of the **general vegetation** of British watercourses. Chapter 12 describes communities of streams on soft rocks, Chapter 13, those on hard rocks, and Chapter 14, those of dykes and canals.

The final chapters consider river plants from the point of view of man, their uses and **benefits**, their **hazards**, and human alterations to watercourses, including **varying flow, maintenance, engineering, catchment management, pollution** and, finally **restoration.**

As mentioned earlier, with such a complex and interrelated subject, some overlap between the material in different chapters is necessary. The principle adopted is that information is always included in a chapter when it is needed in order to understand the point or argument being developed; cross-references are given to related but less directly pertinent information.

TYPES OF RIVER PLANTS

Watercourse plants must, by definition, tolerate or indeed prefer having water round some or all of their parts. Aquatic plants have been

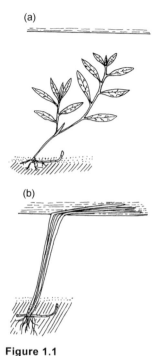

Figure 1.1

grouped in many ways (e.g. Sculthorpe, 1967), but a simple classification for river plants is as follows:

1. *Leaves and stems within or floating on the water*

    They are flexible, moving and bending with the current (Figure 1.1).

    (a) Leaves and stems submerged under water and usually anchored to the soil by roots. The gases needed for photosynthesis and respiration come from the water, while mineral nutrients come mainly from the soil but partly from the water. These plants are particularly vulnerable to strong poisons in the water because a large proportion of the plant is submerged and the leaves are usually translucent, thin and delicate.

    (b) Leaves floating flat on the surface of the water and stems usually rooted in the soil, though some species are free-floating. Gases can be taken up from and released into the air through the upper surfaces of the leaves, and so photosynthesis is not likely to be slowed down by a lack of carbon dioxide in the water. Water transpires (evaporates) into the air, so is pulled into the upper leaf from below. Floating leaves are usually opaque with waxy cuticles on the upper surface and are flexible enough to lie flat on the surface of the water.

2. *Upper leaves or shoots able to grow above the water, lower ones able to grow submerged* (Figure 1.2)

    The leaves and stems are stiff enough to stay erect without being supported by water. The leaves are opaque and most, but not all, can live under water. Gas exchange is mainly through the air but is possible through the water. Water transpired from the upper leaves is replaced by water drawn up from below the stems.

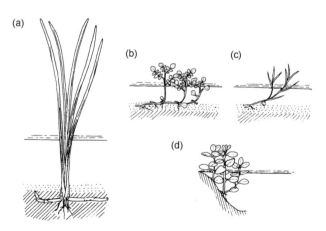

Figure 1.2

Plants falling into this group are:

(a) tall monocotyledons — grasses, sedges and rushes;

(b) short dicotyledons — the fringing herbs — typically found fringing the sides of small brooks;

(c) short monocotyledons, mainly grasses, again frequently at the sides of brooks. A smaller group than (b), though including the 'spoon-leaved' *Alisma plantago-aquatica*;

(d) a very few tall dicotyledons.

3. *Bank plants growing above normal water level, flooded after heavy rain* (Figure 1.3)

These range from emerged aquatics to true land species, and they do not necessarily have any special adaptations for aquatic life.

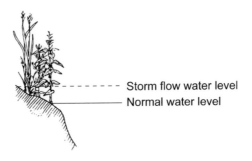

Figure 1.3

Some species occur in only one of these groups, e.g. duck weed (*Lemna minor* agg.) in group 1(b) and nettle (*Urtica dioica*) in group 3, while others may occur in several, e.g. strapweed (*Sparganium emersum*) in groups 1(a), 1(b) and 2(c).

HISTORICAL CHANGES AFFECTING STREAMS

Much of Britain was wooded for several thousand years before man started felling trees, though open grazing land also occurred. For many centuries, however, trees have been removed from near streams, formerly to make open land for pasture and arable farming and nowadays to allow large machines access to channels for maintenance. Streams still flow through woodland, though, and this is well illustrated in parts of North America. Plants grow well in the frequent breaks in the canopy, where patches of sunflecks or open sunlight reach the water, and there are as many species as there are in fully open British streams. Along large rivers the trees shade only the edges of the channels, but plants cannot usually grow in the centre because the depth of the water prevents enough light from reaching the river bed.

In addition to forest clearance another important more recent change over the years is that the water level in lowland Britain has been lowered as wet woodland, swamps, water meadows, flood meadows, etc. have been largely replaced by well-drained farmland. More recently, ground water has been abstracted for domestic water supplies, and this further lowers the water table. In parts of North America, though, the water table is still high, and road-side ditches, unlike those in Britain, still contain water plants. Continental Europe is in between. Streams rising in lowland tree swamps, frequent in lower ground in (non-arid) North America, seem to demonstrate an earlier phase in Europe too (e.g. South Norwegian wood, now). In Britain now, wet woodlands with rising streams are rare, but occur. In Plate 3 the ground level is uneven, stream flow negligible and the water often brown-stained from the peat. Downstream the swamp becomes channelled and eventually turns into a slow-flowing brook. On drier ground, in contrast, the brooks arise as channels which carry flood water. Water is too infrequent to allow aquatic plants to live in the channels and, on steeper ground, too swift to permit land ones to become established. Where springs rise on limestone there is perennial flow from the source, but this too may be swampy. In high-rainfall areas in Britain, rivers start as flood rills running down hills, which soon merge and form perennial streams (Plate 1).

In lowland Britain, channels have been managed by man for many centuries and there is a network of ditches between fields and beside roads on poorly drained soils, particularly in clay country, and, to a lesser extent, elsewhere. Because of the drop in the water table most of these ditches are now dry, though, even after storms. There is no clear boundary between these ditches and the upper part of the stream (Plate 2). As it goes from source to mouth, the channel first bears flood water in winter, then has intermittent puddles in summer and flow in winter and, finally, perennial flow. In the past many of these sources would have been tree swamps, and when the ditch system was made it must have contained water. Thus there has been more change in the upstream than the downstream reaches of these streams (also see Westlake, 1968). Management over the centuries has much decreased flooding from the streams on to the land beside them, but such flooding hardly affects the river plants (unless it alters the amount of scouring). Flow patterns have been artificially altered by falling water tables, culverts, reservoirs, weirs, mills, etc., and also for navigation purposes and to provide urban water supplies. The effects of these changes on the plants are described in later chapters.

In the mountains the course of a stream must necessarily follow the V- or U-shaped valleys. In a wide lowland valley, however, the channel could be anywhere on the alluvial plain, and indeed may have

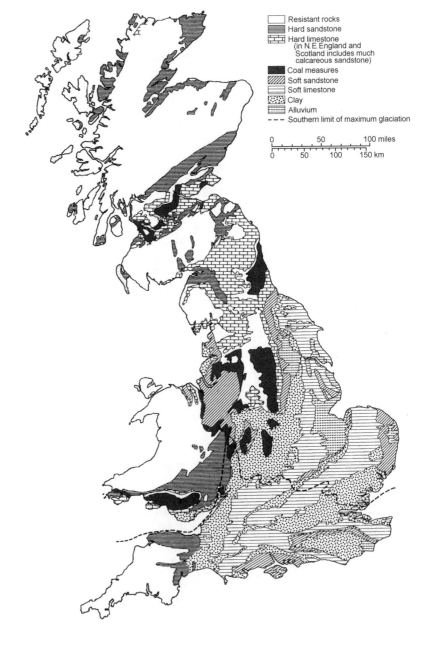

Resistant rocks
Hard sandstone
Hard limestone
(in N.E.England and
Scotland includes much
calcareous sandstone)
Coal measures
Soft sandstone
Soft limestone
Clay
Alluvium
— — — Southern limit of maximum glaciation

Figure 1.4
The main rock types of Britain.
British geology is complex, and
this diagram has been simplified
by omitting small areas of
differing rock types, and where
several types occur close
together by amalgamating these
and labelling them as the type
which affects stream vegetation
the most. Thick boulder clay,
deposited in the Ice Age, covers
some land north of the line
marking the limit of the last
glaciation. Streams on thick
boulder clay over soft limestone
or soft sandstone are,
vegetationally, clay streams. A
detailed geological map should
be consulted for field
investigations. The alluvial plains
in Yorkshire are less flat than
those elsewhere and have only
local areas with the dyke
vegetation characteristic of the
more southerly alluvial plains.
(Modified from a copyright map
by George Philip & Son Ltd.)

been in several different positions in the past. Its present position is likely to be firmly established by channel maintenance, and to have been fixed partly by chance, partly by the location of built-up areas, partly in order to free land for farming and partly by the boundary between properties. Some rivers are braided, having two or more channels. Braiding depends on the physical features of the river, but where there are several channels these can be used for different purposes, e.g. navigation and domestic water supply. Different flow patterns resulting from moving the position of a channel, or from using braided rivers for different purposes, may lead to differences in the river vegetation (see later chapters).

Most towns and villages were sited on streams so that they were provided with a water supply. Consequently sewage and other effluents were discharged into the rivers, and towns in lowland areas released raw sewage into rivers until recently (e.g. until the 1960s along parts of the River Great Ouse). Treated sewage effluent is of course far less damaging than raw sewage, but, unless much diluted, still affects the river plants. Industrial effluents are very harmful in some regions too, formerly particularly in coal-mining areas and near Birmingham. Farming also affects river plants: changing the vegetation and soil texture affects the pattern of storm flow; the ploughing regime affects the amount of silt entering the stream, and thus its substrate and turbidity; and fertilisers and pesticides are also washed into the stream.

STREAM TYPES

The vegetation types of watercourses may be classified according to the flow pattern of their channels and the geology of their catchment area. Rock type influences topography to some extent and affects the chemical composition of the substrate and water, the amount of sediment entering the stream and the physical composition of the substrate. Figure 1.4 shows the main rock types of Britain, grouped as they affect the river plants. The basic groups are the relatively recently formed soft rocks and alluvium, and the hard rocks which are mostly Palaeozoic or Pre-Cambrian. The soft rocks are divided into limestone, sandstone and clay, and the hard ones into limestone, sandstone, coal measures and the resistant rocks. The resistant rocks comprise those rocks (excluding coal measures) which are resistant to both erosion and solution, and include schists, gneisses, (hard) shales, slates, andesites, granites, felsites and basalts. The general topography of Britain is shown in Figure 1.5 and the rainfall in Figure 1.6. Rainfall and hills are both higher in the north and west, on the harder rocks.

Flow patterns are determined by a complex of factors. The dykes and drains of alluvial plains such as the Fenland and Romney Marsh,

Figure 1.5
The general topography of Britain.
(Modified from *Rainfall Atlas of
the British Isles*, 1926.)

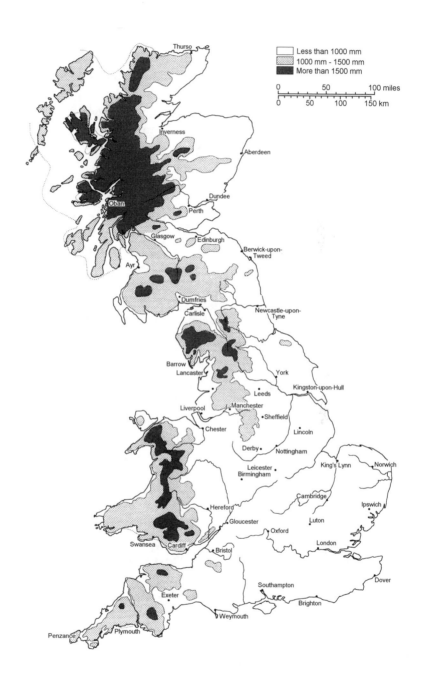

Figure 1.6
The rainfall of Britain.
(Modified from *Rainfall Atlas of the British Isles*, 1926.)

9

together with the canals, are an extreme case, for the channels are nearly flat and water movement is little without sluices and pumps, or, in the case of canals, locks. Vegetation can be abundant. In the other topographical types water is free-flowing, draining under gravity. The vegetation is affected by the force of the water flow and its variations, these in turn being determined by:

1. height of the land, of the hills in general;
2. height of the hills above the stream, i.e. the fall from hill to channel;
3. downstream slope of the channel;
4. seasonal distribution of rainfall;
5. total annual rainfall;
6. porosity of land surface, i.e. how much of the rainfall runs to the streams, and how much passes through the soil and rock to replenish the ground water below;
7. distribution of springs.

The most important of these are usually the fall from hill to channel and the channel slope, while the total annual rainfall is usually the least important factor (in Britain). Local conditions, however, frequently alter these priorities.

Areas classed as lowlands have hills that are not over about 800' (250 m), the height of the hills above the stream channel is usually less than 200' (60 m) and the slope of the channels near their sources can be as little as 1:100 (Figure 1.7). Vegetation in the streams can be abundant, and although storm flows do some damage to plants they are not strong enough to sweep the vegetation away or to move boulders. Upland streams are found where the hills are usually 800'–1200' (250–375 m) high, there is a fall of around 400' (125 m) from hill top to stream channel, and the slope of the upper tributaries is usually between 1:40 and 1:80. The vegetation may become as thick as in the lowlands, but upland streams are liable to the fierce storm flows termed spates, which, when particularly severe, can sweep away almost all vegetation and can move large stones and boulders. Mountain streams usually rise in hills at least 2000' (650 m) high, with falls from hill top to stream channel of 600' (200 m) or more, and the slope of the upper tributaries is often steeper than 1:40 (Figure 1.8). Severe spates, swift flows or unstable substrates usually prevent plants from becoming dense. In the subgroup of extremely mountainous streams the water force is even greater — either because the fall from hill to channel is often over 1000' (310 m), or because rainfall is greater — and plants, if not entirely absent, are very sparse.

Streams change as they flow from their sources to their mouths (Figure 1.9), the channels becoming wider and deeper as more water is

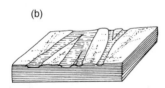

Figure 1.7
Lowland streams.
(a) Single channel.
(b) Braided channel.

Figure 1.8
Mountain stream.

10

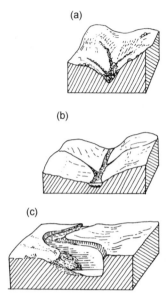

Figure 1.9
Downstream changes in a hill stream.
(a) Source with steep slopes and shallow, small, bouldery channels.
(b) Middle region with gentler slopes and a larger, more gravelly channel.
(c) Lower region, with a large, winding silted, channel in a flood plain.

carried, the hills typically becoming lower, and falls from hill to channel, and channel slopes, becoming less. Thus the flow pattern changes and, also, nutrient status increases. These downstream changes are further complicated when the rock type changes and when the topography is not just a simple transition from hills to lowlands. In general, when this happens, factors causing increased flow override those which decrease flow. For example, if a slow-flowing stream plunges into a gorge, flow and plants immediately become those appropriate to a torrent, while if a swift stream enters a plain it will be a considerable distance before it develops the flow and plants of a channel typical of a plain.

The pattern that the channels make across the land differs in different land forms. It has already been mentioned that in an alluvial plain many channels are man-made and sited for man's convenience, and so are typically straight and form a criss-cross pattern, with small dykes connecting the larger drains (Figure 1.10a). Elsewhere the channels must be sited in the valleys between hills. On chalk and oolite (i.e. soft limestones) streams are sparse because the rock is very porous and so much of the rain passes through the rock to replenish the ground water below, leaving little to reach the streams (Figure 1.10b). In contrast, lowland clay shows a pattern of dense streams (Figure 1.10d), for clay is not porous and most of the rain runs off the surface into the streams. The low hills are also less regular on clay than on chalk and the tributaries vary their direction more. Lowland sandstone shows a pattern intermediate between chalk and clay (Figure 1.10c). The mountain pattern in Figure 1.10f shows the high density of streams typical of a high-rainfall area. The tributaries tend to be parallel because they flow from the side of large mountains. Figure 1.10e is of an upland/low mountainous region with a lower rainfall; here there are fewer tributaries and they are less parallel.

PLANTS AS INDICATORS

River plants are sensitive indicators of the conditions in which they live. Because they are affected by a wide variety of factors, from land form to pollution, if the plants present at a site are known a good deal can be deduced about that site from the plants and, conversely, if the habitat is known, the expected type of vegetation can be predicted. If some but not all of the habitat factors are known then the plants can be used to monitor and assess the remaining factors: for example, when flow pattern, geology, etc. are known, pollution can be diagnosed by the plants.

Since each species has its unique ecological range, the greater the number of species at a site, the more accurate the diagnosis. (This may

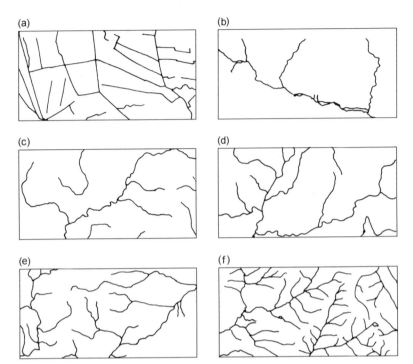

Figure 1.10
Channel patterns in different land forms (all drawn to same scale).
(a) The larger dykes and drains in an alluvial plain (Fenland).
(b) Lowland chalk stream (River Wylye).
(c) Lowland soft sandstone stream (River Tern).
(d) Lowland clay stream (River Chelmer).
(e) Upland streams (Welsh Borders).
(f) Mountain streams (Grampian Mountains).

be species in one 25 m site, or collectively over several sites close together.) Six and more species usually give a good diagnosis, and fewer will do if they are restricted in range, or occur at consecutive sites.

IMPORTANT BRITISH RIVER PLANTS

There are, fortunately, only about fifty river plants which are both widespread and of diagnostic importance in Britain. To this basic list can be added some common bank plants, and some channel species of diagnostic importance in a more limited range of waters. These eighty or so important plants are illustrated here and their habitat preferences summarised, so that this section may be used as a guide to identification and diagnosis both in the field and for readers who are unfamiliar with some of these plants. Names are given here in both English and Latin, though later in the text they are in Latin only. *British water plants* by Haslam, Sinker & Wolseley (1982), can be used to identify the plants of the channels (but not those of the banks, unless these can also grow as emerged aquatics). *British water plants* has many illustrations and most species can be identified without flowers or fruit.

It is, unluckily, not possible to use only a single classification for all these important species, and they are placed in five groups. They are listed according to their typical habitat, but may in some cases be found elsewhere.

Group 1 classifies species according to their general nutrient preferences, with notes about other habitat factors. The nutrient terms used are dystrophic (not-feeding), with negligible nutrients, up through oligotrophic (few-feeding) and mesotrophic (medium-feeding) to eutrophic (well-feeding), with ample nutrients. These terms, and the differences between, for example, mesotrophic limestone and mesotrophic sandstone, are discussed more fully in Chapter 8.

Group 2 lists *Ranunculus* spp.

Group 3 comprises the short semi-emerged dicotyledons or fringing herbs.

Group 4 is of species commonly found in the channel which do not fit into the preceding categories.

Group 5 comprises those species which are frequent on the banks but rare in the channel. (Some of the fourth group may be more common on the bank than in the channel.)

The scale bar to be found on most illustrations is 2 cm long.

GROUP 1   ARRANGED BY NUTRIENT STATUS

A

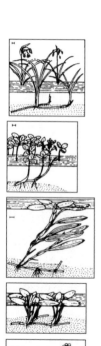

Common cotton grass *Eriophorum angustifolium* ⎫ Smaller
Bogbean *Menyanthes trifoliata* ⎭ streams

Bog pondweed *Potamogeton polygonifolius*

Dystrophic streams of acid peat bogs.

Lesser spearwort *Ranunculus flammula*

Shore weed *Littorella uniflora*   Larger streams

B

 Needle spike-rush *Eleocharis acicularis*

Small to medium oligotrophic streams, often with little spate. Substrate both mineral and acid peat. On resistant rocks or soft acid sandstone.

Floating clubrush *Eleogiton fluitans*

Bulbous rush *Juncus bulbosus*

Jointed rush *Juncus articulatus*

Swifter oligotrophic streams.

C

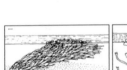

 Intermediate water-starwort
Callitriche hamulata

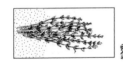

 Alternate-flowered water-milfoil
Myriophyllum alterniflorum

Oligotrophic upstream reaches on resistant rocks or acid sandstone streams. *Myriophyllum alterniflorum* tolerates much spate, often occurring upstream of *Myriophyllum spicatum*, and *Callitriche hamulata* upstream of other *Callitriche* spp.

Hemlock water-dropwort
Oenanthe crocata

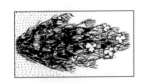

Water crowfoot
Ranunculus aquatilis/peltatus

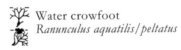 *Ranunculus penicillatus* ssp. *penicillatus*

D

 Monkey flower *Mimulus guttatus* agg.

Red pondweed *Potamogeton alpinus*

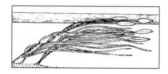

Potamogeton × sparganifolius

 Water crowfoot *Ranunculus fluitans*

Semi-oligotrophic to semi-mesotrophic usually swift waters. *Ranunculus fluitans* also into richer waters. *Potamogeton alpinus* northern, *Potamogeton × sparganifolius* mostly in Scotland.

E

Water-violet *Hottonia palustris*

Frogbit *Hydrocharis morsus-ranae*

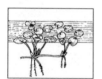

 Ivy-leaved duckweed *Lemna trisulca*

 Water crowfoot
Ranunculus aquatilis/peltatus

Mesotrophic unpolluted dykes (canals). *Lemna trisulca* also in little-polluted chalk brooks.

 Ranunculus trichophyllus

F

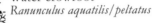

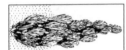

Water celery *Berula erecta* (*Sium erectum*)

Water crowfoot
Ranunculus aquatilis / peltatus

Mesotrophic calcareous streams.

Ranunculus penicillatus ssp.
penicillatus

Ranunculus penicillatus ssp.
pseudofluitans

G

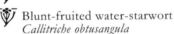

Callitriche

Blunt-fruited water-starwort
Callitriche obtusangula

Common water-starwort
Callitriche stagnalis

Long-styled water-starwort
Callitriche platycarpa
(less frequent)

(a) Common in shallow streams,
particularly on sandstone,
less on limestone, least on
clay streams with scours and
in spatey streams.
Regenerate well from
fragments. (Less *Callitriche
platycarpa*.)
(b) Dykes, canals, etc., least in
eutrophic or polluted ones.
(More *Callitriche platycarpa*.)

Reference illustration section

Canadian pondweed *Elodea canadensis*
In a wide range of habitats, but rare without some eutrophic influence, e.g. clay in catchment, alluvial silt in channel. Absent from dystrophic and very oligotrophic streams, and upstream on chalk. Usually on silt, so in swift waters confined to sheltered banks, etc. Frequently luxuriant in still and slow-moving clear waters. Regenerates well from fragments.

Broad-leaved pondweed *Potamogeton natans*
Frequent in medium sandstone streams with moderate flow and in dykes, etc. on clay. Occasionally in lower reaches of essentially oligotrophic streams and in upper reaches of essentially eutrophic ones.

Water crowfoot *Ranunculus aquatilis/peltatus*, etc.

H

Rigid hornwort *Ceratophyllum demersum*
(a) Semi-eutrophic dykes, canals, etc.
(b) Sheltered parts of slow streams, usually on clay.
Is non-rooted and easily washed away.

Spiked water-milfoil *Myriophyllum spicatum*
When luxuriant, usually on deep eutrophic (little-polluted) silt, or in dykes, canals, etc. on silt or clay, but occurs sparsely into almost mesotrophic habitats.

River water-dropwort *Oenanthe fluviatilis*
On soft limestone with some eutrophic influence such as clay in the catchment, or in chalky clay streams, etc. Usually in a fairly large volume of water.

17

1 Introduction

 Amphibious bistort *Poligonum amphibium*
Often in mesotrophic (or not very eutrophic) non-chalk, and usually large streams or canals. Tolerates some spate, but not a swift normal flow. Absent from eutrophic streams with eutrophic pollution. Shoots usually grow out from the bank and float.

 Perfoliate pondweed *Potamogeton perfoliatus*
Usually in semi-eutrophic streams or canals with a medium or large water volume. In flow, usually on a firm substrate with sediment above. Absent from eutrophic streams with eutrophic pollution.

Water crowfoot *Ranunculus fluitans*

I

 Water plantain *Alisma plantago-aquatica*
Semi-eutrophic to eutrophic places on fine substrate.

 Opposite-leaved pondweed *Groenlandia densa*
In semi-eutrophic streams, usually with a small water volume, particularly in chalk-clay streams, and the middle of clay ones. Less in hard limestone with some spate, and in semi-eutrophic unpolluted dykes.

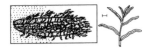 Curled pondweed *Potamogeton crispus*
Usually on semi-eutrophic or eutrophic shallow silt over a hard bed, sometimes on mesotrophic non-limestone silt. Most often in sandstone, chalk-clay and the middle of clay streams and in lower reaches on Resistant rocks. Commonly in streams with medium water volume.

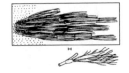 Water crowfoot *Ranunculus penicillatus* ssp. *penicillatus*

 *Ranunculus trichophyllus*

 Horned pondweed *Zannichellia palustris*
In semi-eutrophic streams, often on shallow silt, usually those with rather small water volumes. Most often on chalk-clay streams and in the middle of clay ones. Also in unpolluted dykes, etc.

J

Yellow water-lily *Nuphar lutea*
On eutrophic soft substrates, mostly in streams or canals, etc. with large or moderate water volumes. Characteristic of lower clay streams, eutrophic canals, drains, etc. Less frequent on sandstone. Intolerate of spate.

Great yellow-cress *Rorippa amphibia*

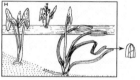

Arrowhead *Sagittaria sagittifolia*
On eutrophic soft substrates, particularly in canals, slow clay streams, drains, etc. Rare on sandstone. Intolerant of much non-eutrophic pollution.

Greater rush or bulrush *Schoenoplectus lacustris*
In eutrophic and semi-eutrophic streams of variable substrate and flow, though little spate. Usually in moderate to large water volumes. Most common in clay streams, frequent in lower chalk streams, rare on sandstone.

Strapweed *Sparganium emersum*
In eutrophic and semi-eutrophic streams on soft, preferably silty soils, and at least moderate water volumes. Characteristic of clay streams; frequent in sandstone ones, both lowland and upland; less common on limestone and elsewhere.

GROUP 2   BATRACHIAN *RANUNCULUS* SPP.
(WATER CROWFOOTS)

There are many hybrids and intermediates, making some identifications doubtful. Excluding *R. circinatus* and *R. trichophyllus*, leaf length is a guide to habitat, shorter-leaved forms are upstream, shallower water; long-leaved, downstream and in deeper water. When occurring together, the shorter-leaved are usually in shallower places.

Ranunculus aquatilis/peltatus

(a) Very short-leaved forms. In small swift streams without severe spates, mesotrophic to oligotrophic, on soft limestone or resistant rocks. Tolerate summer drought on chalk. Can develop terrestrial habit. Also in unpolluted semi-eutrophic or mesotrophic dykes, canals, etc.
(b) Medium-leaved forms. In medium-sized, fairly swift lowland streams or small hill ones, usually mesotrophic to somewhat oligotrophic, rarely on (eutrophic) clay. Often found upstream of *Ranunculus fluitans* in hill streams and, where both occur together, *Ranunculus fluitans* grows in the deeper water.
Ranunculus aquatilis is the more frequent on hard rocks and *Ranunculus peltatus* on soft ones.

19

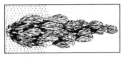

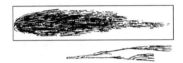

Ranunculus penicillatus ssp. *pseudofluitans*
In medium to large chalk streams, less often on other basic rocks.

Ranunculus circinatus
Uncommon. In unpolluted mesotrophic to semi-eutrophic dykes, canals, etc., sometimes in slow mesotrophic peaty streams.

Ranunculus fluitans
Usually in mesotrophic to semi-eutrophic unpolluted to slightly polluted waters in:
(a) large not-too-spatey hill rivers; and
(b) smaller lowland streams of at least moderate flow.

Ranunculus penicillatus ssp. *penicillatus*
(a) Short- to medium-leaved forms. In swift streams on resistant rocks, particularly in the West and the Pennines.
(b) Medium- to long-leaved forms. In medium-sized mesotrophic to eutrophic streams of at least moderate flow, particularly on limestone-clay streams, less on chalk or upland clay ones, rare elsewhere. In less eutrophic sites it tolerates some pollution.

Ranunculus trichophyllus
Infrequent. Occurs:
(a) in medium-sized clay or part-clay streams;
(b) in canals, dykes, etc.;
(c) in streams on resistant rocks.

GROUP 3   FRINGING HERBS

(Short perennial dicotyledons, usually semi-emerged, also emerged or submerged)

Fools' cress *Apium nodiflorum*

Water celery *Berula erecta* (*Sium erectum*)

Water mint *Mentha aquatica*

 Monkey flower *Mimulus guttatus* agg.

 Water forget-me-not *Myosotis scorpioides*

 Water cress *Rorippa nasturtium-aquaticum* agg.
(*Rorippa nasturtium-aquaticum*, *Rorippa microphylla* and their hybrid; the former is commoner, especially in the south.)

Water speedwell *Veronica anagallis-aquatica* agg.
(*Veronica anagallis-aquatica* and *Veronica catenato*; the former is the commoner.)

Brooklime *Veronica beccabunga*

Note:
(a) Small, usually mesotrophic streams on chalk, hard sandstone, resistant rocks with silting and little water force. Here there are typically at least three species present, often in wide or long fringes at the sides. Often submerged, on chalk frequently right across the channel. Other small streams have less.
(b) Small clay streams often have patches of large, emerged plants, typically one to three species per site.
(c) Banks of larger streams. Small, scattered, often temporary patches may occur in muddy places where the water force is usually low, and the banks have not recently been swept by swift storm waters.
(d) Small- and medium-sized streams on soft limestone frequently have, in addition to (a) above, one or more of: *Berula erecta* present (often as a submerged carpet); *Apium nodiflorum* as a submerged carpet; *Rorippa nasturtium-aquaticum* agg. Dominant over a substantial part of the site.
(e) *Veronica beccabunga* is the most frequent on the resistant rocks (except in the south-west, where it is replaced by *Apium nodiflorum*).
(f) *Myosotis scorpioides* is the most frequent in clay and part-clay streams.
(g) *Veronica anagallis-aquatica* agg. may occur submerged after clay and part-clay streams have been dredged.
(h) *Mimulus guttatus* agg. usually on hard rocks, more often emerged than semi-emerged. It tolerates considerable pollution.

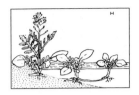

Great yellow-cress *Rorippa amphibia*
In eutrophic streams with little scour, most often clay or part-clay. Also in eutrophic to nearly mesotrophic dykes, etc. Ecologically separate from the others and usually excluded from references to 'fringing herbs'.

GROUP 4   CHANNEL SPECIES NOT INCLUDED IN GROUPS 1 TO 3

Fiorin *Agrostis stolonifera*
Frequent on edges, somewhat less so in the centre, where submerged plants (in shallow water) are often temporary. Often occurs soon after dredging.

Lesser pond sedge *Carex acutiformis*
Infrequent on the edges of dykes and lowland streams, particularly chalk and lower clay ones.

Water whorl-grass *Catabrosa aquatica*
Frequent at the sides of smallish chalk streams, uncommon elsewhere.

Flote-grass *Glyceria fluitans, Glyceria plicata*
Infrequent on edges of smallish streams, rarely in the centre.

Reed grass or reed sweet-grass *Glyceria maxima*
In channels of shallow dykes, at sides of canals and slow large streams, particularly those with alluvial banks; less often on clay, chalk and flatter resistant rocks; sparse elsewhere.

Common duckweed *Lemna minor* agg.
(*Lemna gibba* cannot be distinguished from *Lemna minor* when it is not swollen, and when swollen may grow with *Lemna minor*.)
Often abundant on still and very slow waters, but restricted to sheltered places in swifter streams. *L minuta* is sometimes now present with *L. minor*, but this was not noticed in river surveys in the 1970s and 1980s.

Reed grass, reed canary-grass *Phalaris arundinacea*
Frequent in swift hill streams, on the banks and on intermittently flooded gravel spurs, etc. Also in intermittently flooded ditches and dykes, and on the banks of silt and clay dykes.

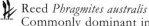 Reed *Phragmites australis*
Commonly dominant in shallow eutrophic and mesotrophic dykes, and on the banks of deeper dykes and drains.

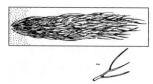 Fennel pondweed *Potamogeton pectinatus*
This (with blanket weed) is a good indicator of pollution. It is frequent in brackish (i.e. clean but salty) dykes. In the clean but peaty sandstone streams of Caithness, it occurs in a different habit, more like that in North America.

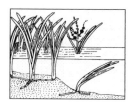 Bur reed *Sparganium erectum*
The most widespread watercourse species. Luxuriant stands are usually on thick silt. In larger streams patches are usually marginal. It avoids severe scours.

Reed-maces, bulrushes *Typha angustifolia* and *Typha latifolia*
Occasionally dominant in shallow dykes, or at sides of lowland, particularly clay, streams.

GROUP 5   BANK SPECIES NOT INCLUDED IN GROUPS 1 TO 4

Great hairy willow-herb *Epilobium hirsutum*
Common except in the higher hills and mountains.

Meadow-sweet *Filipendula ulmaria*
Frequent, especially on chalk and in the hills.

Soft rush *Juncus effusus*
Frequent, especially in the hills and after dredging.

Bramble *Rubus fruticosus* agg.
Common in the lowlands, sparse in the hills.

Woody nightshade *Solanum dulcamara*
Rare except on chalk, where it may grow into the channel.

Nettle *Urtica dioica*
Very common except in the mountains.
(Characteristic of disturbed ground.)

23

Species listed in Groups 1 to 4 which typically also occur on banks out of the water are: *Eriophorum angustifolium*, *Polygonum amphibium*, all the fringing herbs of Group 3, *Agrostis stolonifera*, *Catabrosa aquatica*, *Glyceria* spp., *Juncus articulatus*, *Phalaris arundinacea*, *Phragmites australis*, *Sparganium erectum* and *Typha* spp.

INTRODUCED PLANTS

River plants may be transferred from one stream to another by animals (e.g. on birds' feet) or by man. Introductions by man may be made accidentally, when restocking with fish, or on boots, machinery, etc., or species may be planted deliberately. Deliberate introductions may be ornamental (e.g. pretty water lilies at the bottom of the garden). Or, far, far worse, they may be in larger areas by planners who fail to understand that conservation requires (1) species appropriate to the river type (see later chapters) and (2) ecotypes native to not just Britain, but that local part of Britain. Dutch plants, for instance, are excellent and appropriate for The Netherlands. But Dutch seed or transplants are not native to, say, the English Midlands or Scottish Central Lowlands, and they contaminate the conservation, biodiversity and genetic heritage of rivers there. Accidental introductions from nearby rivers (e.g. on boats) may survive if the plants are suited to their habitat. Garden centres, though, are a hazardous source of accidental introductions. They import pretty aliens, and, inevitably, from their customers and themselves, some reach the river. Most cannot grow well, or at all in British rivers. But some (see below) can do so and, being without the pests or other controls that prevent explosions in their native countries, can become explosive and, to conservation of plants and animals, dangerous. (Alien plants rarely support as many invertebrates etc. as native ones.)

Plants may be introduced to protect banks from erosion. These are likely to be the tall monocotyledons (e.g. *Phragmites australis*) which have a deep network of roots and rhizomes to bind the soil of the bank and dense thick shoots to protect its surface from scour. More commonly, though, plants are introduced to improve fisheries, most often trout fisheries, and *Ranunculus* is usually preferred by the anglers. However, *Ranunculus* will only grow under certain conditions, and introductions into slow clay streams, or mountain streams with excessively severe spates, for example, are likely to prove unsuccessful. Introducing plants is valuable when a stream is recovering from damage but the plants have not yet recolonised by natural dispersal. When the River Mimram was recovering from sewage pollution, small weirs were built to increase water flow locally, wash away accumulated silt and produce fast gravel reaches. In these, *Apium nodiflorum*, *Callitriche* and *Ranunculus* were introduced and grew well (Parkin, 1973). When the River Wear was recovering from pollution from coal mines, *Ranunculus* was introduced in 1959, and spread successfully (Whitton & Buckmaster, 1970).

Before introductions are contemplated, however, the likelihood of explosive growth should be considered, for excessive vegetation can cause flood hazards and hinder angling. *Ranunculus*, for example, causes more flood hazards than any other plant of flowing water, and *Phragmites australis* more than any other plant of shallow still waters, so these should be introduced only with caution. It is probable that introductions within Britain have had little effect on the general composition of British streams, because of the restricted habitat requirements of each species and the likelihood of natural dispersal by animals. A few important and several minor river plants have, however, been introduced from abroad: *Elodea canadensis* and *Mimulus* spp. are now an integral part of British river vegetation. *Elodea nuttallii* (or *forma nuttallii*) has become frequent since the first edition, and a good many *E. canadensis* sites in this book may well now bear both, or *E. nuttallii*. (*forma nuttallii* can be made from *E. canadensis* by suitable chemical treatment, Haslam, 1987, 1990.) *Crassula helmsii* is currently an explosive pest. *Hydrocotyle ranunculoides* may become one also. *Cabomba caroliniana*, *Elodea callitrichoides*, *Lagarosiphon major*, *Myriophyllum aquaticum*, *Sagittaria latifolia*, *S. rigida* and the warmth-requiring *Vallisneria spiralis* fortunately show no sign of becoming invasive, at present. *Azolla filiculoides* is occasionally explosive, but usually satisfactory. *Lemna minuta* is spreading, but it is uncertain whether it is native but formerly overlooked, or introduced. It is not currently explosive.

On river banks three alien species are invasive and potentially explosive. *Heracleum mantegazzianum* is the most troublesome, both because its habit, and the heavy shade it casts, makes an alien type of vegetation, excluding the native, and because the sap is poisonous (rendering the skin photosensitive, and for years). *Fallopia japonica* is less intrusive. *Impatiens glandulifera* is of similar habit and habitat to native tall herbs, *Epilobium hirsutum*, *Filipendula ulmaria*, etc., so is the most easily assimilated (unless monodominant). They are typical of disturbed banks, e.g. those dredged or made of spoil from dredging — like the native tall herbs. (Other introductions occur on banks, e.g. *Impatiens capensis*, but are not, so far, of significant importance to river waters.)

2

Flow, substrate and plant distribution

Water is not only present in rivers but also moving, and the flow of the water is crucial in determining river vegetation. Moving water influences plants directly, and also because it controls the soil; larger particles being found in faster flows. Some plant species grow best in still water, others in swiftly flowing streams. This means that, if habitats are equal in other respects, similar vegetation occurs in streams of similar flow types.

Boulders, stones, gravel, sand, silt and mud, and peat all occur on stream beds. Some plants grow better in the fine-grained silt, mud or peat, while others do better on coarser beds. Plant species may prefer a certain soil type, or may grow there because they prefer the flow type associated with that soil, or because of the particular combination of flow and substrate. Vegetation is related to the substrate on which it grows.

Water movement is one of the most important factors influencing river plants. Flow affects plants directly and indirectly through its effects on the channel bed. One direct effect of flow is that currents move plant parts, and faster currents may batter and tangle leaves, stems and flowers in the water, scour soil from around their roots, and pull plants up. Flow also brings to the plant the gases (dissolved oxygen and carbon dioxide) necessary for respiration and photosynthesis, as well as other dissolved substances such as nutrients, e.g. phosphates and harmful or neutral compounds.

Moving water can, of course, move the soil particles of the substrate; the water velocity needed to move particles on the channel bed depending on the particle size, grading and specific gravity of the soil. Above a critical velocity the soil particles are initially moved along the bed by rolling and saltation, while at higher velocities some of the material is carried away suspended in the water. If water velocity decreases, these rolling particles stop moving and the suspended ones are deposited again. Naturally the larger the particle the faster the flow needed to move it, so that lowland brooks may carry a lot of silt and fine sand but little coarse sand and less gravel, while fast mountain streams can move quite large stones. Most river plants are anchored in the soil and can remain so only when the soil remains in place also. Plants also get most of their nutrients from the soil (though some from the water; see Chapter 8), these soil nutrients being mainly in the fine particles, the silt and mud. Swift flows erode, removing smaller particles, while slow ones do the reverse, accumulating sediment on the bed.

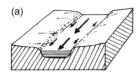

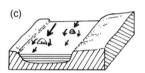

Figure 2.1

FLOW TYPES

In a straight channel without obstructions, the water moves fastest near its centre and more slowly near the banks (Figure 2.1a). As the river bends, the faster flows occur near the outside of the bend (Figure 2.1b). Obstructions such as stones, boulders, plants and bridge piers have a dual effect; they increase turbulence and slow down both the average speed of flow and the speed near the obstructions (Figure 2.1c). Each plant is affected by the conditions of the flow around it and by the water passing through the plant clump itself, but it is, unfortunately, not practicable to measure the flow conditions near many plants over a long period of time. This means that the situation must be simplified and the average flow conditions over a stretch of channel used to describe the hydraulic parameters affecting the plant.

Discharge is defined as the total volume of water per unit time flowing through the channel, and this is one method of describing the flow. However, in a deep channel with smooth sides and a gentle slope to the bed, flow will be slower and less turbulent than in a wide, shallow, steeply sloping channel with a rough bed of boulders, even if the discharge is the same. Thus other measures of flow must be used as well. The speed of the water is another possibility, but since a swift, smooth flow damages plants less than a slower, turbulent one, it is important to consider turbulence as well as velocity.

When the water particles move in smooth paths and one layer of water slides over another, flow is said to be laminar. When the water particles move in irregular paths the flow is said to be turbulent. Flow is laminar when the viscous forces (the forces holding the water particles together) are strong compared with the inertial forces (the forces preventing movement) and turbulent when the viscous forces are weak compared with the inertial forces. The ratio of the inertial forces to the viscous force is called the Reynolds number, so turbulent flow occurs at high Reynolds numbers, and when the channel bed is relatively rough.

The water surface in a channel may be rough, and the flow then appears to be very turbulent. This happens when the ratio of inertial to gravitational forces is high, or when velocities are high and the water is shallow. It appears, therefore, that it may be difficult to define criteria for turbulent flow in natural channels, as these would depend on both the Reynolds number and the roughness of the channel bed.

Useful visual categories of the flow conditions affecting river plants (which can be correlated with physical parameters) are: (1) negligible flow, as in canals, fen dykes, etc. (Plate 14); (2) slow flow, in which trailing plants hardly move (Plate 7a); (3) moderate flow, in which trailing plants clearly move and the water surface is slightly disturbed (Plates 8a, 11); (4) fast flow, (Plate 7b) in which trailing plants move vigorously and the water surface is markedly disturbed (Plate 10); (5) rapid flow, with broken water, 'white water'. In this book, it is combined, in the text, with fast flow. The flow type at any one place often changes very little over long periods of time, though flow will vary during and after storms, or if the water is controlled and the discharge deliberately altered by dredging, river draining works or water storage schemes.

A sixth category of flow must be taken into consideration when assessing the effect of flow on plants: liability to spate. In lowland brooks storm flows do some damage but normally leave most vegetation unharmed; in the highlands, however, the channels and hill slopes are steeper and the rapid spate flows subject the plants to greater forces. Liability to spate can occur when normal flow is fast, moderate or even slow.

As regards the distribution in Britain of channels with these different flow types, channels with negligible flow (flat gradients and low velocities) occur in alluvial plains like the Fenland, Broadland and Romney Marsh, though they also occur in small pockets of drained land throughout Britain; canals are more frequent in England than Scotland or Wales; streams with slow and moderate flow are widely distributed; and fast-flow sites are more frequent in Highland Britain (Scotland, Northern England, Wales and the West Country), liability to spate of course being confined to these regions (see Chapter 5).

VEGETATION CORRELATED WITH FLOW

Watercourses with similar flows have similar vegetation, other factors being equal, so that plant distribution is clearly correlated with flow. Dykes, for example, bear a generally similar vegetation whether in the alluvial plains of South Wales, Sussex, Norfolk or Lincolnshire, and the plants of upland streams of Herefordshire and Lanark are likewise similar, as are those of mountain streams in Snowdonia, the Lake District and the Scottish Highlands. The river habitat is a rigorous one, difficult for plants to live in, and the flow pattern is an overall controlling factor, comparable to the action of drought in the desert, or cold and dark in the Arctic. Thus flow type affects, and may entirely determine, the species present in a habitat, their performance and the relations between them, other factors acting only insofar as they are permitted to by the flow. In very mountainous districts the natural flow is so swift and fierce that it (and the substrate determined by it) are almost the sole controlling factors for the vegetation, but as flows become less fierce in less hilly regions, other factors such as rock type, pollution and management become increasingly influential. Competition between plants, which is such a noticeable feature of land vegetation, is of no importance in the swiftest streams and only of some importance in slower-flowing waters, but may be very important in still waters, where it can determine the general type of the vegetation (see Chapters 3, 5, 6 and 11).

CORRELATION OF FLOW TYPE WITH INDIVIDUAL SPECIES

Species can be grouped according to their response to flow, but these groups are arbitrary in that (as is the case with most other habitat factors) the species show a wide and nearly continuous range of variation. The strength of their preferences varies also. Some distributions are shown in Figures 2.2–2.7. There are two histograms given for each species, the first (on the left) showing the flow type with which the species is best correlated and the second flow type in which the species is most abundant. If a species actually prefers a certain flow type then this will be the one with which it is best correlated, but a plant may be abundant in a

Figure 2.2
Species most closely associated with negligible flow. Histograms I, on the left, show percentage occurrence in each flow type. Histograms II, on the right, show number of occurrences in each flow type.
Flow types are as defined on pages 27/28.
n = negligible; s = slow; m = moderate; f = fast; sp = liable to spate (this category is independent of the others).

Figure 2.3
Species most closely associated with negligible flow to a lesser extent than those of Figure 2.2. Details as for Figure 2.2.

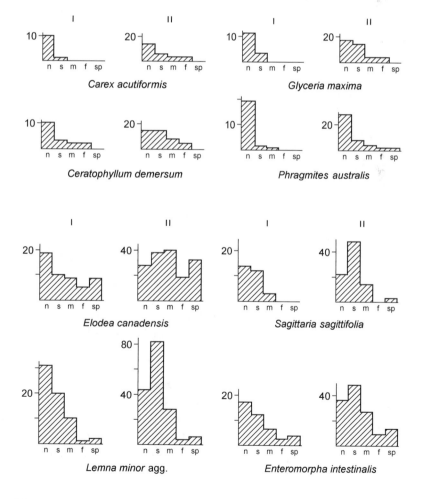

Carex acutiformis

Glyceria maxima

Ceratophyllum demersum

Phragmites australis

Elodea canadensis

Sagittaria sagittifolia

Lemna minor agg.

Enteromorpha intestinalis

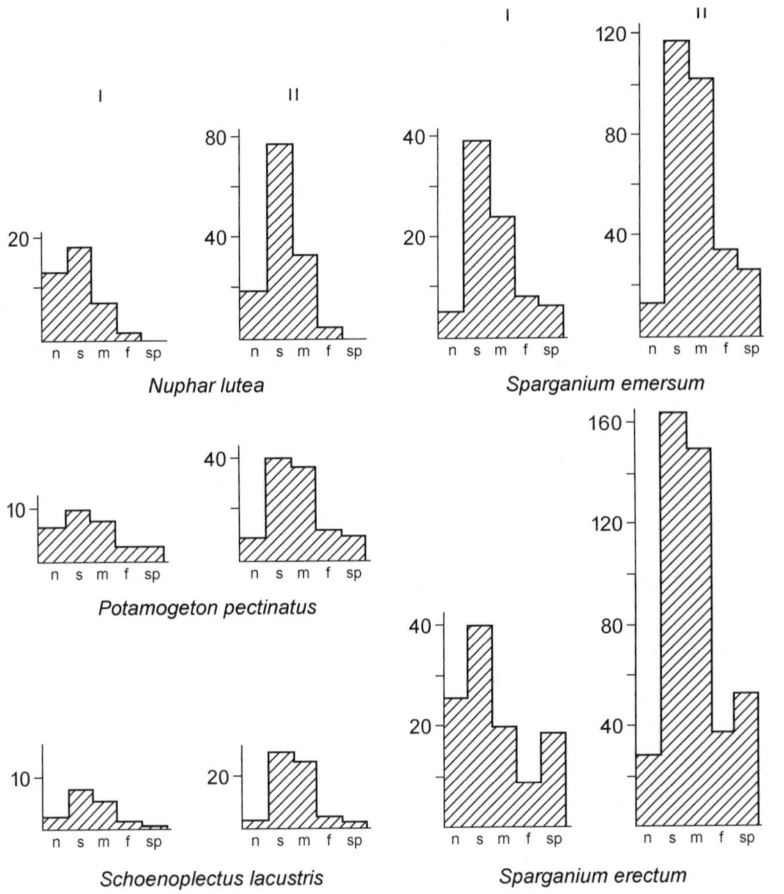

Figure 2.4
Species most closely associated
with slow flow.
Details as for Figure 2.2.

particular habitat because the habitat itself is extremely frequent and not necessarily because it is particularly suitable for the plant.

The species most closely correlated with negligible flow are shown in Figure 2.2. One of these (*Ceratophyllum demersum*) does not have roots or rhizomes and its submerged shoots are easily washed away by fast or storm flows. The other three are tall emerged monocotyledons. These will also grow on the banks above the average water level, and up on the banks they may more often be found by streams with moving water.

Figure 2.3 shows those species that are best correlated with negligible flow but which also occur frequently in other flow types. One (*Lemna minor* agg.) has very small plants which are free-floating on the water surface and are therefore easily removed by currents. The others are submerged but are susceptible to scouring, etc. (see Chapter 3).

The species whose distribution is best correlated with slow flow are shown in Figure 2.4. These include *Sparganium erectum*, the commonest and most ubiquitous watercourse plant in Britain. However, at any one

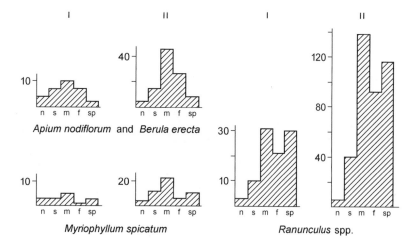

Figures 2.5
Species most closely associated
with moderate flow.
Details as for Figure 2.2.

Apium nodiflorum and *Berula erecta*

Myriophyllum spicatum

Ranunculus spp.

site a plant may be sparse or dense, and the habitat a plant needs for good growth may not correspond to the range of habitats where the species can be found. For example, when plants of this group grow abundantly these dense stands may be best correlated with other flow types, namely:

Negligible flow	*Sparganium erectum*
Negligible to slow flow	*Nuphar lutea*
Slow to moderate flow	*Sparganium emersum*
Moderate flow	*Potamogeton pectinatus*

The species best correlated with moderate flow (Figure 2.5) include those characteristic of chalk streams. Compared with *Ranunculus* spp., *Apium nodiflorum* and *Berula erecta* occur more in fast flow and less in sites liable to spate. They are less well anchored. Abundant populations of *Ranunculus* are, compared to sparse ones,

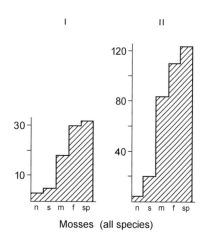

Figure 2.6
Species most closely associated
with fast flow.
Details as for Figure 2.2.

Mosses (all species)

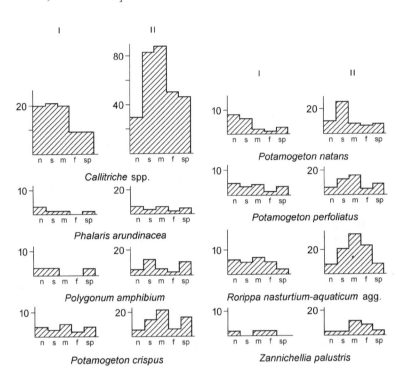

Figure 2.7
Species poorly associated with
flow type.
Details as for Figure 2.2.

more frequent in fast flow. The different *Ranunculus* species have
different habitat preferences, but conclusions about the separate
species are tentative because hybridisation and intermediates are
common, so identification is often difficult. (See also Butcher, 1927,
1933; Holmes & Whitton, 1975 a, b.) Some general conclusions are:

Sometimes occurring in negligible flow:

*Ranunculus aquatilis, Ranunculus circinatus, Ranunculus peltatus,
Ranunculus trichophyllus*

Primary correlation with moderate flow, secondary with fast flow:

Ranunculus penicillatus ssp. *pseudofluitans*

Primary correlation with moderate flow, secondary with spate
liability:

Ranunculus peltatus, Ranunculus penicillatus ssp. *penicillatus*

Primary correlation with fast flow, secondary with spate liability:

Ranunculus aquatilis

Primary correlation with spate liability, secondary with fast flow:

Ranunculus fluitans.

The few plants best correlated with fast flow include the mosses, as
an aggregate group (Figure 2.6), *Myriophyllum alterniflorum, Ranunculus
aquatilis* and *Ranunculus fluitans*. Figure 2.7 shows some channel species
which do not fit into the other groups.

Sometimes, on these histograms, a plant is recorded frequently in one habitat and rarely in another. Such rare records are usually due to some local conditions not shown on the histograms, such as a stream normally kept deep and slow by flood gates being recorded on an unusual occasion when the gates were open. They may also be due to an extension of the range, perhaps because other habitat factors make the site more satisfactory. If a species can grow well, it is more likely to tolerate one unsatisfactory — not lethal — factor.

(These data, as similar data elsewhere in this book, are British. Those for various European countries are given in Haslam, 1987.)

THE FAST FLOW AND THE SPATEY HABITATS

Habitats with fast flow have continuous scour which prevents particles accumulating in the path of the main current, but since the flow is steady, the bed is stable. Spatey reaches in times of spate are subjected to an extremely turbulent flow of great force which disturbs and erodes the bed, but if the normal flow is slow or moderate then fine sediment is deposited between spates.

Fast flow and spates usually occur together, as in many mountain streams, but can be found independently, for spates occur without fast flow in flat places in the hills and near the flood plains of hill rivers, while there is fast flow without spates in the steeper sections of lowland streams. When these two components of swift flow do occur independently they result in different vegetation types, so it can be seen which features of habit and morphology enable certain plants to tolerate which aspect of swift flow.

Plants tolerating fast flow better than spates are more easily uprooted by extra scour and water force, though are more tolerant of being battered and tangled in the water, e.g.

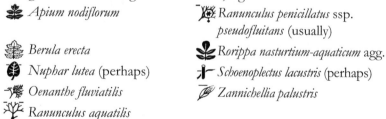

Apium nodiflorum

Berula erecta

Nuphar lutea (perhaps)

Oenanthe fluviatilis

Ranunculus aquatilis

Ranunculus penicillatus ssp. *pseudofluitans* (usually)

Rorippa nasturtium-aquaticum agg.

Schoenoplectus lacustris (perhaps)

Zannichellia palustris

Species tolerating spates better than fast flow may do so because they need fine substrates for rooting and anchorage (see Chapter 3), or are tougher plants, or grow very quickly so that damaged parts are rapidly replaced. They are more tolerant of battering than the last group and are not usually easily uprooted (or if they are can quickly regrow from fragments).

Elodea canadensis

Potamogeton perfoliatus (perhaps)

Myriophyllum spicatum   *Ranunculus fluitans*

Polygonum amphibium   *Sparganium erectum*

Potamogeton crispus

Some species are particularly intolerant of both fast flow and spate. For example:

Carex acutiformis   *Potamogeton pectinatus* (often)

Ceratophyllum demersum   *Sagittaria sagittifolia*

Nuphar lutea   *Schoenoplectus lacustris* (usually)

Phragmites australis

No plants grow where there is both very fast flow and severe spates, but a few can sometimes tolerate a considerable degree of both. For example:

Callitriche spp.   *Potamogeton × sparganifolius*

Myriophyllum alterniflorum   *Sparganium emersum*

Three of these are firmly rooted, two regrow quickly from fragments, three tolerate much battering and one avoids much turbulence.

SUBSTRATE TYPES

Stream beds may be made up of many different kinds of substrate (Figure 2.8). In mountain streams the solid bedrock is commonly exposed, and this is sometimes the case elsewhere (e.g. on clay), though more usually the substrate is composed of particles derived from the rock. These may come directly from the rock in the channel, as with boulders, stones and gravel from hard rocks, sand from sandstone and fine particles from clay, or alternatively the particles may come from the soil or subsoil of the catchment area, being washed in from the stream banks with the run-off water, or coming down from upstream through the scouring of the channel. As well as the inorganic component, organic particles will be present, from the decay of aquatic plants and animals, and from humus, peat and undecayed material washed in from the catchment. Substrates can also be man-made, either intentionally, as in concrete culverts, or inadvertently, as with rubbish dumps.

Natural channels may be incised or alluvial. The incised channel typical of fairly steep catchments scours its bed, unless it meets material it cannot erode, and so the bed is made of material older than the river itself. On this bed river-borne material is deposited when the flow falls and is picked up again and carried on when the flow increases. The alluvial river, found in flatter areas, gradually builds up its own plain composed of deposited sediment. The channel moves within this sediment, and the bed and banks can be eroded more easily. Velocities in the steep channels are usually higher than those in channels with

Figure 2.8

more gentle slopes, and their flows vary more rapidly with the rainfall. These variations in flow cause, in turn, variations in erosion and deposition of sediment, the overall pattern being that of little deposition upstream and much downstream, while in the middle reaches sedimentation occurs in areas of least flow (which include plant clumps).

Most channels have a consolidated bottom (i.e. a hard bed) which is commonly in the subsoil, though it can be man-made as in clay-bottomed canals, etc. Above this there may be sediment deposited which is not consolidated and can thus be moved easily in storm flows. There is usually little fine sediment in the smaller highland streams because of the swift flow, or in chalk streams because the weathering of chalk leads to little sediment. Clay streams usually have the most inorganic sediment, then sandstone, limestone and finally the resistant rocks.

The substrate types discussed here and elsewhere in this book were classified on size as boulders or hard solid rock, stones, gravel, sand and silt. Silt here includes the finer particles of mud, since these cannot be distinguished easily from silt. The additional category used was peat, which forms a very organic soil. In this chapter only fen peat, which is alkaline and moderately rich in nutrients, is considered; bog peat forms a much more specialised habitat which is described in Chapter 13. In the histograms of Figures 2.9–2.13 the substrate types are those which are prominent on the exposed part of the bed at a site, not necessarily those in which the relevant species are actually rooted. Silt

Figure 2.9
Species most closely associated with fen peat substrates. Histograms I, on the left, show percentage occurrence in each substrate type. Histograms II, on the right, show number of occurrences in each substrate type.
Abbreviations for substrate:
p = peat; m = mud and silt;
s = sand; g = gravel; st = stone;
r = rock or boulder.

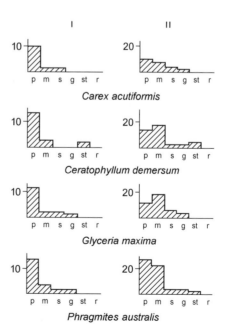

Carex acutiformis

Ceratophyllum demersum

Glyceria maxima

Phragmites australis

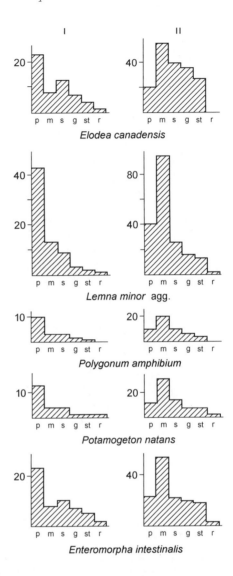

Figure 2.10
Species associated with peaty substrate to a lesser extent than those of Figure 2.9.
Details as for Figure 2.9.

or sand which is almost confined to within plant clumps is not included.

VEGETATION CORRELATED WITH SUBSTRATE

Similar types of soil, if they are equally stable, bear similar vegetation, other factors being equal. There are also similarities between the histograms relating plant distribution and flow and those showing distribution against substrate type (see next section). This is because the particle sizes and the stability of the substrate are largely controlled by flow. For example, faster flows have coarser substrates

36

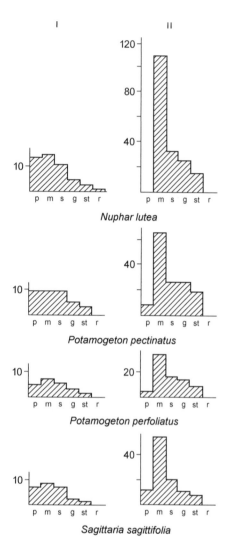

Figure 2.11
Species most closely associated
with silty substrates.
Details as for Figure 2.9.

and streams with widely fluctuating flows have a wide range of scour
and deposition during a season, and so have unstable substrates. Thus
although flow exercises an overall control, the plants may be
responding to the flow, the substrate, or both. Mosses are a good
example. Being without roots they are easily washed away by basal
scour and being short they can be smothered by accumulating silt or
sand. Consequently, mosses occur in places which remain stable and
are not silted. These are usually boulders, etc. (but may be the peat of
fen dykes, where flows are too slow to move the fine soil, or be stray
bricks or bridge piers (Haslam, 1971)) and so the correlation of mosses
with spates and fast flow is due to a causal association between mosses
and the boulders etc. of hill streams.

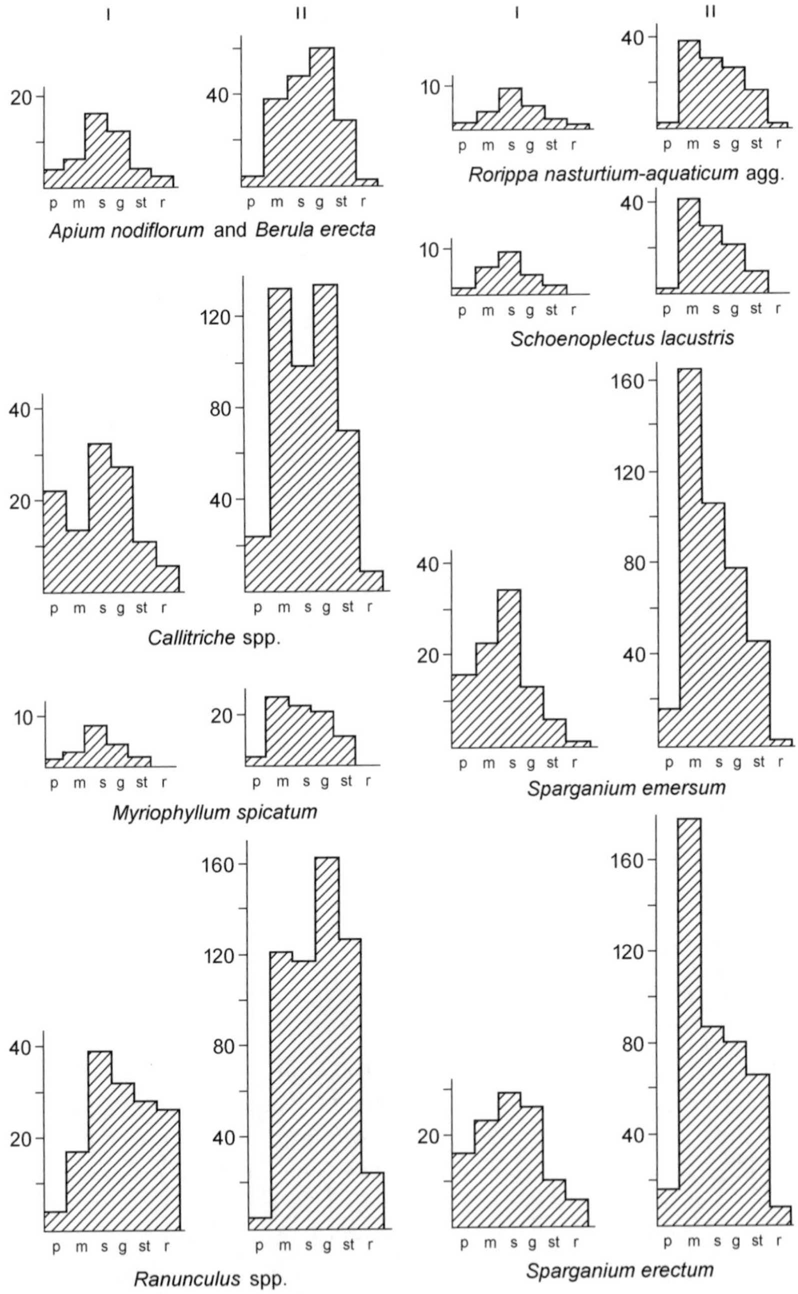

Figure 2.12
Species most closely associated
with medium-grained substrates.
Details as for Figure 2.9.

CORRELATION OF SUBSTRATE TYPE WITH INDIVIDUAL SPECIES

Some plants grow best in fine soil, some among coarse particles. This
is partly a genuine preference of a species for a particular soil, partly a

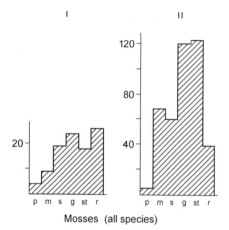

Figure 2.13
Species most closely associated
with coarse substrates.
Details as for Figure 2.9.

preference for a particular flow type (which is necessarily correlated
with substrate) and partly a joint effect of flow and substrate. This last
occurs when, for instance, a plant can grow in its optimum flow type
only when a particular substrate allows it to anchor firmly.

Figures 2.9–2.13 are histograms of plant distribution in relation to
substrate, arranged in the same way as the flow histograms. As with
flow types, species can be arranged in groups with similar responses to
types. The plants show wide range of variation and once again the
grouping is arbitrary. Where several substrate types occur in one site,
each species present is recorded as though it occurred in each substrate
type. This shows correctly that habitats of particular particle sizes can
support particular species, but it also wrongly implies that each species
present grows on each substrate type, which may not be the case (e.g. a
particular species may grow only on the silt banks in a gravel stream).
No angiosperm actually grows on boulders or large stones, though
many grow in streams containing these as well as smaller particles.
Where a species is recorded with a certain substrate type on only a few
occasions, it probably does not grow on this type, but only on other
substrates of the site.

The species most closely correlated with fen peat or organic
alluvium are shown in Figure 2.9. These are the same large,
deep-rooted emerged plants and the non-rooted submerged ones
which are most closely correlated with negligible flow (Figure 2.2), and
will therefore be found in fen dykes, which have both peat beds and
still water.

Figure 2.10 shows the species best correlated with fen peat which
also occur frequently in other soil types, and Figure 2.11 those best
correlated with silt and mud. Most species of fine substrates have long
deep roots, though some (e.g. *Potamogeton* spp.) may grow on shallow

soil. Species often occur in a wider range of soils than those in which they grow well (e.g. *Nuphar lutea*).

Medium-sized particles (sand or gravel) can be found in substrates that are mainly fine, medium or coarse, and the species of Figure 2.12 comprise both deep-rooted members (e.g. *Sparganium* spp.) and shallow-rooted ones (e.g. *Callitriche* spp., *Ranunculus* spp.). If tentative identifications are included for *Ranunculus* spp., then these have the following habitat preferences:

Primary correlation with sand, secondary with gravel:

Ranunculus aquatilis

Ranunculus penicillatus ssp. *penicillatus*

Ranunculus penicillatus ssp. *pseudofluitans*

Primary correlation with sand and gravel, secondary with stone:

Ranunculus peltatus

Relatively high correlation with boulders and stones:

Ranunculus fluitans

Mosses can anchor to boulders and rock, and these are the only macrophyte group to be best correlated with large particles (Figure 2.13).

3

Flow, substrate and how they affect individual plants

Water movement affects plants in several ways. Swift flows pull plants away from the ground; the force needed to do this depending on the species and size of the plant and on the time of year. If a plant is broken above ground then the underground parts are left in place and can regrow, but if the plant is pulled up completely it is washed away and lost from the community. Turbulent flow tangles and batters leaves and stems in the water. In storm flows, silt and other material carried by the water can cause abrasion, and so damage plants.

In general, plants of slow flows and fine substrates have long deep roots which anchor the plants firmly even if the upper silt is disturbed in storms, while plants of faster flows and consolidated gravel substrates usually have tangled roots curling around the gravel particles near the surface, which also remain anchored in this swifter-flowing habitat. When flows are swift enough to move the soil plants may be eroded, the ease of erosion depending on the plant's species and size and on the type of substrate. Where the current is checked silt is deposited and some plants can grow upwards into the loose sediment. When it is washed away then the plants will be washed away also.

Vegetation and flow are normally in equilibrium, the plant species present in any one reach being those which can, in the long run, tolerate both the normal flows and the storm flows of that reach. This is either because there is little damage to individual plants or because any damage is quickly made good.

Individual plant shoots are affected by the flow actually around each of them, and the roots, similarly, by the substrate around each of them. As flow and substrate vary, their effects on shoots and roots vary as well, and so in one river site there may be many microhabitats each with different flows and substrate and thus different vegetation, or the site may be fairly uniform in flow and substrate and have only small variations in vegetation.

The flow pattern within and around a plant varies with both time and space. A plant will usually (though not always) grow from quieter water near the stream bed into swifter water nearer the surface, so the upper parts are likely to be moved more and battered more than the lower ones (Figure 3.1). Large plants tend to impede flow, so, as thick plants grow, patches of quiet water tend to develop in them, while (if discharge remains stable) flow increases between the plants (Figure 3.2). Plants therefore alter the flow pattern of a stream as well as being altered by it. Altering the flow pattern may also alter the substrate pattern, since sediment is more likely to be deposited in the quiet water

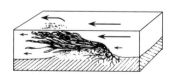

Figure 3.1

41

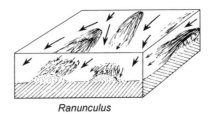

Figure 3.2

Ranunculus

within the plant than between plants, and conversely if the flow is fast enough to cause erosion, this will be greater between the plants (Figure 3.2). When the discharge changes the water level changes and thus turbulence and flow pattern both change. When the water level rises above the plants, turbulence due to the plants usually decreases, and vice versa.

Storm flows have greater force than normal flows; they raise the water level, usually increase turbulence and are more likely to have eroding velocities. They are thus capable of causing major damage. In general, though, plant communities are adjusted to the storm flows liable to occur in a habitat. This may be because the individual plants are not damaged much in storms; or damage may be great to above-ground parts but there is quick regeneration from rhizomes; or some stands may suffer major damage but recolonisation from fragments or fruits is rapid; or although there may be major damage and slow recolonisation the community has a repeating pattern over several decades.

Obstructions, including plant clumps, check flow and increase turbulence. Water velocity is greater beside plant clumps, and least downstream of them (Figures 3.2, 3.3). This means that different habitats suitable for other plants occur around the larger clumps. Downstream of a clump of a trailing plant there will be long waving shoots or leaves, which would hit other plants growing there, so species wishing to grow in shelter do not find this a favourable habitat. Upstream of a clump in shallow streams, however, velocity, water force

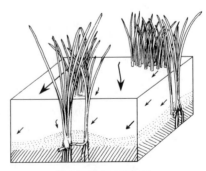

Figure 3.3

Sparganium erectum

and shoot movement are low, yet turbulence, which aids aeration and nutrient supply, is high, and some short species in streams of moderate or fast flow often grow upstream of a clump (e.g. *Berula erecta*, *Potamogeton crispus* when short, and *Zannichellia palustris*). Thus a clump of one species can allow another plant to develop upstream of it in a site which would otherwise have too fast a flow.

Water velocity is very low on and inside a plant clump, dropping sharply from close to (e.g. 3 cm from) the edge. Thick vegetation, whether as clumps or as carpets, has negligible flow inside it unless the flow outside is very turbulent indeed, and in fact as few as four shoots of *Ranunculus* in a path 10 cm wide (the shoots being only *c.* 2 mm wide) can halve the water velocity. Thus an important effect of varying flow patterns and storm turbulence is to bring flow — and therefore the gases essential for metabolism — inside clumps. Some species, including *Ranunculus* spp. (Westlake, 1967) (and probably *Ranunculus fluitans* especially), require considerable water movement for good growth. The outside shoots of a *Ranunculus* clump will grow well if the outside current is suitable even though losses from battering may be great, though the inside shoots are weaker, both because the habitat is less favourable and because they are more liable to be eaten by aquatic snails, insect larvae, etc. The following diagram links the physical effects of flow. Each of these is described separately below.

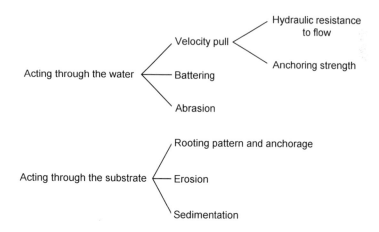

HYDRAULIC RESISTANCE TO FLOW

Any stationary object in moving water resists the movement of that water, so all aquatics offer some hydraulic resistance to flow, though the amount depends on the plant's structure, its size (length, breadth, depth) and shape (branching pattern, leaf and stem shape). The greater the plant's resistance, the greater the 'pull' on it exerted by the water and the more likely it is to be damaged. In general a 'bushy' plant has a high resistance, a streamlined plant a low one, while the bigger a plant is, the greater the impact of the water on it (Figures 3.4, 3.5; Table 3.1). Small plants, if they are long enough, are curled by turbulence and battered (see below). Large plants are less vulnerable, both because their shoots shelter one another and because they usually have longer roots and so are less likely to be uprooted by erosion. They are, however, much more likely to be pulled away from the substrate, because their large size makes them vulnerable to flow forces. Damage depends on three factors: the force of the water, the resistance of the plant (its 'drag', to use an aerodynamic term), and the force needed to break or dislodge the plant. Plant resistance increases rapidly with water speeds, particularly in bushy specimens (Figure 3.5).

Emerged and semi-emerged dicotyledons are bushy and thus have high resistance. Bushy species at the channel edge may be removed by resistance to flow and by erosion (e.g. *Epilobium hirsutum, Mentha aquatica, Myosotis scorpioides*). Some species growing both submerged and emerged (like *Apium nodiflorum* and *Berula erecta*) are usually short when submerged, and taller and bushier when emerged. The short submerged shoots are close to the ground and so are in the zone of the stream which receives little flow anyway (see Chapter 2), being short, they have little hydraulic resistance, and because they are often overlapping, protect each other from flow (Figure 3.6). The emerged shoots are generally larger and set farther apart, and so even though they are flooded only after rain they are more often washed away than are the submerged ones because they offer more resistance to flow. Of the two examples cited, *Apium nodiflorum* has the greater resistance to flow, with more spread-out emerged leaves and sprawling stolons with large terminal shoots. It occurs submerged less often than *Berula erecta*. A different habit is illustrated by *Polygonum amphibium*, which is anchored firmly in the watercourse bank with shoots bearing large tough leaves floating in the water nearby. This plant is associated with slow flow and liability to spate. The high resistance of the floating shoots means they avoid swift normal flows, but because the plants are anchored in the bank, shoots destroyed in storms can be replaced easily. Submerged species are generally more streamlined than emerged ones and thus have lower resistance, though there are exceptions. A submerged species which is exceptionally bushy and so offers a large resistance to flow is *Myriophyllum spicatum* (Figure 3.7). It often grows in rather soft soils and is easily washed away in storms. At the other extreme are the *Ranunculus* spp., with *Ranunculus fluitans* the most so (Figure 3.8). This species is the most characteristic of large highland rivers, liable to frequent spates. *Ranunculus penicillatus* ssp. *penicillatus* is less streamlined and in the hills may occur upstream of *Ranunculus fluitans*.

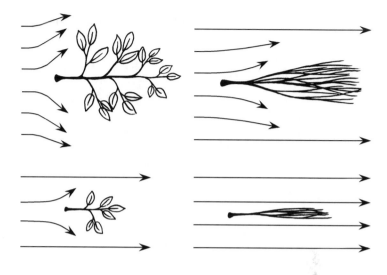

Figure 3.4

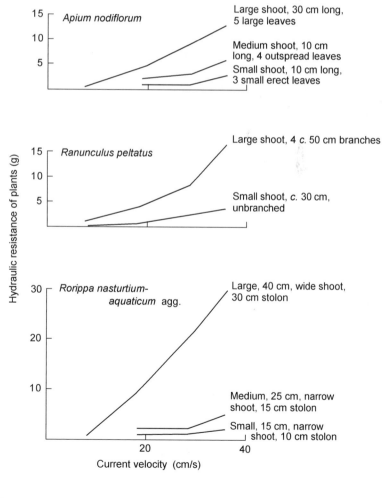

Figure 3.5
The effect of current velocity on
the hydraulic resistance of plants.

45

Table 3.1   Hydraulic resistance to flow of different river plants

Tests were done in a flume tank in water 6.5 cm deep with a surface velocity of 43 cm/s. The plant parts were attached to a spring balance and the pull of plant on the balance was recorded.

(a) Hydraulic resistance of typical shoots (branched if this is typical) c. 30 cm long
1 High resistance

	Apium nodiflorum	Bushy, semi-emergent
	Berula erecta	Bushy, semi-emergent
	Epilobium hirsutum	Bushy, emergent
	Elodea canadensis	Semi-streamlined submergent (when much branched)
	Myriophyllum spicatum	Semi-streamlined submergent (when much branched)
	Nuphar lutea	Very large leaves, floating and submergent
	Ranunculus peltatus	Streamlined submergent (when much branched)
	Rorippa nasturtium-aquaticum agg.	Bushy, semi-emergent

2 Medium resistance

	Elodea canadensis	Semi-streamlined submergent (when less branched)
	Mentha aquatica	Not bushy, semi-emergent
	Myosotis scorpioides	Not very bushy, semi-emergent
	Myriophyllum spicatum	Semi-streamlined submergent (when less branched)
	Polygonum amphibium	Large leaves, floating shoots
	Potamogeton pectinatus	Streamlined submergent (when much branched)
	Potamogeton perfoliatus	Large-leaved submergent (when branched)
	Ranunculus peltatus	Streamlined submergent (when less branched)
	Sparganium erectum	Streamlined emergent

3 Low resistance

	Callitriche spp.	Semi-streamlined but delicate submergent
	Potamogeton crispus	Semi-streamlined submergent
	Potamogeton pectinatus	Streamlined submergent
	Potamogeton perfoliatus	Large-leaved submergent

Table 3.1 Continued

	Species	Description
	Ranunculus penicillatus ssp. *penicillatus*	Streamlined submergent
	Schoenoplectus lacustris	Streamlined emergent and submergent
	Sparganium emersum	Streamlined submergent
	Zannichellia palustris	Delicate submergent

(b) Hydraulic resistance of different shoots of species, to show the effects of shoot size and branching

1 Semi-emerged fringing herbs

	Length (cm)	Habit	Resistance (g)
Apium nodiflorum	55	12 large leaves	40
	35	5 leaves	8
	13	3 leaves	5
Myosotis scorpioides	60	15 side shoots	40
	60	10 side shoots (same plant as above)	40
	60	5 side shoots (same plant as above)	10
	60	0 side shoots (same plant as above)	4
Rorippa nasturtium-aquaticum agg.	100	Well-grown	65
	50	Well-grown	20
	6	Delicate	<0.5

2 Submerged or floating species

	Length (cm)	Habit	Resistance (g)
Callitriche obtusangula	30	Tuft of *c.* 50 shoots	7
	30	Tuft of *c.* 20 shoots	<0.5
Polygonum amphibium	115	11 leaves	15
	25	8 leaves (same plant as above)	4
Potamogeton pectinatus	190	Large bushy shoot	15
	190	Side shoots over 90 cm removed (same shoot as above)	0.5
Potamogeton perfoliatus	110	3 shoots	15
	110	1 shoot	<0.5
Ranunculus peltatus	85	5 side shoots	15
	85	Side shoots removed (same plant as above)	3
Ranunculus penicillatus ssp. *penicillatus*	100	No side shoots, many leaves	8
	200	No side shoots, few leaves	5

Apium nodiflorum

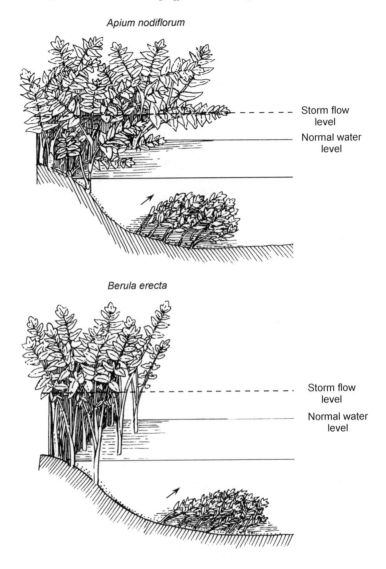

Storm flow level

Normal water level

Berula erecta

Storm flow level

Normal water level

Figure 3.6

Long narrow leaves offer the least hydraulic resistance to flow and thick wide leaves the most. Resistance is also less in flexible leaves than stiff ones. A plant that has both thick, fleshy floating leaves and thin, frail submerged ones is *Nuphar lutea*. When positioned so as to give the least resistance, floating and submerged leaves of the same size offer a similar resistance to flow, but if the floating leaves are twisted they can more than double their resistance, even in a flow of very low velocity (Figure 3.9), and this is one cause of the greater storm damage to floating leaves.

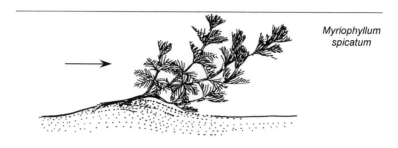

Figure 3.7

Myriophyllum spicatum

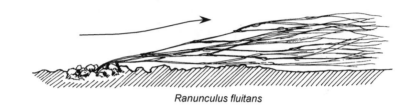

Figure 3.8

Ranunculus fluitans

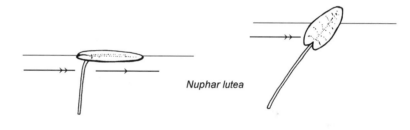

Figure 3.9

Nuphar lutea

It is not always the case that the streamlined plant has the least resistance. For example, size as well as structure affects resistance and although *Ranunculus fluitans* is streamlined and *Apium nodiflorum* bushy, *Ranunculus fluitans* clumps are often 4 m long and 2 m wide while *Apium nodiflorum* often grows as a carpet about 20 cm high. In this case the *Ranunculus fluitans* clump would offer the greater resistance.

Flow pattern also varies across the stream channel and so a plant at the sides, or low on the bed in the middle, offers less resistance than a trailing plant in the centre.

If shoots are broken or eroded from the bed but not washed away from their clump, then these shoots add extra resistance to the rest of the plant, as does debris lodged in plant parts. After rain the increased flow rate and greater amount of debris in the water both increase the likelihood of damage to the plant by increasing its resistance.

ANCHORING STRENGTH

Anchoring strength is the force holding the plant to the ground. If the pull of the water at ground level exceeds the plant's anchoring strength then, depending on the relative strengths of the above-ground and below-ground parts, the plant will either break off at the stem or be completely uprooted. If the below-ground parts are stronger and are left in place when the stem breaks then the shoots can regrow (Figure 3.10), but if the below-ground parts are structurally weaker then the plant will be uprooted and washed away, and so be lost to the community. Table 3.2 shows the results of testing the anchoring strength of different species. The plants used were of a size typical of each of the shallow-water habitats considered. Larger plants have a greater anchoring strength (i.e. more force is required to break them or dislodge them from the soil) than smaller ones, and small or bitten parts can be torn with less force than is shown in Table 3.2. Some species are strongly anchored (e.g. *Sparganium erectum*) while others are easily broken or dislodged (e.g. *Elodea canadensis*).

The anchoring strength of some species varies with season. For example, *Berula erecta* is anchored more firmly in spring and summer than it is in autumn and winter. This is because its rhizomes, which grow mainly in spring, are short-lived, so that in autumn the older shoots are no longer linked by rhizomes and are more easily uprooted. In other species, e.g. *Ranunculus peltatus*, anchorage varies little with season. Substrate also affects anchorage and species which can grow in various substrates are usually more firmly anchored in coarser soils, where their roots can curl round particles that are too large to be moved easily.

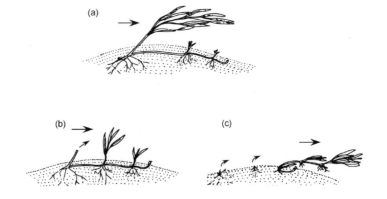

Figure 3.10
Breaking and dislodging.
(a) Undamaged plant.
(b) Breaking. Large shoot broken off, rhizome, roots and small shoots remaining and regrowing.
(c) Dislodging. Large shoot pulled away from the soil and about to drag away the remaining small rooted shoot. No rhizome left for re-growth.

VELOCITY PULL

When a plant is uprooted by flow, this is the result of the interaction of a number of factors, which have been individually discussed above: the force of the current pulling on the plant, the hydraulic resistance to flow of the plant, and the anchoring strength. Together these can conveniently be called velocity pull (see diagram on page 43).

Table 3.2   Anchoring strength

A pull applied to a plant just above ground (in the direction of the flow) may break the stem, leaving roots and rhizomes in the soil, or it may dislodge the whole plant. In these experiments the pull was applied on a spring balance, to shoots of average size for the site. 'Low force' is defined as up to 200 g, 'moderate' as 250-750 g, and 'high force' as greater than this.

Species capable of rooting well in substrates of different textures are usually more firmly held in coarser ones. The terms 'fine', 'medium' and 'coarse' in brackets after species names refer to substrate texture.

(a) Species usually breaking when pulled
1 Breaking with low force

Potamogeton crispus (fine, medium and coarse)

Ranunculus penicillatus ssp. *penicillatus* (medium)

2 Breaking with moderate force

Myriophyllum alterniflorum (coarse)

Oenanthe fluviatilis (medium)

Potamogeton crispus (medium and coarse)

Ranunculus aquatilis (coarse)

Ranunculus peltatus (fine and coarse)

Ranunculus penicillatus ssp. *penicillatus* (fine)

Ranunculus trichophyllus (medium)

Sparganium emersum (medium and coarse)

3 Breaking with high force

Ranunculus fluitans (coarse)

Ranunculus peltatus (coarse)

Sparganium emersum (medium)

(b) Species usually dislodging when pulled
1 Dislodging with low force

Apium nodiflorum (fine)

Berula erecta (fine)

Epilobium hirsutum (medium)

Myriophyllum spicatum (medium)

Phalaris arundinacea (coarse)

Rorippa nasturtium-aquaticum agg. (fine and medium)

Sagittaria sagittifolia (fine)

Zannichellia palustris (medium)

2 Dislodging with moderate force

Apium nodiflorum (medium)

Berula erecta (medium)

Myriophyllum spicatum (medium)

Phalaris arundinacea (medium and coarse)

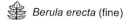

Table 3.2 Continued

 Epilobium hirsutum (coarse)   *Rorippa nasturtium-aquaticum* agg. (fine and medium)

3 Dislodging with high force

 Apium nodiflorum (coarse)   *Phalaris arundinacea* (coarse)

Berula erecta (coarse)   *Rorippa nasturtium-aquaticum* agg. (fine and medium)

Epilobium hirsutum (fine and medium)   *Sagittaria sagittifolia* (coarse)

Nuphar lutea (coarse)

(c) Species which break or dislodge equally when pulled

1 Damaged with low force

Agrostis stolonifera (fine)   *Myriophyllum verticillatum* (fine)

Callitriche spp. (fine)   *Potamogeton pectinatus* (medium)

Elodea canadensis (fine and coarse)   *Zannichellia palustris* (medium and coarse)

Groenlandia densa (medium and coarse)

2 Damaged with moderate force

Agrostis stolonifera (medium and coarse)   *Potamogeton pectinatus* (medium and coarse)

Callitriche spp. (medium and coarse)   *Potamogeton perfoliatus* (coarse)

Elodea canadensis (all)   *Sparganium erectum* (coarse)

Groenlandia densa (medium)   *Zannichellia palustris* (coarse)

Potamogeton natans (coarse)

3 Damaged with high force

Agrostis stolonifera (coarse)   *Potamogeton pectinatus* (coarse)

Carex acutiformis (fine)   *Schoenoplectus lacustris* (fine)

Phragmites australis (all)   *Sparganium erectum* (all)

The species most susceptible to velocity pull are those with high hydraulic resistance and low anchoring strength (compare Tables 3.1 and 3.2). For example:

Very susceptible: *Apium nodiflorum* *Berula erecta*

Susceptible: 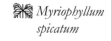 *Epilobium hirsutum* 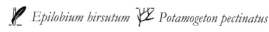 *Potamogeton pectinatus*

Myriophyllum spicatum *Rorippa nasturtium-aquaticum* agg. (extremely susceptible when poorly rooted)

The hydraulic resistances in Table 3.1 are less than they would be in faster flows. Even so, where the measured resistances are below 1g healthy shoots would be unaffected by the usual pull in their normal habitat. As shoots are frequently grouped into clumps or carpets, they shelter each other and lessen the likelihood of damage. A plant with a low anchoring strength but also offering little hydraulic resistance to flow, e.g. *Callitriche*, is less easily removed than one with a very high resistance to flow, such as *Rorippa nasturtium-aquaticum* agg., which has such a high resistance that its relative anchoring strength is low. Two *Sparganium* spp., *Sparganium erectum* and *Sparganium emersum*, form an interesting contrast because although both have rhizomes and long narrow leaves, other morphological differences cause them to respond differently to flow. *Sparganium erectum* has leaves which are strong in summer and rhizomes near the surface of the stream bed, so that when storm flows pull at the leaves the rhizomes can be dragged away and the plant uprooted. *Sparganium emersum*, in contrast, is much frailer, with very thin rhizomes. This is seldom pulled up, mainly because the leaves tear off before any great pull is placed on the rhizomes, though partly because the rhizomes are lower in the soil.

Shallow-rooted short carpets are formed by *Berula erecta*. If a gap is made in the carpet, either from natural causes (see below) or disturbance, then some shoots and roots become separated from the carpet and the combination of the increased velocity pull on the exposed parts and the erosion of exposed soil can result in a large carpet being destroyed. It is possible, therefore, for an intact carpet to continue spreading in a flow swift enough to cause large-scale erosion if a gap is made in that carpet.

BATTERING AND TANGLING

While one component of flow tends to pull plants from the ground, another component — turbulence — tangles and batters submerged parts. Species may respond differently to the two components since different structural features are involved. For example, a tough bushy shoot is more susceptible to velocity pull (e.g. *Epilobium hirsutum*) while a frail one is more susceptible to battering (e.g. *Sparganium emersum*) (Figure 3.11; Table 3.3).

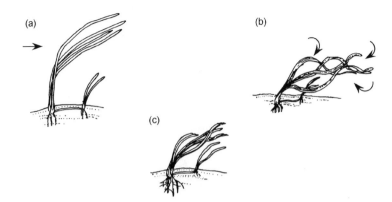

Figure 3.11
Damage by battering.
(a) Undamaged plant.
(b) With turbulence.
(c) With torn leaves.

Small parts are more easily moved by turbulence than large ones, and isolated shoots more than ones in clumps. The possible damage is greatest when shoots are separate and in the zone of maximum turbulence, so that each is individually moved with the force of the whole current. Turbulence varies with channel roughness, configuration, etc. (see Chapter 2), short plants on the bed at the sides of the channel receiving least turbulence (Figures 2.1, 3.2) and long plants in the centre usually the most. When a plant has more than one shoot or large leaf, these protect each other, so plants with susceptible leaves can survive in swift flow provided they are not tangled.

Streams with a continuous high turbulence can support only those species which are tolerant of battering. Where high turbulence is intermittent, occurring only during storms, there may be plant damage during the storm but quick-growing species remaining in place can recover quickly.

The field distribution of various species in relation to flow is shown in Table 3.3 (see also Figures 2.2–2.7). This distribution is usually linked to their tolerance of turbulence, e.g.

Intolerant of battering. Negligible flow   *Potamogeton obtusifolius*
Intolerant of much battering. Fairly slow flows *Sparganium emersum*
Tolerant of battering. Swift flow   *Ranunculus* spp.

However, more species can tolerate battering than would normally occur in fast flow, since distribution is also related to velocity pull, erosion, etc. Some species without anchoring roots, for instance, are confined to slow or still waters although they tolerate battering (e.g. *Ceratophyllum demersum*, *Hydrocharis morsus-ranae*).

Turbulence battering is independent of the size and shape of the leaves. Thick leaves are normally resistant, but thin ones may be either resistant (e.g. *Callitriche* spp., *Elodea canadensis*) or susceptible (e.g. *Potamogeton compressus*, *Potamogeton obtusifolius*). Some species have two

Table 3.3   Susceptibility to turbulence

Tests were performed in flume tanks, typical shoots being placed in different turbulences for different periods.

1 Very susceptible

Potamogeton obtusifolius[a]

2 Susceptible

Potamogeton compressus[a]

Potamogeton friesii[a]

 Potamogeton perfoliatus

Potamogeton pusillus[a]

 Sparganium emersum[b]

 Sparganium erectum
(submerged leaves)

3 Intermediate

 Agrostis stolonifera

Callitriche hermaphroditica[a]

Myriophyllum verticillatum[a]

Potamogeton alpinus

 Potamogeton crispus

 Potamogeton pectinatus

 Sagittaria sagittifolia[b]

 Schoenoplectus lacustris
(submerged leaves)[b]

Sparganium minimum[a]

4 Tolerant

 Apium nodiflorum

 Berula erecta

 Nuphar lutea[b]

 Rorippa nasturtium-aquaticum agg.

5 Very tolerant

Callitriche spp.

Ceratophyllum demersum[a,b]

Elodea canadensis

Lagarosiphon major[a]

Mentha aquatica

Myriophyllum spicatum

Oenanthe fluviatilis

Phalaris arundinacea

Potamogeton natans

Ranunculus aquatilis

Ranunculus peltatus

Ranunculus penicillatus ssp.
penicillatus

Sparganium erectum
(emerged leaves)[b]

a	characteristic of still water
b	characteristic of slow waters
unmarked species	characteristic of moderate or swift water

or more types of leaves with different susceptibilities. For example, most leaves of *Sparganium erectum* are emerged and tough, but there are submerged leaves which occur in spring and on isolated shoots in deeper water (over *c.* 0.5 m) in summer. These are more susceptible and this may reduce the species in faster deeper channels. The early strap-shaped leaves of *Schoenoplectus lacustris* are more susceptible than the later cylindrical shoots. In contrast the early strap-shaped leaves of *Sagittaria sagittifolia* are more tolerant than the later bladed ones.

It is the damaged parts of plants that are the most vulnerable to turbulence: a partly bitten stalk breaks easily, a leaf with a hole tears easily, a stalk bent by a heavy bird breaks easily, and so on. Thus damage initiated during a storm can be continued in the normal flows, or in the next storm, so that losses due to a storm can actually happen some time later. Debris and silt, which are washed down particularly in storms, much accentuate the damage. The tough leaves of *Nuphar lutea*, for instance, tear easily in storms, but the tears only slightly increase in a further six hours of high turbulence.

When whole healthy shoots are damaged, the type of damage depends on the habit of the plant. Long narrow stalks or leaves are bent, and the tissue at the bends is harmed. On flat leaves patches of epidermis are first lost, and then with further turbulence the patches get wider and also deeper as mesophyll is lost, and so large holes develop until finally the whole leaf is lost (Figure 3.12). Young and adult parts are usually equally tolerant, though the young parts are often protected by older ones. However, if dead or dying parts are present in a clump, these are usually harmed first.

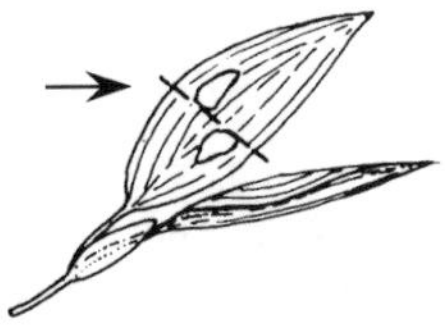

The length of time the turbulence lasts is important, several short periods of high turbulence being less damaging than one long period because the plants can recover and grow again between the storms. *Apium nodiflorum*, for instance, is viable, though damaged, after 6 hours of an extremely high turbulence, but is non-viable after 15 hours.

Many plants that live in flow are damaged by turbulence, and so the relative speeds of growth and loss are important:

Potamogeton pectinatus   Fast flow: plants small, loss equals growth
Moderate flow: plants often rather small in main current, large out of it
Slow flow: plants large, growth exceeding loss

Potamogeton perfoliatus   Largest plants in slower flow than *Potamogeton pectinatus*

Myriophyllym spicatum   Largest plants in both slow flow and faster flow than *Potamogeton pectinatus*

Figure 3.12

🌿 *Ranunculus fluitans*　　Swift large highland rivers: plants often 4 ×
2 m
Torrential flow: plants to about 75 cm long,
with e.g. three shoots
Very turbulent flow: plants to about 75 cm ×
20 cm, but in this site, when turbulence and
battering were decreased, the plants reached
3 m × 1 m in a few weeks.

A number of land plants were also tested for their resistance to battering and were all found to be tolerant, or fairly tolerant — the more susceptible water plants were damaged much more quickly than any land plant. Tolerance to battering is not, therefore, one of the special modifications to life in water.

ABRASION

Damage to plants by abrasion is the result of silt and other particles carried in flowing water hitting exposed leaves and stems as they pass by. All storm damage tends to be increased by silt, sand, or debris in the water, both because these cause abrasion and because, by settling on and catching in plant parts, they increase the plant's hydraulic resistance to flow. Abrasion is least where the leaf surface is smooth, as in *Ranunculus* spp., and high where there are projections such as hairs on the leaf surface. In a hairy plant the upper leaves on a clump can be completely removed by a silty storm flow, leaving bare stems above and leafy ones only where they are sheltered in the lower part of the clump (e.g. *Myriophyllum spicatum*). Leaves with epiphytic algae on them are intermediate between the two extremes, because although the algae cause increased abrasion, they can themselves be washed off as a result without damaging the leaf surfaces (e.g. *Elodea canadensis* and *Potamogeton perfoliatus*).

ROOTING DEPTH AND PATTERNS

Two characteristic rooting patterns occur in rivers: long deep roots, which are characteristic of plants of slow flows; and short curly roots, which are characteristic of plants of faster flows (Table 3.4). There are, of course intermediates, and the actual pattern varies with the size and the species of the plant, as well as the habitat.

In slow flows fine sediments usually accumulate, into which roots can grow deep. As the upper soil is easily disturbed in storms, long-rooted species can remain in place better than short-rooted ones. The roots usually grow straight down (Figure 3.13). In faster flows substrates are usually coarser, and if plants are present then the beds are at least partly consolidated. The plants typically have a dense weft of shallow, often

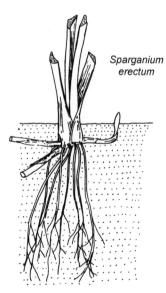

*Sparganium
erectum*

Figure 3.13
A deep-rooted plant.

57

Table 3.4   Rooting depth of river plants

(a) Shallow-rooted species
(most roots in the upper 15 cm of the substrate)
1 Species characteristic of moderate or fast flow

Agrostis stolonifera	*Myriophyllum alterniflorum*
Apium nodiflorum	*Myriophyllum spicatum*
Berula erecta	*Potamogeton crispus*
Callitriche hamulata	*Ranunculus* spp.
Callitriche obtusangula	*Rorippa nasturtium-aquaticum* agg.
Callitriche stagnalis	*Veronica anagallis-aquatica* agg.
Groenlandia densa	*Veronica beccabunga*
Mentha aquatica	*Zannichellia palustris*
Myosotis scorpioides	

2 Species characteristic of negligible or slow flow

Agrostis stolonifera	*Elodea canadensis*
(*Callitriche* spp.)	*Rorippa amphibia*

(b) Deep-rooted species
(many roots deeper than 15 cm into the substrate)
1 Species characteristic of moderate or fast flow

Sparganium erectum

2 Species characteristic of negligible or slow flow

Alisma plantago-aquatica	*Potamogeton pectinatus*
Carex acutiformis	*Potamogeton perfoliatus*
Carex riparia	*Sagittaria sagittifolia*
Glyceria maxima	*Schoenoplectus lacustris*
Nuphar lutea	*Sparganium emersum*
Phragmites australis	*Sparganium erectum*
Polygonum amphibium	*Typha augustifolia*
Potamogeton natans	*Typha latifolia*

horizontal, roots which curl around gravel and stones in the upper soil. The weft is not only securely anchored, but it also helps to consolidate the soil and so increase the plant anchorage (Figure 3.14). A few shallow-rooted species do, of course, grow in slow flow though in somewhat specialised habitats. *Callitriche* spp. and *Elodea canadensis*, which

Ranunculus

Figure 3.14
A shallow-rooted plant.

Figure 3.15

can quickly recolonise from fragments, tend to grow in fine sediment or in more stable soil at the sides of the channel, while in the larger watercourses *Rorippa nasturtium-aquaticum* agg. and small grasses are usually found at the sides when these are stable. In fairly swift shallow streams with coarse beds silt often accumulates at the sides and a temporary shallow-rooted vegetation may grow in this (e.g. *Apium nodiflorum, Mentha aquatica, Rorippa* spp., *Veronica* spp.) until storm flows remove both the substrate and the plants in it. Larger species with deeper roots (e.g. *Carex acutiformis, Sparganium erectum*) anchor below the temporary silt, and are less likely to be affected.

EROSION

Erosion removes soil, and it harms plants when soil around roots is removed or disturbed sufficiently for the plant to be uprooted (Figure 3.15; Table 3.5). Tolerance to erosion differs from anchoring strength in that erosion is concerned with the substrate whereas anchoring strength refers to plant parts, and a plant can have a high anchoring strength but a low erosion tolerance, and vice versa (Table 3.6). When underground parts are exposed or moved by erosion, the plants are vulnerable to velocity pull and further erosion, and are likely to be washed away by moving water. Erosion may actually remove soil, but just churning the soil up *in situ* is as effective in removing the plants. Velocity pull and battering occur during normal and storm flows, while erosion is associated only with storm flows (or dredging, etc.).

The various aspects of erosion are grouped here as the variations at different times of year, the behaviour of different species, and the effects of different types of soil.

Many plants are easily eroded in the spring, when the shoots are growing but there is little rhizome and root. During the summer the vegetation is denser, so the soil below the plants is protected from erosion, and underground parts are larger. Isolated plants and broken plant carpets are susceptible, though. Erosion tends to be greatest in winter when the soil is less protected, as much vegetation has died back, and storm flows are more frequent and have greater discharges. Some species have more seasonal variation in plant structures than others, and therefore more differences in seasonal erosion. For example:

Ranunculus spp.   Usually winter- as well as summer-green, with perennial root wefts. Little variation in erosion susceptibility.

Sparganium erectum Summer-green with deep roots, winter die-back, and slow death of roots in winter. Particularly susceptible to erosion in late winter.

Potamogeton pectinatus Overwinters in the form of small buds and fruits which are not harmed by soil disturbance. Small plants vulnerable in spring. In summer the rhizome system is deep and complex, and difficult to remove, though easy to damage.

The erosion tolerance of various species is given in Table 3.5. Susceptible plants often have small root systems, so that only a little soil need be disturbed before the whole plant is loose. Similarly, larger plants of any species are usually more tolerant than smaller ones, as their root systems are larger. Rhizomatous species are less easily eroded if a rhizome network is present than if shoots are isolated. If other factors are equal, plants able to grow on several substrate types (e.g. *Callitriche* spp., *Rorippa* spp.) are usually eroded more easily on fine soil, as this is moved by slower water flows than coarser particles.

Differential effects of erosion are demonstrated well by *Epilobium hirsutum*, a common plant of stream banks and frequent in channels of narrow lowland brooks with little erosion. It has annual stolons about 20 cm long. When these are even partly held in the compact soil of the bank they are almost immovable, even if the soil around them is lost. However, shoots of the second year's growth, away from the bank, are likely to have no connection with the bank, and are easily eroded, particularly in spring before the roots are full-grown (Figure 3.16). These bushy shoots have a high hydraulic resistance to flow, and of course this increases losses. Eroded shoots may become established farther downstream, but though shoots grow well under water the stolon fragments necessarily lie on the soil, above the ground, and the plants are extremely vulnerable, combining as they do a high resistance to flow, easy erosion and low anchoring strength. Most are washed away before midsummer. In the same way some fringing herbs are stable in ordinary storms if anchored in the bank, but easily washed off if they grow away from the bank.

Soil is consolidated by root wefts and dense rhizome networks and so erosion is made difficult (Figure 3.14). *Zannichellia palustris* is unusually erosion-tolerant for a short-rooted plant in fine soil, since its root weft is extremely intricate. However, if the weft is broken, erosion can be very quick. Even in a soft substrate, the close rhizome network of *Schoenoplectus lacustris* prevents large losses.

The very tolerant species form two groups: those that have root and rhizome wefts firmly entangled in coarse consolidated substrates (though these plants are susceptible to erosion when they happen to occur in unconsolidated soils); and those that have large networks of

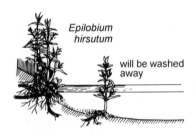

Epilobium hirsutum

will be washed away

Figure 3.16

Table 3.5 Susceptibility to erosion

A horizontal jet of water of constant velocity was directed at the plants, from upstream, to the soil at the base of the shoots, and the time taken for the plant to be eroded was noted. The classification here is based on these times.

The habitats used were typical for each species. Many species, of course, grow in several habitats, and Table 3.7 lists species according to their habitats.

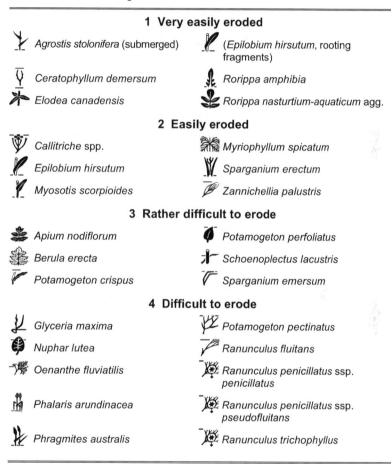

1 Very easily eroded

Agrostis stolonifera (submerged)

Ceratophyllum demersum

Elodea canadensis

(*Epilobium hirsutum*, rooting fragments)

Rorippa amphibia

Rorippa nasturtium-aquaticum agg.

2 Easily eroded

Callitriche spp.

Epilobium hirsutum

Myosotis scorpioides

Myriophyllum spicatum

Sparganium erectum

Zannichellia palustris

3 Rather difficult to erode

Apium nodiflorum

Berula erecta

Potamogeton crispus

Potamogeton perfoliatus

Schoenoplectus lacustris

Sparganium emersum

4 Difficult to erode

Glyceria maxima

Nuphar lutea

Oenanthe fluviatilis

Phalaris arundinacea

Phragmites australis

Potamogeton pectinatus

Ranunculus fluitans

Ranunculus penicillatus ssp. *penicillatus*

Ranunculus penicillatus ssp. *pseudofluitans*

Ranunculus trichophyllus

rhizomes and deep roots. *Nuphar lutea* is an example of the latter. It has deep rhizomes which are sometimes eroded in storms, and these are so large that their high hydraulic resistance to flow means that they are easily washed downstream. *Glyceria maxima*, another of this group, has shallow rhizomes, so that parts losing contact with a firm anchorage are vulnerable.

The effects of substrate type on the erosion susceptibility of various plants are shown in Table 3.7. Erosion is greatest for species

Table 3.6   A comparison of erosion susceptibility and anchoring strength

Tests were carried out as described in Tables 3.2 and 3.5, using the same plants. Categories as used in these tables.

	Anchoring strength	Erosion susceptibility
Apium nodiflorum	Moderate and high force	Rather difficult to erode
Berula erecta	Moderate	Rather difficult to erode
Callitriche spp.	Low	Very easily eroded
	Low	Easily eroded
	Low	Difficult to erode
Eleocharis palustris	Moderate	Rather difficult to erode
Epilobium hirsutum	Moderate and high	Easily eroded
	High	Easily eroded
Myosotis scorpioides	Moderate	Very easily eroded
Oenanthe fluviatilis	Low to moderate	Difficult to erode
Potamogeton pectinatus	Low	Rather difficult to erode
Ranunculus fluitans	Low to moderate	Very easily eroded
	Low to moderate	Difficult to erode
Ranunculus penicillatus ssp. *penicillatus*	Low	Rather difficult to erode
Sparganium emersum	Low	Difficult to erode
Sparganium erectum	High	Easily eroded
	High	Difficult to erode
Zannichellia palustris	Low	Rather difficult to erode

growing in unconsolidated fine soils and is minimised when the plant has deep roots, a root weft, or if plants are attached to the bank. An interesting difference occurs between brooks and dykes, the latter having little flow or scouring so that their fine soil is hardly moved and can be consolidated by roots (Figure 3.17). Once it is consolidated, erosion is difficult. Unconsolidated sand of course erodes rather more slowly than unconsolidated silt. Consolidated sand or stone is firm. When there is a hard bed with loose sediment above, rhizomes in the silt above (e.g. of *Sparganium erectum*) are more easily eroded than those in the hard bed (e.g. of *Schoenoplectus lacustris*). A hard bed of clay is eroded more easily than one of gravel.

Table 3.7   Effect of substrate type on erosion susceptibility

Erosion was tested as described in Table 3.5, in habitats of different texture and type. Erosion classification is as in Table 3.5.

1 Entirely rooted in unconsolidated silt

Very easily eroded

Agrostis stolonifera

Callitriche spp.

Ceratophyllum demersum

Elodea canadensis

Myosotis scorpioides

Myriophyllum spicatum

Ranunculus fluitans

Rorippa amphibia

Rorippa nasturtium-aquaticum agg.

Easily eroded

Epilobium hirsutum

Sparganium erectum

Rather difficult to erode

Glyceria maxima

Sparganium emersum

2 Entirely rooted in a silt or peat which, through lack of disturbance and flow, has become consolidated by dead roots

Easily eroded

Callitriche spp.

Epilobium hirsutum

Rather difficult to erode

Apium nodiflorum

Eleocharis palustris

Difficult to erode

Glyceria maxima

3 Entirely rooted in sand

Easily eroded

Callitriche stagnalis

Rather difficult to erode

Potamogeton perfoliatus

Zannichellia palustris

Ranunculus penicillatus ssp. *penicillatus*

4 In a mixed, somewhat unconsolidated bed

Easily eroded

Agrostis stolonifera

Epilobium hirsutum

Rather difficult to erode

Berula erecta

Callitriche spp.

Ranunculus fluitans

Ranunculus penicillatus ssp. *penicillatus*

Table 3.7   Continued

🦋 *Myriophyllum spicatum*   ⌐ *Sparganium emersum*

🌿 *Potamogeton pectinatus*

Difficult to erode

↲ *Glyceria maxima*   🌾 *Sparganium erectum*

⊥ *Schoenoplectus lacustris*

5 In a mixed, somewhat consolidated bed
Rather difficult to erode

🌿 *Apium nodiflorum*

Difficult to erode

🌿 *Epilobium hirsutum*   ⌐ *Potamogeton crispus*

🌿 *Oenanthe fluviatilis*   🌿 *Ranunculus penicillatus* ssp.
                                       penicillatus

6 In a firm gravel and stone bed, with or without some sediment above
Difficult to erode

🌿 *Berula erecta*   🌿 *Ranunculus penicillatus* ssp.
                                       penicillatus

🌿 *Callitriche stagnalis*   🌿 *Ranunculus trichophyllus*

🌿 *Potamogeton pectinatus*   ⊥ *Schoenoplectus lacustris*

🌿 *Potamogeton perfoliatus*   ⌐ *Sparganium emersum*

🌿 *Ranunculus fluitans*   🌾 *Sparganium erectum*

🌿 *Ranunculus peltatus*

7 Wedged in havens (see text)
Difficult to erode

🌿 *Callitriche* spp.   ⌐ *Sparganium emersum*

🌿 *Myosotis scorpioides*   🌾 *Sparganium erectum*

🌿 *Nuphar lutea*

Figure 3.17
Brook and dyke sections.
(a) A brook: unconsolidated
    sediment at the sides.
(b) A dyke: sediment
    consolidated by the roots of
    living and dead plants.

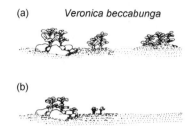

Figure 3.18
Effect of a secure haven on plant damage.
(a) Before the storm.
(b) After the storm.

The effects of erosion may depend on havens, i.e. places where plants may be wedged and secured by stones or similar objects which are not moved during normal storm flow (Figure 3.18; Table 3.7). These havens for plants are most important for the distribution and continuity of many species on softer soils. Here, fringing herbs may be almost restricted to havens in winter, spreading to form new clumps in spring. After storms, only the plants in the havens survive to form the nucleus of new clumps, and so as the haven is in the same place year after year, the clumps also occur repeatedly in these same places. Where there are no havens, however, clumps which have become established at the sides from fragments from upstream are lost in storms, and when the next clumps grow again from new fragments they are likely to be in different places to the previous patches. So, on softer soils, non-erodible havens determine the positions of stable patches of fringing herbs. Similar havens may be important in the centre of the channel (e.g. *Callitriche* spp., *Sparganium* spp.), though more often most of the centre is either firm or soft and the combination of loose silt and local firm stones that provide havens is less common.

A few other points arise from Table 3.7. Silt banks in streams of moderate flow frequently bear *Callitriche* spp. or *Elodea canadensis* which are easily eroded in storms, and regrow from fragments. *Myriophyllum spicatum* has shallow rhizomes, and although it can grow quickly over soft substrates, there are major losses in severe storms. In sandy streams *Berula erecta* and *Callitriche* spp. are more easily eroded from sand than gravel, and then more easily recolonize sand than gravel. *Ranunculus* (and *Potamogeton perfoliatus*) rhizomes are firmly held in the hard floor below the sand, except for young plants not yet established. Root systems often develop differently in different substrates *Sparganium emersum* roots, for instance, grow large in deep nutrient-rich silt, but are smaller in coarser, more nutrient-poor soils. This means the plant is eroded more easily from coarser soils, even though the particles there are eroded less easily.

Much information can be gathered from streams containing several types of substrates, and one such site is shown in Figure 3.19. It was found that vegetation pattern was closely correlated with soil stability. *Potamogeton pectinatus* dominated in deep silt and slow flow (a), its density downstream depending on flow in terms of how many winter buds or fruits were washed down. In spring, young plants were fairly dense on the softer soils, but these are easily eroded, and if storms in May were severe hardly any plants survived, while if storms were absent *Potamogeton pectinatus* could be nearly co-dominant. The softer mixed substrates (b) bore *Sagittaria sagittifolia* and *Sparganium emersum*, and there were sufficient stones present to protect the plants from erosion. Unlike *Potamogeton pectinatus*, these two species have rhizomes living though the winter, so some of the plants occurred in havens. The mosaic of mixed-grained

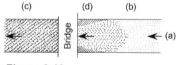

Figure 3.19

65

substrates (c) bore *Sparganium emersum* and *Potamogeton pectinatus* on the softer patches. These have straight roots which anchor by growing deep. On the firmer patches *Oenanthe fluviatilis* and *Potamogeton crispus* grew. These have curly root wefts, anchoring in gravel. The firmest substrate was the hard gravel (d), where *Ranunculus fluitans* was dominant. Shoots grew out on to the softer soils around, but if growth was poor and shoots small, the plants would be washed off in the next storm. Larger plants develop root wefts, which consolidate the soil somewhat and make erosion less easy, yet *Ranunculus fluitans* was effectively confined to the firm gravel at this site, because only there was it resistant to erosion. (In succeeding decades pollution increased, dredging removed the hard bed, and silting increased. Diversity decreased until the pollution-tolerant *Potamogeton pectinatus* was monodominant. A sad loss!)

SEDIMENTATION

When moving water carries suspended particles these are deposited when the flow is checked for any reason, such as the land becoming flatter or plants forming obstructions. Deposited sediment varies from nil to several metres deep, but it is normally unconsolidated and unstable. In some reaches sedimentation may be only inside plant clumps, so that when the clump is damaged or dies this sediment is lost also. Up to 15 cm can be deposited in 2 months in normal flows, though slower rates are more common.

There are two basic responses to sedimentation. Either the plants can keep their rooting level on the hard bed, while sediment builds up above, or they can vary their rooting level so that it remains at ground level, even though this ground level is changing (Figure 3.20). All species vary somewhat between these two alternatives (although individual plants can show just one extreme), but Table 3.8 is a grouping of the common behaviour of some species.

Ranunculus and *Zannichellia palustris* are two hummock-forming species with contrasting responses to sedimentation. In *Ranunculus*, the sediment in the plant clump commonly stays above the root weft, and the thickness of the hummock varies with flow. Sediment is deposited between storms, and removed either during storms or when the hummock is tall enough to reach a zone of faster flow. So in faster currents a point is reached when scour equals accretion. But removal of the upper sediment need not mean removal of the plants. In slow flows silting can continue, and short plants be smothered as a result. In *Zannichellia palustris* the root weft stays around ground level, growing upwards as sediment accumulates. If there is much deposition the plant community is unstable, as both plant and hummock are washed away together.

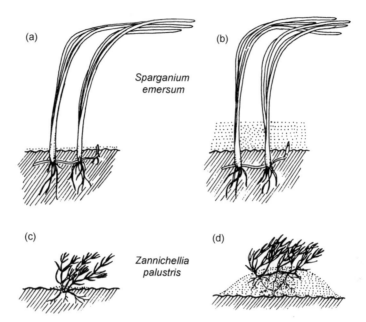

Figure 3.20
Effect of sedimentation.
(a and b) Plants with constant
rooting level.
(c and d) Plants with a variable
rooting level.

Thus the plants most vulnerable to sedimentation are (like *Zannichellia palustris*) shallow-rooted species with a varying rooting level. In these plants, when sediment accumulates, the rhizomes move up from the hard bed, in which they were secure, and as the sediment deepens the roots lose this contact as well, so that the underground parts are entirely in the loose sediment and are easily washed away in storms.

Harm can be done to the plants when shoots are smothered by silt, though this is rare because the short species with constant rooting levels which might be susceptible (e.g. some *Ranunculus* spp.) usually grow where little sediment accumulates anyway, while the constant-level species of silting streams are large and can tolerate thick sediment above their rhizomes. Damage from sedimentation may also occur when flow is altered, for instance by sluice gates. In this case if flow is checked and much sediment deposited, not only will short species with a constant rooting level be smothered (though fragments may grow in the sediment above), but also plants with a variable rooting level will rise with the accumulating sediment to become rooted in the sediment only and, when the gates are opened and the current increased, be washed away along with the sediment. Another source of harm is when silt and mud are deposited on submerged leaves, because this cuts down the light and so decreases photosynthesis. Interestingly, strap-shaped leaves seldom become covered with silt, while wide leaves, and those divided into thread like segments, are often covered. On the other hand, silting of leaves and stems may be an important source of nutrients (see Chapter 8).

Table 3.8   Rooting level in relation to sedimentation

Species vary considerably in their behaviour, and this classification is on typical behaviour only. There are no species which never alter their rooting level.

(a) Plants whose rooting level varies

1 Shallow-rooted species

Apium nodiflorum		*Rorippa nasturtium-aquaticum* agg.	
Berula erecta		*Veronica anagallis-aquatica*	
(*Callitriche* spp.)		*Veronica beccabunga*	
Myosotis scorpioides		*Zannichellia palustris*	

2 Deep-rooted species

Nuphar lutea		*Sparganium erectum*
Potamogeton pectinatus		

(b) Plants whose rooting level remains constant

1 Shallow-rooted species

(*Callitriche* spp.)		*Ranunculus* spp.
(*Potamogeton crispus*)		(*Elodea canadensis*)

2 Deep-rooted species

Carex acutiformis?		*Schoenoplectus lacustris*
Phragmites australis		*Sparganium emersum*
(*Potamogeton pectinatus*)		

Silt banks frequently develop in sheltered places, between major storms, and are churned up during storms. Submerged banks are usually bare if very short-lived, or bear *Callitriche* spp. or *Elodea canadensis* if lasting rather longer. Banks near the water level typically bear fringing herbs. As the unconsolidated silt of these banks offers little resistance to erosion and no firm anchorage, and the clumps have a high hydraulic resistance to flow, they are easily washed away in storms.

Gaps in plant cover allow erosion to take place. When species with a variable rooting level rise with increasing sediment, the unconsolidated sediment is easily washed away if a gap is made by animals, cutting, or changes in flow pattern, etc. Carpets of *Berula erecta* often occur on sand or gravel. In shallow streams (e.g. those 20–30 cm deep) current paths are diverted between these carpets, so while sand accumulates inside the carpets, erosion takes place between them, making the ground level lower. Erosion then proceeds sideways, removing the sand under the edge of the carpet, while the tangled rhizomes and roots of *Berula erecta*

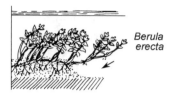

Berula erecta

Figure 3.21

hold a 10–15 cm strip of plants to the main carpet (Figure 3.21). As more sand is washed away under the carpet the plants at the edge are lost too. In deeper water this undercutting does not happen, and the sediment can be deeper before erosion occurs.

Once erosion has occurred, and the plants are lost, there are often other plants present which have newly grown on to the hard bed, and so far have no accumulated sediment, which can continue the population. This leads to plant cycles (Figure 3.22). The fastest cycle seen was in *Zannichellia palustris*, where silt hummocks about 15 cm high developed in 2 months, after which a change in flow pattern brought erosion. In *Berula erecta* the fastest cycle seen took less than a year. The length of the cycles depends upon sedimentation rates. Where this is slow, hummocks also develop more slowly and the plants remain anchored to the hard bed for longer, so that in perennial plants the cycle may take several years, while in annuals the autumn die-back occurs before the cycle is complete. Where there is negligible sedimentation, even perennial plants do not show cyclical development.

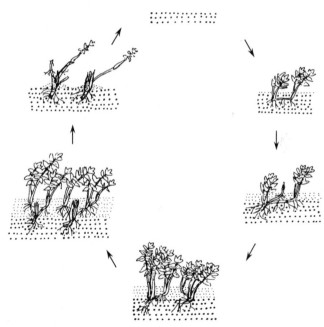

Figure 3.22
Cyclical development of *Berula erecta* carpet in a shallow chalk stream with moderate flow and some sedimentation.

VEGETATIVE SURVIVAL

River plants can often tolerate bad conditions for a long while, though they stay very small. Many can remain alive for a year with living stems only 1–3 cm long (e.g. *Myriophyllum spicatum, Rorippa nasturtium-aquaticum* agg.). Therefore, in general, uprooting is more dangerous to river plants than battering, since a battered plant can remain alive and regrow when conditions improve. In unfavourable conditions, land plants are usually able nearly to halt their growth. Many aquatics, on the other hand, continue to grow at the apex quite noticeably, even though their photosynthesis is negligible and they do not get larger. They merely take food from the lower end of the plant, which dies, and transfer it to the tip, which grows. This means the rhizomes and the anchoring roots may die in order to allow shoot tips to grow. This can be an advantage in still water, as shoots that had been shaded can float to the surface and perhaps grow better. In moving water, however, plants like this are washed downstream, out of the community.

CONCLUSIONS

Plants in natural streams are in equilibrium with the usual flow in the stream, both storm flows and normal flows, and the plants usually recover quickly from the peak and drought flows which may happen in the river. Thus really drastic damage seldom happens. If the plants are damaged in flow the growth rate must, on average, be at least equal to the rate at which the species is lost as a result of the flow. Different plants live in different types of flow: still and slow waters with soft deep soils have mainly deep-rooted and floating plants; faster flows have species which benefit from flow, either because they grow better in it or because they can anchor better to the coarser soils; and in swifter flows plants are increasingly those which can anchor near immovable objects (e.g. *Ranunculus* spp.) or those propagating easily from fragments (e.g. *Callitriche* spp.). Many streams bear no plants (macrophytes) at all, and two possible causes for this are that the flow is too swift and the soil too unstable (see Chapters 5, 6, 11 and 13).

The susceptibility of river plants to the physical components of flow is usually linked to their field distribution. (The correlation is incomplete, though; the physiological and chemical changes with flow variations are described in Chapters 5, 8, 12–14 and 19.) Each species is most closely correlated with the component of flow to which it is most susceptible, for what is important in determining plant distribution is which factor has a lethal effect first as conditions deteriorate. In swift waters the most usual lethal factors are, in order: erosion, velocity pull, sedimentation and battering. These are, however, often linked — for instance, plants of faster currents growing in slow waters are likely to be harmed both by erosion, and by physiological effects of the lack of dissolved gases, etc. reaching the shoots.

The potential hydraulic resistance to flow offered by a plant depends on its structure and size, but its effective resistance depends on its position in the stream, being least if it grows flat in quiet water at the sides of the channel or below an obstruction and most if it is in the fastest current. Plants with a high hydraulic resistance and a low anchoring strength are the most damaged by velocity pull. Even here though, position is important, for a susceptible plant may be protected, by more tolerant plants beside it. Anchoring strength is low when roots are not spread out, when they grow straight in a coarse substrate, when they are short in a fine substrate, or when roots and rhizomes are sparse.

Plants which are most tolerant of erosion usually have a rhizome and root weft in a hard substrate; or deep underground parts; or are protected by immovable objects which provide havens for a few plants in the community and from which susceptible areas can be recolonized after each storm. Tolerance to erosion, battering and some forms of velocity pull increases with increased vegetation cover (except when this leads to sedimentation and therefore poor anchorage), clumps and carpets being less vulnerable than single plants and larger plants providing cover and protection for small ones. However, if the plant cover is broken, damage can spread over a large area.

The amount of sedimentation that plants can tolerate depends both on the species and the sediment. Plants with short roots, which move upwards when sediment accumulates, erode easily and small plants which do not move upwards can be smothered by sediment, while large plants with deep roots are harmed the least by sedimentation.

If parts in the water are harmed the plant seldom dies, as new shoots can grow from below-ground parts. If, on the other hand, a plant is uprooted, it is then lost from the community.

4

River width, drainage order, depth and plant distribution

Width, drainage order and depth are all measures of the size of a stream, and so they usually all increase downstream. Plant distribution is related to width though this is generally because width is in turn associated with flow type, substrate type, depth and shading from the banks, rather than being the result of the changes in width themselves.

As streams flow to the sea tributaries join them and drainage order (Figure 4.5) is a measure of this stream pattern. Some plant species increase as drainage order increases, while others increase as it decreases.

Plants are also related to water depth. Those which have most leaves above the water show the greatest connection with depth, usually growing in shallow places, while floating-leaved and submerged plants can be found in various depths of water. Drought is an important factor in shallow places, and summer droughts may kill some submerged plants.

WIDTH

The narrowest watercourses are some headwater streams and some drainage ditches. These channels may be heavily shaded by tall plants (herbs) on their banks, which prevent the growth of water plants in the channel itself (Plate 13). Hedges on channel banks, which are common particularly in the lowlands, can also produce the same effect (Plate 12). Wider channels cannot be shaded by herbs, or completely shaded by bushes or trees, so provided other conditions are suitable, river plants are able to grow where there are gaps in the tree canopy and in the centre of the channel (see Chapters 1 and 7).

Some plants can anchor firmly to channel banks, but are only loosely attached to the channel beds (e.g. *Epilobium hirsutum* and, in some habitats, *Apium nodiflorum*). They are able to grow perhaps 0.5 m into the channel while remaining anchored to the bank, but if they grow further they are likely to lose contact with the bank and be swept away in storms (see Chapter 3). As 0.5 m is a much greater proportion of a narrow stream bed than a wide one, narrow streams are likely to support relatively more of this group of plants. If washed away, this narrow band of plants can quickly regrow from the populations that remain anchored to the bank.

Small lowland streams do not receive much storm flow. Thus although the discharge increases during storms, the rise in water level is usually small and emerged and semi-emerged plants remain above water level, with storm flow affecting only their lower parts. Velocity pull (Chapter 3) therefore remains low, and damage is also low. In wider streams, where the water level usually rises higher, storm flows are more likely to cover, and then wash away, emerged plants.

The widest watercourses are the lower reaches of large rivers. When watercourses become wider they usually become deeper also, and in wide, deep rivers, plants tend to be near the sides, where the water is shallower, the substrate is often more stable, and they are able to anchor to the banks. Some correlations between plant distribution and channel width are shown in Figures 4.1–4.4. Plants best correlated with channels 1–2 m wide are mainly large deep-rooted species characteristic of shallow still waters, and also ones very easily washed away (Figure 4.1). Those best correlated with channels 2.5–8 m wide form a more varied group. Two species more often grow best in narrow channels, though they may grow well in wider ones also (*Lemna minor* agg., *Sparganium erectum*), while the others, when growing abundantly, are best correlated with medium-width channels (Figure 4.2).

Figure 4.1
Species most closely associated with narrow channels. Histograms I, on the left, show percentage occurrence in each channel width. Histograms II, on the right, show number of occurrences in each channel width.
Abbreviations for channel width:
2   up to 2 m wide
8   2.5–8 m wide
18 9–18 m wide
+   over 18 m wide.

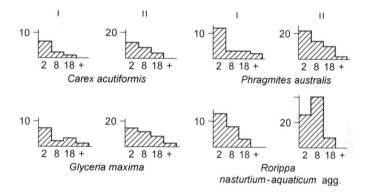

Those best correlated with wide channels are also a varied group ecologically (Figure 4.3); including shallow-rooted species of swift flows, deep-rooted ones of slow flows, and intermediates (see Chapter 3). Using tentative identifications of *Ranunculus* species (see Chapter 2), the preferences of the different species are:

Best correlated with wide channels (including abundant stands):
Ranunculus fluitans, Ranunculus penicillatus ssp. *penicillatus*
Best correlated with medium width:
Ranunculus penicillatus ssp. *pseudofluitans*
Avoids very narrow channels, correlated equally with other widths:
Ranunculus peltatus.

Channel plants not well correlated with width (Figure 4.4) are also varied ecologically. The bank species are even less likely to be directly affected by channel width.

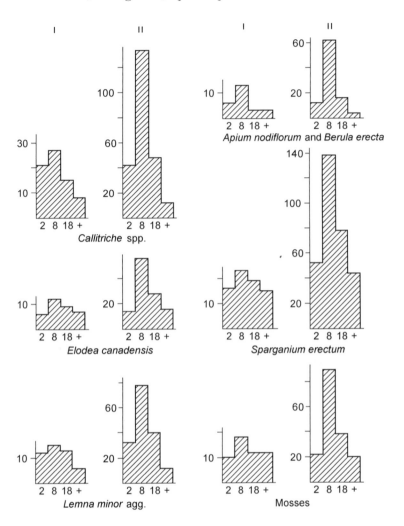

Figure 4.2
Species most closely associated with channels of medium width. Details as for Figure 4.1.

DRAINAGE ORDER

As streams flow towards the sea, tributaries join together. First-order streams, those of Drainage Order 1, are unbranched. For convenience, they are defined as those streams which are shown as unbranched on Ordnance Survey maps, scale ¼ inch to 1 mile (1:250000), in moist climates (Hynes, 1970). Second-order streams are formed by the confluence of two first-order ones, third-order ones from two second-order ones, and so on (Figure 4.5). There are, of course, far more streams of a low than of a high drainage order. If any two of the parameters of drainage order, the number of streams of each order, the mean length of stream of each order or the average drainage area of streams of each order are plotted against each other on semi-log graph paper (graph paper with one logarithmic and one arithmetic scale) then

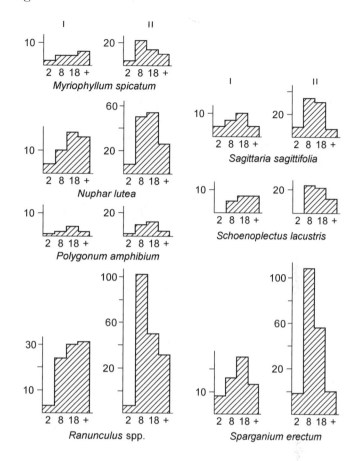

Figure 4.3
Species most closely associated
with wide channels.
Details as for Figure 4.1.

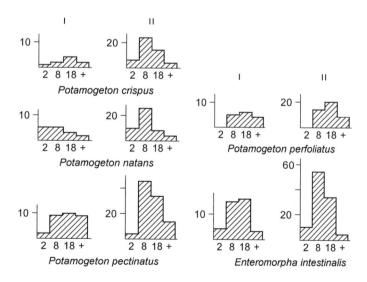

Figure 4.4
Species poorly associated with
channel width.
Details as for Figure 4.1.

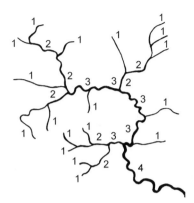

Figure 4.5
Stream order.

a straight line is obtained (Hynes, 1970). An anomaly should be pointed out: if ten second-order streams join a third-order one, the final stream remains of the third order, while if two second-order streams join immediately before flowing into the third-order one, these form a fourth-order stream.

The upper reaches of the smallest streams marked on the ¼ inch Ordnance Survey map are often dry for most of the year when they are in the lowlands, but in the mountains perennial flow often occurs higher than the channel is marked on the map. This is presumably a consequence of the falling water table in the lowlands (see Chapters 1 and 17): formerly perennial flow extended much farther upstream. However, these two types of first-order stream differ greatly in flow pattern and its associated variables, and thus in associated species.

The species best correlated with dykes and canals are shown in Figure 4.6, and are of course those also best correlated with still shallow water on soft substrates (see Chapter 2 and below) (*Potamogeton natans*, however, is a more unexpected member of this group). Those plants best correlated with canals are easily washed away in flowing water, and, unlike the tall emergents best correlated with dykes, die in drought.

Species tending to decrease with increasing drainage order are shown in Figure 4.7. These include the fringing herbs. Species which increase with increasing drainage order, shown in Figure 4.8, include the plants of both large swift rivers (e.g. *Ranunculus*) and large slow ones (e.g. *Nuphar lutea*). The final group in Figure 4.9 shows little association between distribution and drainage order.

DEPTH

Shallow watercourses often dry out in summer. Emergents and semi-emergents can usually tolerate such periods, but floating and submerged plants usually die quickly if dried. (Exceptions include the aerial forms of *Callitriche* and *Ranunculus* in summer-dry – winterbourne – chalk streams.) Short droughts leave living parts of the plant in the soil or on damp mud, and these are able to grow again when the water returns, but droughts long enough to dry out the rhizomes and roots in the top soil are far more damaging, as new growth must come either from deep underground rhizomes or from propagules from outside the community. Some plants can survive in puddles remaining in the lower places, and these can form the nucleus for recolonizing the stream. In hot climates a seasonal drought can be the equivalent of winter in temperate zones, as it is the time of year when the plants are not growing. It has been noted that drying canals in the Sudan for 3½ months had little effect on the final plant growth (Andrews, 1945). In general, however, repeated summer droughts in temperate climates remove

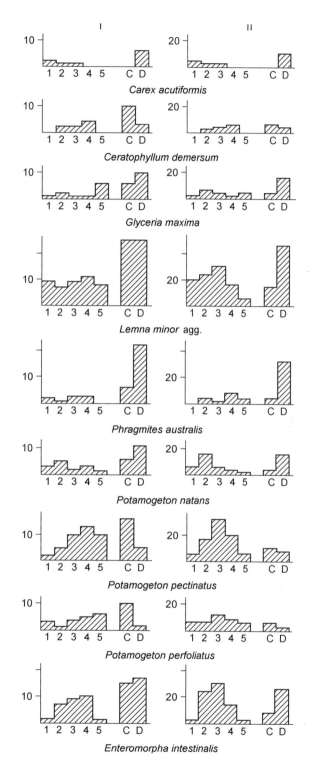

Figure 4.6
Species best associated with dykes, drains and canals. Histograms I, on the left, show percentage occurrence in each type of stream. Histograms II, on the right, show number of occurrences in each type of stream.
Abbreviations:
1–5 drainage orders
C canals and wide drains
D dykes.

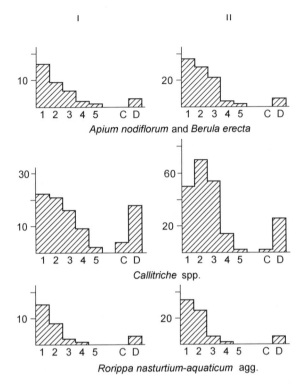

Figure 4.7
Species decreasing with
increasing drainage order.
Details as for Figure 4.6.

submerged and floating plants. A few species can colonise new places quickly, and grow quickly (e.g. *Lemna minor* agg.), and these can take advantage of temporary waters.

Shallow water, rather surprisingly, often harms submerged plants. They grow badly and often die, even though the shoots are in water and have space for growth (so this is a different phenomenon to death from drying, and plants usually survive better in limestone steams). Deep water also causes problems for growing plants. For example, very little light reaches the channel bed (see Chapter 7), and plants may be unable to grow because of this. Also, in still and slow waters particularly, the concentration of dissolved gases may be very different at the top and bottom of deep waters because there is little mixing of the water and the effects of the air do not fully reach the bottom. Most plant-bearing parts of British rivers are less than 1.25 m deep, and at least up to this depth hydrostatic pressure does not appear to affect plant growth. Deep water is necessary, though, for the full development of the larger aquatics such as *Ranunculus fluitans*, whose clumps may reach over 5 m long, 2 m wide and 1 m deep, and *Nuphar lutea*, whose leaves can spread through 1.5 m of water (Figure 4.10). Thus, although most species will grow as smaller plants in shallower places, the provision of space for

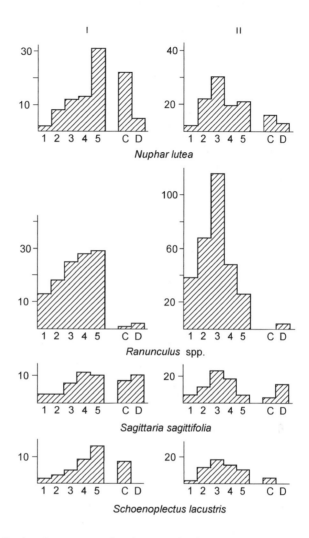

Figure 4.8
Species increasing with
increasing drainage order.
Details as for Figure 4.6.

the full development of submerged plant parts is an important character of deeper water.

Depth can be a limiting factor in the distribution of tall emergents. Some of these plants may be able to live submerged in the water (e.g. *Epilobium hirsutum*) but most cannot because water is physiologically unsuitable for the whole of the shoot. The leaves of *Phragmites australis*, for example, are unable to photosynthesise under water and thus die, so this plant usually grows where at least a third of the shoot is above water level (Haslam, 1973). Another, *Phalaris arundinacea*, needs the whole shoot to be above water for at least part of the summer if it is to grow well (except in some limestone streams). Even the very widespread *Sparganium erectum*, which does have a submerged form, is sparse and infrequent when permanently submerged (see Chapter 3 for the vulnerability of the

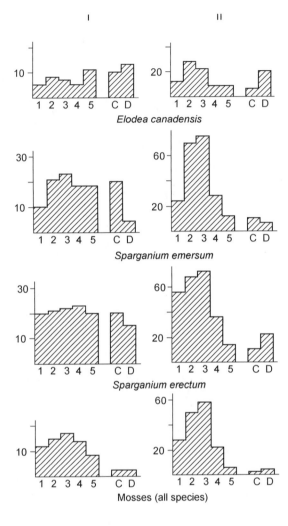

I   II

Elodea canadensis

Sparganium emersum

Sparganium erectum

Mosses (all species)

Figure 4.9
Species showing little association
with drainage order.
Details as for Figure 4.6.

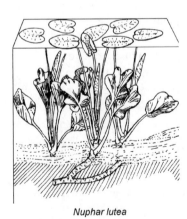

Nuphar lutea

Figure 4.10

submerged form). Most fringing herbs, in contrast, grow well when submerged, provided other habitat factors are suitable (chalk streams are the most suitable). However, these plants, being bushy, have a high hydraulic resistance to flow (see Chapter 3), and if they cannot anchor firmly — if, for example, they are growing in silt — they are washed away in storm flows. Emerged plants, therefore, may be excluded from deep water for either physiological or morphological causes.

The histograms of plant distribution in relation to water depth (Figures 4.11–4.15) show the depth as that of the main part of the river in summer. Consequently the correlations are with river size rather than the actual water depth in which the plants are growing. Emergents recorded in deep rivers are growing in shallow water at the edges and even submergents are often confined to shallow bands at the sides.

The species best correlated with shallow streams are the fringing herbs and mosses (Figure 4.11). Fringing herbs are commoner in the lowlands, where storm discharges are less, and mosses in the highlands, where stable boulders they can attach to are more frequent. The plants best correlated with somewhat deeper streams (Figure 4.12) are submerged or floating ones. *Callitriche* and *Ranunculus* require high light and fairly stable substrates, and diminish in deep water for this reason. Some *Ranunculus* cannot tolerate very shallow water. The correlations for individual species are:

Best correlated with water 35–75 cm deep:

> *Ranunculus aquatilis, Ranunculus penicillatus* ssp. *pseudofluitans, Ranunculus peltatus*

Best correlated with water 80–100 cm deep, though abundant stands are best correlated with depths of 35–75 cm:

> *Ranunculus fluitans, Ranunculus penicillatus* ssp. *penicillatus.*

In fairly deep streams, the best-correlated species come from varied habitats (Figure 4.13). Although *Sparganium erectum* is placed in this group, in deeper watercourses it is found only at the edges. *Myriophyllum spicatum* is a plant of fairly shallow water, growing at the sides of deeper channels, and this is reflected in the correlation of good growth and water under 75 cm deep. The plants best correlated with deep rivers (Figure 4.14) include also those characteristic of slow flow and silty substrates (see Chapter 2), and some that are indifferent to water depth (e.g. the free-floating *Lemna minor* agg., and *Polygonum amphibium*, whose floating shoots anchor in the bank). Finally, Figure 4.15 shows species not belonging to the other groups. These include the tall emerged monocotyledons of ditches and stream edges. Plants of the bank are of course not causally related to the depth of the channel.

Figure 4.11
Species most closely associated with shallow water.
Histograms I, on the left, show percentage occurrence at each depth. Histograms II, on the right, show number of occurrences at each depth.
Abbreviations for depth categories:
30   up to 30 cm deep
75   35–75 cm deep
120   80–120 cm deep
+   over 120 cm deep
T   turbid, probably deep.

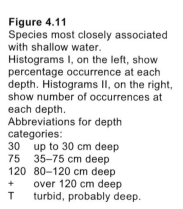

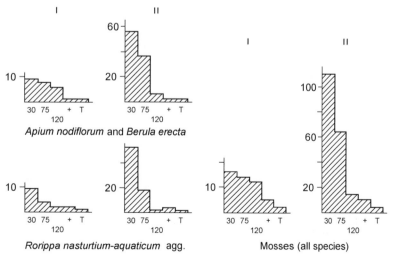

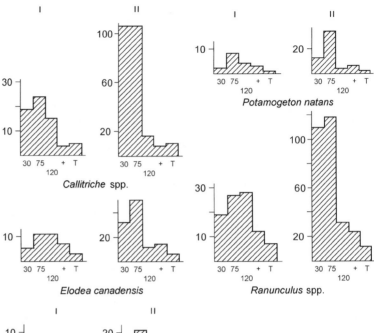

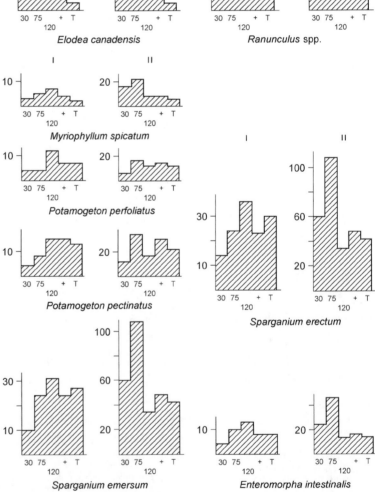

Figure 4.12
Species most closely associated with fairly shallow water.
Details as for Figure 4.11.

Figure 4.13
Species most closely associated with fairly deep water.
Details as for Figure 4.11.

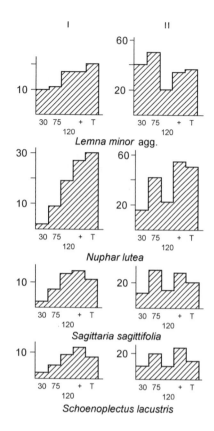

Figure 4.14
Species most closely associated
with deep water.
Details as for Figure 4.11.

Figure 4.15
Species poorly associated with
water depth.
Details as for Figure 4.11.
The tall emergents growing in
shallow water either in shallow
channels or at the edges of
deeper ones also come into this
category: *Carex acutiformis*,
Phragmites australis and *Phalaris
arundinacea*.

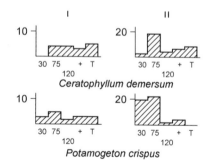

WIDTH–DEPTH ASSOCIATIONS

In becoming larger, watercourses usually become both wider and
deeper. Channel width depends on the discharge carried by the channel
and on the amount of sediment transported (excluding human impact).

Table 4.1   Width–depth associations

---

1 Concentrated in shallow and narrow channels

🌿 *Apium nodiflorum*   🌿 *Rorippa nasturtium-aquaticum* agg.

🌿 *Berula erecta*   🌿 Mosses

2 Concentrated in channels of moderate depth and width

🌱 *Callitriche* spp.   🌱 *Phragmites australis*

🌱 *Elodea canadensis*   🌱 (*Ranunculus* spp.)

🌱 *Phalaris arundinacea*   🌱 *Sparganium erectum*

3 Concentrated in deep though not wide channels

🌱 *Ceratophyllum demersum*   🌱 *Potamogeton crispus*

🌱 *Glyceria maxima*   🌱 *Potamogeton natans*

🌱 *Myriophyllum spicatum*

4 Concentrated in wide and very deep channels

🌿 *Nuphar lutea*   🌿 *Sagittaria sagittifolia*

🌿 *Polygonum amphibium*

5 Wide-ranging

🌿 *Lemna minor* agg.   🌿 (*Ranunculus* spp.)

🌿 *Potamogeton pectinatus*   🌿 *Schoenoplectus lacustris*

🌿 *Potamogeton perfoliatus*   🌿 *Sparganium emersum*

In any set of circumstances, therefore, width is a fixed variable, although it can be varied somewhat by man, or by erosion or silting. Width is only of minor importance to plants (see above), but it is one of the most important parameters indicating the discharge. Depth is of much greater importance to plants but, because it fluctuates greatly, is less satisfactory to estimate for the season as a whole.

Some width–depth results are shown in Table 4.1. The plants best correlated with narrow shallow streams are the fringing herbs and mosses best correlated with shallow water. In the next group are the plants typical of moderate channels. These include both the plants best correlated with rather shallow water and ones best correlated with somewhat narrow channels (see above). The third group is of plants tending to occur in somewhat narrow though often deep channels. This is the first habitat parameter which links *Myriophyllum spicatum* and *Potamogeton crispus*, two species with many resemblances in their field distribution in the lowlands. The species in the widest, deepest channels naturally include some characteristic of deep waters.

When width is linked to depth, the species groups found are more meaningful as diagnostic groups than those for either width or depth separately. The groups in Table 4.1 are of species of streams of increasing size. The different characters of a watercourse must therefore be studied both singly and in combination to understand why plants grow in the habitats in which they do: singly because each factor acts separately, and in combination because there is more than one factor influencing each habitat.

DISCUSSION

Species distribution can be determined for the five physical variables of flow, substrate (Chapters 2 and 3), depth, width (this chapter), and water clarity (Chapter 7). These distributions, though, show optimum occurrences in relation to these variables, not the conditions in which the species inherently prefer to grow. Correlation is not causation! Occurrence is also determined by rock type, nutrient regime, pollution, geographic area (species distribution), management, and these may be the most important. If deep rivers are severely polluted, no species will have peak occurrence in deep water. If rock type leads to unusually unstable substrates (e.g. Apennines), species occurring in flows swift enough to disturb this substrate will be few. With sufficient data, these factors can be understood.

If a species occurs, and is not ephemeral, the habitat of that place — all aspects of it — must be tolerable for that plant. Species usually have a smallish range of a factor in which they can grow very well, a peripheral range which is acceptable, and a wider range of very sparse occurrences. These last are often in microhabitats (e.g. shallow spur in deep rivers). (Since the first edition, a number of extensions to this sparse range have been published.) A species, therefore, may be on its optimum rock type, in its acceptable physical factors, and be able to tolerate the pollution present because of the tough roots developed on the preferred rock type.

A species' response to habitat variables, both separately and cumulatively must be known to understand its autecology. Haslam (1987) describes the distributions and ecology of the frequent species of ten European countries, giving variation, and its causes.

5

Flow patterns and storm damage

Chalk streams have very stable flows, with much of their water coming from ground water springs. Other lowland streams have less stable flows, upland streams vary more and the British mountain streams have the most variation in flow, with their large spate flows and general lack of main springs.

Different plants are damaged differently by storm flows. Some break in the water, and this sort of loss is quickly replaced. Others tend to be uprooted and washed away. Larger plants can shelter and protect smaller or less firmly anchored ones. Storm damage depends also on the type of storm flow and its duration. The longer the storm flow lasts, the greater the harm that is done. In the upper reaches very swift flow scours, breaks, and pulls out plants in the channel. Lower on the river, force is usually somewhat less, but storm flows increase water depth, so that badly anchored plants are washed from the edges of the channel. The speed, force and duration of storm flows vary from place to place and from storm to storm, and thus plant damage is also variable.

River plants are influenced by both the normal and the more extreme flows of their habitat (Chapters 1, 2 and 3). Communities may be determined, for instance, by the presence or absence of severe storm flows. Drought flows can be important if they substantially alter turbulence or silting, but generally have a lesser and more localised effect (for drying effects, see Chapter 4).

Storm flows are important in their frequency as well as their intensity, the frequency of spates which can be tolerated by any particular species depending partly on the rate at which it can regrow after damage (Chapter 2). Because plants present in a natural flow regime are those suited to that regime, they can usually recover from storm and drought flows within a few weeks or, rarely, months, and it is only when (as happens every few decades or centuries) storm flows are exceptionally severe that it may take several years, or even decades, to make the damage good. Flow regimes alter very slowly, except with human interference such as flow regulation and water abstraction. On a smaller scale, though, plant patterns within one site may be much affected by storm or drought flows, as individual small populations are washed away and then replaced by other species, or the space they occupied left bare. Storm flows may differ in their effects as the result of differing amounts of debris they carry and the exact position of current paths, but will always damage a declining population, where plants are poorly anchored, more than they will a vigorous healthy population. The rising phase of a storm discharge does more damage than the falling phase, discharge being equal, because it comes first and therefore removes the weaker shoots, and carries the debris which accentuates the damage by pulling on the plants.

The water regime of a stream is of extreme importance to the vegetation, affecting both the species present and their abundance. As has already been seen in Chapters 2 and 3, water movement acts in many different ways. This chapter looks at the wider aspects, and considers the annual patterns of flow and the overall damage done to vegetation by storm flows, and so links up to the overall influence of topography on vegetation described in Chapters 11, 12, 13 and, to a lesser extent, Chapter 6, and gives some of the evidence for predicting the effects of man's interference with the water regime which is discussed in Chapter 17. Flow comprises a complex of habitat factors. Each must be understood singly before the total effect can be appreciated, but this inevitably leads to some overlap in the information given in each section concerned with flow.

FLOW REGIMES IN DIFFERENT STREAM TYPES

Chalk streams have the most stable flows. This is because much of their water comes from springs, which reduces the fluctuations found in streams fed directly from irregular rainfall. Chalk is relatively porous, acting as a storage reservoir and so the annual peak of flow occurs in March or April after this reservoir has been refilled by the winter rains (Figure 5.1a). In streams other than chalk ones the proportion of run-off water entering the channel increases and that of ground water decreases, so that the flow becomes less stable and more spatey. (Unless, of course, stable effluents make up a substantial part of the flow.) With less underground storage, the annual peak of flow moves earlier, occurring as early as November in the mountains (Jones & Peters, 1977). Soft sandstone has a somewhat porous bedrock also, but less spring water in the streams. Soft clay, on the other hand, is much less porous, so more runoff from the land reaches the streams and the flow is less stable (Figure 5.1b of a mainly clay stream). In clay streams, the still greater instability of flow is matched by the instability of the easily eroded substrate. Much silt is washed in from the land, and deposited silt can be moved in storms. On the hard rocks instability and spateyness increase much more, because the ground is not porous and the rainfall is higher (Figure 5.1c) (Jones & Peters, 1977). The last group of watercourses is those with little flow: the dykes and drains of alluvial plains and the canals. The flow regime is more stable and more predictable, being determined mainly by flood gates, pumps, etc. and storm flows have little effect.

87

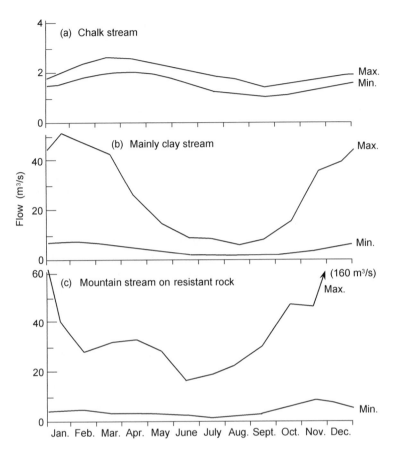

Figure 5.1
Seasonal changes in flow patterns.
Maximum and minimum mean flow
values for:
(a) chalk stream (River
    Lambourn at Shaw);
(b) a mainly clay stream
    (River Great Ouse at
    Bedford); and
(c) a mountain stream on
    resistant rock (River Dee
    at Bala).
(Simplified after Jones & Peters,
1977.)

In chalk streams, storm flows are mild, allowing species to survive and regrow. As a result of the springs, perennial flow occurs nearer the source of the stream than is the case for other (non-boggy) lowland stream types, and thus submerged and floating plants are also able to grow farther upstream. Soft sandstone streams are similar in having little storm damage, but have less water upstream. The instability of substrate and flow in lowland clay streams means they are susceptible to summer drought near the source, so few submerged or floating plants grow near the source except in local pools. In the middle reaches plants are often sparse because of unstable substrates, and in large rivers they tend to avoid the centre for the same reason, or because the water is deep. Other stream types are more likely to have plants right across the bed (if they occur at all) as the water tends to be clearer and the substrate more stable.

In the uplands and mountains, the swifter normal flows and the spates are both controlling influences on plant distribution. The spates have great force in the hills, where they can reduce a complete cover of thick vegetation to a few sparse plants, so the common plants in these areas are ones which do not erode easily and which can grow quickly between spates. In highland streams, flatter reaches have less force of water than steeper ones, so where the substrate is stable the flatter parts have more vegetation (probably of different species) and suffer less storm damage. If, though, these flatter parts have an unstable substrate of silt deposited in normal flows and disturbed during spate, then few plants can survive, and these tend to be ephemeral (potentially temporary species, e.g. *Callitriche* spp., *Lemna minor* agg.) or plants anchored to the banks (e.g. *Glyceria maxima*, *Polygonum amphibium*).

Minor changes in flow may cause minor variations in plant pattern, and conversely changes in plant pattern and growth cause minor variations in flow pattern. For example, plants growing better in moving water (e.g. *Ranunculus*) are benefited by increased current — unless the turbulence is high enough to cause substantial battering. Such small changes are happening continuously, and may benefit or harm individual plants while contributing to the overall stability of the plant community.

TYPES OF STORM DAMAGE

Any plant can be damaged by storm flow, though different species are likely to be harmed in different ways. In Table 5.1 the first group (1a) comprises those species whose early damage is usually to parts in the water by battering and velocity pull. If the shoots grow quickly, long-term damage is unlikely in normal storms. When plants which are normally able to anchor securely to firm substrates grow on soft soils, they are more liable to scour and damage. Recovery then depends on the presence and the growth rate of fragments, and is improved if rhizomes and roots are left in place (e.g. *Callitriche* spp.). A subsection of the group (1b) is the tall emergents whose shoots or leaves are likely to be damaged when bent over by the water or by debris carried in the current. Although individual shoots can be killed in this way, there is usually little total or permanent damage to the plant populations. Bank plants may also be included here, for they are sometimes low enough on the bank to be flooded after storms. Permanent damage is less than to channel plants, though, since they are flooded for less time. If, however, they are torn from the bank by velocity pull (see Chapter 3), the banks themselves may be damaged by erosion. The best protection against this is for the banks to be colonised by deep-rooted and firmly anchored plants which have a low hydraulic resistance to flow (for example, short grasses and alder trees). In the second group of plants

Table 5.1   Types of storm damage

1a Species commonly torn (broken) above the ground

Callitriche spp.

Myriophyllum spp.

Nuphar lutea

Potamogeton crispus

Potamogeton pectinatus

Ranunculus spp.

(*Schoenoplectus lacustris*)

Sparganium emersum

(*Zannichellia palustris*)

1b Species with long leaves commonly bent above the ground

Carex spp.

Schoenoplectus lacustris

Sparganium erectum

2 Species commonly uprooted from the ground

Agrostis stolonifera

Apium nodiflorum

Berula erecta

Callitriche spp.
(in more severe storms)

Ceratophyllum demersum

Elodea canadensis

Epilobium hirsutum

Mentha aquatica

Myosotis scorpioides

Myriophyllum spp.
(in more severe storms)

(*Nuphar lutea*, with local severe
damage)

Ranunculus spp.
(in more severe storms)

Rorippa amphibia

Rorippa nasturtium-aquaticum agg.

(*Sparganium erectum*, with local
severe damage)

Veronica anagallis-aquatica agg.

Veronica beccabunga

Zannichellia palustris

3 Species commonly falling into the stream with clods of earth eroded from the banks

Agrostis stolonifera

Carex spp.

Glyceria maxima

---

in Table 5.1 the usual initial damage is that the whole plant is immediately uprooted and washed away. This may be the result of erosion or velocity pull (see Chapter 3 and below). Most of these species are bushy and poorly anchored, and typically occur in lowland streams and at the edges of small hill streams where danger of uprooting is least. Small losses are tolerable, but heavy losses would eliminate the species from a site. The third category in Table 5.1 is of plants which are often damaged when clods bearing these species slip into the water. This is most likely to happen if the banks are much trampled by anglers or cattle. Minor storm damage can also result from other processes such as abrasion (see Chapter 3).

In small mountain streams the flow is usually too swift for flow-susceptible plants to grow in the channel, so storms cannot have much extra effect. On the edges, though, fringing herbs may grow well (see Chapter 13) in normal flows, though they are damaged in spates. Damage is thus concentrated on the edges of the streams. The other extreme is seen in silted lowland rivers with large deep-rooted plants. Here the vegetation is mainly at the sides, where water force is lower and, because the water is shallower, more light will reach the river bed. Damage may be greater at the centre or at the sides, depending on the stream, but it seldom affects the tall emergents at the edges.

Plant vigour affects the degree of damage they suffer. For example, small or unhealthy plants are less firmly anchored than large robust ones (Chapter 3) and plants which are partly damaged are often more susceptible during subsequent storms. Also, if soft silt or sand has been consolidated by a root weft and the weft is then broken, the whole carpet of plants can be rolled up and eroded away. Similarly if river plants are cut, this exposes the loose sediment that has accumulated under the plants, and this may be washed away together with the plants rooted in it. Plants that have been partly uprooted often have more hydraulic resistance to flow, and so are more easily removed by velocity pull. For instance, *Berula erecta* has stolons which bear clusters of leaves before they bear anchoring roots. If these stolons are waving free in the current, the parent plant is more likely to be swept away than if it had no stolons.

Storm damage is increased by particles in the water, whether in the form of small particles like silt, or large ones like branches. The small particles cause abrasion (see Chapter 3). They occur throughout the water, but in general do less harm than the occasional large particles, which can pull much vegetation away as they sweep by.

Shoals may accumulate during low flows and then be colonised by quick-growing plants (Plate 9). Shoal and plants may then be washed away during the next severe storm. This is part of the constantly changing, yet stable, pattern of river vegetation. Shoals move downstream during high flows, the size of the discharge needed to move them depending on the size of the particles which constitute the shoal. During the falling phase of a storm flow some of the particles may be deposited, and the level of the stream bed thus raised.

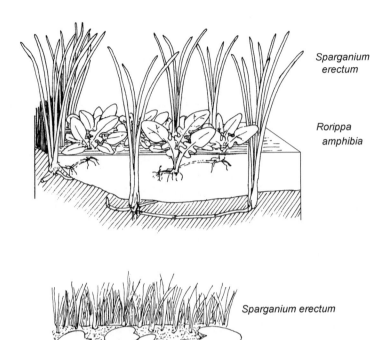

Figure 5.2

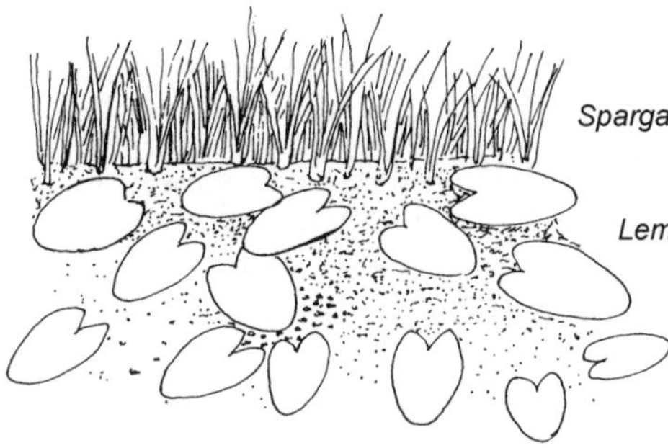

Figure 5.3

There are several other factors which affect storm damage. For example, the main current in one storm may be in a different position to that in a previous storm because of differences in water depth or in the size of plants or other obstructions — so the site of the damage may also vary. Rarely, places usually receiving little water force will receive most of the current, and severe local damage will result. Also, species may interact. An easily moved plant (e.g. *Rorippa amphibia*) may grow into large clumps when sheltered by a taller, firmly anchored species (e.g. *Sparganium erectum*) (Figure 5.2). Then, during a storm flow, the easily moved plant will be washed away, but in the process may damage its protector, which in turn may be bent and broken and have its hydraulic resistance to flow increased by the small plants tangled in it, thus rendering it more likely to be uprooted by velocity pull.

The good growth of *Lemna minor* agg. depends on the absence of swift flows, whether these are storm flows or the normal discharge. It grows quickly, and so takes advantage of temporary suitable habitats, such as those sheltered by large leaves (of e.g. *Nuphar lutea*, *Sparganium erectum*) or indentations in the river bank (Figure 5.3). Even small

92

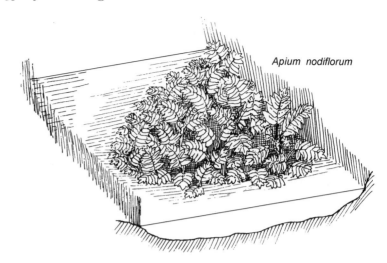

Apium nodiflorum

Figure 5.4

alterations in the flow, e.g. from light rain, can bring moving water to these places and wash off most of the *Lemna minor* agg., while severe storms cause more damage and can completely remove the species from the site. If there are any plants remaining these can re-form the population. Some streams which have intermittent periods of negligible flow (usually in late summer, or from the use of flood gates) may be completely covered with *Lemna minor* agg. at these times. Fringing herbs can grow very quickly in, for instance, small clay streams, where the water is shallow, competition absent, and nutrient status high because rich silt is present and accumulating (see Figure 5.4; see also Chapter 12). Under these conditions plants can grow from a few fragments to clumps *c.* 4 m × 2 m in perhaps 4 months. Because these large clumps accumulate silt the shoots become rooted mainly in this silt and lose contact with the hard bed below, which means they are then poorly anchored. They also have a very high hydraulic resistance to flow, because of their large bushy shoots, and receive the maximum force of the water, because they grow right into the centre of the narrow channel. Thus it is not surprising that such clumps are washed away in the first major storm. A few plants may be left, particularly if these are in havens (see Chapter 3), or new clumps may develop from fragments washed in from upstream. In small clay streams this cycle usually takes (2–)4 to 6(–10) months, depending partly on the plants' growth rate, and partly on the frequency of severe storms. Where the stream bed is harder, and there is not sufficient deposited silt for the plants to become detached from the bed or to grow rapidly because of the nutrients in the silt, the cycle is slower or non-existent. Chalk and mountain streams tend to have permanent populations of fringing herbs, often of small shoots which are only slightly damaged in the usual storm flows, and do not usually have either the luxuriant clumps or the wholesale losses which are so characteristic of the small clay streams.

Long-term changes in catchment management bring long-term, rather than short cyclic, change. Lessening absorption of water by the land greatly increases storm damage, including erosion and lowering of the stream bed. This comes from, e.g., increased hard surface, forest removal, firming of soil, and may be exacerbated by increased soil washed from the land, from more open bare soil and fewer barriers such as ditches and hedges.

DIFFERENT STORM FLOWS

The water force in a stream depends on the discharge, i.e. the mass of water, and the slope of the water surface. The steeper the slope, the greater the force, and the greater the turbulence, and for a given discharge a greater water force means shallower water, and vice versa. The slope of the water depends mostly on the slope of the channel, which is obviously greater in the hills than on the plains, but also depends on the flow at the time concerned, since the water surface is not exactly parallel to the channel bed. The water force affecting the plants is also influenced by the hydraulic depth of the water above them, i.e. the area of the cross-section of the water divided by the length of the wetted perimeter.

When rainfall is heavy and catchment conditions are suitable, the discharge may increase very quickly, leading to a steeply sloping water surface. If discharge increases more slowly during a rising flood the water surface will slope more gently. Given an equal discharge, the steeper flow will have the greater force of the two and do the greater damage. If the slope is the same in two storm flows, the one with the deeper water will have the more force and do the greater damage. The duration of the storm flow is important also, for plants are seldom damaged suddenly, and a storm discharge lasting several days will do more harm than one of equal force lasting less than a day. The poorly anchored plants, frail shoots, etc. will be removed in the first few hours and the degree of loss of semi-resistant parts then depends largely on the duration of a water force strong enough to damage the plants.

The actual damage due to storm flows of known intensity has been recorded from a few streams. One such example is a small chalk (-clay) stream with fringing herbs at the sides and in the centre where this was shallow and gravelly, and *Callitriche* growing in the deeper, slower areas with finer sediment. The effects on the vegetation of three storms are tabulated below:

Peak	Duration	Water slope	Damage
Storm 1			
10 cm above normal flow (vulnerable plants on bank touched only above 8 cm)	*c.* 3 days	Just flatter than in normal flow	(a) Up to and including peak flow (1 day). Removed or partly uprooted fringing herbs shallow-rooted on fine soil (*Veronica beccabunga* and *Rorippa nasturtium-aquaticum* agg. particularly). Carpet and root weft of fringing herbs in centre broken and partly rolled up (*Veronica anagallis-aquatica* agg. particularly). Some *Callitriche* pulled from silt, and broken off in water. (b) Subsiding flow to 7 cm above normal. A little further damage. (c) Subsiding flow below 7 cm above normal (4½ days). Shoots straighten, root wefts unroll, etc.
Storm 2			
25 cm above normal flow	*c.* 1 day	As steep as in normal flow	(a) Up to and including peak flow. A little removal of fringing herbs, and *Callitriche*. Fewer shoots bent, fewer shoots exposed. (b) Subsiding flow below 7 cm above normal. Recovery.
Storm 3			
25 cm above	*c.* 3 days	—	(a) Up to and including peak flow. Considerable damage, particularly to *Callitriche* and *Rorippa nasturtium-aquaticum* agg. some small stands being halved. *Veronica* spp. less damaged than in storm 1 as they were mainly in firmer substrates. (b) Subsiding flow. Recovery.

95

Damage throughout was mainly through velocity pull, pulling plants from the soil and breaking *Callitriche* within the water. A little damage came from erosion, in removing *Callitriche* from finer soil (in storms 1 and 3 mainly) and *Rorippa nasturtium-aquaticum* agg. (in storm 3). The change in the sediment pattern between storm 1, which was in early summer, and storm 3, which was in late summer, is reflected in the greater damage to *Veronica* spp. in storm 1, and *Rorippa nasturtium-aquaticum* agg. in storm 3. In both instances the finer substrates were the most damaged. The storm water was very silty in the earlier stages of the storm flow, but the amount of general removal (rather than disturbance) of the finer soil was too little to cause much damage. It can be seen from the data that damage depended mainly on the duration and depth of the storm flow, though the detailed effects depended also on the sediment pattern at the time of the storm.

Another stream studied was a side channel of a river in a flood plain, which had an almost flat water surface in both normal and storm flows. In storms the water level rose and the water movement increased very slightly, though not enough to cause damage by velocity pull, let alone by erosion or battering. The data from several storms are combined below:

Peak	Duration	Damage
10–30 cm above normal level	One to several days	Some leaves of *Nuphar lutea*, *Sparganium erectum*, etc. bent in water, some broken. *Rorippa amphibia* growing in shelter at the side (some not anchored at all, some poorly anchored in soft silt), floated to new water surface and moved downstream.

In such circumstances as these, storm damage is minimal, and apart from a little damage by water movement, deep flooding, whether for a few hours or a few days, does no effective harm to channel or bank plants.

In a shallow medium-sized clay stream that was investigated, the substrate was of mixed particles, somewhat consolidated, with a layer of silt above. The principal species present were:

Myriophyllum spicatum   *Schoenoplectus lacustris*

Nuphar lutea   *Sparganium erectum*

The data from two storm flows can be summarised as:

Discharge	Damage
Storm 1	
2½ times normal flow	Removed some *Myriophyllum spicatum* and *Sparganium erectum*.

Storm 2

| 4 times normal flow | Removed half the *Myriophyllum spicatum*, washing away most small plants and reduced shoots *c.* 2 m long to *c.* 1 m. Tore or broke over half the *Nuphar lutea* leaves, but there was no noticeable loss of rhizomes. Emerged parts of *Schoenoplectus lacustris* and *Sparganium erectum* were much bent or broken, and a little rhizome uprooted. |

In this case velocity pull was responsible for most of the damage, but erosion, abrasion and flood-bending also caused some harm. The damage done in storm 2, which occurred during the summer, was all made good in about two months. The loss to *Myriophyllum spicatum* was potentially the most serious, partly because this was the only species to lose much rhizome, and partly because the horizontal rhizomes, by which it spreads, grow in only very limited conditions. In the year in question, growth was possible both in spring, when the initial population developed, and in mid-summer, when the recovery took place. If the second growth had not been possible the population could have been seriously reduced by later storms, and if these had been severe the population might even have been lost. Thus it can be seen that the interaction of biology, damage and storm frequency is important (also see Chapter 3).

In the three examples cited above and the one described below, velocity pull was the most important cause of damage in two, battering in one, and the fourth had negligible damage anyway. These were all lowland streams without either spates or temporary shoals of silt, etc., and the data were recorded in summer, which is the time of year when the plant cover best protects the soil from erosion. Erosion is the most important cause of damage to sites where silt, sand or gravel accumulate during low flows. These include plant clumps which, as sediment accumulates, become rooted only in the sediment. Erosion and velocity pull are jointly responsible for most of the autumn wash-out damage, and much spate damage in the hills.

Exceptionally severe storms occur every few decades or centuries and cause severe erosion, with the loss of rhizomes and roots. It may take years, perhaps more than a decade, for the vegetation to recover fully from scour severe enough to cause an unstable substrate (e.g. the River Tees) or new channel. In a silting flow, silt can be deposited on the bed to form a new suitable substrate for plants within a year or two, but if a firm gravel or stone bed is broken then the recovery time is a lot longer.

DOWNSTREAM VARIATIONS IN STORM DAMAGE

The parameters of storm flow affecting plants are the water force, turbulence and depth, and the particles carried, all of which vary along a river.

The upper reaches of lowland streams are now often dry except during storms, and so the storm flows bring force and turbulence to plants which are otherwise not exposed to either (depth is irrelevant). The plants are necessarily emergents, and are mostly bushy. They therefore offer much hydraulic resistance to flow and, as most of them have not developed in flow, they may be insecurely rooted or rooted in loose soil. Quite frequently, tall dense emergents are able to grow near the source of a stream where the storm flow is very little (e.g. *Epilobium hirsutum, Solanum dulcamara*), whereas a little farther downstream (where summer storm flow is greater) plants are both sparser and shorter, and the species found are those offering less hydraulic resistance to flow and often those which have the ability to recover quickly after damage (e.g. *Apium nodiflorum, Veronica beccabunga*).

In the hills, upper reaches of streams usually have a normal flow that is swift and turbulent. The turbulence is usually enough for the additional turbulence of storm flows to have little extra effect, and here the importance of the storm flow lies in its increased force and the increased depth which brings this force to fringing plants growing at the edges of the channel. Channel plants are usually few, but in the infrequent streams where the substrate is stable in the usual spates and normal flow is not too fierce, channel plants may grow thickly (e.g. *Callitriche* spp., *Myriophyllum alterniflorum, Ranunculus aquatilis*). Fringing herbs cannot accumulate much silt, since not much silt is carried in the water, and as they are anchored to a firm substrate they are less easily swept away than in the lowlands. All fringing herbs, however, are bushy and will be swept away if the water force is sufficiently great, so will only grow well in those few mountain streams with an unusually low water force and some accumulation of sediment.

In the middle reaches of both lowland and hill streams the increased turbulence brought by storm flows is important. Plants are tangled and battered and locally pulled from the soil, and temporary and minor damage is common. The increased force is relatively less, though, than in the steeper upstream reaches. At the margins, water force is usually low and hardly affects tall emergents. However, the edges are usually silted and so the fringing herbs, which are shallow-rooted, do not anchor well. When the water level rises these plants are flooded, their soil softens, and because of their bushiness and insecure anchorage they are swept away by water without much force. This is a major reason why fringing herbs decrease downstream, except in chalk streams where the water level is more stable and there is less silting.

The substrate stability in middle reaches of streams varies. Chalk streams usually have a firm stable bed and low storm flows. There is thus little scour and plants typically grow all over the channel. Clay streams, on the other hand, have more silt, a less consolidated hard floor and greater storm flows. In these there can be much scour and few plants in the channel centre. In the hills, rivers with deposited, unconsolidated gravel are very unstable and few or no plants are able to grow, good vegetation only being found when the gravel is consolidated or is stabilised by nearby boulders.

In the lower reaches of rivers, in or near flood plains, there is seldom much force or turbulence in storm flows, and their main effect is to raise the water level, floating off poorly anchored plants from the edges, bending leaves, etc. They frequently deposit silt, though, and this may have a smothering effect (see Chapter 3). The total damage is little.

SEASONAL VARIATION IN STORM FLOWS. TIMING OF DAMAGE

Most river plants die down in winter, so their above-ground parts cannot be harmed by battering or velocity pull in winter storms. The soil may be churned up and washed away, though, uprooting the underground parts of some species (e.g. *Sparganium erectum*). Some plants remain green but have much smaller populations or shoots (e.g. *Nuphar lutea*, *Rorippa nasturtium-aquaticum* agg.) while others stay quite large in winter (e.g. *Berula erecta*, *Ranunculus fluitans*). Most *Ranunculus* species are winter-green, and so offer hydraulic resistance to flow in winter storms. They are unusually resistant to erosion, and in the mountains they are exposed to fierce water in spates. Their second main habitat is chalk streams, where winter storms are the least.

Most aquatics start active growth between March and May. Shoots usually grow before roots, so a storm flow may do more damage in spring than in summer when the shoots are anchored. Also, there is more bare soil in spring, so erosion is more probable. Summer storms are the least likely to cause erosion as the protecting plant cover is greatest. Most die-back is between September and December. Dying shoots are battered and washed away more easily than healthy ones. Tree leaves fall in autumn, and large mounds can accumulate in the streams, to be decomposed and be washed farther downstream.

In summer, the exact timing of damage may be important. In Lincolnshire, a stream has been studied (T. Brabben & K.R.C. Powell, personal communication) which is *c.* 3 m wide, with a usual discharge of 10–40 cusecs (cubic feet of water per second). It is dominated by *Potamogeton pectinatus*, a species growing very quickly in early summer and dying back in autumn. A storm flow of 100 cusecs during rapid growth did a little damage which was quickly replaced. A later storm of 750 cusecs removed perhaps 80% of the vegetation, and although the plants were still growing slowly, the damage happened too late to be replaced. Consequently the late summer vegetation was only about a quarter of that normally expected. The next year, however, the plants grew well. The stored food in most aquatics seems to be enough to initiate more than one year's growth.

Several river plants have a strongly seasonal growth cycle. Damage during rapid growth is fully replaced, but later damage is not, and if the damage recurs several years running it may lead to the decrease or loss of the population (e.g. *Phragmites australis*, *Potamogeton pectinatus*, *Sparganium emersum*). Another group of species can grow at any season, other conditions being satisfactory. In these damage can always be followed by regrowth, but at some times of the year, e.g. mid-winter in Britain, growth is slow (e.g. *Callitriche* spp., *Elodea canadensis*). There is also variation in the seasons in which plants can spread quickly horizontally, colonising unoccupied ground. Examples of typical behaviour are:

Any season	*Callitriche* spp.
Early spring	*Berula erecta*
Early summer	*Groenlandia densa*,
	Myriophyllum spicatum,
	Zannichellia palustris
Late summer	*Apium nodiflorum* (frequent),
	Hippuris vulgaris (hot summers)
Early autumn	*Schoenoplectus lacustris*.

In species with horizontal spread, the timing of the damage can affect its outcome. If it occurs before the spread the losses are quickly made good, provided some plants remain. If, on the other hand, the damage comes at the end of the annual growth period, the stand is left poor and sparse and liable to further damage and perhaps extinction in later storms.

6

Width–slope patterns

The width and slope of a stream, unlike the water speed, depth, etc., remain constant from day to day and nearly so from year to year. Most of the flow, substrate, sedimentation, and depth characters of a stream are summarised in, and can partly be deduced from, the width–slope pattern.

Topography affects the fierceness of flow and thus the distribution of plants. In the mountains the steeper and narrower streams have no large plants, but almost all upland and lowland streams can potentially contain vegetation.

Luxuriant vegetation, however, is confined to certain parts of the width–slope pattern, its distribution depending on rock type and topography.

Different species are found on different width–slope patterns (referred to here as the pattern of the species), and they may occupy some parts of this pattern only in selected habitats — for instance in deeper water, or in places liable to spate, etc. The distributions can usually be interpreted in terms of the habit of the plant. The diagrams in this chapter can be used for predicting the changes in plant distribution that will occur after alterations to the river, such as flow regulation.

The total size of a stream channel is defined by its width and depth. The shape and size in turn depend on the discharge, the amount of bed sediment transported, the substrate type and the roughness of the channel banks. The movement of sediment on the channel bed partly depends on the channel slope. The slope of the river bed, and of the water surface, are usually fixed by the hilliness of the land, and minor man-made alterations, such as flood gates, do not affect the overall pattern.

Width and slope are usually constant, while discharge, sediment and depth may vary from day to day. It is therefore useful to consider width and slope as independent variables. The width used here is approximately that of the channel near a road bridge, and the slope is that on the old 1 inch to 1 mile Ordnance Survey map (1:63 360) above the road bridge. This gives the general slope but not the minor variations: many streams, particularly hill ones, have alternating stretches of faster steeper flows and slower, deeper flatter reaches, and these are not measured separately here.

The roughness of a straight channel depends on the size of the particles of the bed and the banks, the shapes of these (ripples etc. on the bed, undulations in the bank), the river plants and the water depth. If discharge and, consequently, depth much increase, then since slope and width hardly vary, roughness has to decrease. This means that vegetation is removed. Therefore, although flow and substrate interactions damage and remove plants in different ways and in different quantities in different conditions, this plant loss falls within the general physical equation determining roughness.

The width–slope pattern summarises most of the physical characteristics of a river which affect plants, so variations in discharge, substrate, loose sediment, depth and the height from hill top to stream bed can be deduced in part from the width–slope patterns. Since most plant nutrients come from the silt and mud, nutrient preferences can also be deduced, if the flow pattern is known. If slope is fixed, a given amount of turbulence can come either from a shallow slower stream or a deeper swifter one. Plants which require a silting flow or an eroding flow will grow only in particular combinations of depth and flow.

Because of the small size of Britain and the general association of rainfall and altitude, apart from a few minor reservations, the diagrams are valid for all Britain. They do not necessarily apply in other European countries, as rainfall patterns differ; there may be snowmelt, and rock type, landscape, springs and porosity may all differ. New width–slope data need to be collected for each region.

REGIONAL PATTERNS

Regional patterns of plant distribution are shown in Figures 6.1–6.4. In each diagram one line surrounds those stream sites which have angiosperms (ignoring those with only temporary grass clumps or temporarily flooded grass at the edges). When a second outline is present, this indicates sites without angiosperms. Streams are steeper towards the left of each diagram and wider towards the top, so that sites at the upper left have the fiercest flow and those at the lower right the least water movement.

The patterns in Figure 6.1 all have a similar general shape. Figure 6.1a, b and c are of mountainous regions. In each there is a band of streams to the left without angiosperms, because the fall in height from the mountain top to the stream channel is great, the water runs off with great force, and the flow in this outer band of sites is too fierce for these plants to be able to grow. The substrate is affected by the swift flows too. Even over to the right, in the downstream reaches, the substrates are mainly gravel or stone, except in flood plains. If the particles are consolidated into firm beds many species can grow there, but unconsolidated gravel and stone are most unsuitable for plant growth because they are moved in spates, disturbing and squashing the below-ground parts of the plants, which are thus confined to sheltered and stabilised places or are absent altogether. Silt may occur in local sheltered places, and plants requiring either higher nutrient levels or a fine substrate for rooting are confined to these areas.

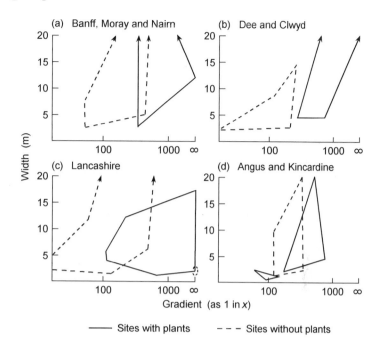

Figure 6.1
Regional width–slope patterns: very mountainous regions. The sites shown in these patterns are from the regions named, but are not necessarily representative of the topography of the whole of these regions. The gradient (or slope) was taken from 1 inch Ordnance Survey maps and is plotted on a semi-log scale, so that 100 represents a gradient of 1:100, 1000 a gradient of 1:1000, and ∞ a gradient substantially less than 1:1000. The channel width is plotted on an arithmetical scale.

Where the patterns of the sites with and without angiosperms overlap, there are several possible causes for this. For example, the streams may have alternating stretches of swifter water without plants and quieter water with them, and of the sites recorded some may be on the swifter and some on the quieter reaches. Alternatively the sites without plants may have fiercer flow because the hills beside them are higher; or the sites without plants may be polluted, shaded, recently dredged, etc.

If a mountainous district includes some lowland regions as well, the lowland sites with plants will be placed on the diagram near the mountainous ones without them (Figure 6.1d). This is because the lowland regions have only a small fall from hill top to stream channel compared with the mountainous regions, and so in the same place on the width–slope pattern flow may be fierce or gentle depending on this fall from hill to channel. In the very mountainous region of northern Scotland, where gradients are very steep and falls from hill to valley are great, most streams do not bear angiosperms. Plants occur in those few channels where the gradients are flatter or — more often — the falls from hill to valley are less. *Juncus articulatus* occurs in fiercer flow than the other species. In flat watersheds the bog streams, with much plant growth, have narrow and nearly flat channels.

Fairly mountainous areas, where the flow is less fierce and the hills less steep than those illustrated in Figure 6.1 are shown in Figure 6.2. Smaller streams in this group may resemble those in the previous

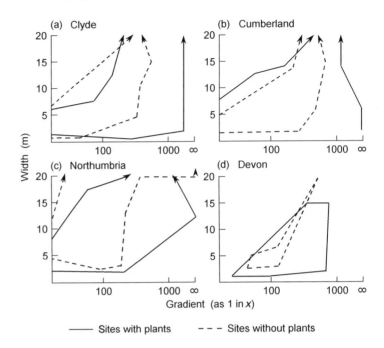

Figure 6.2
Regional width–slope patterns:
mountainous regions.
Details as for Figure 6.1.

——— Sites with plants   – – – Sites without plants

group, but the total pattern differs. Sites with plants occur almost throughout the pattern; plants can grow even in some of the steepest sloping streams. However, most of the sites without plants are in these smaller steeper streams, which are likely to have shallow turbulent water, or greater falls from hill top to stream channel, or to be polluted, etc. Almost all flat or downstream sites have plants, whether these are growing in the channel, on shoals, or as bank emergents.

Upland regions have lower hills (Chapter 1 and 13), less force of water and usually finer substrates (Figure 6.3) than mountainous areas. More silt is produced from sandstone than from the resistant rocks and more can accumulate in upland than in mountain areas. Since upland areas are often sandstone, their increased silt is the result of both these factors. An upland region usually includes some mountain and lowland streams, which unfortunately obscure the pattern. Species which cannot tolerate the extreme flow and substrate regimes of the mountains, but can withstand some spate, are able to grow in the upland streams and as the mountain species can potentially occur here too, these streams more often bear plants, are more species-rich, and more often contain dense vegetation than the mountain streams. If silt is deposited downstream and is usually undisturbed in spates, vegetation can be abundant, though silt which is frequently disturbed bears few plants. As flow becomes less fierce, other factors (such as shade, pollution, recent dredging, etc.) become relatively more important as the overall controlling factors of plant distribution. It is

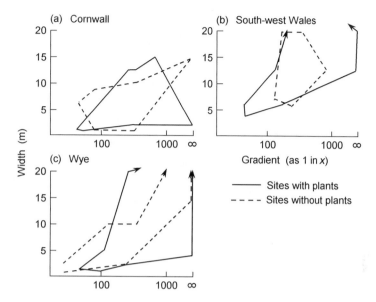

Figure 6.3
Regional width–slope patterns:
uplands.
Details as for Figure 6.1.

only where flow alone is fierce enough to exclude plants from a site that the other possible limiting factors are irrelevant.

Patterns of plant distribution in lowland streams are shown in Figure 6.4, and it can be seen that sites with angiosperms occur throughout the diagram. In this region the storm flows are of much lower force, allowing plants to grow even in the steepest sloping streams. In general species requiring slow flows and fine substrates can do well, though chalk streams have less silt than those on other rock types. In clay streams plants may be excluded as a result of a combination of unstable substrate and unstable flow (see Chapters 5 and 12; shown in Figure 6.4). For example, Essex is entirely clay, and in the pattern from here no sites are empty solely because of the width–slope combination. Pollution, shallowing, shading, channel management practices, etc., may all exclude plants from sites. Shading is of greater importance here than it is in the hills: for example, small brooks often run beside, and are shaded by, hedges (Plate 12).

DISTRIBUTION OF DENSE VEGETATION

The development of a luxuriant river vegetation depends on the interaction of flow regime and geology. In lowlands, catchments often vary in geological type, so although small streams often have catchments of only one rock type, large rivers are often from two or more rock types. The distribution of sites full of plants (on a simple subjective assessment) on soft lowland rocks is shown in Figure 6.5a.

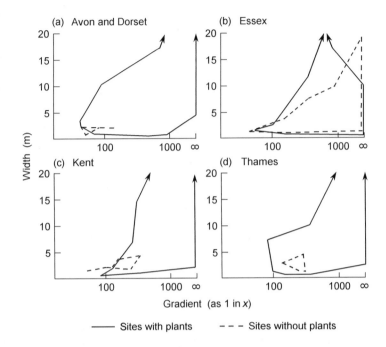

Figure 6.4
Regional width–slope patterns:
lowlands.
Details as for Figure 6.1.

These are in places with the least fierce flows: on flatter and wider sites. This is because in mild flows silt accumulated downstream, and if it is not churned up is able to bear luxuriant vegetation. The upper reaches of clay and sandstone streams have beds which are easily eroded and, particularly on clay soils, much silt enters the streams and can build up in plant clumps, in shoals, etc. However, this is then disturbed in storm flows and consequently these upstream sites are seldom full of vegetation. On chalk, in contrast, the bed is firm, silting is less and a perennial flow extends farther upstream, and thus the steeper streams can be full of vegetation.

The distribution of 'full' sites on hard rocks is shown in Figure 6.5b. The outline for resistant rocks is to the left and above that for soft rocks, that is, on wider and steeper streams. The boulders of steeper hill streams do not move easily, even in spates, and help to stabilise gravel near them, which if it is stabilised and firm can allow the development of a good vegetation. Thus some hill streams on hard rock can bear abundant plants on steeper slopes than can streams on a soft rock. Lower on hill streams, however, the substrate is often deposited unstable gravel or stones, so plants are sparse. In the lowlands, the best downstream habitat for good growth of vegetation is the flatter narrower rivers. In the highlands this habitat is poor, since the substrate tends to be unstable gravel rather than stable silt, but in larger highland rivers, with their greater discharges, the substrates tend to be firmer,

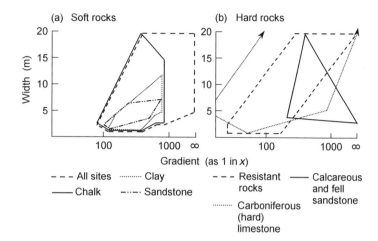

Figure 6.5
Stream sites full of vegetation.
Details as for Figure 6.1.

with little deposition and a consolidated bed that is seldom moved in spates, so here plants are able to grow thickly.

The smaller streams of flatter country on resistant rocks (Figure 6.5b) are often full of plants. Water force is low here, as in other lowlands. On the hard sandstones the pattern of full sites is intermediate between that of the resistant rocks and that of soft sandstone (Figure 6.5a). The full sites on hard limestone (Figure 6.5b) form a larger pattern than on any other rock type. The more extreme points on the pattern are from places without fierce spates and a regulated flow. The very steep sites are from the Cheddar Gorge, which has no spates, and the very wide ones are from the Peak District, where the flows are upland rather than mountainous. Limestone forms a fertile rock, but in mountainous sites it is, as always, the fierce flow that is the factor controlling plant distribution.

SPECIES DISTRIBUTION

Different plant species are found in areas with different width–slope patterns. Figures 6.6–6.11 show the width–slope patterns of various species derived from the vegetation of around 3500 sites throughout Britain. Because many species are very sparse a study of this size may be incomplete, and further study could well add a new habitat (e.g. a new rock type or flow regime) and thus a part to the width–slope pattern. When a few sites stand outside the general pattern, these discrepancies are usually attributable to interference with the flow regime, for instance, a species may occur in quiet water above a weir in a stream otherwise too steep for this species, and such sites have usually been excluded from the diagrams. Most species are more frequent in the

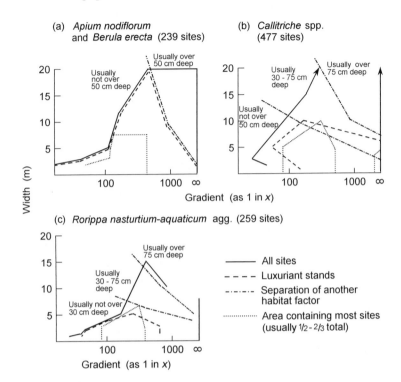

(a) *Apium nodiflorum*
and *Berula erecta* (239 sites)

(b) *Callitriche* spp.
(477 sites)

(c) *Rorippa nasturtium-aquaticum* agg. (259 sites)

Gradient (as 1 in *x*)

Width (m)

——— All sites
– – – Luxuriant stands
–··–··– Separation of another habitat factor
·············· Area containing most sites (usually ½ - ⅔ total)

Figure 6.6
Species of narrower and shallower streams.
Details as for Figure 6.1.

lowlands than the mountains, and consequently the diagrams are more accurate for the lowlands.

Some plants occur in much the same width–slope pattern whether they occur in, say, lowland Essex or highland Aberdeenshire. Variations in the flow pattern as a result of topography are then irrelevant to the distribution. Most of the patterns do differ with topography, though, and these variations are described below. The patterns can often be subdivided according to stream depth, the narrower and steeper sites being shallower than the wider and flatter ones. Wider rivers have a faster flow than narrower ones on the same channel slope. Deeper streams have a faster flow type than shallower ones, other factors being equal. Thus if a plant requires a slow flow type, it grows in deeper water in wider than in shallower streams. Such species require a certain flow-and-substrate regime. If, on the other hand, a plant is almost confined to a single depth category, it is probably influenced more by depth than by flow regime.

Plants typical of upper reaches have width–slope patterns like those illustrated in Figure 6.6. They are concentrated in narrow streams and shallow water.

Apium nodiflorum and *Berula erecta*, grouped together (Figure 6.6a) are most frequent in the steepest streams, though most stands of good performance are placed only a little left of centre of the pattern. In small brooks clumps are often sparse because of the storm flows, which in the hills are spatey and in the lowlands scour the unstable, often dry, substrates. In small lowland brooks without scour, though, taller species can dominate. Abundant populations are mainly found in lowland streams with a firm medium-grained bed (typically chalk streams), for here the plants can anchor and sedimentation is little. In wider streams they are confined to the margins, as a result of the centre having too strong a flow, the water being too deep or too turbid, or the substrate being too coarse or unstable for these plants. The edges usually have fine soil, so that plants are easily washed away in storm flows (see Chapter 5). This means the populations in such streams are often temporary, developing from fragments washed down from upstream, and being themselves swept away in due course.

Rorippa nasturtium-aquaticum agg. has the same overall pattern, but its sites are more frequent in the centre of the diagram, and most of its well-grown populations are in steeper streams. It is excluded from most wide and deep rivers for the same reasons as *Apium nodiflorum*. *Rorippa nasturtium-aquaticum* agg. frequently grows very quickly, growing over any other short or submerged species present. It can cover small channels but, as most shoots are not anchored or poorly anchored, most of the stand is washed away in the next major storm. With this growth habit it does best in the shallowest channels with least fluctuation in depth. It does not grow well when submerged, and so avoids deeper water when it cannot grow on top of other plants. In contrast, *Berula erecta* grows well submerged, rarely shows explosive growth, and does not grow over and smother other fringing herbs. It does best somewhat downstream of *Rorippa nasturtium-aquaticum* agg.

The *Callitriche* spp. (Figure 6.6b) are mainly *Callitriche obtusangula* and *Callitriche stagnalis*, with some *Callitriche hamulata* in more acid places and some *Callitriche platycarpa* in slower waters. There is rather more *Callitriche* in the slightly wider streams, and it is most frequent in steeper ones. Its well-grown, long-lived populations are most often found in somewhat shallow water with a fair flow and a medium-grained firm substrate, or else in somewhat shallow still waters in dykes and canals. *Callitriche* species do, however, occur sparsely in most other stream types, sometimes in only temporary populations (for example, on silt shoals liable to disturbance).

Myriophyllum alterniflorum, though not illustrated, probably belongs with this group of species, although it does occur in wide rivers also. Its main association seems to be with soft water rather than with physical factors.

The next group of plants, shown in Figure 6.7, are those which occur mainly or only in faster flows. In the range studied, depth is of

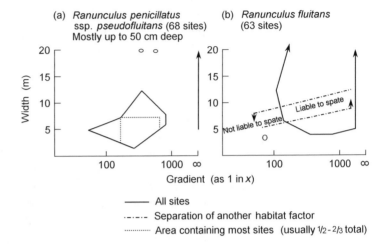

Figure 6.7
Species mainly in swifter flow.
Details as for Figure 6.1.

less importance as a controlling factor. Their pattern is from the lower left to the upper right in the width–slope diagrams, i.e. from steep streams to wide flat streams.

Ranunculus penicillatus ssp. *pseudofluitans* is most frequent, and most often luxuriant, in the steeper, narrower end of its range. It is almost confined to limestone. It usually prefers a considerable volume of water and so does not occur in the very steep streams at the far left of the diagram (if the artificial deep pools of the Cheddar Gorge are excluded). It has a similar range in the lowlands and the hills.

Ranunculus fluitans requires a stable substrate and, for good growth, a large volume of water. It therefore avoids sites where water volume is small (which includes the left of the diagram). It occurs in both lowland and hill sites, but in flatter reaches it is found in narrower streams in the lowlands, and wider ones in the hills. This separation of the width–slope pattern between habitats with and without spates has two causes. First, rivers are spatey in the hills, and spatey rivers tend to be wider for the same volume of flow. A second and more important factor in the distribution of *Ranunculus fluitans* is the difference in the distribution of suitable substrates for its growth between the lowlands and the hills. In lowland streams stable firm substrates tend to be found in medium-width stretches, while in the hills the more spatey flow means that these medium-width streams often have unstable gravel substrates and wide ones are more likely to have consolidated beds.

The plants of Figure 6.8 occur similarly from small narrow to wide flat streams, that is, have a similar band from lower left to upper right of the diagram, as in Figure 6.7. But they also have a band along the right-hand side, which means they grow in flat channels too, both wide and narrow. The sites the plants avoid are the slow-flowing and

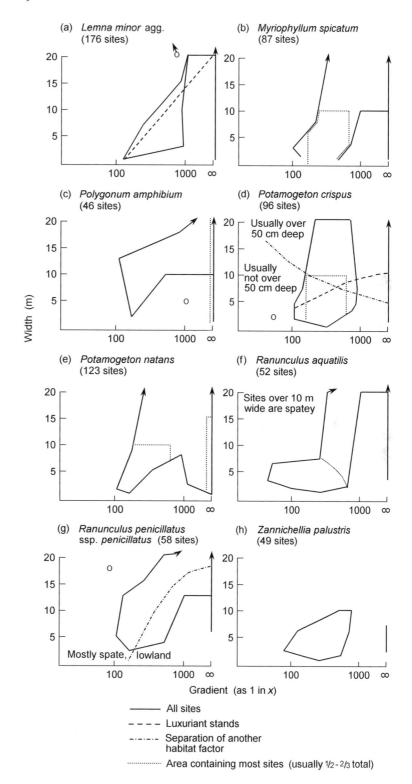

Figure 6.8
Species of a central pattern.
Details as for Figure 6.1.

somewhat narrow streams, where there is unstable accumulating silt in which short-rooted plants cannot anchor and by which low-growing ones can be smothered. Some of this group also avoid the wider more gravelly streams (Figure 6.8).

Myriophyllum spicatum is most frequent in the steeper and narrow part of its range, and the wider sites are in hill rivers. Its morphological characteristics are that it does not have a consolidating root weft, its rhizomes can spread over a wide area and its shoots are bushy. Thus it is probably absent from the low-central part of the diagram because it is vulnerable to velocity pull (see Chapter 3) and cannot remain in, and take full advantage of, small areas of suitable substrate; it is also not able, by means of a root weft, to improve the substrate to its own advantage.

Ranunculus aquatilis and *Ranunculus penicillatus* ssp. *penicillatus* have a broadly similar pattern, and both show a separation between hill and lowland sites (see *Ranunculus fluitans*, above). Both form firm root wefts in stable coarser substrates. *Ranunculus aquatilis* grows in still water in dykes and canals, but there it is likely to be floating and delicate and this form could not survive in flow. Most of its records in narrow streams are in the lowlands, where the flow, particularly from chalk, tends to be stable. Small hill streams have a more variable discharge than lowland ones, and perhaps become too shallow in summer for these species to occur. In mountain streams *Ranunculus aquatilis* is typically found in upper middle or middle reaches, with *Ranunculus fluitans* below, where discharge and depth increase. Where both occur, *Ranunculus aquatilis* grows in the shallower faster parts and *Ranunculus fluitans* in the deeper slower ones. *Ranunculus penicillatus* ssp. *penicillatus* seldom grows in small streams, and does not grow in the narrow still channels of the dykes, etc. The lowland form has longer leaves.

The *Potamogeton natans* pattern may be incomplete, as the species is infrequent. The lower position of the pattern on the diagram shows that it grows in slower waters than the preceding species. The lower reaches and still-water sites (on the right) are mostly lowland, and the wider and steeper ones (on the left) are mainly highland. It needs a fairly soft soil for rooting, though it can grow between stones. It is able to consolidate soil somewhat, though it does not have a dense root weft.

Polygonum amphibium is also infrequent, so may also have a width–slope pattern that is incomplete. The pattern is only for the form with floating shoots (not the emerged form), and as these are anchored in the bank, water depth is irrelevant. It typically occurs in slow waters, though it can tolerate spates by regrowing from the bank. Most sites on the left of the diagram are lowland clay streams, and on those on the right canals and hill streams.

Zannichellia palustris is more frequent in the steeper part of its range, and does not grow in deep water. It grows where some silt or sand will be deposited, the plants accumulating this and stabilising the sediment by means of their root weft. This root weft is broken by storm flows, trampling, etc., and the sediment, along with the plants, can then be washed away. If sediment is deposited very quickly, however, the plant cannot stabilise it, and again both sediment and plant will be eroded. Alternatively the plant grows in sites such as dykes where there is no scour. It has a small habitat range, mainly in the lowlands.

Enteromorpha intestinalis which is a large alga (not shown in the figure) has a rather similar pattern, but occurs in a wider habitat range. It is most frequent, and most often luxuriant, in dykes and drains and is seldom able to grow abundantly in flow because the strands are easily broken and washed downstream.

Potamogeton crispus is spread over most sites except those in the steepest narrowest streams, and in the areas with least stable substrate. It is most frequent in the centre of its range and is rare in flat narrow channels, though it is in these flatter sites that most well-grown populations are found. On a fairly firm medium-grained substrate it can grow well, forming a dense root weft which keeps the soil stable below it: really unstable or coarse substrates are unsuitable for its root weft. Its steepest sites are usually on clay, where silting occurs furthest upstream. Its anchoring root weft, and its ability to stay in discrete patches on suitable substrates, probably account for its wide distribution and its frequency in flatter areas. It is bushy when growing well; giving a high hydraulic resistance to flow, but it is brittle and easily broken above ground by faster flows.

Lemna minor agg. is washed into streams from lakes, ponds and sheltered places upstream. It becomes lodged in any sheltered place, and if conditions are suitable it can grow very quickly. Stands developing during low flows are swept off during high ones. In the wider and steeper rivers the sites are mainly lowland, because water movement at such sites in the hills is too great for it.

The species of the next group, shown in Figure 6.9, have wide overall patterns, though in other respects may vary considerably. Mosses, as a group, are concentrated in narrow steep streams (cf. Figure 6.6). Most sites in such streams (at the far left of the diagram) are from the hills, because this size of stream in the lowlands is often dry in summer or is covered with plants tall enough to shade out mosses.

Elodea canadensis, when luxuriant, is commonest in the unstable silting habitat (lower right of the diagram) most avoided by the species illustrated in Figure 6.8. It grows in the more sheltered places, and because it can quickly regrow from fragments does well in temporary as

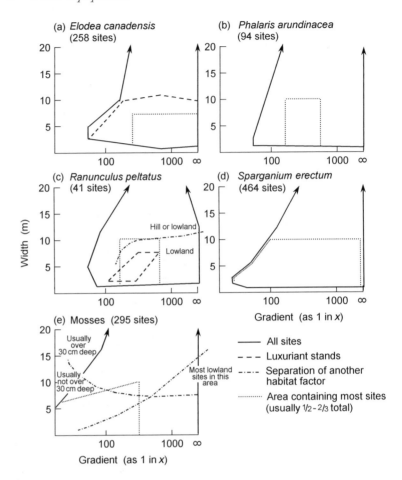

Figure 6.9
Species of wide pattern.
Details as for Figure 6.1.

well as long-term habitats, and can spread widely in the hot summers in which it grows best. The pattern does not have a clear division on stream depth, and this probably reflects the wide range of places in which it can occur, at least temporarily. It seldom grows in the widest rivers. Its roots are short and straight and need soft soil, so are easily pulled up, and this is probably why the species avoids steep mountain streams.

Sparganium erectum is the commonest British river plant. It grows in shallow water and soft soil, and so can be found both in the centre of slow silty channels and at the sides of deeper ones. Luxuriant stands are mostly found in the small siltier channels (left of centre in the diagram).

Phalaris arundinacea is widespread. It does not tolerate permanent flooding and so grows in shallow channels which usually dry in summer, and where flows are not swift enough to erode it from unstable substrates. As often happens, it tolerates long-term submergence best in chalk streams. It is also found on gravel and stone banks and shoals in spatey hill streams — where it is dry in low flows and flooded in high

114

ones, and where it can anchor to the gravel. Elsewhere it occurs on edges and banks, sometimes growing down into the water. Fragments can become established at least temporarily in other places.

Ranunculus peltatus has the widest range of the *Ranunculus* species. In common with the others it has a tough anchoring rhizome and root weft. Like *Ranunculus aquatilis* it can grow in still water as a delicate, often non-rooted form and like *Ranunculus fluitans*, *Ranunculus aquatilis* and *Ranunculus penicillatus* ssp. *penicillatus*, in flatter places it grows in wider channels in the hills than in the lowlands. It frequently occurs in small chalk streams upstream of *Ranunculus penicillatus* ssp. *pseudofluitans*.

Blanket weed (long trailing filamentous algae, most often *Cladophora glomerata*) could also be placed in this group. It is most frequent, and most frequently luxuriant, in streams less than 10 m wide. In these surveys the wider rivers recorded were mainly in the hills and so tended to be too swift for Blanket weed (except in really polluted ones).

The group of plants shown in Figure 6.10 have a similar but smaller pattern, which does not extend into the steeper or wider sites. Most of the tall emerged monocotyledons are included here.

The tall emerged monocotyledons require shallow water, fine soil and little scour. *Carex acutiformis* avoids spates, growing in shallow dykes and at the edges of other lowland channels, particularly on chalk and alluvium. *Glyceria maxima* is also mainly a lowland species, and luxuriant stands are mostly found in fairly flat and narrow watercourses, though it frequently grows along the edges of larger channels. *Phragmites australis* is distributed similarly, though it is less common in streams and much more frequent in dykes. It tolerates even less scour than the others. *Typha* spp. are less common.

Potamogeton perfoliatus grows well in silty substrates with little flow, and in firmer substrates in moderate flows. It has a deep rhizome system, no root weft, bushy shoots which can grow large, and usually grows slowly. These characters exclude it from the steeper and wider channels.

There are only a few records for *Oenanthe fluviatilis*, but it probably belongs in this group. It is typically found in lower parts of chalk streams which have eutrophic influence, so physical factors may be of lesser importance than nutrient status to this plant. It is rather bushy, and forms a root weft in fairly firm substrates.

The main species characteristic of slow flows are shown in Figure 6.11. They have basically similar patterns, well into the flatter reaches to the right, and with sites concentrated to the right, even if they are dense in the lower centre also. Stands of good performance avoid the upper left of the range; i.e. the more extreme flows.

Sparganium emersum extends the furthest into steep streams. It sometimes grows well even in moderate flow, though luxuriant growth

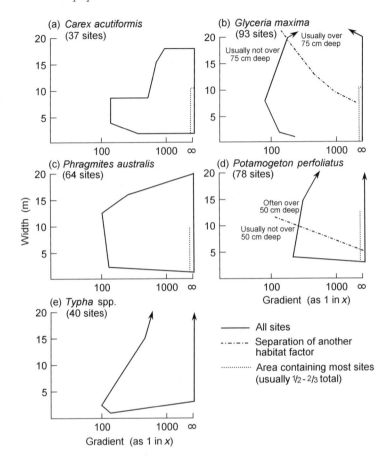

Figure 6.10
Species occurring towards the right.
The tall emergent monocotyledons, *Carex acutiformis, Glyceria maxima, Phragmites australis* and *Typha* spp., grow only in the shallow water with little scour, so are confined to the sides of deeper or more flowing channels.
Details as for Figure 6.1.

is mainly in the flatter sites at the right of the diagram (except in the part avoided by the species of Figure 6.8). Its straight deep roots need soft soil and grow best in fine particles. Its leaves are easily damaged in flow.

Nuphar lutea, Potamogeton pectinatus and *Sagittaria sagittifolia* have similar patterns. All have deep straight roots and tolerate both silting and disturbance of the upper silt (except that *Potamogeton pectinatus* can be swept away in winter and spring; see Chapters 3 and 5). They cannot tolerate much battering. The pattern is clearly divided on depth in Figure 6.11 and this confirms that they have a preference for a definite substrate and flow type. In the steeper parts of the range *Potamogeton pectinatus* is more likely to occur in faster flows and *Nuphar lutea* and *Sagittaria sagittifolia* in slower ones, with *Sparganium emersum* being intermediate.

Nuphar lutea is the commonest in the deeper waters. Most of its abundant stands are in flatter streams, and it is infrequent in streams over 25 m wide (which, in Britain, may often be Highland or navigated and channelled). Its rhizome system is large and deep, but it can be

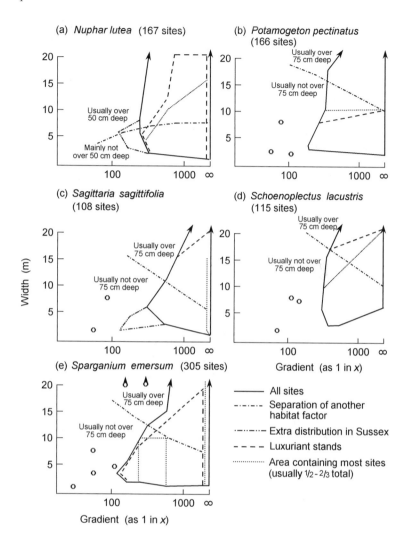

Figure 6.11
Species of slower flow.
Details as for Figure 6.1.

uprooted in severe lowland storms, and, not surprisingly, is absent from mountain rivers. In upland streams it occurs only in the flatter parts (to the far right of the pattern) where deep soft soil may accumulate. As the plants are large they grow better with a large volume of water. *Nuphar lutea* and *Sagittaria sagittifolia* both extend into narrow steep clay streams in Sussex, where quiet silting stretches reach far upstream. *Nuphar lutea* also has a secondary distribution on resistant rocks, in small streams in nearly flat country. Here the sediment is much poorer in nutrients, coming from the neighbouring moorland.

Potamogeton pectinatus can grow well in moderate flow, anchoring in soft deep soil by its complex rhizome system (it does not have a root weft). It is severely battered in faster flows and cannot anchor properly to coarse or firm substrates, so well-grown stands are usually

117

found in narrower streams and it seldom occurs in channels over 25 m wide. It grows somewhat into the hills, but the upland and mountain sites are, of course, the flatter sites to the right of the pattern.

Sagittaria sagittifolia is commonest in drains, canals and larger dykes (bottom right of the pattern). It is damaged by battering, but is less easily uprooted than *Nuphar lutea*. It extends further into the hills than *Nuphar lutea* but less far than *Potamogeton pectinatus*.

Schoenoplectus lacustris has a similar pattern to the other species except that it avoids the habitats with little flow and much silting (bottom right of the pattern). Its roots are straight and often deep and it has dense, nearly superficial rhizomes. This means it is able to anchor both in deep silt, by using its roots, and in stable gravel, with its rhizome mat — an unusual characteristic. Its above-ground parts are versatile also, because there are both strap-like flexible submerged leaves and large stiff emerged shoots; although storm flows break the stiff shoots the submerged leaves are only harmed if there is much turbulence. The proportion of submerged leaves increases in faster flows, where the emerged shoots are more liable to damage. It is found mainly in the lowlands, but can grow well in fast flows without much spate. There is little separation with depth on the width–slope pattern, probably because of the morphological diversity. Bearing in mind this diversity, however, the pattern is small. Its avoidance of mountain streams can be attributed to spate losses through erosion and velocity pull (the latter mostly affecting the emerged shoots), but it is also rare in canals, drains and dykes. In large rivers with stretches of both fast and slow water, as above and below weirs, *Schoenoplectus lacustris* is typically common in the faster flow and *Sagittaria sagittifolia* in the slower.

The last category of width–slope pattern, Figure 6.12, contains only one member, *Ceratophyllum demersum*. This is large, with much hydraulic resistance to flow and no roots for anchorage, and it grows too slowly to be an ephemeral like *Lemna minor* agg. It is therefore confined to the flattest places, to still waters and to lowland streams with a slope of less than 1:1000. It provides a striking final example of the value of width–slope patterns in elucidating the ecology of river plants.

USE OF WIDTH–SLOPE PATTERNS

The width and slope of a channel can be obtained very easily from a visit to the site and a large-scale map. In general, a species will occur within its pattern as illustrated in the preceding figures. It has been seen that the patterns are explicable in terms of the biology and ecology of the plant and thus form a valid measure of plant distribution. They can, therefore, be used to predict changes in plant distribution in rivers which are changing or are likely to change. For example, if the future

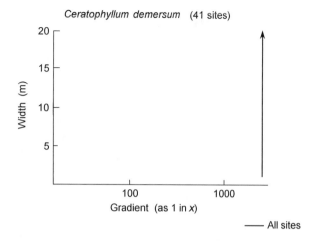

Figure 6.12
Species of the far right.
Details as for Figure 6.1.

depth, normal flow pattern and spateyness are known, the likelihood of any species remaining in or invading a particular site can be assessed (see Chapter 20). Predictions from the patterns are not complete, though, as chemical factors may change as well as physical ones and these are only partly accounted for on the overall patterns. The basic chemical factor is the nutrient regime which is determined partly by the amount of silt present and partly by the nutrient status of that silt (see Chapter 8). If pollution is present, or the water is turbid, or the site has recently been dredged, etc., these factors must also be taken into account, and may result in species not being found at sites within their width–slope pattern that they would otherwise be able to tolerate.

7

Light

Plants need light for photosynthesis, and so their growth can be decreased by lack of light. Because the light reaching submerged plants is lessened by passing through the water, their growth (production) is usually much less than that of emerged plants (see Chapter 9). Light can also be reduced by the shading effect of trees, etc. above the stream, and of the river plants themselves.

SHADING FROM ABOVE

Trees, shrubs and tall bank plants frequently overhang the water, and shade it (Plates 3, 6, 12, 13, 15; Figures 10.14 and 10.15). The field distribution of river plants in relation to shading is shown in Table 7.1. Species which have green shoots in winter are those which tend to be harmed the most by shade. Of the common species of river plants *Ranunculus* spp. are the most light-demanding and *Sparganium emersum* the most shade-tolerant. Many lowland streams were shaded before the woods were cleared for farming (see Chapter 1). Shading is also a simple way of preventing the excessive plant growth (see Chapters 16 and 18) which can cause flooding. A lowland stream is safe for flood prevention if it is not more than a quarter full of vegetation. To keep a *Ranunculus* stream safe from flooding the overhanging trees should let through at most *c.* 60–70% of full sunlight if the shade is uniform (see note in Table 7.1), or *c.* 40–55% of full sunlight in a dapple shade. At the other extreme, a *Sparganium emersum* stream needs more shade to reduce its vegetation, *c.* 40–55% of full sunlight if the shade is uniform and less than 30% of full sunlight in a dapple shade.

SHADING FROM TREES AND SHRUBS

Before Man began to clear the forest (for agricultural land, to use as fuel, and for timber, fruits and nuts and other tree products), much of the land was covered by woodland. There were open areas which were climatically stressed and with large herds of herbivores, e.g., aurochs (more frequent in woodland), buffalo, deer. There were open areas in altitudes and latitudes above the tree line, and in wetlands. (European trees grow only in marshy, or intermittently flooded areas. In North America, trees such as *Taxodium distichum* will form forests in permanent non-scour waters.)

As shown above, river plants do not grow in heavy shade. How, then, did so many types of river vegetation evolve and develop? Just in the expected areas?

120

Table 7.1   Shade tolerance

Divided into groups, from the most tolerant species in Group 1, to the least tolerant in Group 6.

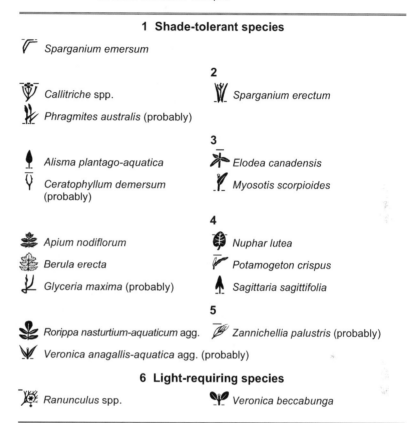

1 Shade-tolerant species

Sparganium emersum

2

Callitriche spp.   *Sparganium erectum*

Phragmites australis (probably)

3

Alisma plantago-aquatica   *Elodea canadensis*

Ceratophyllum demersum   *Myosotis scorpioides*
(probably)

4

Apium nodiflorum   *Nuphar lutea*

Berula erecta   *Potamogeton crispus*

Glyceria maxima (probably)   *Sagittaria sagittifolia*

5

Rorippa nasturtium-aquaticum agg.   *Zannichellia palustris* (probably)

Veronica anagallis-aquatica agg. (probably)

6 Light-requiring species

Ranunculus spp.   *Veronica beccabunga*

Group 1 occurs often in medium continuous shade, and is common in medium discontinuous shade. It occasionally occurs in heavy discontinuous or dapple shade. Group 6 is sparse in medium dapple shade and in light continuous shade.

Shade types are defined as the percentage of full sunlight reaching 1–2 m above water level, between mid-June and mid-September, i.e.

Heavy shade	10–40% full sunlight
Medium shade	45–65% full sunlight
Light shade	70–80% full sunlight

For tree shade to eliminate river plants, the shade and the plants must be present together. In Malta, in the south of Europe, they barely overlap. Native riverside trees are mainly deciduous. The growing season for (most) river plants starts about November (a few weeks after the first heavy rains), when the tree leaves fall. Drying (Mediterranean summer) starts March–May, and the tree shade does not become heavy until May–June. There is no serious conflict.

The main forests of Europe, though, could potentially shade brooks and small rivers. Now, large rivers are channelled and trained so that they are, as much as the discharge permits, narrowed, with quite steep sides. Vegetation bands, if any, are in only the few metres of shallower water at the side. This is not the original pattern. In large American rivers left in a fairly natural state, the river edge may be 1 km and more wide. Indeed, on the landward side there may be shading trees: but these grade to wide bands of reedswamp, grading to mixed then floating and submerged communities. Damage to river plants from trees at the edge is trivial compared with the area of unshadable vegetation. This pattern can be presumed to have also applied in Europe.

The shade cast also depends on the height and habit of the tree or shrub. Taller trees such as English oak (*Querus robur*) of course have shade extending further than a shrubs', like hazel (*Corylus avellana*). Quite as important is the distance the tree can overhang (give permanent heavy shade to) the stream. Oak is far more effective than lombardy poplar (*Populus nigra* var. *italica*) for instance. Then there is the question of completeness of canopy. Beech (*Fagus sylvatica*) has a far heavier shade from each tree than birch (*Betula alba*). Willow (e.g. *Salix alba*) is less likely to form a close canopy than beech, where the canopy of one tree more often overlaps that of the others.

There is, therefore, much variation in shade, so potential effect on river plants, with the habit and morphology of the tree.

The aspect of the stream is also important. One running north-south, with tall shady trees beside, will receive far more sunlight than one running east-west. Coupled with this is the position of the sun. The lower sun of the far north casts longer shadows, so shades more, than the higher sun further south.

River width also determines how much can be shaded: in the past, undredged rivers had more shallow water and islands. There are thus many factors influencing the degree of shade, therefore the presence of river vegetation, on streams and rivers in forests.

In the autumn, tree leaves will fall into the water below, and more may be blown in. This may lead to the covering (shading) of that part of the bed where leaves accumulate, which may smother short plants. The leaves may be swept further downstream, or decay, within a few, or many months. This may thus influence river vegetation through their chemistry. Conifers such as spruces tend to have an acid, and skewing (toxic) effect, birch to have a nutrient-low one, and most of the forest broad-leaved trees have a nutrient moderate effect. Fallen river and bank herbs seem to have little chemical effect.

In present times, with most land unforested, an important factor is whether any trees are present, and if so, where and how many. Separated pollarded willows, so characteristic of (among others) English lowland landscapes, are too sparse to affect the river community but, by overhanging, may well keep plants few or absent under them. A group of birch trees in a Highland valley, though, may cast a little shade that does not change cover and presence, merely decreases productivity.

Given tree shade, this may be from a traditional wood, a plantation, a tree line or band and a hedge (and intermediates).

Walking through traditional forests, there is never continuous shade. There are breaks in the canopy, where a tree fell or some other disturbance took place, and the replacement trees have not yet grown to fill the space. These open glades also occur at the riverside, so there are patches of high light and good vegetation in the river. This is seen well now in the great forests of North America. There are also of course canopy breaks for roads and other human activities. In the past (and still in Canada), in small to medium streams there were scattered beaver ponds, again bringing patches of good vegetation. Where the canopy does not reach across the river, the shade varies with tree height and morphology, and aspect, as described above.

Plantations usually differ, since the trees are planted in close rows, liable to be replaced if dying when young, and usually felled before natural glades (from normal death) occur. Shading is usually heavier, and river vegetation less, though height, habit, aspect and river type may permit some.

Tree lines and bands are more characteristic of the continent than of Britain, though single lines or patches are common in Scotland. Complete shading is likely except where breaks have been made for, e.g., roads. Trees bordering large rivers are common and help to maintain the banks, but these necessarily shade the river less, and may be sparse (or even isolated). The river authorities may remove riverside trees: and then find maintenance costs rise, vegetation becoming a flood hazard or the river width doubling.

Hedges are lines of closely-trained bushes; most often hawthorn or a hawthorn-based mix of old. They are typically 2–5 m high, sufficient to completely shade a ditch or narrow stream beside. Hedges were used to form field and other boundaries, and were thick enough to enclose stock. Typically, a ditch or small brook formed part of the system forming, together, a 'hedgerow'. 'Hedging and ditching' was characteristic winter work on farmland. When fields were made, before there was land drainage, let alone under-field drainage (or serious underground abstraction), numerous small brooks rose and flowed around on the land. These being inconvenient in cultivation, they were diverted to the boundary ditches. Over the centuries, and in particular since *c.* 1850, the land has dried, the ditches have dried, and in recent decades many have even been filled in. They were, though, the first stage of the drainage system which ended at the sea. And they were, and are, often shaded.

Even now, there are river systems (e.g. Sussex) where the upper brooks are shaded by hedges. Here, as surely elsewhere when ditches were wetter, there is good vegetation only where there are breaks in the hedge: for roads, field access, etc.

The hedge pattern, and that of traditional forests, show good river vegetation can occur in a mostly-shaded river system, in the breaks in that shade. River vegetation would have existed in quite sufficient quantities for different types to have developed and adapted. The effect of trees varies also with their seasonal behaviour, height and habit, and with the aspect, depth and width of the river.

SHADING FROM MAN-MADE STRUCTURES

Bridges are the commonest such structures, and river plants are absent or reduced, depending on the intensity of the shade (see above). Buildings cast shade in relation to their height, aspect, relation to the sun's position, and to the width of the river (how far over it the shadow extends). It is very rare for shade from buildings to eliminate river vegetation. A little reduction in productivity, and some skewing towards shade-tolerant species (see above), is the usual result.

SHADING BY AND FROM THE BANK (NOT BY TREES)

It is unusual, but possible, for banks to cast ecologically significant shade, in steep gorges, by cliffs and, in small deepened channels, by the ordinary banks. There can be 2–3 m, low-banked tributaries in woods with good vegetation, but in the cultivated land beside, deepening and straightening make them *c.* 0.5 m wide at the base, with very steep *c.* 2 m high banks: which (with grass, etc.) shade the stream, preventing aquatic or other bottom vegetation. (These are especially frequent in South Norway.)

Similar but lesser shading occurs frequently in any much-drained lowland, where small streams (to *c.* 3 m wide) are well sunk underground, and shading is from both the bank itself, and from the tall herb bank vegetation (*Urtica dioica, Filipendula ulmaria, Rubus fruticosus, Arrhenatherum elatius,* etc.). Small, deepened dykes may be shaded by, e.g., *Phragmites australis* on the banks, and aquatics again be absent.

LIGHT UNDER WATER

When light reaches the water surface, between 5% and 25% of it is reflected back from the surface and does not enter the water. The proportion of sunlight reflected increased as the sun gets lower in the sky. About 6–8% of the diffuse sky light (not the full sunlight) is reflected and this varies much less with the position of the sun (Westlake, 1977). Once below the surface, light is absorbed as it passes through the water. These are three causes of this loss: (1) the water itself; (2) turbidity, due to the particles in the water; and (3) colouring matter in the water. Of these, (1) is stable but (2) and (3) vary greatly. They can be changed in various ways; for instance, river water is more turbid than that of lakes, since rivers drain water from the land, and so plants cannot grow as far below the water level in rivers as in lakes. Plants are usually considered to need at least 1% of full daylight in order to be able to survive (Westlake, 1977).

In clear streams some plants can grow at about 2 m below the surface (even more in clear springs), but they are frequently restricted to shallower water. In lakes, they can grow below the level where they can be seen from the surface, but because streams are more turbid and more coloured, the drop in light is much sharper and, effectively, if plants are present they can be seen from above the water. There are, of course, some exceptions. Pale and large particles hinder viewing more than they hinder the passage of light, and a good deal of vegetation can grow unseen in paper mill effluents and, to a lesser extent, where boats stir up silt.

During storm flows the water is usually turbid from silt being washed in from the land and moved downstream. However, storm flows are infrequent enough during the plants' growing season (i.e. the summer) for the decrease in photosynthesis that they produce probably to have little overall effect on the vegetation (see Chapters 3, 5 and 6 for the other effects of storm flows). Variations in turbidity during normal flows are more important and the productivity of the light-sensitive *Ranunculus* can vary over a two-fold range with these changes.

Turbidity is influenced by rock type. Turbidity is least in chalk streams since chalk dissolves in water and relatively few eroded particles are left to be washed off the land. Resistant rocks also erode very slowly and usually bear clear streams, though material can enter them from drift or soil above the rock. The silting from sandstone is greater, and clay streams are the most turbid, with many small particles in the water. The lower reaches of clay streams, and drains, contain the highest proportion of vegetation with leaves on or above the water. These leaves are not harmed by turbidity.

Small algae (phytoplankton) also make water turbid, as do bacteria and microscopic animals. Algae are present in all streams, but in swift flowing waters the algae are washed along quickly, while slow flows allow rapid reproduction of the algae and so the water may become turbid. In suitable slow rivers, phytoplankton can be very dense and comprise most of the plant life in the river (see Chapter 9), and the lower reaches of clay rivers, and other slow lowland streams, can be very turbid from phytoplankton. Turbidity can also be increased by human interference, both directly, e.g. by coal mine effluents, and indirectly, as when agricultural practices increase the silt being washed from the land (see Chapter 19).

Water may be coloured green-grey in clay streams, particularly in winter. The frequent coloration, however, is brown, the water being stained with peat or humus from the land around. Brown water occurs in some dykes on organic alluvium, and in streams from peaty heath, moorland or blanket bog catchments, such as the New Forest and the northern moors. The only region of Britain with many very dark brown streams is, though, the far north of Scotland, on both resistant rocks and sandstone. Mountain streams are clear where there is little peat in the catchment, e.g. the Lake District.

PLANTS WITHIN WATER

Turbid and coloured water cannot, of course, harm the growth of plants whose leaves are mainly above water level, such as the emergents and most free-floating plants (e.g. *Lemna* spp.). The rooted floating plants receive full light on their floating leaves, but the shoots must first grow up through the water. Plants such as *Nuphar lutea*, which have large rhizomes and much stored food in the soil, can grow well in turbid water, since the young leaves can grow to the surface using food from these reserves.

The tolerance to turbidity of various plants is shown in Table 7.2. Since shading affects the whole plant whereas turbidity affects only those parts in the water, there are differences between Tables 7.1 and 7.2. The

Table 7.2   Tolerance to turbid water

1 Most tolerant of turbid water

	Ceratophyllum demersum		*Polygonum amphibium*
	Lemna minor agg.		*Sagittaria sagittifolia*
	Nuphar lutea		*Schoenoplectus lacustris*

2 Intermediate

	Callitriche spp.		*Potamogeton pectinatus*
	Myriophyllum spicatum		*Sparganium emersum*
	Potamogeton natans		*Sparganium erectum*

3 Least tolerant of turbid water

	Elodea canadensis		*Ranunculus* spp.
	Potamogeton perfoliatus		Mosses

plants most tolerant to turbidity either have parts above the water surface, or are characteristic of deep water (*Ceratophyllum demersum*) or both (e.g. *Nuphar lutea*). The species least tolerant of turbidity all grow submerged, the mosses and *Elodea canadensis* usually growing close to the substrate so that they receive least of the light entering the water. *Ranunculus* spp. are also the least tolerant of shading. The depth distribution and light requirements of several *Potamogeton* spp. have been studied (Spence & Chrystal, 1970a and b) and it has been found that the less light the species needs, the deeper it grows. These species tolerant of low light have the lowest respiration per unit area of leaf and so can stay alive and grow with the least photosynthesis.

In still water the plants may be able to adjust their growth habit in order to decrease self-shading and shading by taller water plants. In currents, however, the habit is determined by the flow, not the light (see Chapter 3), though within these limits as much of the plant as possible will grow in the light (Westlake, 1977), partly because leaves that receive too little light for photosynthesis often fall. The taller a plant can grow, whether within or above the water, the more chance it has of obtaining light if there is competition between the plants. However, while competition may be important in shallow still waters, it has little effect in swift deep ones where flow is again the dominant controlling factor (see Chapter 10).

The taller and wider a river plant grows, the greater its ability to shade plants below. This causes weakening and liability to wash-out, and perhaps even death. Within the water, in flow, habit is much influenced by flow. Exceptions are usually when a species is also emergent. *Rorippa nasturtium-aquaticum*, for instance, can overgrow, mostly as an emergent, *Ranunculus* spp., in chalk streams. (Here, washout occurs only in severe storms or when the *Ranunculus* is weakened e.g. by shade.) In more unstable and swifter flow, bushy overgrowth is washed off at an early stage.

In considerable flow, many water-supported species form trailing clumps (e.g., *Callitriche* spp., *Myriophyllum spicatum*, etc.). There is little mutual shade. Blanket weed, however, overshades these.

In still waters, those reaching higher may remove those below, particularly when they grow faster than those around. Those responsible may have at least their upper leaves floating or emergent (e.g., *Hottonia palustris*, *Callitriche platycarpa*).

Floating leaves or plants are more effective at shading those below. *Nuphar lutea*, in slow or still water, occupies space with its submerged leaves, and shades it with its floating ones: effective. The strap-leaved *Sparganium emersum* is (like other strap-leaved species) usually too sparse to form a canopy, but can occasionally do so and shade effectively.

Small floating plants like *Lemna* spp. and *Azolla filiculoides* can dominate in suitable habits (still or near-still water, warmth, reasonably clean).

Scramblers which root in river or pond and can grow, scramble, up the bank as well, are primarily not European. *Crassula helmsii* (Australian) is naturalised in Britain and spreading fast, smothering and killing native plants below. *Hydrocotyle ranunculoides* (American) is introduced to Britain, and may likewise become invasive. Others, like *Micranthemum umbrosum* (American) are not yet in England. In their native habitats there are checks and balances such as grazers or diseases, and they are not invasive.

Where an emerged plant can grow, it will shade out the submerged and floating, and any shorter scramblers. Tall emergents shade out short ones. Emerged plants grow upright (except in deep storm flows), so habit is independent of flow. Presence is dependent, though, on flow as well as depth, etc. In sufficiently swift or unstable flow, emergents are restricted to sheltered niches: if any.

Emergents are therefore usually at the edges, where water is shallower and more sheltered. The short bushy fringing herbs, e.g. *Rorippa nasturtium-aquaticum*, can spread easily, be washed out easily — and be shaded and killed by taller plants.

The tall monocotyledons, e.g., *Sparganium erectum*, are slower to invade, anchor more firmly, and shade any other river plant: but are swept off in severe flows. Other habits include the tall, wide-leaved *Rumex hydrolapathum* (more like an American habit), and *Rorippa amphibia*. This last anchors badly, and is easily washed away. It thus grows well in the shelter of *Sparganium erectum*: until this grows large enough to shade it out.

The shading and weakening of one river plant by another, and the re-invasion of emptied ground, is part of the ordinary variation, the changeless change, of the river.

The taller shades the shorter. This applies equally to tall trees, and to plants in the middle of the water shading those on the substrate. Within the river, however, plant-to-plant shading is merely part of the changeless change of the river community: that species invade, increase, are washed out, and re-invade, for reasons of light as well as flow, etc. (Haslam, 1987).

Within the water, light is always less, as light is reflected from the surface, more if the sun is low (Scandinavia, early morning, etc.). Natural and man-made turbidity (non-toxic) and colouring further reduce the light to, so productivity of, river plants.

River plant species themselves vary in their tolerance to shade. On the small scale this seriously influences community species, cover and productivity. On the large scale, the amount of river shaded enough to skew vegetation but not enough to eliminate it, is too small to be significant.

8

Nutrients and rock type

River plants (except for free-floating ones) take up nutrients from both soil and water, the soil usually being the more important source. Most soil nutrients are in the silt particles, so the soil texture affects its nutrient status. As well as the stable silt, temporary silt deposited in, on, or under plant shoots can be an important source of nutrients, particularly to plants in somewhat nutrient-deficient habitats.

The silt from different rock types differs in nutrient status. The flow regime controls silt deposition, and different rock types differ in the amount of silt entering the channels. These three factors control the nutrient pattern of stream types, and each stream type has a characteristic vegetation which can be linked to this nutrient pattern. Streams on Resistant rocks are often oligotrophic, those on chalk and sandstone tend to be mesotrophic, and clay streams are often eutrophic.

ROCK TYPE

River plants need, for their growth and development, both the gases oxygen and carbon dioxide (or another form of dissolved carbon: bicarbonate), and dissolved mineral nutrients such as calcium, potassium, phosphate and nitrate. The minerals are taken up from the water and the soil, and oxygen and carbon from the water, the air and (for carbon) the soil. When nutrients are absorbed, the area immediately surrounding the site of uptake (e.g. the water around each leaf) is depleted of nutrients, so uptake becomes progressively more difficult. However, water movement (and diffusion) brings in fresh supplies of nutrients, so that moving water is, for plants, richer in nutrients than still water. It seems probable that flow is more important for the carbon supply to submerged plants than for the mineral supply, because carbon is one of the nutrients most likely to be limiting for the growth of submerged shoots (Westlake, 1973). All animals and plants use oxygen for respiration, while photosynthesis uses carbon dioxide and produces oxygen. The presence of green plants usually increases the total oxygen supply of the river because of the oxygen released during the day when the plants are photosynthesising; this improves the habitat for fish. In some circumstances, though, plants can actually decrease oxygenation, as when there is much decaying plant material (the micro-organisms which effect the decomposition use oxygen in respiration), or when much of a plant clump is too shaded by its upper shoots to photosynthesise, or when the water becomes very warm.

129

Chemical data frequently vary with the laboratory doing the analyses. Comparing different data sets, the relative order in each (species associated with low, medium, high concentrations) is likely to be valid and stable. But, e.g. 15 p.p.m. NO_3-N from one laboratory need not mean the same concentration as 15 p.p.m. from another. The water analyses were from a variety of laboratories. The silt analyses were all from the same laboratory. However, for later (1980s to 2000s) and more accurate analyses, see Bibliography.

NUTRIENT UPTAKE

Water plants can obtain their mineral nutrients from the soil or from the water. Free-floating plants which are near the water surface (e.g. *Lemna minor* agg.) necessarily obtain all their nutrients from the water, while tall emerged plants on the banks (e.g. some *Phragmites australis* must obtain all their minerals from the soil. Other groups can use both soil and water nutrients, though under experimental conditions (Bristow & Whitcombe, 1971) a plant's entire nutrient intake may come from either the water or the soil, and, at least for short periods, this is adequate for growth. Nutrients can be taken up by roots, stems and leaves, and uptake by roots and by shoots may be independent, each being unaffected by the nutrients surrounding the other (shown for phosphorus, Bristow, 1975).

Soil contains more nutrients than the same volume of water, and within the soil the water present contains more nutrients than the water above ground (e.g. 6–20 times per unit wet weight of silt). The nutrients are held in the silt, so as roots take up nutrients from the soil water they are replenished from the silt. (The concentrations of exchangeable nutrients in wet silt are around three to six times higher than those in the soil water alone, exchangeable nutrients being defined as those which are extractable from the soil with ammonium acetate and are considered to be available for uptake by plants.)

Since the soil is richer in nutrients than the water, this is the main source (Bristow & Whitcombe, 1971; Bristow, 1975; Denny, 1972; Nicholson et al., 1975). However, in chalk stream water there is more nitrogen and phosphorus than is needed for the growth of dominant *Ranunculus*, and the amount of phosphorus removed from the water is the same as that held in the *Ranunculus*. *Ranunculus* can also grow well, at least for short periods, with nutrients supplied only from below. Low levels of water nutrients may lead to poor plant development in experiments (Bristow & Whitcombe, 1971), and it is suggested that development is poor below *c.* 11 p.p.m. of nitrate-nitrogen and *c.* 30 μg of phosphate-phosphorus (Westlake, 1975). If it is the soil and not the water nutrients which are very low, more roots may develop in the water above ground, which increases the amount of nutrients taken up from the water (Bristow, 1975) and the temporary silt. In streams, water nutrients often seem adequate for survival but not for good growth. For instance, plant fragments can live for many months in the water, staying healthy but small and not growing well or luxuriantly, e.g.

Apium nodiflorum	*Myriophyllum spicatum*
Berula erecta	*Ranunculus* spp.
Callitriche spp.	*Rorippa nasturtium-aquaticum* agg.
Myosotis scorpioides	*Veronica beccabunga*

These are common in the floating fringe of middle reaches of chalk streams (see Chapter 10, Figure 10.2), and also occur elsewhere. If, and only if the fragments become anchored, they can increase in size and start to spread. (The floating fragments usually have roots, so this poor growth is not due to lack of growth hormone developed in roots.) Soil nutrients are essential for normal growth.

It seems that only part of the plant need be in a nutrient-rich place. For example, if one part of a bed is silty and another is nutrient-poor (e.g. clean-washed sand), a rhizomatous plant which can grow well only in the silty part can, at least in experiments, move nutrients along its rhizomes so that shoots can grow well in the nutrient-deficient area. As rhizomes may be short-lived, those shoots will eventually be cut off from the high nutrient source, and further growth in the deficient area will be unsatisfactory: unless, of course, silt has, by then, been deposited.

Submerged plant parts can, as mentioned above, all obtain nutrients from the soil or the water, but the morphology and habit of the plant may determine which of its parts are more important for uptake. Leaves and stems may have a thick water-repellent fatty cuticle, in which case mineral uptake is difficult, or this cuticle may be very thin or negligible (Table 8.1) Woody rhizomes and rootstocks do not, of course, absorb much nutrients. Many aquatics can, under experimental conditions, grow well initially with few or no roots, but roots are the parts best adapted for nutrient uptake. In general, deep-rooted species (see Chapter 3) have all their roots in the ground, while shallow-rooted ones often have them above ground as well. Roots in the water reach much the same nutrient supplies as the lower shoots there, but roots in the soil grow well beyond the rhizomes, reaching different nutrient supplies. When soil nutrients are inadequate, roots may develop more above ground (Bristow, 1975), increasing the proportion of nutrients obtained above ground. The development of individual roots is also influenced by soil type. If a plant grows best in eutrophic places (e.g. *Sagittaria sagittifolia*, *Sparganium emersum*), its roots are longer and wider in silt than in a soft mixed-grained substrate.

Table 8.1   Amounts of cuticle in different species

1 Very little or negligible cuticle

Callitriche spp.

Ceratophyllum demersum (leaf)

Elodea canadensis (leaf)

Groenlandia densa (leaf)

Hottonia palustris (leaf)

 Myriophyllum spicatum (stem)

 Nuphar lutea (submerged leaf)

 Potamogeton crispus

Potamogeton lucens (leaf)

Rorippa nasturtium-aquaticum agg. (some leaves)

Sagittaria sagittifolia (submerged leaf)

Schoenoplectus lacustris (submerged leaf)

Zannichellia palustris

2 Little cuticle

Apium nodiflorum

Ceratophyllum demersum (stem)

Elodea canadensis (stem)

Groenlandia densa (stem)

Hottonia palustris (stem)

 Lemna minor agg.

 Mentha aquatica (leaf)

Nuphar lutea (submerged petiole)

Ranunculus aquatilis (leaf)

Ranunculus peltatus (broad leaf)

Rorippa nasturtium-aquaticum agg. (some leaves, stems)

Sparganium emersum

Sparganium erectum (submerged leaf)

Spirodela polyrhiza

Veronica beccabunga

3 More cuticle

 Agrostis stolonifera

 Carex acutiformis

Hydrocharis morsus-ranae

 Mentha aquatica (stem)

 Myriophyllum spicatum (leaf)

 Nuphar lutea (floating leaf)

 Phalaris arundinacea

Potamogeton lucens (stem)

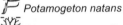 Potamogeton natans

 Ranunculus aquatilis (stem)

 Ranunculus peltatus (stem)

 Rorippa nasturtium-aquaticum agg. (emerged stem)

Schoenoplectus lacustris (emerged)

Sparganium erectum (emerged leaf)

Uptake can vary in different seasons. Roots of winter-dormant plants usually start growing in spring or early summer, some weeks after the shoots have emerged. Tall emergents such as:

 Phalaris arundinacea

 Phragmites australis

 Schoenoplectus lacustris

Sparganium erectum

absorb little through their thick rhizomes or aerial parts, so effective nutrient uptake occurs only when living roots are present. This seasonal uptake can be important in relation to pollution. Following the winter flooding by sea water of a bed of *Phragmites australis*, spring growth of the shoots was normal, but when the new roots grew and were influenced by the salt, the shoots developed badly and many died. If in contrast, a pollutant can both enter and be lost from a habitat while it cannot be effectively absorbed by the plants, no harm results.

In conclusion, mineral nutrients necessary for plant growth, and pollutants damaging to this, can be taken up by plants from both the soil and the water. In general, soil is more important because it contains more nutrients and usually more roots. Water uptake is probably needed for the optimal growth of submerged plants and is usually enough to keep plant fragments alive (these contain nutrients before being detached) though not enough for their normal growth. In some circumstances water uptake is more important than soil uptake, as when poisonous pollutants are in the water but hardly affect the soil, or when the soil is particularly nutrient-deficient and water nutrient-rich. Dependence also varies with habit, tall emergents being necessarily almost entirely dependent on soil nutrients, while submerged, rooted floating, and short semi-emergents obtain nutrients mainly from the soil (though the proportions vary with the habitat and, presumably, the species concerned) and free-floating plants near the surface depend on water uptake.

SOURCES OF NUTRIENT SUPPLY

Water

When stream water is derived from springs it contains the same nutrient concentrations as the ground water in the aquifer from which it originated. When stream water is derived from rainfall running off the land, however, it contains dissolved substances picked up from the soil. Thus nutrients in run-off are basically related to the rock type of the catchment. However, different influences may come from the surface layers, acid bog, superficial deposits, land altered by fertiliser, pesticides, and with altered use (to and from forest, and that conifer or broadleaf; moor; flower-rich meadow; ley; different crops; etc.). Run-off from hard surface bears no relation to the rock type. The last main source of water nutrients is from effluents from sewage works, etc. (see Chapter 19). There is some exchange of nutrients between soil and water, so long-term changes in chemical habitat factors tend to influence both, though in the short-term nutrient concentrations in water tend to fluctuate more than those in the soil. As mentioned above, the effective nutrient supply to the plant is increased when the water is moving.

Stable substrate of the channel bed

The substrate likewise contains and supplies nutrients. It is composed of particles of different sizes and of varying proportions (see Chapters 2 and 3). Silt particles, which contain most nutrients, occur around and between larger particles, as well as in silt beds, etc. From this nutrient-rich silt the water within the soil becomes nutrient-rich also (see above). The total store of nutrients is greatest in a silt bed and least in clean-washed sand, or the clean-washed stone beds of mountain streams, etc. Substrates with little silt can be nutrient-deficient for plants (though sands and gravels which appear non-silty may in fact contain considerable amounts of silt on and between the particles). In addition, substrates of similar texture, derived from different sources, may differ in both the concentrations and the ratios of the nutrients they contain (see below). The nutrients usually reflect those of the rock types of the catchment (with the same reservations referred to above, for water).

There is no clear separation between the substrates described here and the temporary silt discussed in the following section, but the distinction is useful ecologically because although both supply nutrients, one does so on a long-term the other on a short-term basis. Both are derived from erosion of the channel bottom, falling material from the channel banks, sediment washed in from the catchment and, in downstream reaches, sediment transported from upper reaches. As loose silt is moved the most easily, and is very nutrient-rich, it can have an independent effect.

Temporary and unstable silt

Where the stable substrate is nutrient-rich, supplying the nutrients needed for the luxuriant development of the plants present, temporary silt is irrelevant, but elsewhere it is of great importance. Plants contain stores of nutrients which can be moved to new parts of the plant and supply it for some while, and in a low-nutrient habitat good growth and development can be achieved with temporary silt, which allows intermittent good uptake and accumulations of nutrient reserves.

Stream water carries fine particles, especially during storm flows, and these are deposited where flow is checked (see Chapters 2 and 3). When silt is deposited on a plant part the nutrient supply to, and uptake of, that leaf, stem or root will be much increased. Silt is caught

most easily on individual leaves if these are large (e.g. *Nuphar lutea*) or
hairy (e.g. *Myriophyllum spicatum*), or, as in *Elodea canadensis*, they are
made hairy by filamentous algae growing on them. Shoots near the
ground, particularly if within a clump of at the side of a channel, receive
the least flow (Chapter 3) and so frequently collect silt. This silt may be
washed off soon after a storm or may remain for some time.

Plant clumps accumulate silt (Figure 3.2). For example:

Apium nodiflorum	*Ranunculus* spp.
Callitriche spp.	*Rorippa* spp.
Elodea canadensis	*Veronica* spp.
Myriophyllum spp.	*Zannichellia palustris*
Potamogeton pectinatus	

This silt may be in firm hummocks, or in the form of silty water trapped
between shoots. Changing flow patterns and storms move this silt, thus
renewing nutrient supplies. The above-ground roots (see above) are
mainly in this silty area, and usually belong to silt-trapping species.

When plants are newly established, their few and small shoots
cannot trap silt well. If the nutrients of the stable substrate are
inadequate, therefore, growth will be greatly stimulated once the plant
is able to trap silt. Frequently species cannot grow, or grow well, unless
bands of temporary silt are present or can be accumulated by the
plants. These species include, on coarse or low-nutrient substrates:

Callitriche spp.	*Myriophyllum* spp.
Elodea canadensis	*Potamogeton crispus*
Groenlandia densa	*Zannichellia palustris*

An extreme example was seen in clean-washed sandy gravel of a
chalk brook, where frequent cutting had made the vegetation dwarf,
shoots being very short and small. The plants included:

Apium nodiflorum	*Ranunculus peltatus*
Callitriche spp.	*Veronica beccabunga*

These remained dwarf for over a year after the cutting ceased. Then the
flow pattern changed and silt was deposited along the sides of the
channel. Within a few months the plants were growing well, spreading
quickly, and had shoots of normal size.

Silting decreases the light reaching the leaves, thus decreasing
photosynthesis. This may be harmful if most leaves are covered, but is
immaterial when most photosynthesis is carried out by leaves higher in
the water (e.g. *Nuphar lutea*). (The non-rooted *Ceratophyllum demersum*
usually has silt around the lower shoots and may indeed have some
shoots buried in silt.)

Organic matter

Decomposing organic matter is provided by dead river plants and animals, trees and other plants which overhang the channel, dropping leaves, etc. into the water and material washed in from the land. When in the form of small particles, it forms a part of the temporary silt (as well as of the stable substrate). Decaying organic matter produces both mineral nutrients and organic substances. On peat lands, of course, peat particles are washed into the channels, and this is particularly important for plants where acid peat particles are deposited in a stream. Apart from the peat lands, the silt of chalk streams tends to have the highest proportion of organic matter, probably because chalk streams contain much plant life, and because decomposing chalk leads to little mineral silt. Some organic substances enhance, or are necessary for, the good growth of aquatics. This is an additional reason for the chemical importance of silt for the plants.

PLANT DISTRIBUTION IN RELATION TO WATER NUTRIENTS

Plant distribution and luxuriance are determined by a complex of chemical, physical and biotic factors, and the individual nutrients in the water, or indeed the total nutrients there, are only a small part of this complex. Plants are likely, in fact, to be better correlated with flow type or depth than with any or all water nutrients. As the soil is usually the more important nutrient source, there are unlikely to be waters so low in nutrients that plants cannot grow well. Also, waters too nutrient-rich for any plant growth are unlikely to occur without human interference. Within these extremes, different species have different nutrient ranges with which they are best correlated, and within these, narrower ranges in which they can grow luxuriantly. Water nutrients fluctuate during the year, so many samples must be analysed in order to obtain a good estimate of the average nutrient content of the water. In some circumstances, seasonal variations may be crucial. (In ponds, the rootless *Ceratophyllum demersum* can occur if there is high nitrogen present for part of the year only, Goulder & Boatman, 1971). Water analyses of rivers and large brooks, supplied by the (former) River Authorities and River Purification Boards have been correlated with plant distribution, and Table 8.2 summarises the typical nutrient preferences of some widespread species. (The ranges correspond to the highest peak of the left-hand histograms in Chapters 2 and 4.) The division of plant species into groups according to nitrate-nitrogen and phosphate-phosphorus levels in the water corresponds quite well with those groups postulated in Chapter 1. When the plants are classified according to levels

Table 8.2   Plant distribution in relation to water chemistry

The species are listed under the concentration with which they are best correlated. Concentrations are in parts per million (p.p.m.) unless otherwise stated. Water analyses supplied by River Authorities and River Purification Boards, so combined from different laboratories: see note at start of chapter.

1 Alkalinity (as calcium carbonate)

Below 50	Mosses	
170–250	*Apium nodiflorum* and *Berula erecta*	*Potamogeton natans*
	Callitriche spp.	*Potamogeton pectinatus*
	Ceratophyllum demersum	*Potamogeton perfoliatus*
	Enteromorpha intestinalis	*Ranunculus* spp.
	Oenanthe fluviatilis	*Rorippa nasturtium-aquaticum* agg.
	Potamogeton crispus	*Sparganium emersum*
Over 250	*Callitriche* spp.	*Schoenoplectus lacustris*
	Lemna minor agg.	*Sparganium emersum*
	Nuphar lutea	*Sparganium erectum*
	Rorippa nasturtium-aquaticum agg.	*Zannichellia palustris*
	Sagittaria sagittifolia	
Poorly correlated	*Elodea canadensis*	*Myriophyllum spicatum*

2 Biological Oxygen Demand

2.5–4	*Apium nodiflorum* and *Berula erecta*	*Potamogeton perfoliatus*
	Callitriche spp.	*Ranunculus* spp.
	Enteromorpha intestinalis	*Rorippa nasturtium-aquaticum* agg.
	Lemna minor agg.	*Sagittaria sagittifolia*
	Myriophyllum spicatum	*Schoenoplectus lacustris*
	Nuphar lutea	*Sparganium emersum*
	Potamogeton crispus	*Sparganium erectum*
	Potamogeton natans	*Zannichellia palustris*
	Potamogeton pectinatus	Mosses
Over 4	*Sagittaria sagittifolia*	

3 Chloride

Below 15	Mosses	
15–35	*Apium nodiflorum* and *Berula erecta*	*Ranunculus* spp.
	Elodea canadensis	

137

Table 8.2   Continued

35–65	*Callitriche* spp.	*Potamogeton natans*
65–100	*Enteromorpha intestinalis*	*Sagittaria sagittifolia*
	Nuphar lutea	*Schoenoplectus lacustris*
	Oenanthe fluviatilis	*Sparganium emersum*
	Potamogeton pectinatus	*Sparganium erectum*
Over 100	*Ceratophyllum demersum*	*Potamogeton pectinatus*
	Lemna minor agg.	
Poorly correlated	*Myriophyllum spicatum*	*Zannichellia palustris*
	Rorippa nasturtium-aquaticum agg.	

4 Nitrate-nitrogen

Below 1	*Myriophyllum spicatum*	*Ranunculus* spp.
1–3	*Lemna minor* agg.	*Potamogeton perfoliatus*
	Myriophyllum spicatum	
3–6	*Apium nodiflorum* and *Berula erecta*	*Rorippa nasturtium-aquaticum* agg.
	Nuphar lutea	*Sagittaria sagittifolia*
	Oenanthe fluviatilis	*Sparganium erectum*
	Potamogeton perfoliatus	
Over 6	*Enteromorpha intestinalis*	*Schoenoplectus lacustris*
	Nuphar lutea	*Sparganium emersum*
	Potamogeton pectinatus	*Sparganium erectum*
	Sagittaria sagittifolia	*Zannichellia palustris*

5 Ammonia-nitrogen

Below 0.1	*Apium nodiflorum* and *Berula erecta*	
0.1–0.3	*Apium nodiflorum* and *Berula erecta*	*Potamogeton natans*
	Callitriche spp.	*Potamogeton pectinatus*
	Elodea canadensis	*Ranunculus* spp.
	Enteromorpha intestinalis	*Rorippa nasturtium-aquaticum* agg.
	Lemna minor agg.	*Sagittaria sagittifolia*
	Myriophyllum spicatum	*Schoenoplectus lacustris*
	Nuphar lutea	*Sparganium emersum*
	Polygonum amphibium	*Sparganium erectum*
	Potamogeton crispus	Mosses
Over 0.3	*Lemna minor* agg.	

Table 8.2   Continued

6 Nitrite-nitrogen

Below 0.05	*Elodea canadensis*	*Ranunculus* spp.
	Myriophyllum spicatum	Mosses
0.05–0.1	*Callitriche* spp.	*Sagittaria sagittifolia*
Over 0.1	*Lemna minor* agg.	*Schoenoplectus lacustris*
	Nuphar lutea	*Sparganium emersum*
	Potamogeton pectinatus	*Sparganium erectum*

7 Phosphate-phosphorus

Below 0.03	*Apium nodiflorum* and *Berula erecta*	*Potamogeton natans*
	Callitriche spp.	*Ranunculus* spp.
	Elodea canadensis	Mosses
0.03–1.2	*Lemna minor* agg.	*Potamogeton pectinatus*
1.2–3.0	*Nuphar lutea*	*Sparganium emersum*
	Sagittaria sagittifolia	*Sparganium erectum*
	Schoenoplectus lacustris	
Over 3.0	*Enteromorpha intestinalis*	*Myriophyllum spicatum*

8 pH

Below 7.5	*Elodea canadensis*	
7.5–8.0	*Apium nodiflorum* and *Berula erecta*	*Ranunculus* spp.
	Lemna minor agg.	*Sagittaria sagittifolia*
	Nuphar lutea	*Sparganium emersum*
	Potamogeton crispus	*Sparganium erectum*
Over 8.0	*Enteromorpha intestinalis*	*Potamogeton perfoliatus*
	Nuphar lutea	*Schoenoplectus lacustris*
	Potamogeton crispus	*Sparganium emersum*
	Potamogeton pectinatus	*Sparganium erectum*
Poorly correlated	*Callitriche* spp.	*Potamogeton natans*
	Ceratophyllum demersum	*Rorippa nasturtium-aquaticum* agg.
	Myriophyllum spicatum	*Zannichellia palustris*
	Oenanthe fluviatilis	

9 Total dissolved solids

Below 350	*Apium nodiflorum* and *Berula erecta*	*Potamogeton natans*

139

Table 8.2   Continued

	Elodea canadensis	*Schoenoplectus lacustris*
	Myriophyllum spicatum	*Sparganium erectum*
	Polygonum amphibium	
350–500	*Callitriche* spp.	*Ranunculus* spp.
	Enteromorpha intestinalis	*Rorippa nasturtium-aquaticum* agg.
	Potamogeton perfoliatus	*Zannichellia palustris*
Over 500	*Ceratophyllum demersum*	*Potamogeton pectinatus*
	Lemna minor agg.	*Sagittaria sagittifolia*
	Nuphar lutea	*Schoenoplectus lacustris*
	Potamogeton crispus	
Poorly correlated	*Oenanthe fluviatilis*	*Sparganium emersum*

10 Total hardness (calcium carbonate plus magnesium carbonate)

Below 100	*Myriophyllum spicatum*	*Ranunculus* spp.
	Polygonum amphibium	Mosses
100–350	*Enteromorpha intestinalis*	*Potamogeton natans*
Over 350	*Enteromorpha intestinalis*	*Sagittaria sagittifolia*
	Lemna minor agg.	*Schoenoplectus lacustris*
	Nuphar lutea	*Sparganium emersum*
	Potamogeton pectinatus	*Sparganium erectum*
Poorly correlated	*Callitriche* spp.	*Potamogeton crispus*
	Elodea canadensis	*Potamogeton perfoliatus*

of chloride, nitrite-nitrogen and total dissolved solids, the correlation is less good, and there is no such relation in the groups with common requirements for alkalinity, pH and total water hardness. (There were, however, no analyses from dystrophic or oligotrophic streams with acid peat in the channel; see soil analyses below.) Ammonium-nitrogen and Biological Oxygen Demand are the two parameters most widely accepted as indicators of water quality for domestic use, but they are generally irrelevant to plant distribution. (There are too few records of the major cations — calcium, magnesium, potassium and sodium — to determine correlations. For soil data, see below.) Water nutrients cannot account for all trophic variations between species. For instance, middle reaches of swift gravelly stretches of part-limestone lowland streams may have:

 *Ranunculus* spp.   Fringing herbs

while in the slow silty stretches alternating with these, typical species include:

Myriophyllum spicatum   *Schoenoplectus lacustris*

Within a single river, the River Tweed, plant distribution has been correlated with five nutrient parameters (Table 8.3; Holmes & Whitton, 1975b). There is some general correspondence between the nutrients and the trophic preferences of the plants which are described elsewhere in this book (alkalinity, Table 8.2, is often well correlated with conductivity, Table 8.3). Of course, only a few rock types are included in the system.

Table 8.3   Plant distribution in relation to water chemistry in the River Tweed

Data from Holmes & Whitton (1975b).

---

1 Negatively correlated with conductivity and calcium
Myriophyllum alterniflorum

2 Negatively correlated with conductivity
Ranunculus aquatilis agg.

3 Not correlated
(with conductivity, calcium, phosphate-phosphorus or nitrate-nitrogen)

Callitriche spp.	*Potamogeton pectinatus*
Elodea canadensis	*Potamogeton* x *suecicus*
Potamogeton × *olivaceus*	*Ranunculus circinatus* + hybrid
Potamogeton × *salicifolius*	*Ranunculus penicillatus* var. *penicillatus*

4 Correlated with one of the following:
conductivity, calcium (Ca), or nitrate-nitrogen (NO_3-N)

Potamogeton lucens (conductivity)	*Potamogeton perfoliatus* (NO_3-N)
Potamogeton natans (Ca)	*Potamogeton pusillus* (NO_3-N)

5 Correlated with two or three of these parameters

Potamogeton brechtoldii (conductivity, Ca)	*Zannichellia palustris* (conductivity, Ca, NO_3-N)
Ranunculus fluitans hybrid (conductivity, NO_3-N)	

6 Correlated with conductivity, calcium, phosphate-phosphorus and nitrate-nitrogen

Myriophyllum spicatum	*Potamogeton crispus*

NUTRIENT PATTERNS IN SILT

Different rock types differ in the nutrients present in the silt of their channels. The star diagrams in Figure 8.1 summarise the results of a countrywide survey of nutrient levels. On the star diagrams, the line joins the average concentrations of each nutrient. The error marks on the diagrams (the standard error of the mean) show how variable the records are. If the error mark is close to the line, the nutrient levels are similar in the samples analysed. (When the error is not marked at all, as in Figure 8.4, it is too large to be shown on a diagram of this size, and the average is a less reliable measure of the nutrients found.) Table 8.4 is complementary to Figure 8.1, listing the hardness ratio of each rock type. The hardness ratio is the combined calcium and magnesium present in the site divided by the combined sodium and potassium (Seddon, 1972) and has proved very useful in interpreting lake and river (Haslam, 1987) vegetation in terms of nutrient status for plants. Both ratios and quantities of nutrients are important in determining how plants react to the chemical regime. The total nutrients present depend both on the nutrient levels in the silt and on the amount of silt present. Ratios are independent of the amount of silt. If these two parameters are used together, a coherent pattern of nutrient regimes and plant communities emerges.

Table 8.4   Seddon's hardness ratio of silt from different watercourse types

The hardness ratio is $\dfrac{calcium + magnesium}{sodium + potassium}$

In brackets after each value is the standard error of the mean, a measure of the variability of the results.

Rock or soil type	Hardness ratio
Peat dykes	1.4 (0.2)
Silt dykes	2.0 (0.6)
Soft sandstone streams	2.5 (0.2)
Resistant rock streams	2.6 (0.3)
Clay streams	3.6 (0.3)
Hard sandstone streams	4.9 (0.6)
Chalk streams	4.9 (0.8)

In Figure 8.1 and Table 8.4, the first division is between alluvial dykes (on peat and silt) and streams. Dykes have a very low hardness ratio, low ammonia-nitrogen, and very high calcium, magnesium, sodium, potassium, chloride, and, to a lesser extent, sulphate-sulphur.

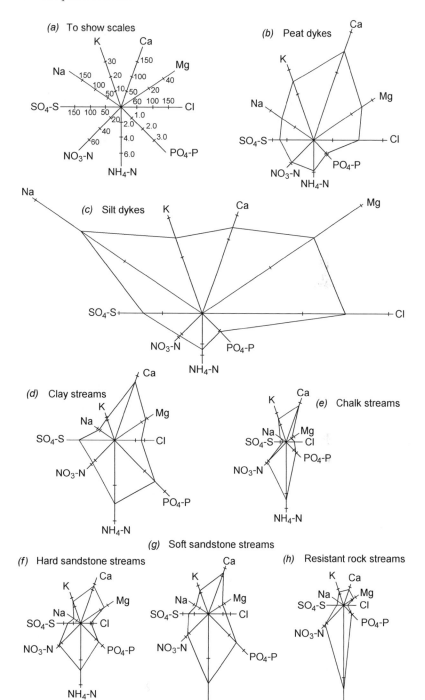

Figure 8.1
Star diagrams of nutrient patterns for different stream types. The scales shown in (a) give nutrient levels (in p.p.m.) in water extracted from silt. The lines join the average values for each nutrient. The two small marks indicate the standard error of the mean, a measure of the variability of the results. Where no such marks are shown, the error is too large to be placed on a diagram of this size.

Ca	calcium
Mg	magnesium
Cl	chloride
PO₄-P	phosphate-phosphorus
NH₄-N	ammonia-nitrogen
SO₄-S	sulphate-sulphur
Na	sodium
K	potassium.

143

This combination of low hardness ratio and high nutrient levels is unusual. Peat dykes at the most mesotrophic end of the range, may have as the principal species:

Hottonia palustris   *Utricularia vulgaris*

Potamogeton alpinus

and these presumably occur in this nutrient-rich environment because of the low hardness ratio. Silt dykes have higher nutrient levels, and a slightly higher hardness ratio. They do not have the plants especially characteristic of nutrient-poor sites, and may have species commonly found in eutrophic (clay) sites, such as (see Chapter 14):

Enteromorpha intestinalis   *Sagittaria sagittifolia*

Nuphar lutea   *Sparganium emersum*

Dykes contain an unusual variety of plant communities (see Chapter 14) and this could be partly due to their unusual nutrient regime.

Clay streams are the most nutrient-rich, their silt containing the most calcium, magnesium, sodium, phosphate-phosphorus, chloride and sulphate-sulphur; they have a medium hardness ratio. The characteristic species of their most eutrophic downstream reaches (see Chapters 1, 11 and 12) are here described as eutrophic (strictly, euthraphent).

Chalk has a high hardness ratio (more because the sodium content is low than because the calcium is high) and magnesium, phosphate-phosphorus, chloride and sulphate-sulphur are very low. Calcium-dominated regimes reduce the available phosphorus, etc., so the actual nutrient levels for the plants are, except for calcium, very low indeed: in fact resembling those in (the low-nutrient) resistant rock streams. On limestone, this combination of low nutrients and high hardness ratio is here termed mesotrophic, and the species characteristic of upper and middle reaches of chalk streams are described as mesotrophic (strictly, mesotraphent). There is some overlap of these species with mesotrophic dykes, e.g.

Lemna trisulca   *Ranunculus aquatilis*

There is more overlap between chalk brooks and silty upper brooks on resistant rocks (which are nutrient-rich for their rock type), with soft sandstone streams, and with the upland brooks on hard sandstone (see Chapters 11–13). Hard sandstone is the rock type nearest in nutrient status to chalk, being similar in most nutrients and in hardness ratio. It does not, though, have enough calcium to become calcium-dominated: other nutrients are not reduced. It has more magnesium, phosphate-phosphorus, chloride, sulphate-sulphur and less potassium, and so is of slightly higher nutrient status. This is especially true in the lower reaches, as hard sandstone produces much more inorganic silt than chalk (see below). Soft sandstone has a very low hardness ratio, but high levels of calcium, potassium, sodium and phosphate-phosphorus, and fairly high levels of chloride and sulphate-sulphur. The final nutrient status can presumably be considered similar to that of chalk, but it is different in that it has a low hardness ratio, low calcium dominance and high nutrients, instead of the reverse. The vegetation is mainly mesotrophic, but with more eutrophic plants than occur on chalk. These are presumably influenced by the high nutrient levels (as well as by the greater amount of silt; see below).

Streams on resistant rock are very low in most nutrients (particularly so in calcium, phosphate-phosphorus, chloride and sulphate) and the hardness ratio is as low as on soft sandstone. These streams are the most nutrient-poor, being low in both nutrients and hardness ratio. The country on resistant rocks varies from arable land to blanket bog, channels on blanket bog containing the least nutrients of all, being the most dystrophic, with chemicals added from the bog. Without this peat, resistant streams are merely very low in nutrients. The average nutrient levels of a few blanket bog channels are (in p.p.m.):

Calcium 1.5   Magnesium 2   Sodium 25

Potassium 3   Nitrate-nitrogen 4   Ammonia-nitrogen 4

Phosphate-phosphorus 0.4 Chloride 35   Sulphate-sulphur 8

Hardness ratio 0.6

(Nitrogen levels are as high as in other stream types.)

The dystrophic (dystraphent) species of this habitat include:

    Drosera anglica   *Littorella uniflora*

    Eriophorum angustifolium   *Menyanthes uniflora*

When there is both acid peat and mineral sediment on the channel bed, the nutrient levels are slightly higher and the typical oligotrophic species include:

  Callitriche hamulata   *Juncus bulbosus*

    Eleocharis acicularis   *Myriophyllum alterniflorum*

 Eleogiton fluitans

The star diagram in Figure 8.4a shows the nutrient pattern in which such species occur. Oligotrophic habitats are usually streams on fairly flat moorland or bog, but can be swift highland ones with very little sediment, or upper non-silted reaches of streams on acid soft sandstone, e.g. in the New Forest. Streams with less or no peat have the higher nutrient status shown in Figure 8.1b.

Interestingly, nitrogen levels vary little between stream types, but vary considerably from place to place within them. This is most probably because decomposing organic matter produces considerable nitrogen in all channels, but the amount of dead plants or animals in any one site will vary. Table 8.5 shows that manganese tends to be higher on hard than on soft rocks.

Table 8.5   Manganese contents of silt from different watercourse types

Values are in p.p.m. and the figure in brackets is the standard error. Methods as for Table 8.6.

Peat dykes	0.5 (0.2)
Silt dykes	0.6 (0.1)
Chalk streams	0.5 (0.3)
Clay streams	0.5 (0.1)
Soft sandstone streams	1.0 (0.2)
Resistant rock streams	3.5 (2.0)
Hard sandstone streams	3.5 (1.1)

When silt is analysed from channels from mixed rock types, such as clay and soft limestone, or hard sandstone and resistant rock, its nutrient status is intermediate between that of the two types considered separately.

Using the combination of nutrient levels and hardness ratio, the comparative nutrient status of the rock types is:

Low   **High**

Resistant   Resistant   Chalk   Clay
with peat   Sandstone

NUTRIENT STATUS OF DIFFERENT STREAM TYPES

Trophic status depends both on the quality and the quantity of the nutrients present, and differences in the nutrient status of silt between rock types are enhanced by the different amounts of silt produced:

Low   **High**

Hard limestone   Chalk   Soft   Hard   Clay
Resistant rock   sandstone   sandstone

It is the flow regime of each reach, however, that determines how much of this silt is actually deposited in the channel, and is thus available to influence plants.

Passing downstream along a river, flow generally becomes slower, and silt tends to increase. It is temporary silt that is often important for plant nutrition in upper and middle reaches, while silt in the middle and lower reaches is more stable. Also, the nutrient status of the silt, sometimes in relation to most of the major nutrients, often increases downstream, particularly in rivers on resistant rocks. Downstream increases in anions or conductivity in river water, though, can also be attributed to changes in rock type or the entry of agrochemicals, hard surface run-off and effluents rather than to silt. As a result of these changes in nutrient status the vegetation of British streams shows a consistent shift towards species of more eutrophic preferences as one passing from upper to lower reaches (also see Chapter 11). There are three stream types in which downstream eutrophication is particularly marked. The first of these is streams on Resistant rock rising on blanket bog, which when they receive mineral silt from the more fertile land downstream may change from being dystrophic to mesotrophic channels. Secondly, on hard sandstone, mountain brooks are clean-washed, with negligible silt and, sometimes, oligotrophic plants. Farther down, however, flow may be checked sufficiently to allow thick nutrient-rich silt to accumulate on the bed. Thirdly, streams rising on a nutrient-poor rock type and flowing on to a nutrient-rich one will show a sharp increase in nutrient status.

The classification of British stream types shown in Figures 8.2 and 8.3 is by nutrient status and flow type. The nutrient factors, summarised here, are:

Nutrient status of silt (and water)

Amount of silt entering the channel

Amount of this silt which can remain in the substrate

(Coal Measures, calcareous sandstone and hard limestone streams are included in Figure 8.3, even though the nutrient data for these types are incomplete.)

Flow, of course, affects plants directly (see Chapters 2–6), as well as affecting the silt deposition, and other factors also differentiate between stream types. Some, such as the stability of the hard bed, are described elsewhere in this book (see Chapter 3). A minor but important factor may be the slope (and stability) of the bank. For instance, soft sandstone brooks, in contrast with those on chalk or hard sandstone, often have banks which are too steep for abundant fringing herbs at the sides (Figure 10.2).

The importance of Figures 8.2 and 8.3 is that each category has its own characteristic vegetation type, recognisable and classifiable as such (see Chapters 11–14). The main controlling factors of British stream vegetation (excluding human impact) are flow type and geology, and these can be interpreted in terms of topography, water inflow, silting and nutrient status (and other minor factors such as bed stability, turbidity, etc.).

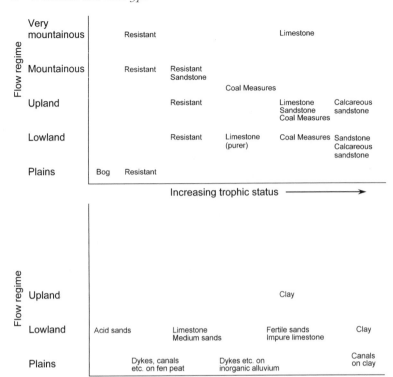

Figure 8.2
Stream types on hard rocks.

Figure 8.3
Stream types on soft rocks.

DISTRIBUTION OF SPECIES IN RELATION TO SILT NUTRIENTS

Dystrophic and oligotrophic species are confined to a narrow range of habitats, with a narrow and characteristic nutrient status. Dystrophic nutrient levels are given above. Figure 8.4a is a star diagram showing the low nutrient levels of the sites in which oligotrophic species occur (for nitrogen, see above). Figure 8.4b, for sites with mesotrophic species, is a larger pattern, and that for eutrophic species (Figure 8.4c) is larger again. These species groups can be identified and separated on nutrient status. However, mesotrophic and eutrophic species have wide and sometimes overlapping ranges, and there are also species groups intermediate between these (see Chapters 1, 12, etc.) and it is difficult to get clear separations on nutrient regimes (particularly on such a small number of samples). Star diagrams for some species are shown in Figure 8.5. Contracted patterns (narrow ranges of these nutrients which vary considerably within the mesotrophic–eutrophic range) are illustrated in (a) and (b) (*Ranunculus* spp. and mosses), and wide patterns with high nutrients in (c) and (d) (*Alisma plantago-aquatica* and *Enteromorpha intestinalis*). (Mosses and *Enteromorpha* both have at least some access to silt nutrients.) Species with particularly low values for a single nutrient are shown in (e) and (f) (*Myriophyllum spicatum* for

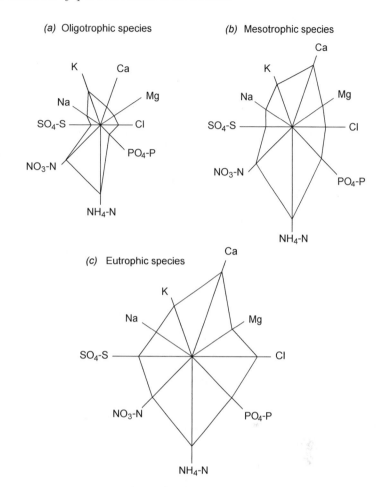

Figure 8.4
Star diagrams of nutrient patterns for different species groups. Details as for Figure 8.1. (a) Represents all sites containing oligotrophic species; (b) all sites containing mesotrophic species; and (c) all sites containing eutrophic species.

magnesium, and *Potamogeton crispus* for phosphate-phosphorus), and with particularly high values of one nutrient in (g) and (h) (*Potamogeton pectinatus* for chloride, and *Sparganium erectum* for ammonia-nitrogen. *P. pectinatus* extends its range to brackish water).

Plants also vary in their distribution according to hardness ratio. Using the average of all sites in which any given species was found, the following generalisations between hardness ratio and type of species can be made:

Hardness ratio	Types of species
0–1	Dystrophic, oligotrophic and dyke species
1–2	Mainly oligotrophic and dyke species
2–4	A varied group, including eutrophic species
4+	Mainly limestone species, including fringing herbs

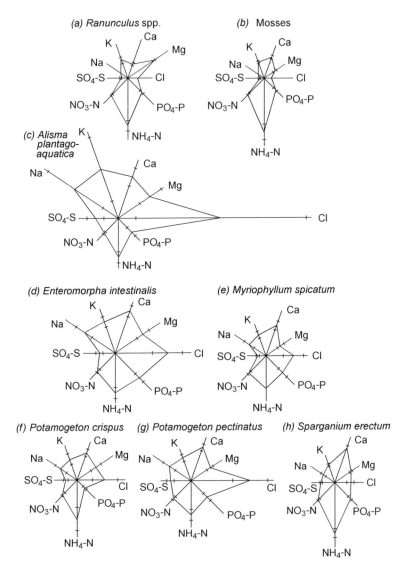

Figure 8.5
Star diagrams of nutrient patterns for individual species (or aggregates). Details as for Figure 8.1 except that in order to make the standard errors small enough to show on the patterns, the site with the highest nutrient levels in each instance has been omitted from the calculations.

It again appears that silt nutrient content and hardness ratio jointly determine nutrient status for plants, so that, for instance, clay species require a medium hardness ratio but very high silt nutrient levels, while chalk species are characteristic of a high hardness ratio and low nutrient contents. Calcium dominance reduces the availability of e.g. phosphate and nitrate, so effectively further lowering nutrient status.

Plant distribution in relation to silt chemistry is shown in Table 8.6, and should be compared with the water chemistry data in Table 8.2. Both tables show mesotrophic and eutrophic plants only (apart from part of the aggregate — mosses). Sodium and chloride levels are important in

Table 8.6   Plant distribution in relation to silt chemistry

The species are listed under the concentrations with which they are best related. Concentrations are in p.p.m. Data are of water extracted from silt and analysed on Atomic Absorption Spectrometer, Flame Photometer, and Hach Fieldlab DR/EL2.

1 Calcium

Below 50	Mosses	
50–100	(*Carex acutiformis*)	*Potamogeton crispus*
	Ceratophyllum demersum	*Potamogeton pectinatus*
	Myriophyllum spicatum	*Ranunculus* spp.
	Phalaris arundinacea	*Sagittaria sagittifolia*
100–150	*Apium nodiflorum*	*Potamogeton crispus*
	(*Carex acutiformis*)	*Potamogeton pectinatus*
	Elodea canadensis	*Rorippa nasturtium-aquaticum* agg.
	Glyceria maxima	*Schoenoplectus lacustris*
	Lemna minor agg.	*Sparganium emersum*
	Mentha aquatica	*Veronica beccabunga*
	Nuphar lutea	
150–300	(*Carex acutiformis*)	*Potamogeton perfoliatus*
	Mentha aquatica	*Schoenoplectus lacustris*
	Myosotis scorpioides	*Sparganium emersum*
	Potamogeton pectinatus	
Over 300	*Phragmites australis*	*Enteromorpha intestinalis*
	Polygonum amphibium	
Poorly correlated	*Alisma plantago-aquatica*	*Sparganium erectum*
	Callitriche spp.	

2 Chloride

Below 20	*Callitriche* spp.	*Rorippa nasturtium-aquaticum* agg.
	Carex acutiformis	*Veronica beccabunga*
	Elodea canadensis	Mosses
	Mentha aquatica	
20–40	*Apium nodiflorum*	*Phalaris arundinacea*
	Carex acutiformis	*Potamogeton perfoliatus*
	Elodea canadensis	*Ranunculus* spp.
	Myosotis scorpioides	*Rorippa nasturtium-aquaticum* agg.
	Myriophyllum spicatum	*Sparganium erectum*

151

Table 8.6   Continued

40–60	*Glyceria maxima*	*Rorippa nasturtium-aquaticum* agg.
	Nuphar lutea	*Sagittaria sagittifolia*
	Phragmites australis	*Schoenoplectus lacustris*
	Potamogeton crispus	*Sparganium emersum*
60–80	*Glyceria maxima*	*Enteromorpha intestinalis*
	Nuphar lutea	
Over 80	*Alisma plantago-aquatica*	*Phragmites australis*
	Ceratophyllum demersum	*Potamogeton pectinatus*
	Lemna minor agg.	

3 Magnesium

Below 5	*Apium nodiflorum*	*Phalaris arundinacea*
	Callitriche spp.	*Ranunculus* spp.
	Carex acutiformis	*Rorippa nasturtium-aquaticum* agg.
	Myriophyllum spicatum	*Veronica beccabunga*
5–10	*Elodea canadensis*	*Potamogeton pectinatus*
	Lemna minor agg.	*Sagittaria sagittifolia*
	Nuphar lutea	*Sparganium emersum*
	Potamogeton crispus	*Sparganium erectum*
10–20	*Glyceria maxima*	*Schoenoplectus lacustris*
	Nuphar lutea	*Sparganium erectum*
20–40	*Alisma plantago-aquatica*	*Schoenoplectus lacustris*
	Ceratophyllum demersum	*Sparganium erectum*
	Lemna minor agg.	Mosses
	Polygonum amphibium	*Enteromorpha intestinalis*
40+	*Ceratophyllum demersum*	*Phragmites australis*

4 Nitrate-nitrogen

Below 3	*Alisma plantago-aquatica*	*Mentha aquatica*
	Callitriche spp.	*Phalaris arundinacea*
3–4	*Callitriche* spp.	*Potamogeton crispus*
	Ceratophyllum demersum	*Potamogeton pectinatus*
	Mentha aquatica	*Rorippa nasturtium-aquaticum* agg.
	Myriophyllum spicatum	*Veronica beccabunga*
	Nuphar lutea	Mosses
	Phragmites australis	*Enteromorpha intestinalis*
	Polygonum amphibium	

Table 8.6   Continued

4+	*Elodea canadensis*	*Rorippa nasturtium-aquaticum* agg.
	Lemna minor agg.	Mosses
Poorly correlated	*Apium nodiflorum*	*Ranunculus* spp.
	Carex acutiformis	*Sagittaria sagittifolia*
	Glyceria maxima	*Sparganium emersum*
	Myosotis scorpioides	*Sparganium erectum*
	Potamogeton perfoliatus	

5 Ammonia-nitrogen

Below 2.5	*Callitriche* spp.	*Polygonum amphibium*
2.5–5	*Ceratophyllum demersum*	*Lemna minor* agg.
5–10	*Mentha aquatica*	*Potamogeton crispus*
	Nuphar lutea	*Rorippa nasturtium-aquaticum* agg.
	Phalaris arundinacea	*Enteromorpha intestinalis*
	Polygonum amphibium	
10+	*Apium nodiflorum*	*Phalaris arundinacea*
	Lemna minor agg.	*Sparganium erectum*
	Mentha aquatica	*Enteromorpha intestinalis*
	Myosotis scorpioides	
Poorly correlated	*Alisma plantago-aquatica*	*Potamogeton pectinatus*
	Carex acutiformis	*Ranunculus* spp.
	Elodea canadensis	*Sagittaria sagittifolia*
	Glyceria maxima	*Schoenoplectus lacustris*
	Myriophyllum spicatum	*Sparganium emersum*
	Phragmites australis	Mosses

6 Phosphate-phosphorus

Below 1	*Alisma plantago-aquatica*	*Polygonum amphibium*
	Ceratophyllum demersum	*Ranunculus* spp.
	Elodea canadensis	*Rorippa nasturtium-aquaticum* agg.
	Glyceria maxima	*Sagittaria sagittifolia*
	Nuphar lutea	*Schoenoplectus lacustris*
	Phalaris arundinacea	
1–2	*Mentha aquatica*	*Polygonum amphibium*
	Myriophyllum spicatum	*Rorippa nasturtium-aquaticum* agg.
	Nuphar lutea	*Sagittaria sagittifolia*

153

Table 8.6   Continued

	Phragmites australis	
2–3	*Callitriche* spp.	*Schoenoplectus lacustris*
	Myriophyllum spicatum	*Sparganium erectum*
	Potamogeton pectinatus	*Veronica beccabunga*
	Ranunculus spp.	*Mosses*
3+	*Myosotis scorpioides*	*Rorippa nasturtium-aquaticum* agg.
	Phalaris arundinacea	*Sparganium erectum*
Poorly correlated	*Apium nodiflorum*	*Potamogeton perfoliatus*
	Carex acutiformis	*Sparganium emersum*
	Lemna minor agg.	*Enteromorpha intestinalis*
	Potamogeton crispus	

7 Potassium

Below 10	*Alisma plantago-aquatica*	*Ranunculus* spp.
	Polygonum amphibium	*Veronica beccabunga*
	Potamogeton perfoliatus	*Mosses*
10–20	*Elodea canadensis*	*Ranunculus* spp.
	Lemna minor agg.	*Sagittaria sagittifolia*
	Potamogeton pectinatus	*Schoenoplectus lacustris*
	Potamogeton perfoliatus	*Sparganium emersum*
20–40	*Alisma plantago-aquatica*	*Glyceria maxima*
	Carex acutiformis	*Lemna minor* agg.
	Ceratophyllum demersum	*Rorippa nasturtium-aquaticum* agg.
40+	*Callitriche* spp.	*Enteromorpha intestinalis*
	Lemna minor agg.	
Poorly correlated	*Apium nodiflorum*	*Nuphar lutea*
	Mentha aquatica	*Phalaris arundinacea*
	Myosotis scorpioides	*Sparganium erectum*

8 Sodium

Below 20	*Callitriche* spp.	*Ranunculus* spp.
	Mentha aquatica	*Veronica beccabunga*
	Phalaris arundinacea	*Mosses*
20–40	*Apium nodiflorum*	*Ranunculus* spp.
	Myosotis scorpioides	*Rorippa nasturtium-aquaticum* agg.
	Nuphar lutea	*Sparganium emersum*

Table 8.6   Continued

	Potamogeton crispus	
40–60	*Alisma plantago-aquatica*	*Sagittaria sagittifolia*
	Elodea canadensis	*Schoenoplectus lacustris*
	Glyceria maxima	*Sparganium emersum*
	Nuphar lutea	
60–100	*Sparganium erectum*	
100+	*Alisma plantago-aquatica*	*Potamogeton perfoliatus*
	Ceratophyllum demersum	*Sagittaria sagittifolia*
	Lemna minor agg.	*Enteromorpha intestinalis*
	Phragmites australis	
Poorly correlated	*Carex acutiformis*	*Potamogeton pectinatus*
	Myriophyllum spicatum	

9 Sulphate-sulphur

Below 10	*Myosotis scorpioides*	Mosses
10–30	*Apium nodiflorum*	*Rorippa nasturtium-aquaticum* agg.
	Callitriche spp.	*Schoenoplectus lacustris*
	Carex acutiformis	*Veronica beccabunga*
	Phalaris arundinacea	Mosses
	Ranunculus spp.	
30–80	*Ceratophyllum demersum*	*Potamogeton pectinatus*
	Myriophyllum spicatum	*Potamogeton perfoliatus*
	Nuphar lutea	*Sagittaria sagittifolia*
	Phragmites australis	*Sparganium emersum*
	Polygonum amphibium	*Enteromorpha intestinalis*
	Potamogeton crispus	
80+	*Alisma plantago-aquatica*	*Lemna minor* agg.
	Apium nodiflorum	*Nuphar lutea*
	Elodea canadensis	*Potamogeton pectinatus*
	Glyceria maxima	*Sparganium emersum*
Poorly correlated	*Mentha aquatica*	*Sparganium erectum*

separating these two groups (also see Figure 8.4 and, for chloride, Table 8.2) and some separation is shown with magnesium, potassium and sulphate-sulphur but not with the other nutrients. Differences in nitrate-nitrogen and phosphate-phosphorus levels in the water are more important ecologically than similar differences in silt.

PLANT NUTRIENT CONTENTS

Oligotrophic species, and the grouping of all species from oligotrophic sites, contain very low levels of calcium, potassium, nitrogen and phosphorus. The wide-ranging mesotrophic and eutrophic species, in contrast, each have widely varying nutrient contents. However, if all plants sampled on each rock type are grouped, the values are much more stable.

In resistant rock streams plants have very low calcium, potassium, nitrogen and phosphorus levels (though those from the more fertile sites contain higher levels than those from the oligotrophic ones); in chalk streams plants are low in magnesium; in both clay and sandstone streams plants have high levels of potassium, nitrogen and phosphorus, but plants on clay are rich in sodium while those on sandstone are rich in magnesium and low in sodium (also see Casey & Downing, 1976).

DISCUSSION

Plant communities and vegetation types are described in Chapters 12–14. They are closely related to rock (and soil) type, which in turn determine the nutrient status of the silt in the channel substrate. The association between species and bedrock is through the community type, and both the quality and the quantity of the silt can be linked with this. As far as individual mesotrophic to eutrophic species are concerned, the quantity of silt is too variable to be assessed and the species usually occur in a wide range of habitats, not well related to individual nutrients of the silt or water. The type of variation is shown well by considering communities containing three or more fringing herbs. Such communities typically occur in chalk brooks (high hardness ratio, low nutrient contents), upland hard sandstone brooks (similar to chalk but higher in some nutrients, often lower in silt bands), silty sheltered mountain brooks on Resistant rocks (low hardness ratio, rather low nutrients but ample silt), some soft sandstone brooks with gently sloping banks (low hardness ratio, fairly high nutrients) and sheltered upland hard limestone brooks (chemically probably like chalk, with some silt present). All these are mesotrophic habitats, but are classified as such because of different combinations of nutrient characters, the link being with the rock type and silt content rather than with, say, calcium or phosphate levels separately. If these fringing herbs are considered as individual species rather than as a group, each has a much wider habitat range and thus a yet wider nutrient range. In other words, communities have smaller nutrient ranges than do their component species. It must be borne in mind though that nutrients are only one of the complex of factors determining plant distribution, and must not be considered in isolation from other factors such as flow.

There are also other complications which are not considered in Tables 8.2 and 8.6. For example, it appears that if plants have adequate nutrients for part of the time, e.g. from temporary silt, this is sufficient for continuous good growth. It is also possible for nutrients to be present in too high amounts. In particular, if several nutrients are jointly present in high concentrations in water they are more toxic than if only one is at a high level. Plants growing over-lush because of excess nutrients are particularly liable to wash-out, since their shoots are large but weak, and their roots, small for the size of shoot. Also, there is as yet no relevant evidence on relationships between carbon sources and the distribution of river plants.

ROCK TYPE AND RIVER VEGETATION

Rock type influences nutrient status, both directly and indirectly, as discussed above. It also has other profound influences on habitat, and consequently on river vegetation. Habitat is, of course, the integration of many different influences. (Human impact may be anything from minor to overriding importance, and is mostly omitted here.) While water force is the primary natural influence, this is partly determined by rock type. It is also due to the effects of glaciation, tectonic movements and suchlike.

Riverscape and topography

Excluding geological events, topography is determined by rock type. Soft rocks erode faster than hard ones, so form lowlands in conditions hard rocks would remain as hills. The type of riverscape also depends on rock type: rolling chalk downs differ from much flatter, and indeed smaller-scale, clay country; very hard slates and limestones produce more jagged and cliffy hills than the gentler gneiss ones.

Rock type affects weathering, and so affects riverscape
* through hardness (resistance to erosion),
* through the way it erodes (mostly mud and silt from clay, much boulder and stone from many Resistant rocks),
* through its liability to solution (limestone dissolves, so produces less sediment).

Rock type affects flow
* through topography,
* through how this influences rainfall,

- through the absorption of rainfall (aquifer and not, flash floods and not).

From these influences the characteristic and distinctive riverscapes develop. And from the variation in rock type come the diversity of features in the river, the diversity in habitat, in flow regime, substrate and nutrient regime, in river and bank shape. Water force depends on topography, therefore on rock type, as well as on rainfall and climate.

Quantity of water

A river is a stream of water. Therefore water is a pre-requirement! Due to drainage and abstraction in the past century or two, smaller streams are increasingly drying and, if not kept open by storm flow, disappearing. Abstraction is from aquiferous rock where, therefore, streams are drying greatly. So this form of drying is influenced by rock type, both as to total water, and as to its regime and type. Spring water reflects the chemistry of the rock below (and unfortunately, pollution), and adds stability to water flow, depth and force. Excluding human impact, rock type also influences,

- through topography,
- springs,
- seepages,
- run-off and abstraction.

High ground catches more rain, and there can be drier areas beyond such hills. Thus topography influences stability of discharge. Porous rock and land surface stabilise discharge by absorbing rain, and either releasing it slowly or letting it seep down to the water table below (losing these and making surfaces impermeable increases damaging flash floods).

Unconsolidated sediment

Loose sediment in the river depends (excluding impact) on the amount of sediment released by eroding rock and land upstream, and, secondly on the stability of discharges, both of which depend on rock types. If nutrients are deficient in the hard bed, the following are among species unable to grow well without temporary (i.e. unstable) silt:

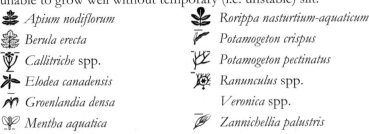

Apium nodiflorum   *Rorippa nasturtium-aquaticum*

Berula erecta   *Potamogeton crispus*

Callitriche spp.   *Potamogeton pectinatus*

Elodea canadensis   *Ranunculus* spp.

Groenlandia densa   *Veronica* spp.

Mentha aquatica   *Zannichellia palustris*

Myriophyllum spp.

(Also see above.)

Rock type and river vegetation

Plant stability

The ability of a plant to remain in the same place, year after year, is an important element in the development patterning and maintenance of a plant community. This ability is influenced by rock type directly, as well as by the factors discussed above and in other chapters.

Species	Rock type in which a plant community is	
	Stable	Unstable
Apium nodiflorum	Chalk, sandstone, middle clays	Other rock types
Callitriche spp.	Chalk, lowland sandstone	Clay
Elodea canadensis	Lowland clay (moderately)	Other rock types
Nuphar lutea	Lowland clay	Other rock types
Potamogeton pectinatus	Polluted chalk	Other rock types
Ranunculus spp.	Limestones	Other rock types
Sparganium emersum	Lowland clay, sandstone, and mild pollution	Other rock types

These species are part of the communities in which they are stable, but may also be integral parts of communities in which they are unstable, e.g., *Callitriche* spp. Here the plants are lost and invade again, rather than remaining for long periods, under ordinary conditions (excluding dredging, major summer storms, accidental severe pollutions, etc.).

Channel shape

The shape of the channel and bank (again excluding impact) is less directly connected to rock type. Topography influences water force, so channel shape. Land composition also influences channel shape (granite versus clay, for instance). Both also influence braiding of channels. Unstable flows lead to wide, shallow-edged channels, and unstable substrates lead to shallow banks and shoals.

Substrate

In regard to substrate texture and stability, rock type influences particle size (e.g., sandstone versus gneiss), and, as already seen, the amount of sediment washed in. Rock type often determines land surface (unless there is, e.g., alluvial overlay). These all then influence erosion of both consolidated and unconsolidated sediment, so also washout, so also re-colonisation and patterns, of vegetation.

159

Nutrients

- Rock types differ in the amount of nutrients released from the rock, to both sediment and water.
- Rock types differ in the relative amounts of different nutrients they release.
- Most of these, and other nutrients are in silt or water, less in water, and levels are low indeed in (non-silty) sand, gravel and stone.
- Therefore silt and mud, consolidated or not, are crucial in determining nutrient status. The proportions of nutrients (calcium-rich, etc.) are the same on silty and non-silty places, but in nutrient-poor places only the silty allow good growth.

Organic matter, which significantly affects nutrient regime, is partly influenced by rock type (e.g., blanket bog is mostly on resistant rock, fen peat has lime-influenced run-off, clay usually bears nutrient-rich vegetation).

Conclusions

Rock type is a major determinant of river vegetation, acting as itself (including substrate and soil types, if different),

- through topography, which it partly influences,
- through flow regime, which again it partly influences,
- and, to some extent, human impact is altered by rock type (e.g., low-nutrient rock is not the first choice for agriculture).

The many habitat niches of pristine rivers are decreased as human impact increases uniformity. Species assemblages become more restricted and distinctive to each rock type (e.g., the 'unstable' species of the display above are gradually unable to be part of the community. That becomes increasingly restricted to the 'stable' species, and these are the main ones distinctive of each rock type). Species requiring habitats now gone, e.g. those of riffles, disappear. So do those near the limit of their habitat range, when habitats change to being just a little too nutrient-rich, just a little too shallow, just a little too sedimented, etc. As human impact becomes more intensive, it overrides and lessons the influence of rock type, by e.g. pollution (including agrochemical and hard surface run-off), channelling, (deepening, straightening), lining, abstraction and overmuch silting.

The influence of rock type is interwoven through all patterns and behaviours of river plants.

9

Productivity

Productivity, the rate at which the vegetation increases, is greater for emerged than for submerged plants, mainly because the submerged plants receive less light. The total production of river plants in streams is very variable and depends on how much of the stream is occupied by plants at all and the relative proportions of emerged plants, submerged plants and algae.

The *production* of vegetation is the weight of new organic matter made by plants over a given period of time, *productivity* is the rate at which this organic material is formed and the *biomass* is the total weight of plants present at any one time. Productivity is very variable in different rivers, some having no macrophytic vegetation, some a little and others being choked with plants. Among aquatics, most of the research so far has been on the largest amount of production — and the maximum biomass — which can occur, rather than on the variations between different plant species and the effect on production of differences in habitat such as substrate texture, trophic status, etc.

The main division of river plants according to production is between the emerged and the submerged plants. Emergents receive full sunlight, and because their lower parts are in water their production, unlike that of most land plants, is rarely hindered by shortage of water. Thus the production of tall emergents is usually higher than that of any other type of vegetation and they also have a high productivity. Submergents, in contrast, receive much less light, since a proportion of it is reflected or absorbed during its passage through the water above them, and they may often suffer from a shortage of carbon (see Chapter 8). Their production is therefore very low, averaging only about a tenth of that of the tall emergents (Table 9. 1).

Production depends both on features of the plant's habitat, and on the rate at which green shoots can fix carbon and energy into organic compounds under optimum conditions. As can be seen from Table 9.1, the amounts of carbon fixed (per unit dry leaf weight per hour) in emergents and submergents are similar, so the difference in productivity between the two groups is a result of differences in habitats, not their biochemical efficiency (Westlake, 1975). There is too little evidence at present to determine whether variations in habitat within the two main groups cause variations in production.

The production in a chalk stream, Bere stream, has been studied (Westlake *et al.*, 1972) and the results are summarised in Table 9.2. The

Table 9.1   Production of water plants in good conditions

	Maximum biomass (kg organic wt per m^2)	Annual net production (kg organic wt per m^2)	Productivity (g dry wt per m^2 per day)	Carbon uptake (mg per g dry wt per hour)
Emergents	4–10	4–6	12–48	3–9
Submergents	0.4–0.7	0.5–0.8	2–10(–25)	2–10(–20)

Adapted from Westlake (1975).
Data refer to temperate regions.
Emergents are tall species such as *Phragmites australis* and *Typha* spp. and do not include short emergents such as *Myosotis scorpioides*. Submergents include *Chara* spp. and *Myriophyllum spicatum*.

Table 9.2   Production in Bere stream .

(a) Production (metric tonnes organic matter per year) for the whole stream	
Submergents (mainly *Ranunculus*)	8
Emergents (mainly *Rorippa nasturtium-aquaticum* agg.)	5
Algae	6
Tree leaves, etc.	2
Bank plants, etc.	1
From watercress beds	38
In spring water	17
(b) Annual net production (kcal per m^2 per year) at one site	
Submergents (mainly *Ranunculus*)	550
Emergents (mainly *Rorippa nasturtium-aquaticum* agg.)	1800
Algae (in water and on bed)	700

Adapted from Westlake *et al.* (1972).

stream is fairly small, with a moderately swift flow and plants growing right across the channel. *Ranunculus penicillatus* ssp. *pseudofluitans*, a submergent, is the main dominant, growing most in spring and early summer. *Rorippa nasturtium-aquaticum* agg., a fringing herb, increases greatly in late summer, particularly at the sides, and partly overgrows the *Ranunculus*. More of the stream is covered by the submergent and in the stream as a whole its production is the higher, but the productivity of the fringing herb is much the greater and where the habitat is suitable for it the biomass of the vegetation is mainly *Rorippa nasturtium-aquaticum* agg. There are also algae present, growing and suspended in the water. Their production is about half that of the larger plants. As in many chalk streams, commercial watercress beds occur near the source, and fragments from these are washed into the stream.

Table 9.3   Production[a] in the Thames

Acorus calamus (tall emergent)	Site 1	23.7		Site 2	16.4
Nuphar lutea (rooted floating)	Site 1	0.1		Site 2	27.6
Tree leaves, etc.			79		
Algae in water (phytoplankton)			4388		

Adapted from Mann *et al.* (1972).

a   Annual net production and input of tree leaves etc. (kcal per m^2 per year).

To a lesser extent organic material enters the stream as leaves, etc., from overhanging trees and bank plants. When the plants and animals die, their remains take some time to decompose completely, and some of this dead organic matter is washed downstream.

A study has been made of production (downstream) in the River Thames (Berrie, 1972; Mann *et al.*, 1972), the results of which are shown in Table 9.3. The River Thames is a large slow eutrophic lowland river, with a very different vegetation from the chalk stream. The water is deep and turbid, and so the larger plants are able to grow only on the shallow edges. The slow eutrophic waters are very suitable for the growth of floating algae, though, and in the reach studied they accounted for most of the production. The organic matter contributed by the larger plants comes partly from the tall emergent *Acorus calamus* and the floating-leaved rooted *Nuphar lutea*, but mainly from tree leaves dropping into the water. Where trees overhang the water these have the double effect of increasing the tree leaf content of the site and decreasing the river plants as a result of shading. *Acorus calamus* grows in shallow water, while *Nuphar lutea* is usually in water 0.5–2 m deep, so that the proportions of each, and indeed the total biomass of the two, depends on the slope of the channel below water level.

10

Plant patterns

A few river channels have uniform vegetation from one bank to the other, but in most the plants found at the edges are different from those in the centre. Some channels have essentially similar species growing in much the same positions and to much the same size each year, while in others there are large changes from year to year, or even between early summer and late summer. This type of variations can be the result of differences in factors which are physical (e.g. flow, substrate texture), chemical (e.g. the nutrients in the silt) or biotic (e.g. shading by larger plants, grazing by animals). It is easier to list the causes of such patterning than it is to classify plant behaviour, and some phenomena, for example the pattern of fringing herbs, are due to more than one cause. A final controlling factor on vegetation patterns is that any one site will only support a limited number of species and only some of these will be capable of luxuriant growth in a given habitat.

This chapter brings together descriptions of the sort of plant patterns which can be seen within sites — the emerged plants at the sides of the channel and the submerged ones in the middle; the decrease in vegetation under trees; and the differences at the same site when it is observed in May and in August, for instance. Most of these patterns are governed by the factors such as channel depth, flow, substrate and shading which have already been discussed in previous chapters. However, the patterns due to storm flows, fully described in Chapters 5 and 3, are not repeated here, nor are e.g. mosaics due to substrate stability. Here we consider the patterns from the point of view of plant behaviour, rather than as an effect of a physical factor such as flow, and the study of river vegetation as a whole, which is continued in Chapter 11 with a discussion of the changes which occur along a river system, and in Chapters 12–14 with an examination of the different plant communities and vegetation of various stream types. The small-scale plant patterns described here occur within the larger-scale ones described later, and are irrelevant to the diagnosis of a site as being e.g. a chalk stream, an upper reach or a polluted habitat.

ACROSS THE CHANNEL

Cross-sections of channels vary in shape, from, at one extreme, deep canals with uniformly deep water between piled banks, to small chalk or hill streams with a shallow channel and gentle side slopes at the other (Figure 10.1). River plants can potentially live on all angles of substrate and at all water depths commonly found in Britain, though concrete or

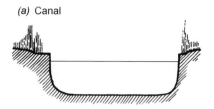

(a) Canal

(b) Small chalk stream

Figure 10.1
Contrasted channel shapes.
(a) Canal (deep water, piled
    sides)
(b) Small chalk stream.

piled slopes cannot, of course, bear rooted plants. More importantly, plants often cannot grow in deep water, either because the substrate is unstable, or because in turbid water too little light reaches the bed (see Chapters 3, 4, and 7). The next sections show some typical variations in vegetation with the slope of the bank above and below water level, the slope of the bed, and the general size and flow regime of the channel. The plant communities themselves are described in Chapters 12–14.

CHANNEL BANKS

High banks may be man-made to prevent flooding, for example in the flood plains of large rivers, or, and commonly, they may be the result of a lowering of the ground water level for drainage. Where wetlands have been drained for arable farming, the water may be as much as 2 m below ground level (Figure 10.2a), but in little-drained streams ground level and water level almost coincide and banks will be very low (Figure 10.2b). Lowland chalk streams have a very stable flow and also often have very low banks, in little-drained land. Sandstone banks are slightly higher, and clay ones are higher still, the land usually being well drained. The low banks associated with mountain streams means that they may flood land beside the river downstream unless they are artificially embanked or drained.

Banks vary in steepness as well as in height, and this can influence vegetation. For example, narrow channels with steep banks 1–2 m high may be completely shaded by tall herbs on the bank, whereas if banks of the same height slope more gradually there may be enough light for plants to grow in the channel. In wide channels, however, channel vegetation is hardly influenced by the slope of the bank above the water.

Bank plants in the lowlands are usually tall, but may be short when they are grazed (e.g. by sheep on the Romney Marsh), sprayed with herbicides or regularly cut (as on some tow paths). Most lowlands are of moderate to high nutrient status, and the disturbance caused by dredging raises nutrient status higher, so allows tall herb vegetation. In the mountains the plants are short. Scattered trees are widespread

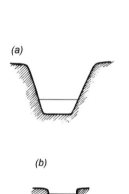

(a)

(b)

Figure 10.2
A cross-section of a dyke
(a) with the water level well
    below ground level; and
(b) with the water level almost at
    ground level.

165

along lowland streams, and are often also found in valleys in the highlands. The main groups of tall bank plants are those of dry land, damp ground, and of habitats intermittently flooded (Figure 10.3). Of those species in the last group, some seldom grow far from the water (e.g. *Carex acutiformis*, *Sparganium erectum*), others often grow well up the bank (e.g. *Glyceria maxima*, *Phalaris arundinacea*), while yet others vary markedly in habitat (e.g. *Phragmites australis* grows well up the banks of dykes, but elsewhere is seldom far from the water).

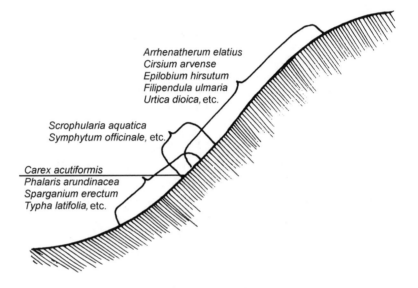

Arrhenatherum elatius
Cirsium arvense
Epilobium hirsutum
Filipendula ulmaria
Urtica dioica, etc.

Scrophularia aquatica
Symphytum officinale, etc.

Carex acutiformis
Phalaris arundinacea
Sparganium erectum
Typha latifolia, etc.

Figure 10.3
The habitat preferences in relation to water level of the main groups of bank plants.

At the edge of the channel, river plants, if present, may be tall emerged monocotyledons or fringing herbs. Rarely, other large broad-leaved plants may occur (e.g. *Alisma plantago-aquatica*, most frequent in somewhat small clay streams; and *Rumex hydrolapathum*, most frequent in canals), or small grasses may be prominent (as opposed to present but inconspicuous). When both tall and short plants can grow at the edge, the tall will shade and kill the short. However, the habitat preferences of the tall monocotyledons and the fringing herbs, while overlapping, do differ. The tall monocotyledons (except sometimes *Phalaris arundinacea*) require or prefer a soft fine substrate in which their deep roots and large rhizomes can anchor, and, being slow-growing perennials, need habitats which are stable, preferably for some years. They are also, being tall and deep-rooted, less likely to be harmed by fluctuating water levels and are thus more able to colonise steep slopes. The fringing herbs, in contrast, can invade temporary habitats, and can root in both fine and coarse substrates (though they can anchor more firmly in coarser ones). They

166

offer much hydraulic resistance to flow and their root systems are short, so on fine soils they are likely to be floated off in storm flows (see Chapter 5). They require fairly gentle slopes for the proper development of clumps, though fragments can become lodged on steeper banks.

CHANNEL BEDS

Within the channel itself it is possible for emerged, floating and submerged plants to grow, and some characteristic patterns are shown below. The basic habitat preferences of the tall monocotyledons and fringing herbs are the same as those described for the channel edges. Tall monocotyledons are characteristic of shallow water and deep soft soils, with little scour but possibly some drying. This means they are usually found at the sides of watercourses, sometimes on stable shoals and islands and occasionally right across the channel. They are commonest in clay streams and shallow dykes, where also they are most likely to dominate. Fringing herbs grow well in shallow water, at the sides of the channel or in the centre, particularly on firm gravel in moderate flow (see above), and especially in chalk and sandstone streams. Clay streams tend to have much fine sediment, so that clumps are easily washed away, while streams on Resistant rocks tend to have too fierce a flow and too little sediment for their good development. Fringing herbs grow well, and can develop into clumps, from fragments lodged on obstructions in the channel, though such clumps may be easily washed away.

Rooted submerged and floating plants may cover all the bed, as is quite common in small brooks. In a larger river, though, they are often confined to the shallower water at the sides. These water-supported plants can be patterned across the channel in various ways. Free-floating plants are usually less important. They are necessarily commonest in still and slow waters, their pattern tending to depend on shelter, i.e. the wind and current in relation to the positions of plants, banks and other obstructions. They may occur locally in faster flows, as when *Lemna trisulca* grows tangled with submerged shoots in small chalk streams. The third group of floating plants are those with floating shoots anchored to steep banks; and these are necessarily found close to these steep banks.

DIRECTION OF FLOW

In still water plant parts will grow out in all directions, but in a current they will be patterned according to the direction of flow, the plants usually being longest in the direction of the current, shortest vertically, rooted mostly at the upstream end, and with shoots trailing downstream (Plates 8–11). Current, then, determines both the pattern of the population and what spaces between plants are available for colonisation. It similarly affects rhizome growth. In still and slow waters the rhizomes often grow in all directions (e.g. *Nuphar lutea*), while in faster flows growth is often most across the channel with only a little growth upstream and variable development downstream (e.g. *Berula erecta*, *Groenlandia densa*, *Myriophyllum spicatum*, *Potamogeton crispus*, *Ranunculus penicillatus* ssp. *penicillatus*).

ALONG THE CHANNEL

In most natural channels bends produce patterns of erosion and sedimentation (Figure 10.4), which in turn lead to the patterns of vegetation along the channel. The erosion on the bends may actually undercut the banks, and then clods fall into the water. If these bear species which can grow submerged (e.g. *Agrostis stolonifera*, *Epilobium hirsutum*) then the plants will start to grow where the clods fall, but will probably soon be washed downstream, where they may again lodge and grow. More importantly, on the channel bed itself places liable to the most erosion usually have different vegetation, but the differences do depend on the habitat. In the mountains, for instance, the areas that are eroded most may be bare, while sheltered ones have fringing herbs. Again, in quieter streams the fringing herbs may be on the most-eroded parts with tall monocotyledons in the sheltered places, and in very slow flows tall monocotyledons may be present throughout. For variations with fluctuations in flow and substrate regimes, see Chapters 2, 3 and 6.

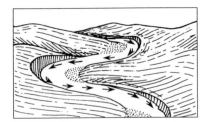

Figure 10.4

PROTECTION

Often, plants are unable to grow in an open habitat because the flow is too fast or too turbulent, or the substrate too unstable, etc., though they can grow well in that site if local protection is provided from these unfavourable factors. Such protection may be given by a large plant. In faster flows current force is decreased just upstream of a clump while turbulence remains high, and species characteristic of somewhat slower flows may grow here (Figure 10.5) (e.g. *Groenlandia densa, Potamogeton crispus, Zannichellia palustris* above *Ranunculus*). Some plants of slower waters which tolerate low light can grow as isolated shoots within large clumps, where they are sheltered (e.g. *Elodea canadensis* and *Potamogeton crispus* in *Ranunculus*).

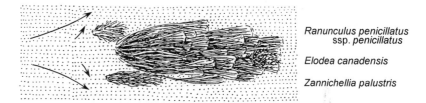

Figure 10.5

Ranunculus penicillatus ssp. *penicillatus*

Elodea canadensis

Zannichellia palustris

Emergents often accumulate silt between them, forming hummocks and providing shelter for other plants. These populations may be permanent, or temporarily growing in the shelter while recolonising from fragments (Figure 10.6; Plate 4). Examples of these are *Schoenoplectus lacustris* and *Sparganium erectum* providing protection; *Nuphar lutea* and *Myriophyllum spicatum* as permanent populations in the shelter; *Ceratophyllum demersum* as a temporary submergent; *Rorippa amphibia* and *Rorippa nasturtium-aquaticum* agg. as temporary emergents.

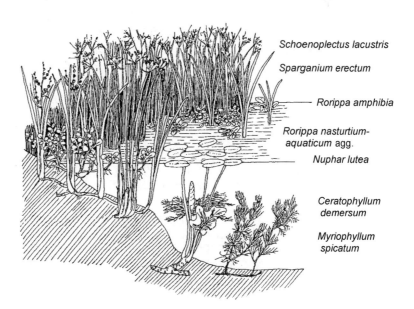

Figure 10.6
Tall emergents sheltering short, poorly anchored emergents and submerged and floating plants (lower reach of clay stream, River Great Ouse).

Schoenoplectus lacustris

Sparganium erectum

Rorippa amphibia

Rorippa nasturtium-aquaticum agg.

Nuphar lutea

Ceratophyllum demersum

Myriophyllum spicatum

169

Any plant with parts at the water surface may trap viable propagules. Fringing herbs are often held and grow for a while, sometimes explosively, but their roots are seldom long enough to anchor in the soil and though they may survive mild storms they are likely to be dispersed in the next severe storm flow. Fragments of trailing plants can lodge well on firm small obstructions, such as stones or stakes, where they can remain with the ends trailing (Figure 10.7; Plates 8, 9) (e.g. *Myriophyllum* spp., *Potamogeton* spp., *Ranunculus* spp.). For fragments to become rooted to the ground, they must be near enough to the ground for a month or two. Even temporary plants may, however, reach over 1 m × 0.5 m before being washed away. Indentations in the stream bank, boulders and other obstructions can all provide local protection, allowing plants to grow which could not tolerate the main current.

Figure 10.7

SHADING FROM ABOVE

Channels are most often shaded by trees and bushes, though bridges and buildings may have local effects and, as has already been mentioned, tall bank herbs can shade narrow channels (see Chapters 7 and 18; Plates 3, 6, 12, 13, 15). Patterns of shading lead to patterns of plants, since although no river plants can live under heavy shade, some species are more shade-tolerant than others. For example:

   Berula erecta – Ranunculus
      In light shade *Berula erecta* increases
   Nuphar lutea – Sparganium emersum
      In light shade *Sparganium emersum* increases.

   In any one site shade patterns may vary with time, as when a tree falls and gives full light to a previously-shaded place. Plants will then invade and increase in size until the community becomes stable. In one example, fringing herbs and *Callitriche* invaded a place previously without plants, and within two years a stable pattern had formed.

BRIDGE AND WEIR PATTERNS

Bridge piers and other structures in the water may slow the water upstream, cause swirling and turbulence around them, and perhaps faster flows or deep pools downstream. Weirs also have slower water upstream and faster water downstream of the structure, and as they are often sited at bridges the effect of the two together is additive. Near large bridges, therefore, there is likely to be a range of flow, and consequently substrate, types. This means that such bridges are useful for studying the varieties of plant communities which can occur within the overall chemical regime of each stream (e.g. Plate 7).

SEDIMENTATION AND PLANT CYCLES

Sedimentation varies both along the length of a stream and within individual sites. Where sedimentation varies, plants may vary also. In practice such plant patterns occur only where the sediment is silt or sand, since loose gravel and stones are unsuitable for plant growth. The deposited sediment may form shoals, on which plants can then grow, or in faster flow it may accumulate only inside plant clumps, not between them. Sand is deposited in faster flows than is silt because the particles are heavier. Silt is more nutrient-rich, and its presence in a clump may lead to shoots growing larger and denser, so some form of pattern can emerge from variations in the type of sediment. Also, deposition may vary across a channel, e.g. sand in *Berula erecta* in the middle, silt in *Rorippa nasturtium-aquaticum* agg. at the sides.

Shoals build up in shelter, and may be temporary, long-term or cyclical, depending mainly on the flow regime although plant cover can help to stabilise them. In deeper water they are first colonised by quick-growing submergents, while shallow ones are invaded by fringing herbs. Tall monocotyledons and more slow-growing submergents invade if the shoal persists. Regular disturbance or erosion leads to cyclical patterns. The cycle of fringing herbs, where this depends on silting, plant growth and storm flows, is described in Chapters 3 and 5.

Unusual sedimentation can alter plant distribution. A bare stretch of hard gravel bed observed for 5 years became silted during exceptionally low flows in one summer. *Zannichellia palustris* (with sparser other species) invaded and spread, and because of the extra trapping of silt by the *Zannichellia palustris* plants the silt became 5–20 cm deep. This depth was unstable and was swept away in the autumn storms, and as the general flow increased at that time, the area remained bare. Similar patterns occur with other species.

The true plant cycles depending on the morphology of the dominant plant, however, occur when the stream has a hard bed, the plants are short-rooted and sedimentation is sufficient for plants to become rooted only in the sediment. Species which move their rooting level completely into the sediment are washed away easily, while those staying more firmly in the gravel are less damaged in storms, so that differential damage and cycles result. Cycles of *Ranunculus* (which is firmly rooted) and *Rorippa nasturtium-aquatilis* agg. (which is poorly rooted) are described in Casey & Westlake (1974). *Berula erecta* and *Zannichellia palustris* (which are sediment-rooted) may also show patterns with *Ranunculus*. In cycles, it is the age of the plant patch which is important, not that of the individual rooted shoot, because it is on the age of the clump (as well as flow and substrate regime) that the depth of sediment present depends. Sediment usually accumulates most in summer and wash-out is most in winter; damaging storms can occur at any season. Some cycles tend to be annual, controlled by the general growth and weather cycles (as in the firmly rooted *Ranunculus*; see Casey & Westlake, 1974), while others are much more dependent on the minor fluctuations during the growing season, and several factors here affect the duration of the cycle.

Hummocks of sediment accumulate under *Zannichellia palustris* (Figure 10.8). As these rise they become more exposed to damage from flow, trampling, etc. Erosion of the top leads to erosion of the whole hummock leaving plants on the firm bed to form the nuclei of new hummocks. This plant is summer-green, so cycles are ended in the autumn anyway. Carpets are formed by *Berula erecta* (Figure 10.9). This is winter-green, so cycles may take a year or more. It spreads most in spring, so then many shoots are joined by living rhizomes and are difficult to move. Anchoring strength is less in autumn and winter, and storm flow of equal discharge will wash away more *Berula erecta* in autumn than in spring (see Chapters 3 and 5). The faster the sedimentation, the faster the cycle, provided the sediment can be stabilised by the root weft. Cycles can last anything between about two months and several years.

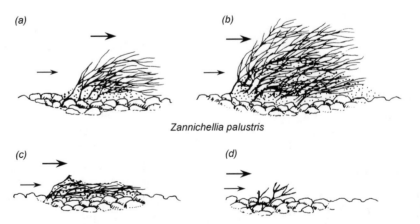

Figure 10.8
Development and erosion of hummock of *Zannichellia palustris*.

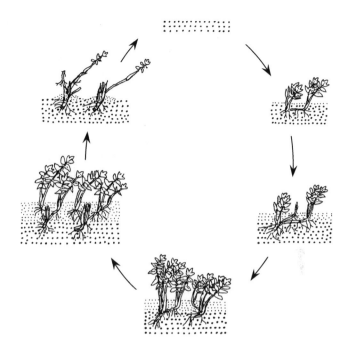

Figure 10.9
Development and erosion of a
carpet of *Berula erecta*.

Cyclical changes are of much botanical interest, but are uncommon unless the ordinary changes between spring and autumn are included. They occur with a combination of shallow water, a hard bed, sediment deposited in plant clumps though not much outside them, no severe spates, and storm flows occurring only infrequently. Most sites are on chalk, with sandstone and chalk-clay ones ranking next. The cycles are ended by storm flows. This is in contrast with cycles on land, which are more usually determined by the growth cycle of the dominant plant. This again emphasises the control which flow exerts on river plants.

POOR ESTABLISHMENT

When plant patches are firmly established in a site, properly anchored and growing well, they are likely to remain for some while — perhaps for many years, if not disturbed by severe storm flows, dredging, trampling, etc. However, many plants are transients, so that plant patterns occur because of their coming and going. Poor establishment may be because the plants are not held in the substrate, or because the substrate is itself a temporary habitat.

Most river plants can grow from the fragments washed down in storm flows, provided these are of a suitable size. A few (e.g. *Potamogeton pectinatus*) need a rhizome portion, but most can grow well from just

173

shoots, though some trailing species (e.g. *Ranunculus*) grow best from fragments from the lower part of the plant. Often portions only a few centimetres long are viable (e.g. *Callitriche*). Plants which can live in shallow water at channel margins, can often grow well there from fragments. These may become anchored, or they may form a floating fringe. A band of floating plants up to about 1 m wide is particularly characteristic of medium-sized chalk streams. Because they are not rooted in the nutrient-rich soil the plants remain small, but a fringe can survive until the next very severe storm flow and may last for two years or more, though trimmed and kept in place by the current. (Because the plants are separate, some can be moved without affecting the rest.) This vegetation pattern contrasts with the large luxuriant single-species patches of rooted fringing herbs that are so characteristic of small clay streams (see Chapters 3 and 5).

Passing downstream, the lack of shallow water and increased silting and floods mean it is increasingly difficult for fragments to anchor, and so relatively more of the clumps of fringing herbs (*Callitriche*, etc.) are temporary. *Callitriche* spp. and *Elodea canadensis* both propagate well from fragments, and both are characteristic of temporary silt shoals. Large populations can form, be churned up by storm flows, and then recolonise.

Other patterns caused by poor establishment are described elsewhere in this chapter, and in Chapter 3.

AGEING

Most aquatics propagate vegetatively, and although clumps and patches may move, the death of such patches (as opposed to individual shoots) from old age seems improbable. One aquatic, *Phragmites australis*, has been estimated to live over 1000 years in large marshes (see Rudescu *et al.*, 1965). Some plant patterns are, however, related to the age of the plant. For example, most fringing herbs have below-ground parts which live less than a year. Thus if they are to persist at a site, new shoots must continually develop beside the old ones as they die. This regrowth may be outside or inside the area of the patch in the previous year, and so the patch may move. This alteration in distribution is more pronounced in the channel centre than it is at the edge. This is because the edges comprise a smaller habitat and so new growth is more likely to be within the area of old plants. It also follows that plants with long-lived rhizomes (such as *Nuphar lutea*) will move around any given site less. Ageing can affect the survival of emerged plants anchored in the bank but growing out into the channel. As mentioned in Chapter 3, they are able to remain in place while still joined to the bank by a strong rhizome, but are likely to be washed away once this rhizome dies.

SEASONAL AND ANNUAL CHANGES

Vegetation often varies from early summer to later summer, and from one year to another. These changes are due both to differences in the growing pattern of the plants, and to differences in habitat, flow pattern, temperature, etc. The changes described here are those of the growing seasons, not the differences between winter and summer forms.

In the south of Britain some species usually reach their maximum size in early summer, others in mid- or late summer. Local conditions may alter this pattern, however.

Early species: *Berula erecta, Callitriche* spp., *Hottonia palustris,*
Ranunculus spp.

Late species: *Apium nodiflorum, Ceratophyllum demersum,*
Potamogeton spp., *Rorippa nasturtium-aquaticum* agg.,
Sagittaria sagittifolia

Streams which contain plants from both these groups usually look very different in May and September (Figure 10.10; Casey & Westlake, 1974; Westlake *et al.*, 1972).

Some populations vary in position and luxuriance from year to year. Those which vary most are species which have intermittent rapid or explosive growth, or have some character, such as poor anchorage, which potentially causes large losses. Such species are frequently those that propagate well from fragments. Plant patches retaining their position and size may show the reverse characters, or may be confined to a substrate or flow regime occurring in only a small part of the stream (e.g. a silt shoal, or fast flow below a bridge). Patches restricted to certain substrates are particularly common in chalk-clay streams, as these tend to have variable substrates. When such mosaics occur, plant clumps remain stable because shoots moving outside them get swept away (see Chapter 3).

Plants which form trailing clumps in moving water (e.g. *Callitriche, Oenanthe fluviatilis, Ranunculus*) usually keep their shape. This shape can be determined by internal factors or by small-scale variations in substrate etc. If substrate and other factors permit, though, the clump may move slowly. During the growing season the clump may be destroyed by cutting, trampling, etc., leaving scattered patches of shoots which can each form the nucleus of a new clump (Figure 10.11). The position of these clumps may be different from that of the original one, and indeed clump and bare soil areas may be reversed, substrate and flow permitting. From year to year, therefore, the position and pattern of the plant clumps vary.

The growth of the plants themselves may cause seasonal variations in habitat. In shallow streams plants alter the current pattern as they grow during the summer, which leads to increased erosion in some

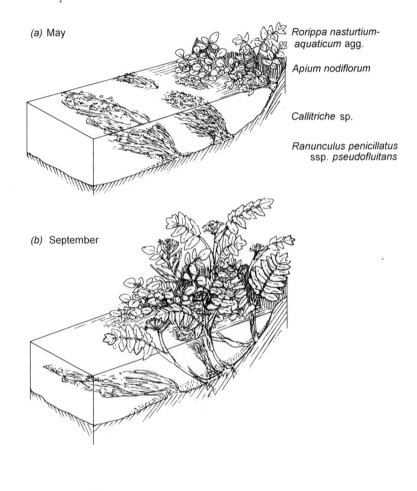

(a) May

*Rorippa nasturtium-
aquaticum* agg.

Apium nodiflorum

Callitriche sp.

Ranunculus penicillatus
ssp. *pseudofluitans*

(b) September

Figure 10.10

Figure 10.11
Movement of *Ranunculus* clumps
after cutting.
(a) Uncut plants.
(b) After cutting, with only a few
    viable tufts of shoots.
(c) New plants.

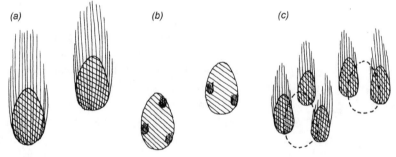

(a)   (b)   (c)

places and greater shelter and sedimentation in others. These changes
may then affect the existing plants and the position of any new ones.

Annual variations in water depth and flow may lead to annual
changes in the plants. Channels drying in summer will lose their
submerged plant parts and land species may invade; this change is

reversed on flooding. If flow becomes slower in late summer, slow-flow species will show a relative increase (e.g. *Lemna minor* agg.), and faster-flow species a decrease (e.g. *Ranunculus* spp). The interaction between flow and substrate may cause annual variations in *Ranunculus*. In clay, or near-clay streams *Ranunculus* is often absent because the silt is unsuitable for anchorage and makes the habitat too nutrient-rich. In years of low flows, however, *Ranunculus penicillatus* ssp. *penicillatus* may appear in those sites where more turbulent water and reduced silt allow the plant to anchor to the hard bed below and provide it with a lower nutrient supply. The *Ranunculus* appears in parts of the channel which are normally empty.

Minor changes between one year and another can also be caused by temperature. For example, *Elodea canadensis* grows much better in exceptionally hot summers, and in e.g. 1975 often grew very well, particularly in northern Britain. It was more frequent and more luxuriant, extending its habitat range into faster flows where, because of the losses, it could not survive if growth was slow. Heat waves may kill plant parts in still water, where the temperature rises most (e.g. *Myriophyllum verticillatum*).

COMPETITION

The overall controlling factors in the distribution of river plants are flow and substrate, and competition is, in consequence, much less important in river communities than in typical land communities. It does occur, however, and it alters the pattern of plant growth. The effect can be due to the mere presence of one species making the habitat less suitable for another species. For example, if a *Sparganium erectum* patch develops upstream of a *Ranunculus* clump, the *Ranunculus* grows badly because the *Sparganium erectum* shelters it from flow and may cause silt to be deposited on it (Figure 10.12). Tall plants kill short ones by shading them, and emergents can smother submergents by the silt they accumulate. So if both can grow well in any one place, it is the taller which survive. Tall emergents shade short ones, emergents shade floating and submerged species, floating plants shade submerged ones, and submergents high in the water shade those below (Figure 10.13). Compensating for this, both flow and human interference remove mostly the taller plants, so the end result is that the overall plant pattern remains stable although the detailed arrangement in any one place may vary.

An interesting example of competition, in a form more characteristic of water plants than land plants, occurs between *Ranunculus* and *Berula erecta*. In chalk streams which flow too fast for the good growth of *Berula erecta*, this species can colonise the sheltered

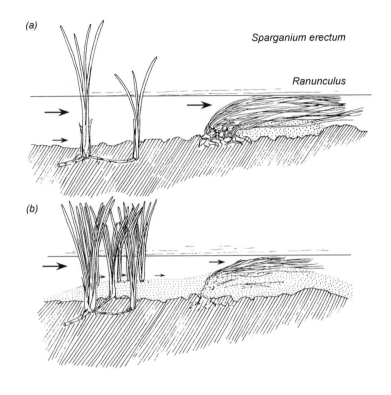

Figure 10.12
Sparganium erectum damaging *Ranunculus*.
(a) Establishment of *Sparganium erectum* upstream of a well-grown *Ranunculus* clump.
(b) Thick clump of *Sparganium erectum* causing silt deposition in, and lack of flow to, the *Ranunculus* clump, which is growing badly.

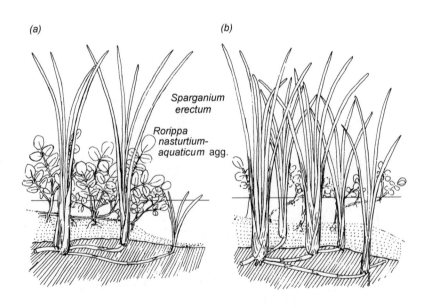

Figure 10.13
Sparganium erectum shading and killing *Rorippa nasturtium-aquaticum* agg.
(a) Early stage.

patch upstream of *Ranunculus* clumps. Once established, *Berula erecta* can spread downstream, over the *Ranunculus* and perhaps on the ground as well, tangling and rooting in the firmly anchored *Ranunculus* clumps. In due course, however, the shading effect of the *Berula erecta* weakens the *Ranunculus* and both species are washed away (Figure 10.14).

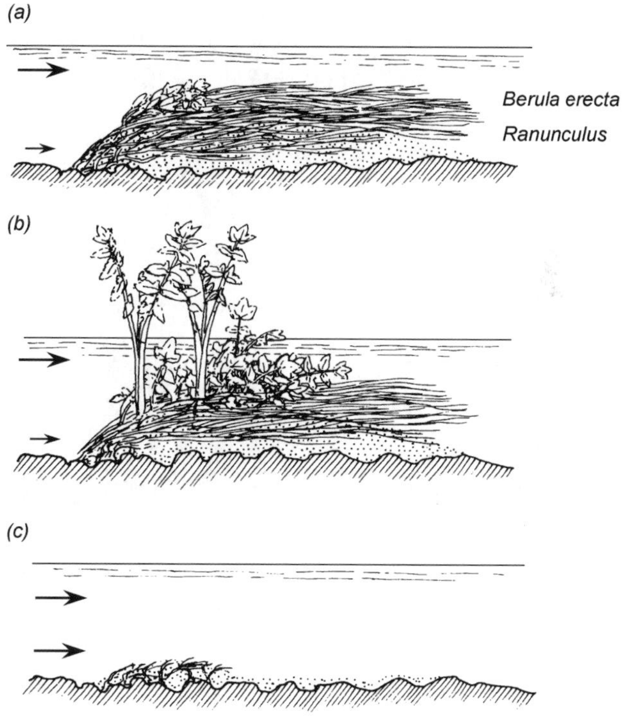

Figure 10.14
Berula erecta shading and harming *Ranunculus*.
(a) *Berula erecta* colonising a *Ranunculus* plant.
(b) The well-grown *Berula erecta* shading *Ranunculus*. Most *Berula erecta* roots are in the *Ranunculus* plant or the loose sediment below this. *Berula erecta* weakens *Ranunculus* and increases its hydraulic resistance to flow.
(c) *Ranunculus* is washed away, taking *Berula erecta* with it, as the latter is not rooted independently. The few remaining *Ranunculus* shoots can re-grow.

MANAGEMENT

This has an overriding effect on vegetation when river depth, flow, substrate and chemistry are affected. Such management creates new habitats, and the vegetation alters accordingly. Some large-scale effects of management are also described in later chapters.

Some small-scale effects of management on plant patterns are that killing large bands of tall monocotyledons at the sides of silting rivers means that the silt accumulated by the plants is then eroded and submerged or floating plants invade instead. Cutting part rather than all the channel leads to differential growth and invasion. Some species (e.g. *Berula erecta*, *Ranunculus peltatus*) become dwarf under frequent cutting (see Chapter 8). Trampling by animals or man can lead to plant patterns influenced by disturbance.

INTERPRETATION OF INDIVIDUAL SITES

This section demonstrates how the principles described above and in earlier chapters work out in the river.

Figure 10.15 is a small chalk stream, slightly dredged and drained, but still with summer water level near ground level, and gentle slopes permitting good fringe vegetation. Although the water is shallow, there is sufficient scour to restrict emerged vegetation to the edge, and grazing, cutting or scour have kept down tall monocotyledons, allowing fringing herbs to dominate there. The low, calcium-dominated nutrients keep these plants small, so there is mixed dominance (of five species). *Berula erecta* is also growing submerged, something possible only in high-calcium water. The water-supported species (*Ranunculus*) is bent over and trailing in the flow. Species diversity is good.

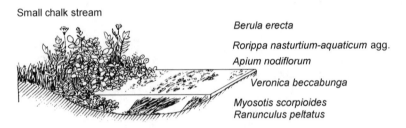

Small chalk stream

Berula erecta

Rorippa nasturtium-aquaticum agg.

Apium nodiflorum

Veronica beccabunga

Myosotis scorpioides
Ranunculus peltatus

Figure 10.15
Small chalk stream: gravelly bottom; fairly fast flow; gently sloping banks.

Figure 10.16 is of similar size (a little smaller), also limestone, but a much harder, steeper and more northern limestone. There is the same mixed-dominance fringing herb fringe, though the spate flows (as well as northern climate and lower nutrient status) keep the plants small, and prevent water-supported plants from growing in the channel. (A stable water regime means water-supported plants can grow in shallower water.)

Small hard limestone stream

Filipendula ulmaria
Mimulus guttatus

Veronica beccabunga

Rorippa nasturtium-aquaticum agg.

Figure 10.16
Small hard limestone stream: coarse substrate with some fine soil in shelter; swift flow.

Figure 10.17 is a continent away, on fairly soft limestone in Ontario (Canada). The pattern is similar, mixed fringing herbs (mostly alien), though also some monocotyledons, both in the side, and

Figure 10.17
A limestone brook, with some fall in water level in summer but with perennial flow. It is species-rich with limestone plants (e.g. fringing herbs, *Callitriche palustris, Ranunculus longirostris*) and others (e.g. *Eleocharis erythropoda, Potamogeton foliosus*) (Ontario).

Eleocharis erythropoda
Rorippa nasturtium-
aquaticum
Myosotis scorpioides
Veronica catenata
Callitriche palustris
Ranunculus longirostris
Potamogeton foliosus

surprisingly, *Ranunculus* in very shallow water. The channel is more dredged, and a summer drop in water is considerable. The similarity, yet disparity, of small limestone streams is noteworthy.

Figure 10.18 is a medium to large chalk stream, which has been dredged (steep banks below water) but not too much drained (low bank above water). Here tall monocotyledons have not been reduced (by management or scour), so these have become dominant, shading out fringing herbs. The band is narrow, as there is only a narrow habitat. There is mixed dominance.

Medium to large chalk stream

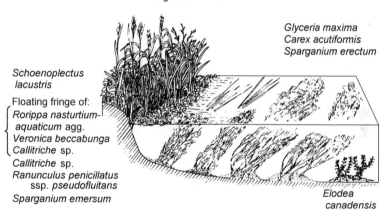

Glyceria maxima
Carex acutiformis
Sparganium erectum

Schoenoplectus lacustris

Floating fringe of:
{ *Rorippa nasturtium-*
aquaticum agg.
Veronica beccabunga
Callitriche sp. }
Callitriche sp.
Ranunculus penicillatus
ssp. *pseudofluitans*
Sparganium emersum

Elodea canadensis

Figure 10.18
Medium to large chalk stream: gravelly bottom; moderate flow; low banks; tall monocotyledons in narrow banks only; submerged plants throughout the channel.

Fragments of fringing herbs and *Callitriche*, detached upstream, have collected to form a floating fringe in the sheltered edge. Because they obtain nutrients only from the water, they remain small, but can live satisfactorily here for a long time. (Any placed so they can root in the soil, can survive and grow.) The channel is fairly full of plants, mostly *Ranunculus*: as typical of limestone streams. The picture show how different plants and different species grow together, forming very characteristic shapes and patterns. The firm gravelly bottom and clear water (unlike the more turbid clay water) allow vegetation in water considerably deeper than that portrayed.

Figure 10.19 is, like 10.16, a mountain stream, with the same rather 'spiky' appearance from having small monocotyledons in with the

181

Small hard sandstone stream

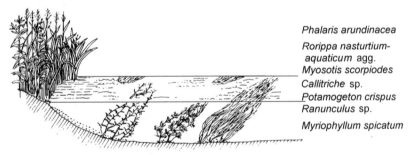

Veronica beccabunga
Apium nodiflorum
Mentha aquatica

Callitriche sp.

Figure 10.19
Small hard sandstone stream:
sandy and gravelly bottom; swift
flow; gently sloping banks.

fringing herbs. The stream is hardly managed. *Callitriche* grows in the channel. Low-nutrient resistant, or low-nutrient calcium-dominated streams, have *Ranunculus* exceeding *Callitriche*. Sandstone has lower calcium so less suppression of other nutrients so, has — in smaller streams — *Callitriche* exceeding *Ranunculus*. In the high-nutrient clay streams, *Callitriche* is frequent, *Ranunculus* almost absent (unless damage is very low).

Figures 10.20 and 10.21 show medium-sized sandstone streams, hard mountain, and soft lowland respectively. These are much alike. The lowland stream has eroded meanders (see above), with emerged aquatics (fringing herbs) — here grazed — only on the sedimenting opposite bank. Both are shallow enough for plants across the channel, and *Callitriche* is still just exceeding *Ranunculus*. Further downstream, the deeper water and increased hill spates favour *Ranunculus*. Several other submerged species are also present, giving high-diversity communities.

Medium-sized hard sandstone stream

Phalaris arundinacea

*Rorippa nasturtium-
aquaticum* agg.
Myosotis scorpiodes
Callitriche sp.
Potamogeton crispus
Ranunculus sp.

Myriophyllum spicatum

Figure 10.20
Medium-sized hard sandstone
stream: silted in sheltered parts;
gravelly bottom in exposed ones;
moderate flow; banks not steep.

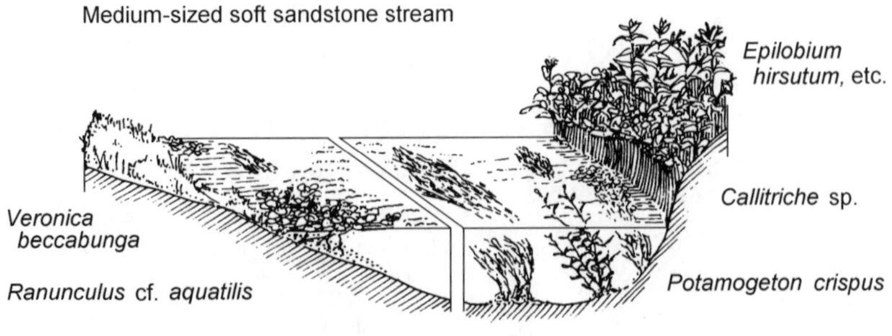

Medium-sized soft sandstone stream

*Epilobium
hirsutum*, etc.

Callitriche sp.

*Veronica
beccabunga*

Ranunculus cf. *aquatilis*

Potamogeton crispus

Figure 10.21
Medium-sized soft sandstone
stream: sandy and gravelly
bottom; moderate flow; steep or
gently-sloping banks.

Figures 10.22–10.25 illustrate various types of lowland clay stream. Silting, more in sandstone than limestone (other factors being equal) is more again on clay: where the rock (clay) is primarily silt (including mud). Being in the agricultural lowlands, most clay streams have been dredged, and the land is drained. This means banks above water are mostly both steep and high (steep: steep dredging; high: drained). Silt accumulates on the bottom, more so with intensive agriculture and lack of planning, and silt is removed by dredging every few years (see Chapter 19).

Small clay stream

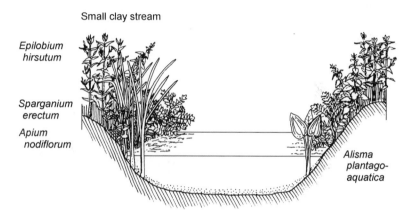

Epilobium
hirsutum

Sparganium
erectum

Apium
nodiflorum

Alisma
plantago-
aquatica

Figure 10.22
Small clay stream: silted bottom; steep banks; slow flow.

Medium-sized clay stream with fairly fast flow

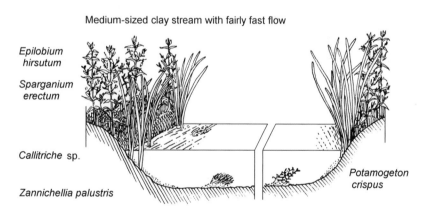

Epilobium
hirsutum

Sparganium
erectum

Callitriche sp.

Zannichellia palustris

Potamogeton
crispus

Figure 10.23
Medium-sized clay stream with fairly fast flow: gravelly bottom; steep banks; very sparse plants.

When banks are high, and ungrazed, etc., tall herbs replace the emerged aquatics a little above water level (nutrient rich: see above), so the band of aquatics here, is narrow. Tall monocotyledons are the commonest group (see above). In the small streams, the more nutrient-rich of the fringing herbs (especially *Apium nodiflorum*) may occur, and with the high nutrients, grow large and lush. Wide-leaved short aquatics, like *Alisma plantago-aquatica* (higher) on the land side and *Sagittaria sagittifolia* in (deeper) water may also be edge plants.

183

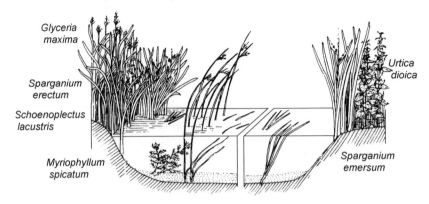

Medium-sized clay stream with slow flow

Glyceria maxima

Sparganium erectum

Schoenoplectus lacustris

Urtica dioica

Myriophyllum spicatum

Sparganium emersum

Figure 10.24
Medium-sized clay stream with slow flow: silted bottom; large or low banks; much vegetation; tall monocotyledons in large patches or bands.

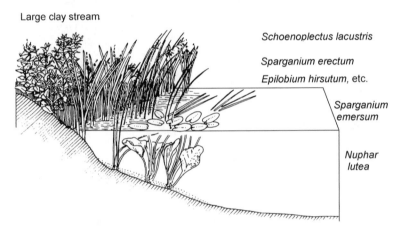

Large clay stream

Schoenoplectus lacustris

Sparganium erectum

Epilobium hirsutum, etc.

Sparganium emersum

Nuphar lutea

Figure 10.25
Large clay stream: centre too deep and turbid or unstable for plants, slow flow; low banks; tall monocotyledons in large patches or bands.

Small clay streams have usually been much drained and shallowed, and water-supported species are typically absent. Chalk streams have natural winterbournes, that dry in summer, with ecotypes of *Ranunculus, Callitriche*, etc., adapted to this. But clay streams used to have considerable water all year, and it seems such strains have not developed.

In the middle-size of clay streams, water-supported species grow across the channel, but in large ones the turbid water and unstable, silted, much-dredged substrates usually confine species to the edge. Most clay streams have slow flow. Those with locally faster flow (unless deep) have too much scour for much vegetation. Species preferring large volumes of water, e.g., *Nuphar lutea*, are common. In such large streams, upstream clay species like fringing herbs and *Callitriche* become very sparse. Occasional gentle banks permit them to occur, but usually the steep banks, varying water level and their lush growth exclude them.

The patterns described here are so obviously related to habitat that it is easy to suppose they are universal. This is not so.

If one genus is singled out as the common dominant of European streams, this is *Ranunculus*. *Potamogetons* and others are frequent, but much less prominent. Across the Atlantic, though, the position is reversed. Figures 10.26 and 10.27 show this. The former is from the Canadian Shield, the latter from Wisconsin, both in habitats which, in Europe would have dominant *Ranunculus*. The general pattern is the same, but the submerged genera differ.

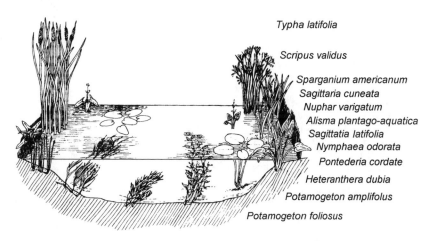

Figure 10.26
Species-rich stream on Canadian Shield (Ontario). Note the distribution of emergents, both monocotyledons and dicotyledons, and that plants occur across the whole channel.

Typha latifolia

Scripus validus

Sparganium americanum
Sagittaria cuneata
Nuphar varigatum
Alisma plantago-aquatica
Sagittatia latifolia
Nymphaea odorata
Pontederia cordate
Heteranthera dubia
Potamogeton amplifolus
Potamogeton foliosus

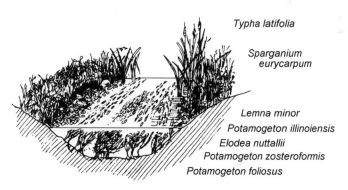

Figure 10.27
Species-rich brook of moderate flow (Wisconsin). The proportion of submerged species, in both number and in bulk of vegetation, is very high for North America.

Typha latifolia

Sparganium eurycarpum

Lemna minor
Potamogeton illinoiensis
Elodea nuttallii
Potamogeton zosteroformis
Potamogeton foliosus

Figure 10.28 shows the spread and imminent dominance of tall monocotyledons across a shallow, silting channel. Once dominant, ponding may occur, and if the land is not drained (i.e., stream beds deepened), crop harm may occur.

Another interesting difference in North America is the bands of short but deep-rooted wide-leaved monocotyledons in place of fringing herbs (which are rare). Figures 10.29 and 10.30 can be contrasted with Figures with fringing herb, and the occasional, e.g.,

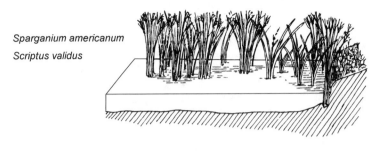

Sparganium americanum
Scriptus validus

Figure 10.28
A shallow silty stream with tall monocotyledons extending across the channel (e.g. *Scirpus validus, Sparganium americanum*) (Ontario).

Alisma plantago-aquatica. Fringing herbs are easily dislodged and re-colonise fast, also easily. The wide-leaved are the reverse. From, at least, Ontario to Florida fringing herbs are mainly European introductions, and are mostly found in calcareous springs or small streams. Is this sufficient explanation?

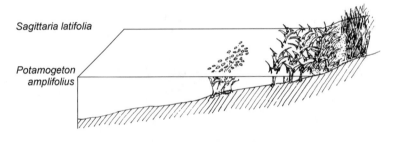

Sagittaria latifolia

Potamogeton amplifolius

Figure 10.29
A stream with shallow silty sides, partly exposed in July, with a wide band of short emergent (*Sagittaria latifolia*) and sparser floating or submerged species confined to the sides (e.g. *Potamogeton amplifolius*) (Ontario).

Figure 10.30
River with much seasonal fluctuation in water level, and a band of *Sagittaria latifolia* on dry mud in mid-July (Quebec).

Other patterns, those of, e.g., tall monocots, water lilies, and trailing submergents, are the same in both continents.

Over great areas of North America stream management and drainage have been little, and rivers like Figure 10.31 still have the wetland behind that, once, was also usual in European streams.

Figure 10.32, showing a river drying in late summer, is in fact from North America, where this phenomenon, the adaptation of water-supported species to land conditions, is frequent. The same occurs, though, in drought years in Britain (e.g., 1976 and 1992), even though the conditions occur so seldom.

Typha latifolia
Sparganium eurycarpum
Scirpus validus
Zizania aquatica
Nuphar variegatum
Sagittaria cuneata

Lemna minor
Potamogeton nodosus
Heteranthera dubia
Ceratophyllum demersum
Elodea nuttallii

Figure 10.31
Species-rich, slow-flowing
stream with a wide swamp
fringe (Wisconsin).

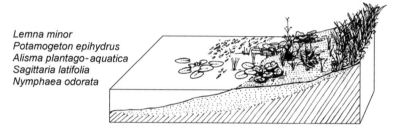

Lemna minor
Potamogeton epihydrus
Alisma plantago-aquatica
Sagittaria latifolia
Nymphaea odorata

Figure 10.32
Silted river with plants
on drying mud in July (Vermont).

Figures 10.33–36 are of hill resistant rock streams. All are liable to spate, and swift flow, two to really fierce flow. The amount of vegetation, in these little-managed streams, is controlled by the force and scour of the water. This contrasts with the lowland streams. There is as much diversity as in the other streams, but here it is largely due to the rock and stone pattern, rather than to the plants. When present, the macrophytic plants of course contribute, but they are often sparse or absent. Mosses are present, at least in the splash zone, in all but the strongest flow. The silt and soil produced as substrate by resistant rock is less suitable for anchoring than that of other hill types. It tends to be less cohesive, less stable, often shallower, and of lower nutrients.

In the man-made channels of negligible flow, dykes, drains and canals, most diversity comes from vegetation (Figures 10.37–39). Banks are usually steep (to take up less valuable agricultural space), and, in drained land, dykes are excavated well below ground level. Canals have high water levels, as they do not flood, and they are puddled where water could seep out. Fringing and similar herbs grow well on shallow, gentle edges, tall monocots on steeper (but stable) edges. Steep banks under water rarely bear vegetation. Here the water-supported plants are not bent by flow, so form a different pattern to that in most rivers.

It is easy for a tall water-supported plant, here upright, to shade another, shorter one. Abundant or dominant species often change every month or two, in a sequence determined by both the season of the year and the conditions of that particular year. (Disturbed channels have little vegetation and demonstrate less of this phenomenon.)

187

Small resistant rock stream with very fierce flow

Figure 10.33
Small resistant rock stream with
very fierce flow: coarse substrate;
gently slopping banks; large fall
from hill to channel and steeply
sloping channel; no river plants.

Small resistant rock stream with less fierce flow

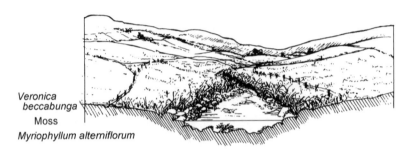

Veronica
beccabunga
Moss
Myriophyllum alterniflorum

Figure 10.34
Small resistant rock stream with
less fierce flow: as Figure 10.33
but with less steep falls from hill
to channel, and a less steeply
sloping channel.

Large resistant rock stream with very fierce flow

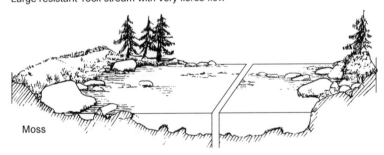

Moss

Figure 10.35
Large resistant rock stream with
very fierce flow: coarse bouldery
substrate; very swift flow.

Medium to large resistant rock stream with much less force of water
than Figure 10.35

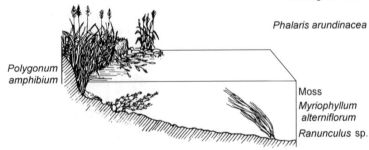

Phalaris arundinacea

*Polygonum
amphibium*

Moss
*Myriophyllum
alterniflorum*
Ranunculus sp.

Figure 10.36
Medium to large resistant rock
stream with much less force of
water in middle reaches: coarse,
non-bouldery substrate; fairly
swift flow; less steep hillsides,
etc. (*Polygonum amphibium* is
included to show habit only. It
occurs in shelter, and as regards
both flow and trophic status
rarely overlaps with *Myriophyllum
alterniflorum*.)

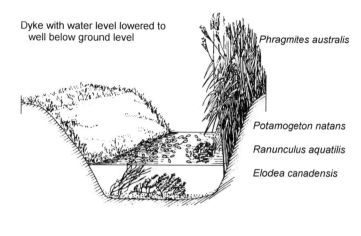

Figure 10.37
Dyke with water level lowered to well below ground level: negligible flow: dredged sufficiently recently to prevent growth of tall monocotyledons on the bed; one bank grazed, or treated with herbicide and covered with short grasses, the other unmanaged and dominated by *Phragmites australis*; channel plants included to show different habits.

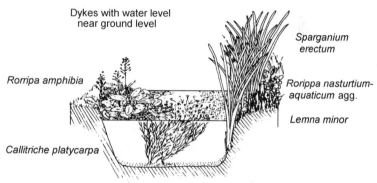

Figure 10.38
Dyke with water level near ground level: negligible flow; dredged sufficiently recently to prevent growth of tall monocotyledons on the bed; fringing herbs able to grow on the shallow bank; other channel plants included to show different habits.

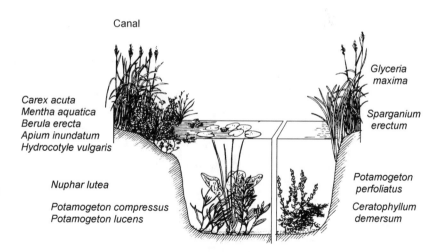

Figure 10.39
Canal: negligible flow; slightly silted floor; species-rich. The shallow ledge forms a favourable habitat, being shallow and affected little by boats. Disused canals may be full of plants, ones that are used somewhat have fringes of plants, and much use results in the disappearance of vegetation.

Looking back at the vegetation of the sites portrayed, patterns can be recognised. Once recognised, they can be recognised in the field, and so, be understood.

189

INTERPRETATION OF SITES USING SPECIES LISTS

The plant is always right (A.S. Watt). If a plant grows in a river, the conditions of that river are proper for that plant; except that fragments or introduced plants may live temporarily; and in changing conditions plants may survive where they could not colonise. Consequently, interpreting with many, or diagnostic species is the most accurate. Everywhere, species have their own distinctive habitat ranges, and so knowledge of species gives interpretation of habitat. That is, each species has a unique habitat range: rock type, topography, water regime, channel type, climate, land use, pollution, etc. A river has numerous components, which act singly or in combination, e.g., plant depth ranges are modified by durations and turbidity; flow ranges depend also on substrate and chemical regime (influencing root development and anchoring ability). Pollution tolerance varies with both its composition and its concentration, and the plants' rooting pattern and flow resistance of shoots. Knowing plant behaviour, a site species list interprets the habitat.

Geographic variation causes complications when large regions are concerned. For instance, in Britain, *Sparganium erectum* penetrates into fairly swift hill streams. Further east, further from its centre of distribution, it is increasingly restricted to the lowlands. In comparable hill streams, its presence in Britain and absence in Germany do not diagnose different water regimes, but different behaviour in different geographic regions.

Rivers with unusually low interference, of course, have numerous habitat niches varying in, e.g., flow, depth, substrate (both chemistry and rooting habitat). Their water quality reflects rock type and low-impact catchment vegetation, and in this wider habitat more species can occur (e.g., Sipos, 2001, Sweden; Haslam, 1987, Sardinia; Haslam, 1978, North America). As damage increases, niches are lost, fewer species occur, and these are those best suited to each restricted habitat, and diagnosis is more accurate. With more damage, there is little or no vegetation, and so it is often impossible to use plants for assessment. Non-vegetation evidence is needed to give the reason for the absence of plants, e.g., excessive pollution, shading, disturbance, rapid water. It may, however, be possible to diagnose using several near-by sites which, collectively, have a coherent picture of the vegetation.

An example shows the use of species lists. The site is 30 m long, in a non-pristine river. The average cover is 75%.

Present are: Tall monocotyledons: *Glyceria maxima, Phalaris arundinacea, Sparganium erectum*. A fringe of three frequent species.

Short emergents: *Berula erecta, Glyceria fluitans, Mentha aquatica, Mimulus guttatus* agg., *Myosotis scorpioides, Veronica anagallis-aquatica,*

V. beccabunga. A frequent to abundant fringe of seven species, mixed together (mixed dominance).

Water supported species: *Berula erecta*, frequent, in a carpet; *Callitriche stagnalis*, occasional; *Elodea canadensis*, occasional to locally frequent; *Potamogeton crispus*, occasional; *P. perfoliatus*, occasional; *Ranunculus* sp., abundant. Six species in all.

Diagnosis: Middle reach of a lowland limestone river, probably 6–15 m wide, the centre partly less than 50 cm deep, partly at least 75 cm, averaging moderate flow, with clear water. The banks are (mostly) not steep. Edges are wide and shallow. The centre of the bed is partly firm gravel, partly softer, and there is some silt at the side. There is no major disturbance, shading or channelling, though there has been shallowing (drying) and perhaps a little grazing. The water is chemically calcium influenced (i.e. calcium-rich, with other nutrients too low to fully reduce the calcium influence). Pollution is low or absent.

A site like this would be rated as Very Good whatever index was used. By studying species ecology, though, diagnosis can be much fuller. Sixteen species in a 30 m reach is very good, particularly when there are no pollution-favoured species and only the normal proportion (four out of sixteen) of pollution-tolerant ones (Haslam, 1987). All three habit groups of tall monocotyledons, short emergents and water-supported species are represented. The highest number, both absolutely and relatively, is of the short emergents (six bushy fringing herbs, one grass). Therefore there is enough space for this, a wide edge habitat, and shallow water at the edge. Something is preventing the tall monocotyledons invading and shading out the short plants. This could be shallowing (exposing soil, which tall monocots have not had time to colonise), unequal grazing, recent wash-out, unusual lining, fencing, or other, less likely factors.

There are only six water-supported species. This is small in relation to the nine emergents. Their cover is high. Recent shallowing is deduced, with perhaps a little grazing. There are no rarer species such as *Groenlandia densa* and *Lemna trisulca*. This supports a diagnosis of within-water damage. Absence of species can only rarely be used as primary evidence, but it can be helpful in support.

Looking at more detailed plant behaviour, *Glyceria maxima* is associated with silt, so there is silt at least at the sides. It is not a fast-flow species, unlike *Phalaris arundinacea*, which has a wider range. *P. arundinacea*, except in lime, though, is unflooded at least in late summer. Both anchor to the bank: so, if stable, the banks are at least partly earthen. *Sparganium erectum*, being beside the bank, is easier to dislodge in storms. Being so common, it merely diagnoses sufficient soil space and texture for its shallow rhizomes and deep roots, and infrequent wash-out. A good fringe of tall monocotyledons means firm banks, penetrable by roots and rhizomes, not greatly cropped or disturbed.

There are six fringing herbs, bushy short emergents, forming a mixed and wide fringe. Mixed dominance comes with low nutrients which keep the plants small, not growing to large monodominant clumps. As many as six species means limestone, and because of the poor anchorage in mountain limestone, lowlands.

Mimulus guttatus agg. has the lowest nutrient range. The site cannot be more nutrient-rich than a middle limestone river. *Mentha aquatica* is slightly more nutrient-rich in range, being mainly in hills or lowland limestone. *Myosotis scorpioides* is the most nutrient-rich. Within a range of calcareous lowland habitats (upper or middle reaches), all six species are interchangeable.

Berula erecta is not just in the emerged fringe, but is present also as a submerged carpet. A submerged carpet means lime, and stable but active flow, shallow water (up to about 50 cm) which is usually clear. Pollution is always present in agricultural, settled, lowlands, but here it is mild, insufficient to overset the calcium-dominated influence of the water. As a carpet, *B. erecta* occurs in upper and middle reaches. (With other nutrients increased by some clay or pollution, *Apium nodiflorum* can carpet instead.) *B. erecta* roots are short and curly, so it can carpet only where there is firm ground without much wash-out. Even there, silt collects round the shoots, new roots grow in the silt, the plants — and silt — are washed out, and the fresh cleaned gravel can be re-colonised.

Ranunculus (Batrachian) dominates the river bed. It anchors like, but more firmly than, *B. erecta*: curling round superficial stable stones and gravel. *Ranunculus* is usually in fairly clear and flowing water. (Different species differ within this. Some, like *R. peltatus* can even grow, in limestone, in shallow flow in winter, dying back in summer: winterbourne ecotypes. At the other extreme, *R. fluitans* inhabits deep and often spatey rivers.) *Callitriche obtusangula+stagnalis* is wide-ranging, usually in shallow water (whether at the edges or in the centre). It has very dense, thin, shallow roots, and spreads rapidly by fragments. Wash-out both removes and spreads the plants. Where it can anchor very well, it can dominate shallow streams. This means a suitable chemical as well as water environment (e.g. sandstone with only moderate wash-out). As mentioned earlier, in small brooks, much *Ranunculus* little *Callitriche*, as here, means lime, and much *Callitriche*, little *Ranunculus*, sandstone or altered lime.

Potamogeton perfoliatus needs adequate space, a water depth of at least 75 cm. This indicates a middle or downstream species. The water is usually clear (clean or slightly polluted). Its substrate is soft enough for deeper roots to penetrate, yet firm enough to maintain anchorage.

P. perfoliatus occurring with a carpet of *Berula erecta* means depth is variable, *B. erecta* in shallow water, *P. perfoliatus* in deeper, e.g. a pool-and-riffle system, or an uneven cross section.

Potamogeton crispus has deep, straight roots, longer than those of *Elodea canadensis*. These anchor well in penetrable substrates. *P. crispus* may occur on silty edges of otherwise hard (or eroding substrates, or in the centre of more mixed beds. It avoids strong calcium dominance, so in a chalk stream occurs where downstream eutrophication or incoming pollution has lessened this.

Considering the *Berula erecta* carpet, the *Potamogeton perfoliatus* and the *Elodea canadensis* plus *P. crispus*, the presence of a shallow water firm gravel habitat plus a deeper water one, with a more penetrable bed, is deduced.

A different example comes from a mountain river, where, in the smaller streams, no (30 m) site has a sufficient either diversity or cover for the plants to be used for diagnosis. However, aggregating ten sites, the species recorded were:

Agrostis stolonifera	in 5 sites
Mentha aquatica	in 2 sites
Mimulus guttatus agg.	in 4 sites
Petasites hybridus (not large)	in 4 sites
Phalaris arundinacea	in 3 sites
Veronica beccabunga	in 2 sites
Mosses (agg.)	in 8 sites
Blanket weed	in 1 site and the sole species

Cover always under 10%.

Blanket weed is pollution-favoured, and this stream has no other species present. This single site is moderately to severely polluted. That can be diagnosed from the vegetation. Being just the one site, it should be separated from the others.

The species remaining, collectively, are not a pollution-tolerant assemblage (as with the example above, the proportion of tolerants is that of clean sites). The high frequency of mosses shows the presence of rock or boulders, large particles not moved in ordinary storms. While this could be rip-rap or bridges, the other species (see below) indicate a mountain stream.

Agrostis stolonifera is frequently found at edges where storms have eroded and eaten into banks (and clods fall) or where banks are low and the grass is on these, and grows out into the water. While it also occurs in lowlands, it is more characteristic of highlands where there are fewer tall species to shade out this very short grass.

Phalaris arundinacea is the tall monocotyledon which extends the furthest up into mountain streams, so, here without, say, *Sparganium erectum*, a mountain stream is likely.

These three (mosses, *A. stolonifera* and *P. arundinacea*) all indicate but do not prove, a mountain stream. With all three together, the probability is high. Since the other species present, the short edge herbs, indicate the same, the collective conclusion is: mountain.

Petasites hybridus, when reaching its full size, may occur in streams on soft rocks, but here it is smaller than that. This means mountain or resistant rock streams (or, of course, both). This plant is firmly anchored and tolerates much spate flow, so the record could be from any part of the river, upstream or downstream. Downstream, it is probably on shoals and shallow edges (high on the banks, leaves are usually bigger).

With no water-supported species apart from mosses, the river and its bed are unsuitable for larger plants. This could be for various reasons, many of which are ruled out:

- Species composition is wrong for severe or even moderate pollution.
- These species and no others are wrong for a larger or downstream river.
- So many species means there is no continuous heavy shade.
- *Phalaris arundinacea*, *Petasites hybridus* and mosses are not typical of invasion after recent dredging.
- So many edge species show no continuous and great disturbance, such as trampling, paddling, etc.
- In very swift, white water conditions, fringing herbs would be swept away.
- In deep water, channel plants (e.g. *Ranunculus* spp., *Myriophyllum* spp.) would be expected to be present.

The most plausible deduction is that the streams are too shallow for water-supported species apart from mosses. Because of the swift and unstable flow, plants need rather deeper water, more space, than they do in lowland streams.

The fringing herbs are those of the nutrient-poor end of the range (see above). *Apium nodiflorum* and *Myosotis scorpioides* would indicate more nutrient-rich habitat, and *Berula erecta*, a more calcium-dominant one. They are easily washed away, so as they are the main species present, they may suffer some storm flow, but no great scour and wash-out. This means upper, not lower, reaches of a river.

Diagnosis: Deducing from the species list, the habitat is that of a small upper mountain stream, liable to upstream spate only, and on resistant rock or limestone — or very mountainous (alpine) sandstone (sandstone carries more vegetation, see Chapter 8, it has more, and more nutrient-rich silt). The water is shallow, clear, and as nearly clean as can be found in Britain.

ORGANISATION OF PLANT COMMUNITIES — SUMMARY

Organisation operates within the framework set by the habitat. This framework is more important than in land habitats because it has, in addition to soil and air, water as a medium of growth, and flow has great importance, both directly and indirectly via its control of substrate stability and texture.

Communities are organised. They have spatial and temporal patterns, patterns in architecture, of occupation of space, vigour of growth, competition and dependency. Competition is primarily by shading (leading to weakening and wash-out). Dependency is primarily for shelter from flow. Mosaics, spatial variations of substrates and flows, allow species of many physical habitat preferences to occur together. Pristine rivers often have very many niches, but human impact usually increases uniformity.

Stable rivers show 'changeless change' with constant wash-out and loss, and as constant re-invasion from species of the same community assemblage. Loss maintains communities, preventing overgrowth and the disappearance of shorter or weaker species.

1. *Organisation by patterned habitat — substrate (also see, e.g., Chapter 3)*
   Causes
   a) texture (including nutrient variation, silt highest). Species with different rooting patterns occur in different textures, so mosaics of textures lead to mosaics of plant pattern.
   b) species forming hummocks and raised carpets are more stable if deposition is little, and if roots remain in the firm beds below.
   c) stable stones form havens, from which sheltered species can spread: and be washed back in storm flows.
   d) eroded, so bare banks add to heterogeneity. Ephemerals usually colonise first (e.g., fringing herbs and *Callitriche* spp., depending on water level.

2. *Organisation by patterned habitat — water*
   Flow is the main organiser of pattern, a river being a habitat with water moving in one direction (see Chapters 2–6).
   a) variation in direct effects, of varied flow type, depth, turbulence, size, shape and position of channel.
   b) variation in indirect effects of flow: particle size (textured), stability, and pattern with, e.g., rock type, topography. For instance, in a range of flow from whitewater to slow, *Ranunculus* would be: in whitewater absent; then found in sheltered niches; then in the main channel; then in swifter open niches; and finally, in the slowest flow, it would again be absent.

3. *Organisation by patterned habitat — nutrient and pollution regimes*
   Causes

a) change in rock type leading to changes in vegetation (see Chapters 8, 11 and above).

b) variation in silting. Silt contains more solutes, of both nutrients and pollutants. In low-nutrient streams shoals may allow colonisation by higher-nutrient species (e.g., *Potamogeton crispus*). Some species occur in silted channels even in oligotrophic plains (e.g., *Glyceria maxima*).

In middle reaches, pool/riffle systems may be more polluted and more nutrient-rich in pools than in riffles, because pools have more silt. Vegetation varies accordingly.

c) small changes may be important. *Berula erecta*, dominating a chalky stream, was replaced by *Apium nodiflorum*, starting on the (silted) banks, under moderate pollution (which weakened *B. erecta*).

d) polluting effluents entering form, in larger rivers, a diagonal pattern across a river: marked by difference in vegetation.

e) pollution entries and downstream purification lead to vegetation patterns.

4. *Organisation by dynamic processes of plant growth*

River plant communities are dynamic. The plants constantly colonise, grow, become mature, are washed out and recolonise (by lateral growth or new propagules). (Not all become mature, not all are lost through wash-out — may be eaten, etc., but this is the typical pattern.)

Weaker plants are washed out due to:

- fierce storm flow
- age
- disturbance
- winter die-back or killing
- being eaten
- niche alters and becomes unsuitable, and
- human impact influencing all (e.g., dredging, cutting, grazing, biocides, disturbance, pollution, shade).

Replacement propagules from a vast range of water and land plants continually reach sites. Many do not lodge. Few grow to maturity.

In stable conditions, incoming species able to establish and grow are from the same community assemblages as those leaving. 'Changeless change' is a basic process in communities. Wash-out and replacement are needed to maintain the heterogeneity of communities. All plants grow, and continue growing: unlike animals, whose growth is finite. So sites would be overgrown by the faster-growing and taller species if there was no wash-out to maintain the dynamic balance. Major habitat changes, e.g., dredging, may change flow, substrate, etc. sufficiently to remove the original community, and that which enters, in due course, is new.

Cycles from colonisation to loss may be quick (a few months) or slow (several years). They are quicker if the species can grow quickly (e.g., *Lemna minor*, fringing herbs) than if they grow slowly (e.g., complex rhizomes, especially if attached firmly to the bank). Cycles are also quicker (even if perhaps cut off before they are complete) if there is frequent disturbance (e.g. boats); much sedimentation; loose, unconsolidated substrate; many spates; and if winter cold and storms arrive when the cycle is still young. Cycles are also slower with numerous habitat niches; firm banks and beds, medium substrate; and low disturbance from maintenance.

Both plant characters and habitat characters therefore influence cycles.

Species most variable from year to year usually have intermittent rapid (explosive) growth and/or some character, such as poor anchoring, which potentially causes large losses, and they frequently propagate well from fragments. Species likely to retain their position from year to year may have the opposite characters to the above, or be restricted to a sparse niche habitat.

Clumps move because parts with old stems are washed out, or they over-grow, or lose contact with their firm anchorage, and are washed out with re-growth centred elsewhere, or their niche habitat changes (e.g., erosion, disturbance), or the plants have created a habitat unsuitable for themselves (e.g., shelter). Or just because the plants get bigger!

Communities also change because different species grow — so occupy more space — in different seasons, and at the same season in different years. All species vary in their speed of growth with habitat. For instance, in one site, (i) no May heat wave led to no explosive growth. (ii) May heat wave plus sparkling flow, led to dominant (explosive) *Ranunculus* spp. (iii) A May heat wave, but plus negligible flow, led to (explosive) dominant *Lemna minor* agg.

In changing conditions, many entering species are ones better suited to the new conditions, so, with constant replacement of the original species the community changes.

5. *Organisation by one species being dependent on another*
   Causes
   a) A plant can create shelter in which other species can thrive. The sheltered plant may: remain dependent, or be lost if the shelterer becomes a shader, or become independent once properly established, or it may grow enough to shade and kill the shelterer.

b) All settled plants allow fragments to lodge on or by them, and potentially these become established. Without the existing plants, most fragments would be washed through.

6. *Organisation by one species competing with another*

Causes

a) Shade. Whenever one plant can grow taller and above another and shade it, the shaded one is weakened and may be lost. The power of a river plant is limited because larger and bushier plants are more easily washed out, leaving unshaded bare habitat. Competition depends on (i) the plant's shading ability, then (ii) the potential species growth and (iii) the habitat allowing this growth, and (iv) on the tolerance to shade of each species.

b) Root toxins. These are of little importance compared with, say, wetlands, but perhaps aid the spread of, e.g., *Glyceria maxima*, *Typha* spp.

7. *Other factors*

Many other factors organise plant communities, particularly the more direct forms of human impact (drainage, lining, weirs, etc.). The effects act through flow, depth, substrate, etc., as described above.

11

Downstream changes

Passing downstream from the source a river normally gets larger, the flow slower and the substrate siltier; thus the vegetation changes also. In the hills, fringing herbs and Callitriche *tend to occur in shallow, fairly stable and fairly swift water in the upper reaches, and they decrease as water level fluctuations increase lower down. Tall monocotyledons and submerged plants increase in the lower reaches where there is more silt and less scour. In the lowlands, where the flow is less strong, there is more vegetation and submerged plants occur further upstream, up to the limit of perennial flow. Plants of slow flow are common and often luxuriant in the lower reaches, much more so than in the mountain streams.*

From the source to the mouth of a stream the habitat changes, and, of course, the plants change too. The main downstream changes are that the parameters of channel size, including width, depth and drainage order, increase; the proportion of fine sediment and the trophic status increase; water movement and the amount of light reaching the channel bed tend to decrease; and the nature of storm flows alters (see Chapter 5). Superimposed upon these general trends there may be marked variations in any one stretch of the stream as the result of changes in topography, geology, human interference, etc.

The changes in plants from swift upstream to slow downstream stretches in several British rivers were described in about 1930 (Butcher, 1927, 1933) and some northern rivers have been studied about 1970 (Whitton & Buckmaster, 1970; Holmes & Whitton, 1975a,b; Whitton & Dalpra 1968; Holmes *et al.*, 1972). (See Bibliography for other rivers, particularly, for Britain, Haslam 1982, 1987; Holmes 1983, 1985.). Figure 11.1 shows the downstream increases in species of slower flow or higher nutrient status, and decreases in the species of the reverse habitat.

This chapter centres round vegetation maps of whole rivers (Figures 11.2–11.18). Each of these shows the river pattern and the species present at selected sites along the length (usually at road bridges). The rivers illustrate the vegetation of the main British stream types, showing a typical example of a lowland clay stream, an upland hard sandstone stream, etc. The actual plant communities of these stream types are described in Chapter 12 for streams on soft rocks (mainly lowland ones), and in Chapter 13 for streams on hard rocks (mainly upland and mountain ones). These three chapters thus form a unit, this chapter describing the downstream progressions, and the others the plant communities of each stage and of the stream types as a whole.

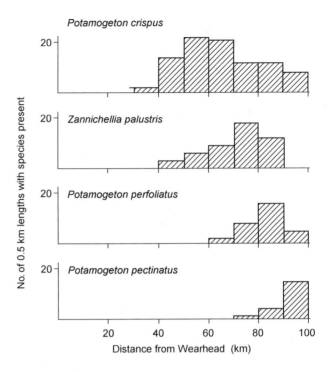

Figure 11.1
Downstream changes in species
frequency in the River Wear.
(Adapted from Whitton &
Buckmaster, 1970.)

STREAMS OF DIFFERENT TYPES

No one river can show all the possible progressions of plants from
source to mouth. Some typical progressions are shown in Figures
11.2–11.18, which comprise:

- Very mountainous, resistant rock, River Oykell (Figure 11.2)
- Mountainous, resistant rock, River Vyrnwy (Figure 11.3)
- Mountainous and plain, resistant rock, River Dart (Figure 11.4)
- Upland hard sandstone, River Tone (Figure 11.5)
- Upland hard sandstone and clay, River Leadon (Figure 11.6)
- Lowland chalk, River Itchen (Figure 11.7)
- Lowland chalk, River Darent (Figure 11 .8a–c)
- Mountainous and lowland, limestone and clay, River Derwent
  (Figure 11.9)
- Lowland sandstone, River Meese (Figure 11.10)
- Lowland sandstone, River Blythe (Figure 11.11)
- Lowland clay, River Chelmer (Figure 11.12)
- Upland clay, River Chew (Figure 11.13)
- Lowland clay and alluvium, River Axe (Figure 11.14)
- Lowland chalk and fertile sandstone, River Avon (Figure 11.15)
- Mountainous, resistant rock and hard sandstone, River Tweed
  (Figure 11.16)

- Mountainous, resistant rock and hard calcareous rock, River Clyde (Figure 11.17)
- Upland, resistant rock and hard sandstone, River Lugg (Figure 11.18)

As a summary, Table 11.1 lists the characteristic species of upper and lower reaches of some different stream types.

Table 11.1 Characteristic species of the upper and lower reaches of different stream types

(Species in brackets tend to occur more towards middle reaches.)

1 Resistant rocks
(i) Upper reaches

Juncus articulatus — (Short-leaved *Ranunculus*, e.g. *Ranunculus aquatilis*)

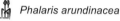

Myriophyllum alterniflorum — *Veronica beccabunga*

Phalaris arundinacea — Mosses

(ii) Lower reaches

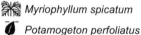

(*Elodea canadensis*) — *Ranunculus fluitans*

Myriophyllum spicatum — *Sparganium emersum*

Potamogeton perfoliatus — *Sparganium erectum*

2 Hard sandstone
(i) Upper reaches

Apium nodiflorum — *Rorippa nasturtium-aquaticum* agg.

Callitriche spp. — *Veronica beccabunga*

(ii) Lower reaches

Callitriche spp. — *Ranunculus* spp.

Elodea canadensis — *Sparganium emersum*

Potamogeton crispus — *Sparganium erectum*

3 Hard limestone
(i) Upper reaches

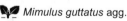

Mentha aquatica — *Veronica beccabunga*

Mimulus guttatus agg. — Mosses

Rorippa nasturtium-aquaticum agg.

(ii) Lower reaches

Callitriche spp. — *Ranunculus* spp.

Groenlandia densa — *Zannichellia palustris*

Myriophyllum spicatum

Table 11.1   Continued

4 Chalk
(i) Upper reaches

 *Apium nodiflorum*

Mentha aquatica

Myosotis scorpioides

Phalaris arundinacea

 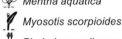 Short-leaved *Ranunculus*, e.g. *Ranunculus peltatus*

Rorippa nasturtium-aquaticum agg.

Veronica anagallis-aquatica

Veronica beccabunga

(ii) Lower reaches

Callitriche spp.

Elodea canadensis

Glyceria maxima

Lemna minor agg.

Myriophyllum spicatum

Ranunculus penicillatus ssp. *fluitans*

Schoenoplectus lacustris

Sparganium emersum

Sparganium erectum

Zannichellia palustris

5 Soft sandstone
(i) Upper reaches

Apium nodiflorum

Callitriche spp.

Epilobium hirsutum

Phalaris arundinacea

Sparganium erectum

Veronica beccabunga

(ii) Lower reaches

Callitriche spp.

Glyceria maxima

Lemna minor agg.

Potamogeton perfoliatus

Ranunculus spp.

Sparganium emersum

Sparganium erectum

6 Clay
(i) Upper reaches

Apium nodiflorum

Callitriche spp.

Epilobium hirsutum

Phalaris arundinacea

Sparganium erectum

Veronica beccabunga

(ii) Lower reaches

Elodea canadensis

Enteromorpha intestinalis

Lemna minor agg.

Nuphar lutea

Polygonum amphibium

(Potamogeton perfoliatus)

Rorippa amphibia

Sagittaria sagittifolia

Schoenoplectus lacustris

Sparganium emersum

Sparganium erectum

The downstream changes described below are discussed firstly as they apply in general to streams of a particular type (mountain streams, etc.). The features considered can be seen from the river diagrams. Next, a very brief description is given of the rivers illustrated for each stream type (most of the necessary information being on the diagram). A typical stream is always given here, and when there is a particularly interesting unusual stream showing relevant features, this also is included and described. The full descriptions of the composition of river vegetation are given in Chapters 12 and 13 and are mostly illustrated in Chapter 10, and so are not repeated here.

The surveys presented in this book were carried out in the 1970s. Since plant behaviour does not change, all the ecology and interpretation here remain correct. However, there has been much human impact since, both directly on the rivers (more channelling, more pollution, etc.) and indirectly through catchment management affecting run-off (more intensive agriculture and drainage, more development and hard surface, etc.). This means the species now present at individual sites are not necessarily those in the Figures. In stable conditions species lists are likely to vary annually, but to do so within the total assemblage of the relevant community. With a long-term change of habitat, the community changes (see Haslam, 1987, 1990, 1997).

Therefore the river surveys described should be considered as accurate representations of the river types in question, but not as the species or communities necessarily present now at each site recorded on these named rivers.

Some rivers were re-surveyed up to the early 1990s, and many, into the mid-1980s.

Explanation of Figures 11.2–11.8

These diagrams of the vegetation along whole rivers illustrate the general vegetation patterns of the main types of British rivers. (In Chapter 19 some characteristic effects of pollution are discussed.) Each site is recorded from a bridge, whose approximate position is marked on the diagram (see Haslam, 1987, for details and discussion of this method, and Haslam 1982 for (scales) maps and descriptions of several hundred rivers).

1. Comparing near-by sites shows the type of variation found within the same community: a number of species are potentially present at each site, but only some of these occur at any one site.
2. Comparing sites along the length of the channel shows the changes in species composition and species diversity from the source to the mouth.

3. The definitions of lowland, upland and mountain streams, in terms of height of hill, fall from hill to channel and slope of channel, are given in Figure 13.1. The rainfall varies, being less in the lowlands of south and east England, and greater in the north and west of the country. It is only in the far north of Scotland (River Oykell, Figure 11.2) that rainfall variation has much effect on the vegetation. The high rainfall there increases the mountainous nature (for plants) of the stream type.

4. The effects of geological variations, in Figures 11.15–11.18, are described only briefly in the text, but can be seen in more detail in the diagrams.

5. At each site the widespread species are shown by the symbol used elsewhere in this book, and listed again below. Plants of doubtful identity (including possible hybrids) are given the symbol of the species they are closest to. Any other essential information, such as very recent dredging, is also given.

6. At each site, the species present are listed in the following order: tall monocotyledons: fringing herbs; other emergents; water-supported higher plants; mosses and algae. Symbols in boxes indicate the species is present in quantity.

7. Symbols in brackets are for sites on streams too small to be shown on maps of this scale.

8. *Glyceria fluitans* is included in 'small grasses' except in Figures 11.2 and 11.4.

9. Where a stream is braided, the different channels are marked (1), (2), etc.

List of symbols

Y	*Acorus calamus*	🌿	*Nuphar lutea*
Y	*Agrostis stolonifera* and other small grasses	🌿	*Oenanthe crocata*
▮	*Alisma plantago-aquatica*	🌿	*Oenanthe fluviatilis*
🌿	*Apium nodiflorum*	🌿	*Phalaris arundinacea*
🌿	*Berula erecta*	🌿	*Phragmites australis*
ʃ	*Butomus umbellatus*	🌿	*Polygonum amphibium*
🌿	*Callitriche* spp.	🌿	*Potamogeton crispus*
🌿	*Carex acutiformis/riparia*	🌿	*Potamogeton lucens*
🌿	*Carex* spp.	🌿	*Potamogeton natans*
Y	(*Catabrosa aquatica*, see *Agrostis*)	🌿	*Potamogeton pectinatus*
🌿	*Ceratophyllum demersum*	🌿	*Potamogeton perfoliatus*

Elodea canadensis	*Ranunculus fluitans*
Eleocharis acicularis	*Ranunculus omiophyllus*
Eleocharis palustris	*Ranunculus peltatus*
Eleogiton fluitans	*Ranunculus* spp.
Epilobium hirsutum	*Rorippa amphibia*
Equisetum palustre	*Rorippa nasturtium-aquaticum* agg.
Eriophorum angustifolium	*Rumex hydrolapathum*
(*Glyceria fluitans*, see *Agrostis*)	*Sagittaria sagittifolia*
Glyceria maxima	*Schoenoplectus lacustris*
Groenlandia densa	*Scirpus* spp.
Hippuris vulgaris	*Sparganium emersum*
Iris pseudacorus	*Sparganium erectum*
Juncus articulatus	*Spirodela polyrhiza*
Juncus bulbosus	*Symphytum officinale*
Juncus effusus (and other spp.)	*Typha latifolia*
Lemna minor agg.	*Utricularia vulgaris*
Lemna trisulca	*Veronica anagallis-aquatica* agg.
Mentha aquatica	*Veronica beccabunga*
Menyanthes trifoliata	*Zannichellia palustris*
Mimulus guttatus agg.	Mosses
Myosotis scorpioides	Benthic algae
Myriophyllum alterniflorum	Blanket weed (trailing algae)
Myriophyllum spicatum	*Enteromorpha intestinalis*
Ranunculus aquatilis	Other species

Mountain streams: general

In mountain streams mosses are frequent, except in the fiercest flow, but most tributaries are without angiosperms, these only occurring when the tributary is protected from severe spate flows. The species present vary from those typical of bogs, when the sediment present is acid peat, to the usual fringing herb and *Callitriche* communities, when the sediment is nutrient-rich. Tributaries nearly or quite in the lowlands below, which have very small catchments and negligible scour, can bear tall emergents. Plants are sparser or absent in reaches with the greatest force of water, whether this force is from normal flow or from spates.

The force is due to the fall from hill top to stream being particularly great, or to the stream slope being particularly steep, or to the rainfall being both high and irregular.

In these mountain streams submerged plants enter somewhat lower than the fringing herbs, the position depending on the water depth and force. The leaf size of *Ranunculus* increases downstream. If luxuriant vegetation develops in middle or lower reaches, the dominant plants are probably *Ranunculus*. Nutrient status increases downstream. (This is apart from the presence of any tributaries from bogs.) Species of low trophic status (e.g. *Myriophyllum alterniflorum*) occur in upper reaches only, and are effectively absent from fertile rocks (e.g. limestone). The more eutrophic species are normally confined to lower reaches (e.g. *Sparganium emersum*). The comparative length of 'upper' and 'lower' zones varies with substrate and flow type. Downstream eutrophication is greater the longer the river, other factors being equal. Fringing herbs and *Callitriche* decrease downstream, being found in shallow, fairly stable waters. Tall monocotyledons at the edges increase downstream, as banks with deep nutrient-rich soil increase.

Plants of mountain streams show downstream variation with changes in water force, water volume, trophic status and substrate stability.

Mountain streams: individual descriptions

The very mountainous stream in Figure 11.2 has strong normal flows and frequent, very fierce spates. These keep the channel nearly bare, even mosses being sparse. Plants can grow near the mouth, where water force is least, and in small tributaries from bogs receiving little run-off. The general absence of plants is due to the fierce flow, and not to low nutrient status.

A typical mountainous stream on resistant rock is shown in Figure 11.3. (This is typical if the reservoir is ignored.) Small tributaries which are flatter or have less fall from hill top to stream bed usually have fringing herbs. Short grasses may be washed into the channel from the banks, but then on the channel bed the plants are usually poorly anchored and temporary. *Phalaris arundinacea* grows well on banks, gravel bars, etc. where it is intermittently flooded. Somewhat downstream, a short- or medium-leaved *Ranunculus aquatilis* enters. Lower, where the water volume is larger and the flow less strong, this is replaced by the long-leaved *Ranunculus fluitans*. The only species showing eutrophic influence are confined to the downstream flatter parts which have the most fine sediment and the least water force. Small tributaries in the foothills are dominated by tall emergents because there is no swift storm flow. The mountain stream in

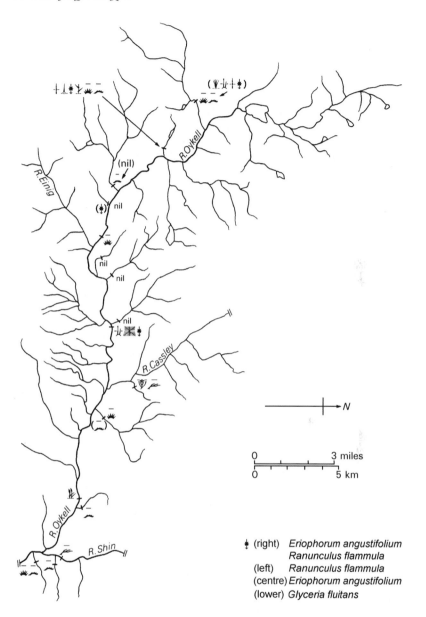

Figure 11.2
Very mountainous river on
resistant rock. River Oykell
(North Scotland); 1974.

✹ (right)	*Eriophorum angustifolium*
	Ranunculus flammula
(left)	*Ranunculus flammula*
(centre)	*Eriophorum angustifolium*
(lower)	*Glyceria fluitans*

Figure 11.4 rises on a high-level plateau (plain) with moorland
vegetation. The drop in land level from the moor to the stream is very
small so fierce flow is absent, and oligotrophic plants (Chapters 1, 8
and 13) grow well. When the river leaves the plain the ground drops
steeply, and the stream is a typical mountainous one. Lowland
tributaries have tall emergents, as before.

207

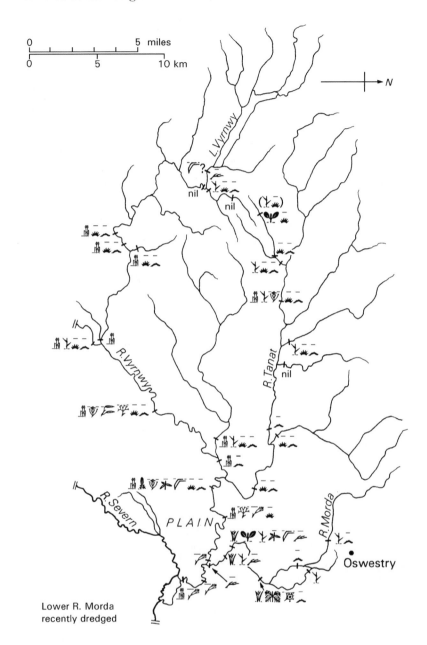

Figure 11.3
Mountain river on resistant rock.
River Vyrnwy (Severn); 1973.

Lower R. Morda
recently dredged

Upland streams: general

Upland streams have a lower water force than mountain ones and thus
have more fine sediment and a higher trophic status. Many upland
streams are on sandstone, and so necessarily have more fine sediment
than streams on resistant rocks. Oligotrophic species are absent, even

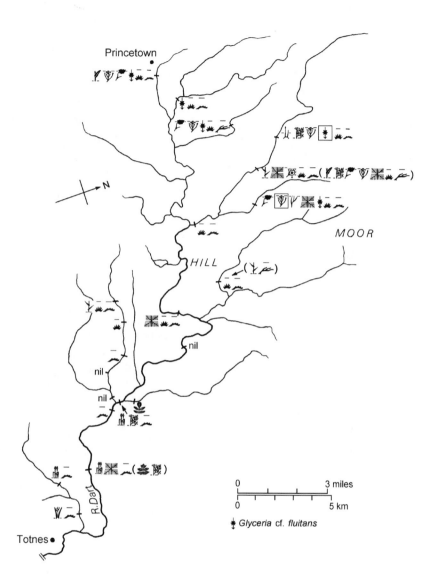

Figure 11.4
Stream on resistant rock rising on
moorland, and becoming
mountainous lower. River Dart
(Devon); most records 1973.

on resistant rocks. Fringing herbs potentially occur in all tributaries. Upper reaches do not have fierce spates as they do in the mountains, nor do they dry in summer as often happens in the lowlands. Submerged plants are frequent. Spates are still present, though, and these can sweep away even plentiful vegetation.

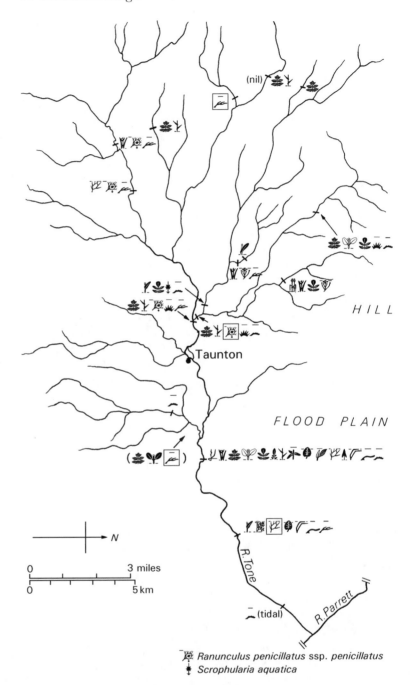

Figure 11.5
Upland river on hard sandstone,
with a flood plain. River Tone
(Somerset); most records 1973.

　Ranunculus penicillatus ssp. *penicillatus*
　Scrophularia aquatica

Upland streams: individual descriptions

A typical upland sandstone stream is shown in Figure 11.5. It has a
well-developed and species-rich fringing herb vegetation, and *Callitriche*
and *Ranunculus* grow high into the hills. Where plants are sparse or

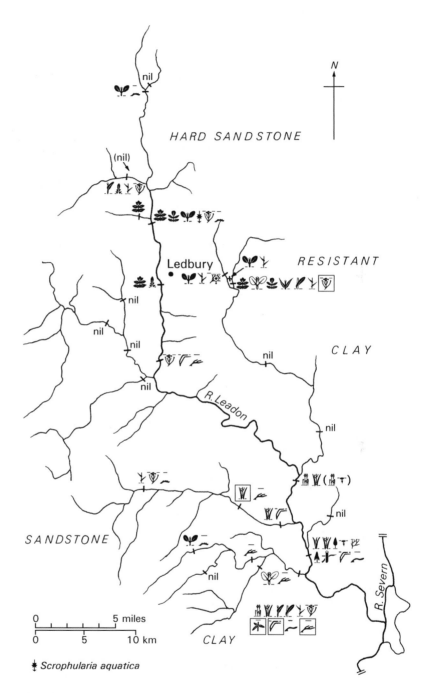

Figure 11.6
Upland river rising on hard
sandstone (and locally on
resistant rock), flowing on to clay
below. River Leadon (Severn);
most records 1973. (Upper
tributaries on the right are on
resistant rock.)

Scrophularia aquatica

absent this is more because of shade than because of fierce spates.
Downstream, silt increases, flow decreases and eutrophic species enter.
In Figure 11.5 this transition is sudden, as the stream enters a flood
plain (and there is pollution from Taunton).

211

Figure 11.7
Lowland chalk river. River Itchen (Hampshire); most records 1973.

The stream in Figure 11.6 is a less common type, being upland above and lowland below. There is much less vegetation. The main stream is polluted (see Chapter 19). Deep storm flows, silting and the consequent unstable substrates reach far into the tributaries. Part is shaded. The fall from hill top to stream is less (often <200'; <60 m) and this allows silting and *Sparganium emersum* to occur in upper reaches. Good vegetation occurs in two stable habitats: fringing herbs, etc. in

212

stable small hard-rock tributaries with good anchorage, gently sloping banks and low silting; and a eutrophic channel flora in the flood plain in stable slow silted reaches not liable to much disturbance during storms.

Other upland streams with spates are shown in parts of Figures 11.16, 11.17 and 11.18, and one on clay, with lesser storm flows, in Figure 11.13. This last is described below with the other clay streams.

Lowland chalk streams: general

Chalk streams are lowland, without spates and many small ones have dried. They show little fluctuation in depth and little silting. Fringing herbs typically occur throughout, in species-rich populations. In shallow parts they grow on the bed as well as at the sides. The non-eutrophic species (see Chapters 1, 8 and 12) occur throughout the stream, while semi-eutrophic species are common in lower reaches and may be sporadic above. In small brooks, *Ranunculus* spp. are short-leaved (e.g. short-leaved *Ranunculus peltatus*, *Ranunculus peltatus* × *Ranunculus trichophyllus*). As the water volume increases, medium-leaved forms take over (typically *Ranunculus penicillatus* ssp. *pseudofluitans*). This is the same progression of growth forms as in the hill streams. If short-leaved winterbourne forms are absent, small brooks are without *Ranunculus*, for medium-leaved forms cannot tolerate either the very shallow water or the intermittent drying that winterbourne forms can. Submerged plants grow farther up than in other stream types. This is mainly because of the perennial springs at the sources, but also because the submerged *Callitriche* and *Ranunculus* can survive on damp mud. (Gravelly stretches of winterbournes dry out quickly, and bear fringing herbs or, if dry for longer, no aquatics.)

Plants of chalk streams show downstream variation with changes in trophic status, water depth and substrate stability.

Lowland chalk streams: individual descriptions

Figure 11.7 is of a typical chalk stream, which was described earlier in Butcher (1922). Figure 11.8 shows a chalk stream recently severely damaged by a decrease in its water flow. The damage is discussed in Chapter 17. Fringing herbs are sparse and submerged plants almost absent by the end of the drought period. There is little downstream variation.

Mixed mountain and lowland, limestone and non-limestone streams: individual descriptions

An unusual combination of mountain and lowland streams, with limestone and non-limestone influences, is shown in Figure 11.9. The upper tributaries are mountain limestone ones, with little vegetation, but when these enter the flat Vale of Pickering the water force

213

Figure 11.8a
Lowland chalk river. River Darent
(Thames); 1969.

Sevenoaks

R. Darent

Dartmouth

N

0   3 miles

0   5 km

Ranunculus is *R.* cf. *aquatilis*
fringing herbs, and possibly
other species, under-recorded

R. Thames

decreases and is no longer the controlling factor. The chemical status is
both limestone and eutrophic. *Ranunculus* dominates, with some
Potamogeton pectinatus. The streams, though, are still spatey, fluctuating in
depth, and the fringing herbs which are so abundant in lowland
limestone streams are very sparse because of these fluctuations.

214

Figure 11.8b
Lowland chalk river. River Darent
(Thames); 1972.

Ranunculus is *R*. cf. *aquatilis*

Lowland sandstone streams

Lowland sandstone streams are rather like chalk ones, but species diversity
is less (more frequent damage), fringing herbs are less frequently found on
the channel bed, and submerged plants extend less far upstream (because

215

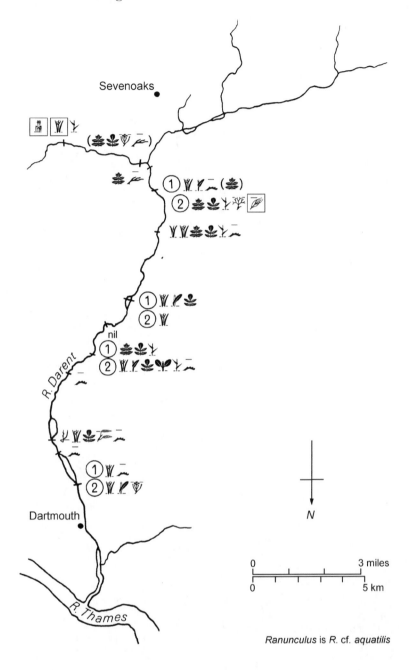

Figure 11.8c
Lowland chalk river. River Darent
(Thames); 1974.

Ranunculus is *R.* cf. *aquatilis*

the upper parts often dry in summer). There is downstream
eutrophication, though this is not shown very well on the short streams
in Figures 11.10 and 11.11. Figure 11.10 has the faster flow.

Lowland and upland clay streams: general

In clay streams the upper tributaries are ditches which are not normally scoured much, and tall emergents are common. Next, where discharges are larger and there is some scour, fringing herbs and tall emergents are sparse. These, possibly with *Callitriche*, continue well into the zone of perennial flow downstream. Clay streams have more silt, a clay bed is more eroded, and their flow regime is more unstable than other lowland streams. These factors lead to poor anchorage, much storm loss, and consequently little vegetation in the middle reaches where scour is greatest. Narrower streams are often shaded by hedges. Fringing herbs are sparse in middle reaches and are uncommon downstream because of the silting and flooding. Eutrophic and semi-eutrophic species enter farther up than in other stream types, being found as soon as the substrate is sufficiently stable and silty for the survival of the species concerned.

In the middle reaches, flow type is often variable. Some (rare) zones have swift flow, coarse substrates and few plants. Other areas have moderate to fast flow, fairly firm gravelly beds and little silting, and these bear the semi-eutrophic species of faster flows (e.g. *Zannichellia palustris*). These species are unable to grow in upper reaches because there is too little water, or in lower ones because there is too much silting. The slower middle and the lower reaches bear as eutrophic a plant community as can exist in natural conditions in this country. The plants often grow on deep silt.

Plants of clay streams show downstream variation with changes in water flow and depth, substrate type and stability, and trophic status.

Lowland and upland clay streams: individual descriptions

The stream in Figure 11.12 is a typical lowland clay stream. That in Figure 11.13 is an upland stream, not entirely on clay but, as regards the plants, effectively on clay. The flow is greater than in the lowland stream and so silting is less. This means that fringing herbs can grow farther downstream, and *Ranunculus* can grow in places hilly enough to provide a firm anchorage, a moderate flow and little silting. Eutrophic plants still enter well upstream. The stream is unfortunately not long enough to show a full downstream eutrophic vegetation, though this progression can be seen in Figure 11.6 where the lower part is on clay.

The stream in Figure 11.14 also rises in hilly clay. In the upper reaches flows are swift, and short-leaved *Ranunculus* grows well. The stream is still small when it enters the flat alluvial plain and it is very soon similar to the drains that rise within the plain. This contrasts with the streams in Figures 11.3 and 11.9 when they are in plains. In these the volume of swift water is much greater and the vegetation remains

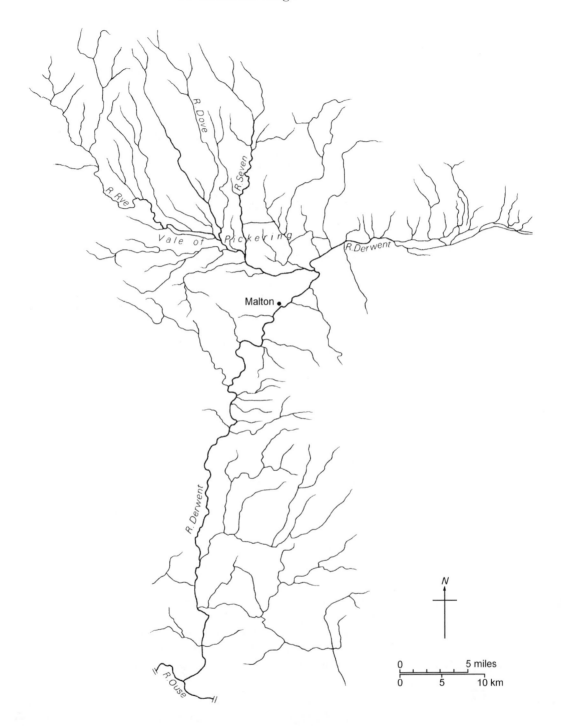

Figure 11.9
River rising on mountain limestone, flowing into an alluvial plain, then passing downstream on to lowland clay (etc.).
River Derwent (Yorkshire); most records 1973.

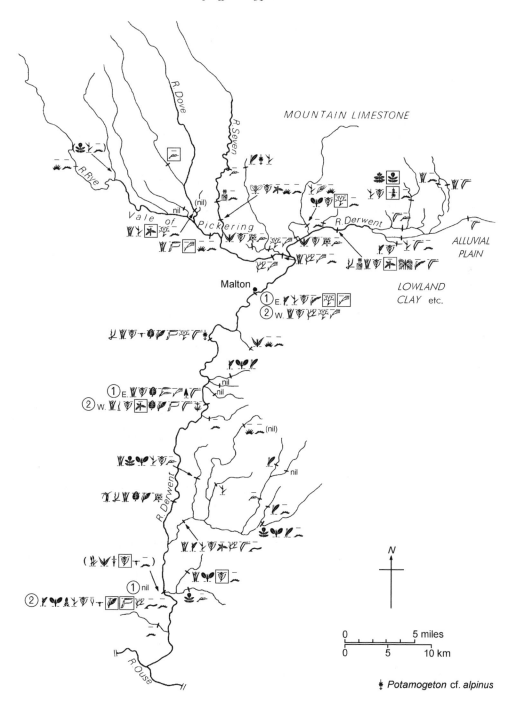

Figure 11.9
Continued

Potamogeton cf. *alpinus*

219

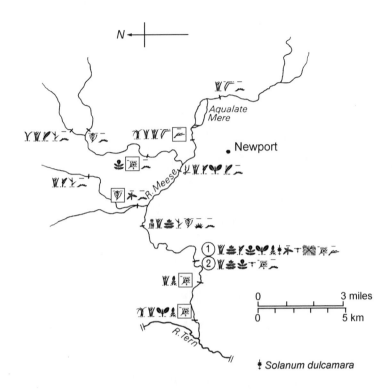

Figure 11.10
Lowland river on soft sandstone.
River Meese (Severn); most
records 1972.

that of moving water. The only difference between the stream in Figure 11.14 and the channels of the plain is that the stream vegetation is slightly more eutrophic, presumably because more silt is present. The Cheddar Gorge stream, on hard limestone, is a tributary. In the Gorge the stream bears a chalk stream vegetation, though this is much affected by human interference. It has a short-leaved *Ranunculus* in the shallower swifter zones, and a medium-leaved species in the deeper slower areas. When the stream flows into the plain, *Ranunculus* is still present, though in an unusual form, growing as a short carpet across the channel bed.

Conclusions

It can be seen, therefore, that vegetation does change downstream. This is attributable mainly to changes in:

- flow regime;
- trophic status and silting;
- water depth;
- substrate stability; and
- the human impacts of pollution, drainage, etc.

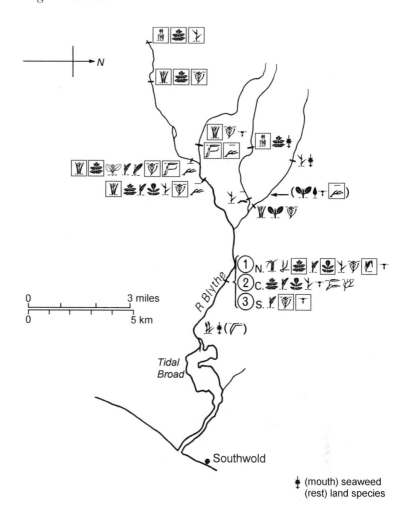

Figure 11.11
Lowand river on soft sandstone. River Blythe (East Suffolk and Norfolk); most records 1972.

✳ (mouth) seaweed
(rest) land species

The natural trends apply to all streams, but the actual effect on the vegetation depends on the other habitat factors influencing each stream. If rivers flow over several rock types, for instance, the vegetation shows a combination of downstream variation and geological variation (see below; and Chapters 12 and 13).

CHANGES IN BEDROCK

General principles

When bedrock changes, flow regime, substrate type, silting and trophic status may all change too. Changes in flow regime are due to changes in topography, and the effects on vegetation are described in Chapters 2, 3, 5, 6, 12, 13, 14 and 17. When a stream crosses a geological boundary, the dissolved substances and suspended particles in the water that are

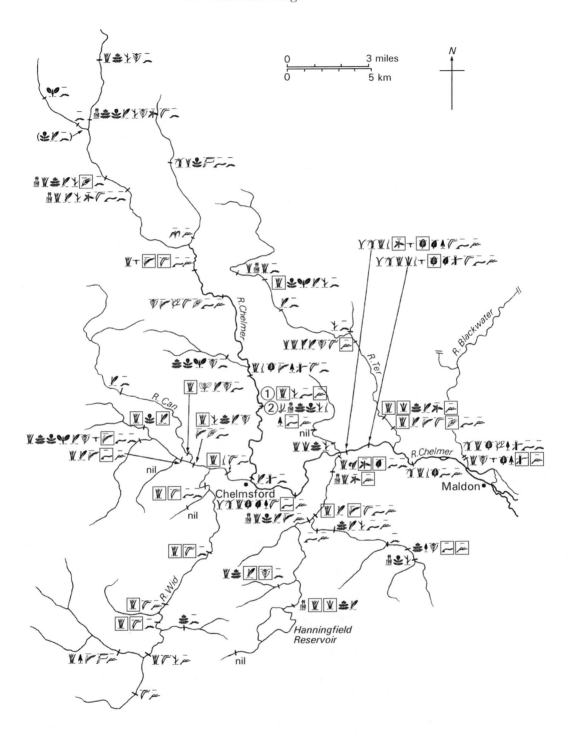

Figure 11.12
Lowland clay river. River Chelmer (Essex); 1972.

222

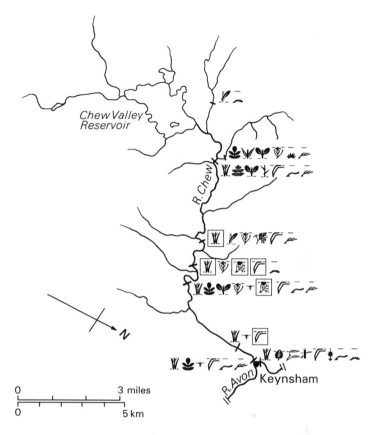

Figure 11.13
Upland clay river. River Chew
(Bristol Avon); most records
1972.

Ranunculus is *R. peltatus* or *R. trichophyllus*

derived from the original rock type will be carried over the boundary towards the mouth of the stream. The relative amount of these found beyond the boundary on the new rock type decreases as material enters from this new rock, the greatest change occurring when a tributary entirely on the new rock flows into the stream. Consequently the influence of the original rock type diminishes downstream.

The effect on the plants depends on how much the rock types differ in their influence on the plants, and on how the rock types are distributed within the catchment. There is, for instance, no change on passing from clay bedrock to thick boulder clay over a different rock type, or again little change on passing from one resistant rock to another (schist, hard shale, gneiss, granite, etc.), unless topography alters also (see, however, Holmes, 1983). There is most change in the lowlands when passing between chalk and clay, and in the hills when passing between sandstone and resistant rocks.

The trophic status of a site depends on the whole catchment, and a second rock type has more effect the more of the catchment it covers.

223

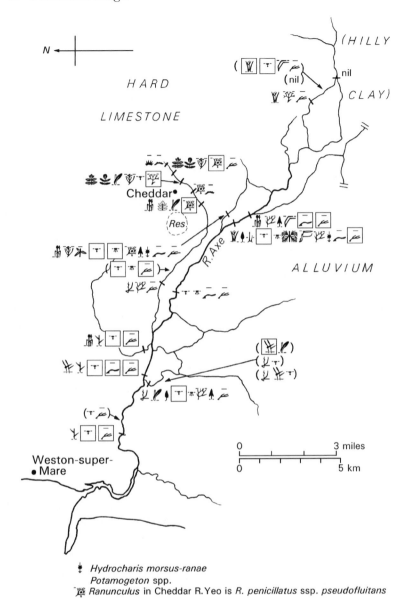

Figure 11.14
River rising on slightly hilly clay, but soon flowing into an alluvial plain. One tributary on hard hilly limestone. River Axe (Somerset); most records 1972.

‡ *Hydrocharis morsus-ranae*
  Potamogeton spp.
✼ *Ranunculus* in Cheddar R. Yeo is *R. penicillatus* ssp. *pseudofluitans*

It also has more effect the closer it is to the source of the stream, the least effect being seen when it is sited away from the stream at the downstream end of the catchment. When streams cross to a new rock type, they at first bear the same vegetation as the original rock type because the sediment and water are both derived from this. The original type of vegetation extends farther downstream the larger the river is, since large streams carry more sediment, etc. The change in a river starts either after several miles on the new rock, or when the first tributary of any size enters from the new rock, if this happens first.

R. Bourne, perennial flow starts below Idmiston
‡ in brooks, land species
Ranunculus: R. Wylye, *R. peltatus*, changing to *R. penicillatus* ssp. *pseudofluitans*
   R. Naddar, *R. trichophyllus* and a medium-leaved form;
   R. Ebble, *R.* cf. *aquatilis;* R. Avon, *R.* cf. *penicillatus* ssp. *pseudofluitans*

Figure 11.15
Lowland river influenced by chalk, fertile sandstone and clay. River Avon (Avon and Dorset); most records 1972.

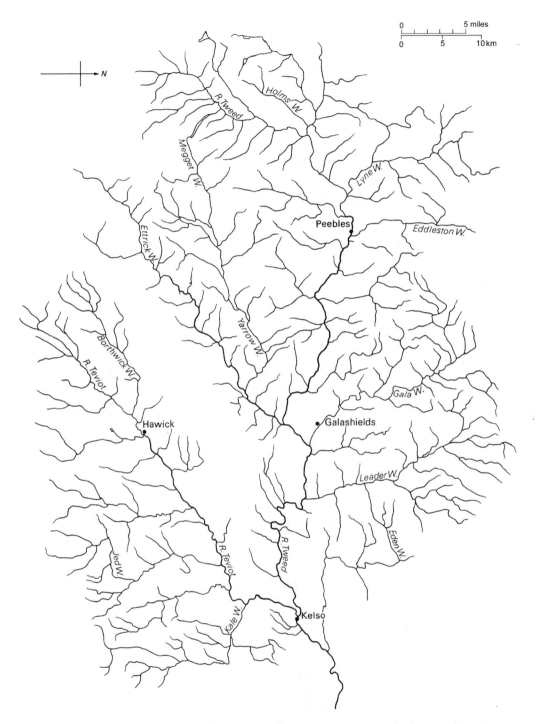

Figure 11.16
Mountain river influenced by resistant rock and hard sandstone. The bedrock is resistant except for streams marked as being on hard sandstone. River Tweed; most records 1973.

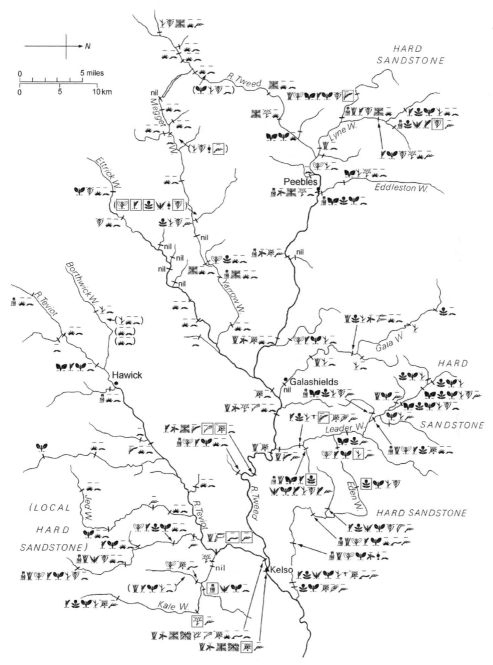

Ranunculus: in upper parts *R. aquatilis;* in lower reaches *R. fluitans* (or hybrid); and in middle and lower parts *R. penicillatus* ssp. *pseudofulitans*
Glyceria cf. *fluitans* is frequent in smaller streams and recorded under '⅄'

Figure 11.16
Continued

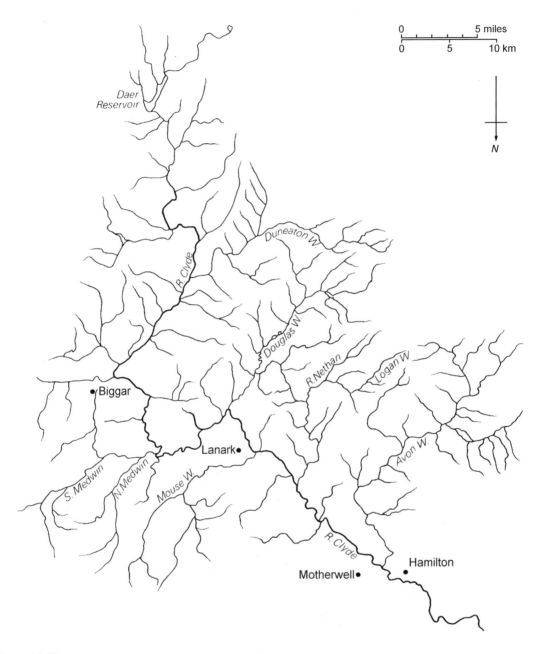

Figure 11.17
Mountain river influenced by resistant rock, hard limestone and calcareous sandstone. River Clyde; most records 1972. Mouse Water, North Medwin and South Medwin are mostly on calcareous sandstone or hard limestone. Douglas Water is influenced by hard limestone. River Avon, though with considerable hard limestone, show little influence of this because of the hilly moorland topography.

Figure 11.17
Continued

After this the influence of the new rock increases, both with the length traversed and with the number and size of tributaries entering (Figures 11.15–11.18).

229

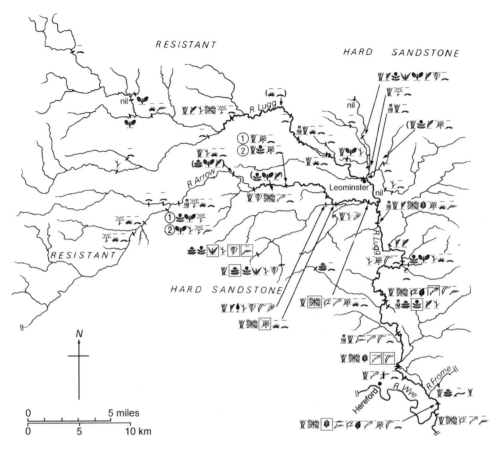

Ranunculus: R. cf. *aquatillis* above: *R. fluitans* in lower R. Lugg,
and *R. penicillatus* ssp. *pseudofluitans* in R. Arrow and part of lower R. Lugg

Figure 11.18
Upland river influenced by resistant rock and hard sandstone River Lugg (Wye); most records 1972.

Soft rock (lowland) catchments

A chalk-clay river never changes completely to the vegetation appropriate to the downstream rock, perhaps because the British examples of such rivers are too short (Figure 11.15). The vegetations of chalk and sandstone streams are more similar to each other than either is to clay streams, and so there is less effect on passing from chalk to sandstone or vice versa. Nevertheless a stream rising on a fertile sandstone (e.g. greensand) and then flowing on chalk contains some eutrophic (i.e. sandstone) plants throughout its length. Small amounts of a less fertile sandstone placed at the side of the catchment, however, have little or no effect. In the reverse case, where a stream rises on chalk and flows on to sandstone, the effect of the chalk quickly disappears.

(Calcium cannot remain dominant and decrease the availability of other nutrients.)

Hard rock (mountain and upland) catchments

In the mountains two further factors influence the effects of changes in bedrock. First, a fierce flow can override all other habitat factors. It does not matter what plants can potentially grow on each rock type if the water force prevents all of them from growing. This often happens with catchments of hard limestone and of resistant rocks. (Where water force decreases enough for plants to grow, if limestone is present then *Ranunculus* is probably more likely to be present also, and the *Ranunculus* is more likely to be *Ranunculus penicillatus* ssp. *pseudofluitans*.) The second factor is that streams have a low trophic status on resistant rocks. In a chalk-clay interaction both rocks have a strong trophic influence and mixed effects result, but when resistant rock streams interact with others the only result is to dilute the influence of the second rock. Where streams of roughly equal size from resistant rock and sandstone join, the downstream vegetation is similar to that of the more fertile tributary. Where the sandstone tributary is very small compared with that from resistant rock, though, the downstream influence of the sandstone may be negligible, particularly if the flow is swift and spatey with little silt deposited (Figure 11.16). (The plant distribution in River Tweed is much more fully described in Holmes & Whitton (1975a,b), where further controlling factors are considered.) However, a small area of fertile rock may have far-reaching effects below a boundary. Figure 11.17 shows one such example where vegetation intermediate in trophic status between the short fertile tributaries and the long infertile ones occurs for many miles downstream of the confluence. Figure 11.18 shows the overriding influence of sandstone, when present in a large proportion of the catchment. Fringing herbs can appear very soon after a stream passes from resistant rock to sandstone (Figures 11.16 and 11.18) because the banks on which they grow (in the larger streams) are mainly on sandstone soil once the boundary is crossed.

DOWNSTREAM PROPAGATION

Viable fragments, fruits and winter buds of river plants are washed downstream by the current. Many do not become lodged at all, while others lodge so far downstream that the habitat is too different for good growth and the plant dies (e.g. *Ranunculus* lodging in the slow flow and deep silt of a stream in a flood plain). A few, however, may lodge on obstructions and then grow and become established (see, e.g. Chapter 10). Plant parts which cannot become permanently established may lodge and grow for a few weeks or months. Some

Ranunculus clumps in slow reaches develop like this and clumps of fringing herbs downstream are often formed from shoot fragments washed from above. Although the clumps do not grow large and are soon washed away, new fragments arrive from upstream and form new clumps. Even upstream stands of fringing herbs may start from such fragments. *Rorippa nasturtium-aquaticum* agg. populations are particularly frequently started from fragments, and watercress beds upstream are important in providing *Rorippa nasturtium-aquaticum* agg. populations in the main river (Parkin, 1973).

Lakes sometimes occur along a river. They do not normally alter the general vegetation, except where they act as settling tanks for streams with much sediment pollutions, etc. They do, however, usually have a different and richer flora, and sometimes lake species extend somewhat into the river below the lake, usually as temporary populations established from fragments.

Plants which usually or sometimes form temporary populations are much affected by downstream propagation (e.g. *Callitriche* spp., *Elodea canadensis*, *Lemna minor* agg.). In the River Tweed river system the distribution of *Potamogeton* spp. which suggests downstream propagation from whatever site the species first entered the river (Holmes & Whitton, 1975a,b). In contrast, in Dorset chalk streams different physiological strains of *Ranunculus penicillatus* ssp. *pseudofluitans* occur in a downstream progression — which indicates that *Ranunculus penicillatus* ssp. *pseudofluitans* is not propagating here by fragments (Dawson, 1980).

After severe losses of plants, e.g. from fierce spates or dredging, recolonisation is partly from plants upstream and partly from underground parts left in place. Propagation from washed-down plant parts is made easier in these circumstances, since the habitat is initially empty and so the places most suitable for plant growth are available for colonisation. Also, if the affected zone is short, it is likely to have a similar environment to the zone immediately upstream of it, and so fragments washed down are likely to be of species which will grow well in the bare habitat.

Plates

Plate 1 (above)
Mountain-rising stream
(Sutherland). Note bends and
swift flow. River plants occur only
in the flood plain, some distance
beyond the end of the slope,
where both normal and spate
flows are less fierce.

Plate 2 (right)
Lowland-rising stream
(Hertfordshire). Due to
abstraction (and draining) in the
catchment, this is now dry except
in storm flow.

Plate 3
Tree-swamp rising stream, now very rare in Britain, but still common in (less-impacted) North America (North Carolina). Undrained, with low banks, and variable water level. The water is slow, dark and peat-stained, but as the peat is fertile, river plants can grow well.

Plate 4 (right)
Downstream of a lowland river below a weir or piered bridge. Fragments of fringing herbs and other submerged and emerged plants are caught on obstructions, and are growing well (in the absence of storm flow).

Plate 5 (below)
Lowland river (Cambridgeshire) with pollard willows. Ungrazed bank (left) with tall herbs, and grazed bank (right) with short grasses, but damaged by trampling by horses.

Plate 6
Woodland stream shaded and
with its banks stabilised and
strengthened by alder (*Alnus
glutinosa*) and needing little
maintenance (Germany).
(Photograph kindly supplied by
Drs A. Krause and
W. Lohmeyer.)

Plates

Plate 7
Lowland streams showing the
effect on habitat of altering water
(flow, depth, substrate) by a
construction.

(a) Reach well away from any
construction, with very slow flow.
Species include *Glyceria
maxima*, *Apium nodiflorum* and
Rorippa nasturtium-aquaticum
agg., *Nuphar lutea*, *Sparganium
emersum* and *Lemna minor*.

(b) Downstream on a similar river
with initially swift and shallow
water, resulting from obstruction
by a bridge. *Ranunculus* is
abundant, *Sparganium erectum*
a frequent fringe.

238

Plate 8
Lowland chalk stream to show
the effect of drought
(Hertfordshire).

(a) Normal (May 1975). Dense
Ranunculus, species-rich, good
flow, gravel substrate.

(b) Same site in drought (July
1976). Sparse and small
Ranunculus and *Sparganium
erectum*, little other vegetation,
little flow and thick silt.

239

Plate 9
Lowland stream (Wiltshire).
Phalaris arundinacea clump
providing protection for
Callitriche.

Plate 10
Potamogeton pectinatus in its
typical form in a
badly-polluted Midlands
stream (Warwickshire).

Plate 11
A stream choked with plants
(Michigan). A common sight in
Britain, rare in middle-latitude
America. The summer water
table here is, unusually, as stable
as in Britain. *Potamogeton
pectinatus* is in its (very different)
North American form. Also
Eleocharis erythropoda agg.,
*Heteranthera dubia, Phalaris
arundinacea, Pontederia cordata,
Potamogeton* c.f. *gramineous,
Sparganium americanum* and
Typha angustifolia.

Plate 12
A brook shaded by a hedge
(Hertfordshire).

Plate 13
A brook shaded by tall herbs
(Gloucestershire).

243

Plate 14 (right)
A canal with emergent tall
monocotyledon fringes, but too
much boat traffic for other
vegetation (Wolverhampton).

Plate 15 (below)
A stream shaded and its banks
established by alder (*Alnus
glutinosa*). Much animal habitat
from the roots (Germany).
(Photograph kindly supplied by
Drs A. Krause & W. Lohmeyer.)

Plate 16
Much drained fenland
(Cambridgeshire). Deep, straight,
artificial channel. Water level has
to rise very high before there is
any hazard from plants and flood!

Plate 17
Cutting *Ranunculus* by scythe
(Cambridgeshire). Satisfactory
for conservation, angling and
flood hazard, but
labour-intensive.

Plate 18
A weed cutting boat. Satisfactory
for conservation if done with care
(see Chapter 16), for flood
hazard, and usually for angling.
(Photograph kindly supplied by
Rolba Ltd, East Grinstead,
Sussex.)

Plate 19a
A modern centre drive 3.75 m wide weed cutting bucket suitable for mounting on any excavator.

Plate 19b
The bucket in use, clearing a river bank. (Photos courtesy of the manufactures Engineering & Hire Ltd, Laughterton, Lincolnshire.)

12

Vegetation of streams on soft rocks

Streams on soft rocks can be, and often are, choked with plants. They can be classified by flow regime and nutrient status. Chalk streams have clear water, fairly swift and stable flow, and firm gravelly substrates. They are species-rich, with a lot of Ranunculus *and fringing herbs. Soft sandstone streams are siltier, with less species diversity and often less vegetation. They have more* Callitriche, *eutrophic species extend further upstream, and fringing herbs, and often* Ranunculus, *decrease. Clay streams are the commonest type. They tend to have less flow, a less stable substrate, more silt and more turbid water. Upper reaches are often shaded, or choked by emergents. Eutrophic (clay) species grow throughout the zone of perennial flow, and chalk species are sparse. If catchments contain two or more rock types, the vegetation is influenced by each in those parts where the stream has flowed over the different rock types.*

The soft rocks of the lowland south and east of Britain comprise the soft limestones of chalk and oolite, the clays, and the soft sandstones of Mesozoic, Tertiary or, if they are present in large quantity, Quaternary age. (The Triassic sandstones of hills in the north-west are here classed as hard rocks.) Watercourses influenced mainly by alluvium are described in Chapter 14. There are no (normal) severe storm flows in streams on soft rocks, so potentially they can contain choking vegetation. Figure 12.1 shows the relationship between the main stream types, which is discussed more fully later in the chapter. Much basic ecological information about these streams is also given in earlier chapters.

The communities are described here with a view to helping understanding and interpretation. They are not intended to be a

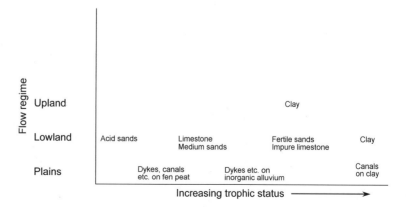

Figure 12.1
Stream types on soft rocks.

classification. Classifications of British river communities are described in full in Haslam (1987, 1997), Haslam and Wolseley (1981) and Holmes (1983, 1985). These should be consulted by those interested in methods of analyses.

CHALK STREAMS

Chalk is a very pure fine-grained limestone. Many streams which are classified for geographical or fishery purposes as chalk streams differ in their plants from the streams solely on chalk, and are botanically classed as streams of mixed catchments (e.g. River Great Stour in Kent, River Frome in Dorset). A chalk stream can, however, have small amounts of sandstone, drift or alluvium in the catchment, or some clay-with-flints on the hills, without affecting the plants.

Chalk usually forms rolling hills (Downs) up to 250 m *c.* 800' (Figure 12.2). Much of the brook water comes from springs, and so the flow is fairly swift. Little silt is washed in from the land and much of the silt in the upper reaches is organic in origin. The silt within plant clumps, and the silt shoals downstream, are less than in other streams on soft rocks. The bed is usually firm and gravelly, with a little deposited sediment. The water is unusually clear, seldom being coloured or turbid except in storms. Because of its origin in springs the water temperature is more stable than that of other stream types. The relatively high winter temperatures promote the growth of *Rorippa nasturtium-aquaticum* agg. and allow the species to be grown commercially in winter. The relatively high spring temperatures encourage the early growth of *Ranunculus*, etc. However, the stable temperature has little overall effect on the vegetation. In drying brooks, the high summer water temperatures in pools do not harm the plants and so do not alter the character of the vegetation.

Figure 12.2
A chalk landscape.

Width-slope patterns for individual stream types (Figures 12.3, 12.5, 12.7, 13.3, 13.5, 13.7 and 13.9) cannot be directly compared with those described in Chapter 6. Large rivers, especially in the lowlands, usually have more than one rock type in the catchment, so the patterns for the separate rock types apply mainly to small streams. The width-slope pattern for an individual species cannot be larger than that for the stream type (Figure 12.3). Small chalk brooks are often *c.* 2 m wide with a slope steeper than 1:200; larger brooks are often c. 4 m with a slope of *c.* 1:400; and rivers may reach *c.* 20 m wide with a slope of 1:1000. There are, of course, more small brooks than large rivers (Figure 12.3a). Even the rivers, though, are seldom over 1–1.5 m deep and have a stable firm bed which allows good anchorage, and under such conditions plants are able to grow right across the channel. Relatively more of the large than the small channels are full of plants, and there are only a few sites in which angiosperms are sparse or absent (Figure 12.3a). The characteristic species are shown in Table 12.1. Additional habitat notes are given below.

Table 12.1   Chalk stream species

(a) Channel species
Undamaged channels contain higher frequencies
Occurring in at least 40% of sites recorded

Ranunculus spp. *Rorippa nasturtium-aquaticum* agg.

Occurring in at least 20% of sites recorded

Apium nodiflorum *Myosotis scorpioides*

Callitriche spp. *Sparganium erectum*

Mentha aquatica *Veronica anagallis-aquatica* agg.

Occurring in at least 10% of sites recorded

Berula erecta *Veronica beccabunga*

Lemna minor agg.

Other species which, though sparse, are characteristic of some part of the range

Elodea canadensis *Oenanthe fluviatilis*

Glyceria maxima *Phalaris arundinacea*

Groenlandia densa *Schoenoplectus lacustris*

Lemna trisulca *Sparganium emersum*

Mimulus guttatus agg. *Zannichellia palustris*

Myriophyllum spicatum Mosses

(b) Bank species

Occurring in at least 40% of sites recorded

 Epilobium hirsutum   *Urtica dioica*

Occurring in at least 20% of sites recorded

 Phalaris arundinacea

Occurring in at least 10% of sites recorded

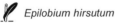 *Apium nodiflorum +*   *Rorippa nasturtium-aquaticum* agg.
Berula erecta

 Carex acutiformis   *Sparganium erectum*

Filipendula ulmaria

Notes on Tables 12.1–12.5, 13.1–13.5, 14.1–14.2

The data in these tables come from surveys of watercourse sites (mostly from bridges) carried out between 1969 and 1974. Sites with severe pollution were discarded and all other sites (upstream and downstream, mildly polluted, shaded, recently dredged, etc.) were included. The tables are intended as summaries only. Ecological subdivisions are discussed in the text, particularly in Chapters 8 and 11–14. Because sites that are shaded, recently dredged, etc. are included, species frequency is less than in well-vegetated rivers (see figures in Chapter 11).

Some categories of plants have been omitted or grouped in the tables. Mosses are considered as a group only; *Enteromorpha intestinalis* is the only named alga included; and the small grasses and, (*Agrostis stolonifera* and, less commonly, *Catabrosa aquatica* and *Glyceria* spp.) are omitted as the earlier records did not distinguish between temporary plants on fallen clods and permanent populations. On the banks, the only species recorded were those which also occur in the channel and those which are characteristic of (drier) marshes.

The species are listed in frequency categories, of species occurring in at least 40%, 20–39% and 10–19% of the sites recorded of that geological type. If plants are sparse in a stream type, a further category of 5–9% is added.

Chalk streams which are permanently dry near the source bear land plants there. Winter-wet brooks bear sparse land plants and aquatics, the proportion of aquatics increasing with the length of the flooded period. The channel is seldom covered with aquatics if it is dry for more than late summer. Apart from land plants, the plants of the drier channels are usually:

 Mentha aquatica   *Urtica dioica*

 Myosotis scorpioides   *Veronica anagallis-aquatica* agg.

 Phalaris arundinacea   *Veronica beccabunga*

Rather lower, the following enter:

 Apium nodiflorum   *Rorippa nasturtium-aquaticum* agg.

In the zone flooded for most of the year, the following can come in:

 Berula erecta   (*Lemna trisulca*, rare)

🌱 *Callitriche* spp.   🦋 (*Mimulus guttatus* agg., infrequent)

🌿 *Lemna minor* agg.   ✿ *Ranunculus* spp., short-leaved

By this stage, *Urtica dioica* is only on the bank, and *Phalaris arundinacea* is mainly so. The term 'fringing herb' is conveniently used to describe, collectively, the short semi-emerged dicotyledons *Apium nodiflorum*, *Berula erecta*, *Mentha aquatica*, *Mimulus guttatus* agg., *Myosatis scorpioides*, *Rorippa nasturtium-aquaticum* agg., *Veronica anagallis-aquatica* agg. and *Veronica beccabunga*. These form clumps, usually based on the sides even in small channels, but also extending into the middle. *Apium nodiflorum* and *Berula erecta* may form submerged carpets over a good deal of the bed, and *Rorippa nasturtium-aquaticum* agg. may form emerged carpets in flooded parts with stable low flows. *Callitriche* and short-leaved *Ranunculus* grow in the centre. The *Ranunculus* species is commonly *Ranunculus peltatus*, though *Ranunculus aquatilis*, *Ranunculus trichophyllus* and intermediates may also occur. All can, in winterbournes, tolerate drying in late summer, and often develop aerial leaves in shallow water or on damp ground. Such brooks are typically covered with vegetation unless they are cut or otherwise managed.

With perennial flow the following can be found:

🌾 *Sparganium erectum*   🌿 Mosses

🌱 (*Hippuris vulgaris*, uncommon)

Brooks with perennial flow from the source may contain any of the above species. The typical pattern of plants in the channel is shown in Figure 10.15. Fringing herbs with occasional *Sparganium erectum* occur at the sides, the fringing herbs being mixed together, or in small, often contiguous patches, and not growing very large or luxuriant. Any of the species may extend into the channel in shallow water. Submerged carpets of *Apium nodiflorum* and *Berula erecta* are common and emerged ones of *Rorippa nasturtium-aquaticum* agg. occur occasionally. *Callitriche* and *Ranunculus* are more prominent than in shallower brooks, and with increasing depth and flow *Callitriche* becomes concentrated at the sides.

In middle reaches (Figure 10.18), *Ranunculus* is the main channel dominant, and is here in medium-leaved forms which cannot tolerate drying. *Ranunculus penicillatus* ssp. *pseudofluitans* is the commonest, but *Ranunculus penicillatus* ssp. *penicillatus*, *Ranunculus aquatilis*, *Ranunculus peltatus* and intermediates also occur. *Callitriche* is usually present but inconspicuous. The fringing herbs become increasingly concentrated at the edges as scour and depth increase in the centre. *Apium nodiflorum* and *Berula erecta* still form large submerged carpets in shallower channels (usually those less than 40 cm deep, though carpets are occasionally in water *c.* 75 cm deep), but *Rorippa nasturtium-aquaticum* agg. seldom forms carpets because the plants are so easily washed away. *Lemna trisulca* and *Mimulus guttatus* agg. are usually absent.

At the margins there may be a band (up to *c*. 1 m wide) of floating fragments of fringing herbs and *Callitriche* (Figure 10.18), and there may also be a narrow band of tall monocotyledons on the bank, usually *Glyceria maxima* and *Sparganium erectum*, though *Carex acutiformis* and (in small patches) *Phalaris arundinacea* are also characteristic. Bands of tall monocotyledons and of fringing herbs are usually mutually exclusive, though sparse fringing herbs may be found on the channel side of a fringing herb band, and patches of tall monocotyledons may occur behind fringing herbs.

In the downstream or siltier parts of these middle reaches, species not especially characteristic of chalk streams first appear. *Elodea canadensis* is usually found in species-rich sites, and may grow just as small shoots within other clumps. It is luxuriant only in the more eutrophic places such as silt shoals.

In the lower reaches, where the channel is deeper, fringing herbs are excluded from the bed and *Callitriche* usually occurs in shallow or sheltered places. The water is still clear and fairly swift, the bed remains firm and stable (suitable for plants with shallow root wefts) and plants can usually grow right across the channel. *Ranunculus* is the usual dominant, often *Ranunculus penicillatus* ssp. *pseudofluitans*, sometimes *Ranunculus penicillatus* ssp. *penicillatus* or other species. Their leaves are typically longer than in the middle reaches.

The distance from the water to the top of the bank, in lesser-drained areas, is less than in other stream types, often only *c*. 0.5 m. The banks are steep with little silt, and the fluctuations in water level are greater. Because of this, fringing herbs are seldom prominent, though small patches, often temporary, are usually present where they can anchor. The narrow band of tall monocotyledons which appeared upstream is now likely to be continuous unless the zone is grazed.

Nutrient status increases in the lower reaches, allowing the entry of semi-eutrophic and eutrophic species.

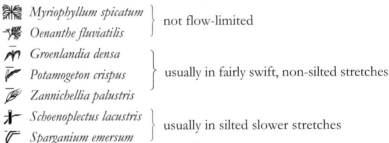

Myriophyllum spicatum	not flow-limited
Oenanthe fluviatilis	
Groenlandia densa	
Potamogeton crispus	usually in fairly swift, non-silted stretches
Zannichellia palustris	
Schoenoplectus lacustris	usually in silted slower stretches
Sparganium emersum	

One or more of these occur in *c*. 15% of all sites recorded. *Groenlandia densa* does also rarely occur in upper parts with only slight indication of a non-chalk influence, but apart from this the presence of any of these species in upper or middle reaches, or of many or large amounts of them in lower reaches, indicates eutrophication, probably from man's activities. (They can also occur in silted flood plains, where there is, for example, a more eutrophic rock in the catchment that has been overlooked.)

The difference between upper, middle and lower reaches is one of stream size and vegetation physiognomy, and is controlled by the topography and water regime rather than by the actual distance from the source. The typical downstream-patterning of a large chalk stream in good condition is shown in Figure 11.7. Upper reaches which are winter-wet and summer-dry usually have one or two aquatic species per site. Upper brooks with perennial flow have about four species per site and undamaged lower reaches at least nine species. A small number of sites have 10 or more species in normal conditions. A healthy chalk stream looks roughly full (25% or more) of plants throughout the zone of perennial flow. Many sites are damaged and bear fewer species.

The width-slope patterns for the more characteristic plants are show in Figures 12.3b–g, demonstrating the wide habitat ranges and the downstream variation.

Apium nodiflorum + *Berula erecta, Callitriche obtusangula* + *stagnalis* and *Ranunculus* spp. grow well in all sizes of chalk stream. Luxuriant stands of *Callitriche* have a smaller pattern, avoiding the extremes of flow and the purer lime water (calcium-dominated). Short-leaved *Ranunculus* species occur upstream of medium-leaved forms, as is demonstrated here for *Ranunculus peltatus* and *Ranunculus penicillatus* ssp. *pseudofluitans*, the two most frequent chalk species. The central parts of the habitat range can bear both species. *Ranunculus aquatilis, Ranunculus penicillatus* ssp. *penicillatus, Ranunculus trichophyllus*, hybrids and intermediate forms occur less frequently.

The other fringing herbs, Figure 12.3c, are restricted to brooks with less extreme width-slope characters. *Myosotis scorpioides* and *Veronica* spp. are more confined to the fringes than *Apium nodiflorum* and *Berula erecta*, though they also may occur on the bed of brooks, and *Mentha aquatica* is almost confined to the fringes. Emerged fringing herbs collect silt and grow more luxuriantly in it, so because silting is little on the chalk, shoots of fringing plants are often smaller than on clay. The low silting and the firm bed to the channel are the main reasons why fringing herbs grow better in channels here than they do in other streams. *Sparganium erectum* is somewhat restricted (Figure 12.3e), probably because silting is low and flow is swift.

The slow-flow eutrophic species (Figure 12.3f) are confined to wide flat streams with the most silt. Those more characteristic of faster flow (Figure 12.3g) occur in somewhat narrower and steeper streams,

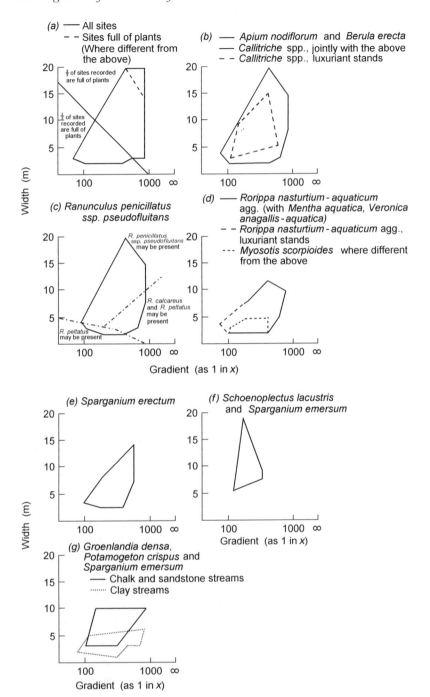

Figure 12.3
Width–slope patterns in chalk streams. Here, and in the comparable figures in this chapter and Chapter 13, large rivers are usually excluded, as they so often flow over more than one rock type. Consequently the species sites occurring to the right of the patterns in the figures in Chapter 6 are usually absent. The patterns for each rock type should be compared with pattern (a) on each figure, as this is the pattern for the total sites included for that rock type. Gradient and width are represented as in Figure 6.1, etc.

though they do not grow as far upstream as on sandstone and clay. Small swift chalk streams are unsuitable for eutrophic species because of their trophic status, substrate and flow.

Downstream patterning is described in Chapter 11 and is illustrated in Figure 11.7, which also shows typical plant communities in different sites.

Chalk outcrops are found in the south and east of England. The most westerly chalk streams are tributaries of the River Frome, Dorset. They extend eastwards to Kent, and north through the Berkshire Downs and Chilterns to Hertfordshire and Cambridgeshire. The next main outcrop is in Lincolnshire, where most streams of the Wolds are on mixed catchments, and the most northerly outcrop is in Yorkshire, the River Hull being the main chalk river there. There is little variation between the plants found in streams in different geographical areas. However, *Apium nodiflorum* is a common channel species in Dorset, while in Hampshire and Berkshire, *Berula erecta* is the more abundant. *Ranunculus penicillatus* ssp. *pseudofluitans* is more frequent in the south-west. The River Hull, Yorkshire, has lower hills than the others, and a large part of the catchment is covered by alluvium: only small parts have a pure chalk vegetation.

Chalk Downs sometimes rise sharply from flatter ground on other rock types (e.g. the Sussex Downs with greensand and clay in the vale below). The chalk streams are then very short, often summer-dry, and narrow, making it difficult to diagnose chalk vegetation. Wetter brooks usually bear the characteristic fringing herbs and have the characteristic sparkling water.

OOLITE STREAMS

Oolite is the other common soft British limestone, though oolite streams are less frequent than chalk ones. The total area is less, much of it is covered by boulder clay outcrops, so that the catchments are mixed limestone-clay and often only short brooks are influenced solely by oolite.

Oolite is less pure than chalk and more polluted, so more semi-eutrophic and eutrophic species grow in the channels. Some brooks have the same vegetation as chalk ones of a similar size. Usually, however, there is less:

Callitriche spp.   *Ranunculus* spp.

and more

Enteromorpha intestinalis   *Sparganium emersum*

Myriophyllum spicatum   *Sparganium erectum*

Nuphar lutea

There is usually less vegetation in the channels and a higher proportion of sites are almost without macrophytes.

The main outcrops are the Cotswolds, Northamptonshire Wolds, and the ridges projecting north from the latter into Lincolnshire. (There are smaller outcrops joining these areas and running south into Somerset. The streams of the North Yorkshire Moors on Coralline oolite are classed as hard limestone and described in Chapter 13.) The other soft limestones are of only local importance, e.g. bands in the Corallian, so it is very rare to find streams of any size exclusively on these limestones. In mixed catchments the vegetation is the same as for oolite.

SANDSTONE STREAMS

Sandstone hills can be as high as chalk ones, but the ground is usually lower with the streams flowing more slowly (Figure 12.4). There are often at least intermittent patches of boulder clay, so it is not easy to determine the vegetation of exclusively sandstone streams. The vegetation described here as characteristic could be slightly influenced by clay.

Figure 12.4
A soft sandstone landscape.

Sandstone streams are partly fed by underground aquifers, so their flow type is nearer that of soft limestone than is that of other rock types. However, sandstone has more very narrow brooks, and brooks are often closer together than they are on chalk. Because of the fewer springs and greater run-off more brooks rise on steeper slopes than is the case on chalk (Figure 12.5a), but more of the stream length is on flatter ground and, as it happens, Britain has no large rivers on soft sandstone. There is more loose sand and silt in the streams, and the downstream increase in silting is greater. Consequently the potential damage from scour is also greater. When the firm bed is on sandstone itself, this is more easily eroded than the firm bed of a chalk stream. The water tends to be more turbid but still with little colour, and though water temperature is more variable this is probably of little significance to the plants (see above).

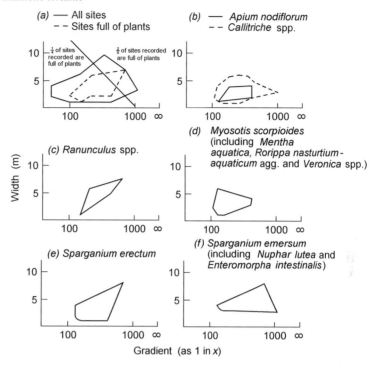

Sandstone streams

Figure 12.5
Width–slope patterns in sandstone streams. For details see Figure 12.3. For *Groenlandia densa, Potamogeton crispus* and *Zannichellia palustris* see Figure 12.3g.

The smallest sandstone brooks are often 1–2 m wide with a slope steeper than 1:100, and the largest truly sandstone streams are seldom over 8 m wide with slopes of *c.* 1:750. There are relatively fewer sites which are full of plants, and relatively more which are effectively without angiosperms. Also, the width-slope pattern for sites choked with plants is smaller than that for all sites taken in total, showing that luxuriant vegetation does not occur in more extreme habitats. Because of the less stable bed, less stable flow and more turbid water, downstream reaches with plants growing right across the channel are less common than on chalk (Figure 12.5a), and the habitat is generally less suitable for plant growth. The characteristic species are shown in Table 12.2. The typically chalk species are less frequent, though *Callitriche* has increased and the eutrophic species are commoner. The loss in chalk vegetation is, however, greater than the gain in eutrophic vegetation.

Fringing herbs

These are less frequent and in smaller populations than in chalk streams. *Apium nodiflorum, Berula erecta* and *Rorippa nasturtium-aquaticum* agg. no longer form extensive carpets over the channel. All show greater decreases downstream than they do on chalk.

Table 12.2 Soft sandstone species[a]

(a) Channel species
Undamaged channels contain higher frequencies

Occurring in at least 40% of sites recorded

 Callitriche spp.

Occurring in at least 20% of sites recorded

 Myosotis scorpioides   *Sparganium erectum*

 Sparganium emersum

Occurring in at least 10% of sites recorded

Apium nodiflorum   *Ranunculus* spp.

 Epilobium hirsutum

Other species which, though sparse, are characteristic

Alisma plantago-aquatica   *Nuphar lutea*

Elodea canadensis   *Potamogeton natans*

 Mentha aquatica   *Veronica beccabunga*

(b) Bank species
Occurring in at least 40% of sites recorded

 Epilobium hirsutum   *Urtica dioica*

Occurring in at least 10% of sites recorded

Filipendula ulmaria   *Sparganium erectum*

 Phalaris arundinacea

a   See notes to Table 12.1

Non-emergents

Ranunculus decreases, and the increase in *Callitriche* cannot compensate for the decline in the other carpet-forming species. Luxuriant *Callitriche* is characteristic of sandstone, with the higher other nutrients and lower calcium. The *Ranunculus* spp. are more diverse, and rarely include *Ranunculus penicillatus* ssp. *pseudofluitans*. *Potamogeton natans* is characteristic, though infrequent.

Characteristic of small upper brooks

 Epilobium hirsutum   *Sparganium erectum*
Phalaris arundinacea   Other tall herbs

Sandstone streams

Entering somewhat lower, with more water and scour

🌿 *Apium nodiflorum*   🌱 *Veronica beccabunga*

Entering in the zone of perennial flow

🌱 *Mentha aquatica*   *Ranunculus* spp.

🌱 *Myosotis scorpioides*   🌱 *Veronica anagallis-aquatica* agg.

Downstream

Eutrophic species occur mainly in lower reaches, but can extend upstream to the limits of perennial flow. In general they are commoner and occur further upstream than on chalk (because silting occurs further upstream and pollution is often more). Mosses, on the other hand, are much scarcer because there is a small proportion of stable bed. This is a different downstream progression to that on chalk, attributable to the differences in substrate, flow and water quality. Species diversity is usually lower than on chalk.

On the banks there is an increase in

🌿 *Epilobium hirsutum*   *Urtica dioica*

Filipendula ulmaria

and the fringing herbs, etc. decrease. The width-slope patterns (Figures 12.5b–f and 12.3g) show that less of the potentially colonisable area is occupied by the chalk species and more by the eutrophic ones.

In the width-slope pattern, fringing herbs and *Ranunculus* occupy less of their potential areas than on the chalk. This is also true for *Callitriche*, even though this is more frequent on sandstone. *Sparganium erectum* has a large pattern. The eutrophic species of slow flows have a wider habitat range, extending into steeper and narrower brooks. Downstream patterning is described in Chapter 11, and Figures 11.10 and 11.11 show typical plant communities in different sites.

The larger outcrops of soft sandstone are the Tertiary sands of southern England, the greensands rather more to the north and east, the Crags of East Anglia, and the Mesozoic sandstones of the Cheshire-Shropshire region. Other outcrops are smaller, or have more clay in the stream catchments. Sandstone streams vary more in their vegetation than do chalk streams. Where the land is nearly flat (hills rarely up to 60 m (200')) and flows are slow, *Ranunculus* is likely to be absent. The acid sands of the New Forest bear oligotrophic species upstream, e.g.

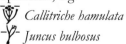

🌱 *Callitriche hamulata*   *Myriophyllum alterniflorum*

🌱 *Juncus bulbosus*

Downstream eutrophication is rapid because of the silting, and the vegetation soon becomes eutrophic. Some greensand has a high trophic status and the vegetation is then more nearly that of clay streams.

CLAY STREAMS

Clay is the commonest rock of lowland Britain, and large rivers as well as small brooks can occur on exclusively clay catchments (Figure 12.6). The large rivers have, however, been omitted from the analyses here in order to keep these comparable with the chalk and sandstone data. Clay has a strong influence on river vegetation, and clay communities occur also when small outcrops of other bedrock are in the catchment, and when thick boulder clay overlies other rock types. This demonstrates well that, within the lowlands, flow pattern is less important for plants than rock types. Streams on thick boulder clay over chalk receive water from springs in the chalk, but the substrate is derived from boulder clay and it is this which (almost) determines the trophic status. Clay streams have an unstable flow pattern (see Chapter 5). The non-porous land surface leads to the brooks being close together and flows being very dependent on run-off. There is more storm scour than on chalk or sandstone. Much silt enters the streams and is deposited in the lowlands, giving, together with an erodible firm bed, an unstable substrate to the channel.

Figure 12.6
A clay landscape.

In clay country the land is usually low, but in some parts hills reach 250 m (*c.* 800'). Because of the more spatey flow and the unstable silt, hilly clay streams have a different character, and are here classed as upland rather than lowland (Figure 12.1) — in contrast to chalk and sandstone streams, which are all classed as lowland. Whether upland or lowland, the small brooks are usually on steep slopes, as they are dependent on run-off. In the upper reaches the channel bed is often the solid clay, and this is more easily eroded than other firm beds. Even gravel beds on clay are less stable than those on chalk. Even in these upper reaches deposited silt is more important, and sand less important than on the other rocks, and deep silt commonly occurs in lower reaches. The water tends to be more turbid than in the other streams, and is often somewhat grey, particularly in winter. Water temperature fluctuates more, but again this is only of minor importance.

Small clay brooks are often 1–2 m wide with a slope steeper than 1:80, while the largest clay rivers are over 20 m wide with slopes flatter than 1:1000. Clay is usually much-drained. Comparing clay with sandstone, the proportion of sites full of plants is about the same and, again, full sites do not occur in the whole width-slope range (Figure 12.7a). The full sites are in the most silted habitats. However, there are even more effectively empty sites, though this is partly due to the increased tree shading, and even fewer sites with plants right across the channel. The latter are frequent only in slow silted streams with water less than 1 m deep, which provide a substrate that is relatively stable (for species growing well in deep silt) and allow enough light to reach the channel bed.

The characteristic species are shown in Table 12.3. In general the chalk species are much fewer, and though the eutrophic species have increased, the gain is on average less than the loss. The downstream decrease in fringing herbs and *Callitriche* is faster than on sandstone, contrasting markedly with the small decrease on chalk. The fringing herbs are effectively confined to the edges, and in shallow water they form the luxuriant, silt-accumulating, nutrient-rich and short-lived clumps described in Chapters 3, 5 and 10. They do not form the stable carpets across the channel which are so characteristic of chalk streams. The eutrophic species extend far upstream, and show greater frequency and diversity than those on clay or sandstone. In large rivers plants are usually confined to the sides (see Chapters 5 and 10). In lower reaches tall monocotyledons are frequent. These tend to form wide and intermittent bands, but in quiet open places the fringe may be continuous. (Chalk streams typically have narrow continuous bands, and sandstone ones show an intermediate pattern.)

Characteristic of small upper brooks

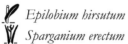 *Epilobium hirsutum*   Land species
Sparganium erectum

Entering somewhat lower, with more water and scour, and less choking by plants

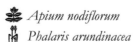 *Apium nodiflorum*   *Veronica beccabunga*
Phalaris arundinacea

261

Table 12.3   Clay species[a]

(a) Channel species
Undamaged channels contain higher frequencies
Occurring in at least 40% of sites recorded

 Sparganium erectum

Occurring in at least 20% of sites recorded

 Apium nodiflorum   *Sparganium emersum*

Occurring in at least in 10% of sites recorded

 Callitriche spp.   *Nuphar lutea*

 Epilobium hirsutum   *Phalaris arundinacea*

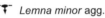 *Lemna minor* agg.   *Rorippa nasturtium-aquaticum* agg.

Other species which, though sparser, are characteristic of part of the range

 Alisma plantago-aquatica   *Rorippa amphibia*

 Butomus umbellatus   *Sagittaria sagittifolia*

 Enteromorpha intestinalis   *Schoenoplectus lacustris*

 Glyceria maxima   *Typha latifolia*

 Potamogeton crispus   *Zannichellia palustris*

 Potamogeton perfoliatus

(b) Bank species
Occurring in at least 40% of sites recorded

Epilobium hirsutum   *Urtica dioica*

Occurring in at least 20% of sites recorded

Phalaris arundinacea

---

a   See notes to Table 12.1

Notes to Table 12.3
As more clay stream sites are small than are large, the characteristic species of the larger clay streams, *Sagittaria sagittifolia*, etc., are not among the most frequent. Upper sites, with little sediment and a relatively low nutrient status, contain most of the *Apium nodiflorum*, *Callitriche* spp., etc. (see text). The characteristic species of chalk and soft sandstones, in contrast, occur on small as well as large streams.

Entering just above or below the zone of perennial flow

Callitriche spp.

Entering in the zone of perennial flow

In swifter flow: *Potamogeton crispus*   *Zannichellia palustris*

If lime is present: 🌿 *Oenanthe fluviatilis*

In slower flow: 〰 *Enteromorpha intestinalis* ⴕ *Schoenoplectus lacustris*

🍃 *Nuphar lutea* 𝟋 *Sparganium emersum*

🌱 *Sagittaria sagittifolia*

Large rivers characteristically bear mainly deep-rooted eutrophic species

〰 *Enteromorpha intestinalis* (shallow-anchored) 🌱 *Sagittaria sagittifolia*

🌿 *Elodea canadensis* (shallow-rooted) ⴕ *Schoenoplectus lacustris*

✴ *Lemna minor* agg. (free-floating) 𝟋 *Sparganium emersum*

🍃 *Nuphar lutea* ⵞ *Sparganium erectum*

In less eutrophic parts there may also be

🕯 *Alisma plantago-aquatica* 🌰 *Potamogeton perfoliatus*

🌿 *Polygonum amphibium* Fringing herbs

With some organic or industrial pollution there may also be

🌿 *Potamogeton pectinatus*

ⵞ *Sparganium erectum* is important throughout, in contrast to chalk streams. It can choke the channel in flatter narrower brooks and can dominate, and indeed create, silt banks downstream.

🌿 *Elodea canadensis* is more frequent, and more frequently luxuriant, than on chalk or sandstone.

🌿 *Potamogeton natans* may occur in upper reaches which receive little silt and little pollution.

Species diversity is as high as on chalk, some downstream sites having 10 or more species. The most frequent number of angiosperms present (including the large number of species-poor small streams), in sites with river plants, is three, similar to that of sandstone. This number, however, is artificially lowered by pollution and other damage. Because towns are most often sited on clay, more clay streams suffer from high pollution than do chalk and sandstone ones, and an important effect of pollution is to decrease species diversity (see Chapter 19).

On the banks, there is, in comparison to chalk, an increase in:

Epilobium hirsutum *Urtica dioica*

Filipendula ulmaria

The fringing herbs, etc., characteristic of chalk decrease, and so do the tall grasses and *Sparganium erectum* which are frequent on sandstone banks.

The width-slope patterns (Figures 12.7b–f, 12.3g) show the restricted habitat distribution of the chalk species, and the increased distribution of the eutrophic ones.

Apium nodiflorum has as restricted a distribution as on sandstone, but *Rorippa nasturtium-aquaticum* agg. and *Veronica* spp. have a wider range, *Veronica* spp. extending into steeper streams. *Ranunculus* is more restricted than on sandstone and its most frequent species are *Ranunculus penicillatus* ssp. *penicillatus* and *Ranunculus trichophyllus*. These are characteristic of little-polluted streams. The *Callitriche* pattern is like the sandstone one, and more restricted than that on chalk. The populations are, however, of much sparser plants than before, and they are less frequent in lower reaches. *Sparganium erectum* is very widely distributed. The eutrophic species of faster flow grow further upstream than they do on chalk or sandstone (Figure 12.3f). The species of slow flow occur wherever silt can accumulate, and show a very different pattern to that on chalk. *Enteromorpha* has a large pattern for the first time. Like other submergents it avoids small brooks likely to dry in summer.

Downstream patterning is further described in Chapter 11 and Figures 11.13–11.15.

The upland streams have much less silting compared with the lowland streams and there is an increase of:

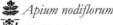 *Apium nodiflorum*    *Rorippa nasturtium-aquaticum* agg.

 *Callitriche* spp.   ✿ Mosses

✿ *Ranunculus* spp.   (Other fringing herbs, to a lesser extent)

These are more frequent than in lowland streams and also extend farther downstream. The eutrophic species may be less frequent than in the lowlands.

Clay is found in those parts of south and east England which are not on limestone or sandstone or in alluvial plains.

STREAMS OF MIXED CATCHMENTS

Large lowland rivers derived from more than one rock type are usually slow-floating and silted, and frequently somewhat polluted. They are very similar to large clay rivers in their general vegetation, though a few more mesotrophic species may be present. Where smaller rivers are concerned, however, mixed catchments result in river vegetation which reflects the geology of the catchments and the proportion of each rock type. A chalk stream rising on fertile sandstone, e.g. River Avon, Wiltshire (see Figure 11.15) shows some eutrophic influence throughout. An equally small amount of acid sandstone at the source or of any sandstone downstream and at the sides, has little effect. When

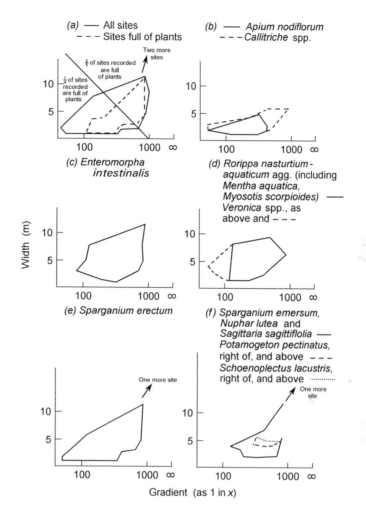

Figure 12.7
Width–slope patterns in clay streams. For details see Figure 12.3. For *Groenlandia densa*, *Potamogeton crispus* and *Zannichellia palustris* see Figure 12.3g.

sandstone and chalk occupy roughly equal portions in the catchment, the river vegetation is intermediate between that of chalk and that of sandstone. When clay occurs in a sandstone catchment, or vice versa, it has a noticeable influence on the plants.

Many streams are mixed limestone-clay. This clay may be solid or drift (Quaternary, boulder clay, etc.), but there are only a few differences in the plants. When boulder clay overlies limestone, and when solid clay occurs upstream of limestone, *Apium nodiflorum* and perhaps *Callitriche* spp. are likely to be more frequent than where limestone is upstream of clay. Comparing solid with drift clay, *Ranunculus* spp. are apt to be more frequent on the solid clay. When passing from mainly limestone to mainly clay catchments, chalk species decrease and clay ones increase, but the habitats in which alterations occur differ for different species.

Chalk species decreasing towards clay

🌿 *Apium nodiflorum*   Steady decrease throughout

🌿 *Berula erecta*
🌼 *Ranunculus penicillatus* } Usually lost before a half-clay
   ssp. *pseudofluitans*   catchment is reached

Most frequent in mixed catchments

🌿 *Groenlandia densa* (perhaps)   🌿 *Potamogeton pectinatus* (pollution-
                                      favoured)

🌿 *Myriophyllum spicatum*   🌿 *Potamogeton perfoliatus*
🌿 *Oenanthe fluviatilis*   🌿 *Zannichellia palustris*
🌿 *Potamogeton crispus*

Several of these species occur in chalk streams with eutrophic influence, and in clay ones with little deposited silt.

Clay species increasing away from chalk

🌿 *Sparganium erectum*   Main increase after a half-clay catchment is
                           reached

🌿 *Nuphar lutea*   } Main increase when clay influence first
🌿 *Sparganium emersum*   } starts with little clay in catchment

When boulder clay intermittently overlies chalk, the river plants are sparse in swifter flows because of the silty unstable substrate, but are (part-) limestone in type. The *Ranunculus* spp., however, do not usually include *Ranunculus penicillatus* ssp. *pseudofluitans*. When the rock boundary is crossed, the distance on the new rock that elapses before the plants change varies with the size of stream and the tributaries entering (see Chapter 11).

Limestone upstream, clay downstream (two examples)

1. Clay species entering 2 miles and a town downstream of the rock boundary.
2. Still chalk vegetation 2 miles downstream of boundary. After 8 miles and the entry of both chalk and clay tributaries, stream with semi-clay vegetation in slower silted reaches and semi-chalk vegetation in swifter gravel reaches.

Clay upstream of limestone (two examples)

1. Chalk species entering 2 miles downstream of the rock boundary.
2. Larger stream. After 5 miles and the entry of a chalk stream, chalk, clay and intermediate species present. After 9 miles and two more chalk tributaries a mainly chalk vegetation, but clay species still present.

Clay brooks with intermittent bands of Corallian limestone have limestone species for several miles below the band if at least half the catchment is limestone, and these are luxuriant where the catchment is three-quarters limestone.

STREAM CLASSIFICATION

The watercourses on soft rocks and alluvial plains, except for streams on mixed catchments, are classified in Figure 12.1. The vertical axis shows flow regime. There are minor differences in flow pattern between lowland chalk, sandstone, and clay streams, but these are small compared with their differences from upland and mountain streams. The hill heights on upland clay are no greater than those on chalk both reaching around 250 m (*c.* 800'). However, the greater run-off; more spatey and swifter flow, and the less silted and unstable substrate in upland compared with lowland clay streams means there is a real difference in the vegetation, and such a difference is not found within the chalk streams. The horizontal axis in Figure 12.1 represents trophic status (described in Chapter 8). Chalk streams are mesotrophic, with remarkably little eutrophic influence even in the lower reaches. Acid sand may be oligotrophic, but most sandstone streams are intermediate in nutrient status between those of chalk and of clay.

13

Vegetation of streams on hard rocks

Streams on hard rocks are often spatey in highland areas, and usually contain only a little vegetation. Like the streams on soft rock they can be classified by flow regime and nutrient status. Streams on resistant rocks where there is bog peat in the substrate bear nutrient-poor species. The upper reaches of mountain streams normally have fierce flow and thus there are few river plants.

Scour-tolerant species increase downstream, and Ranunculus *is usually the only plant which can be luxuriant. Coal Measures streams are often polluted and species frequency is low. Limestone streams have fringing herbs in the upper reaches and, when water force is low,* Ranunculus *can be luxuriant in lower reaches. Species diversity is low. Hard sandstone streams are much more silty, and so although plants are few where there is strong flow, vegetation can be luxuriant where scouring is less and silt can accumulate. Fringing herbs,* Callitriche *and* Ranunculus *occur in the upper reaches, and* Ranunculus *and more eutrophic species in the lower reaches.*

The rocks termed here as hard are those of north and west Britain. They comprise the hard limestones, mainly Carboniferous ones, the hard sandstones, mainly Old Red Sandstone (but including hilly Mesozoic sandstones, etc.), Coal Measures, and the resistant rocks. Resistant rocks include the old (Pre-Cambrian and Palaeozoic) shales, slate, gneisses and schists, together with later igneous rocks (basalt, etc.). They are all resistant to erosion and solution and, if topography is similar, bear fairly similar vegetation.

The relationship between the different stream types is shown in Figure 13.1. This resembles the classification on soft rocks (Figure 12.1) except that because the range of topography is greater, from plain to mountain, there is more separation with flow regime. (Figure 13.1 is more fully described below.)

The rainfall and its seasonal distribution determine the amount of water reaching the streams as run-off. The force of this water is influenced by the height of the nearby hills, the fall from these hills to the stream bed and the slope of the stream bed. Of these three, the fall from hill to stream is usually the most important for vegetation type. An example is the North Yorkshire Moors, which are only *c.* 300 m (1000') high, but have vegetation typical of mountainous areas in their streams because the fall to the valleys is that characteristic of the mountains (over 200 m; 600'). Local conditions may alter this. For example, a stream

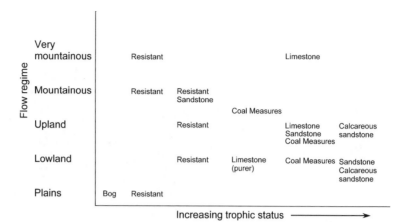

Figure 13.1
Stream types on hard rocks.

running down a very steep mountain-side has the same absence of plants as a flatter stream in a steep gully.

	Hill height (usual)	Fall to stream (usual)	Slope of upper streams (typical)
Lowlands	Up to 250 m (800')	Up to 60 m (200')	Flatter than 1:100
Uplands	250–370 m (800–1200')	90–150 m (300–500')	1:40–1:80
Mountains	600 m (2000') and over	At least 180 m (600')	Steeper than 1:40
Very mountainous	600 m (2000') and over	At least 300 m (1000') or rainfall very high	

Where water force is low the vegetation may be dense (as it is on the soft lowland rocks). In mountain streams spates can cause severe damage, and these and the swift normal flows usually prevent dense vegetation developing. There is an intermediate situation in the uplands, where vegetation may grow thickly (as in the lowlands) but may also be severely damaged by spates (as in the mountains). Water force is greatest in the sub-group of very mountainous streams, and here river plants are usually absent. As plants are usually much sparser and rarer on hard than on soft rocks, the width–slope patterns quoted in this chapter are less reliable than those in other chapters. Much basic ecological information about these streams is also given in Chapters 10 and 11.

Figure 13.2
A stream in blanket bog.

STREAMS ON RESISTANT ROCKS

Streams on lowlands, plains and bogs

Bog streams occur in blanket bogs in almost flat riverscapes (e.g. parts of the Scottish Highlands) and are on, or contain, acid bog peat (Figure 13.2). They are characterised by having very little force of water. They tend to have little water movement except after rain, to be shallow, and to have water stained by the peat of the land near by. The typical species of these streams are also found in the bogs For example:

Eriophorum angustifolium	*Potamogeton polygonifolius*
Menyanthes trifoliata	*Ranunculus flammula*

(*Sphagnum* spp. occur in similar channels which have still water except after rain.)

On the moorland plains (e.g. Dartmoor), acid peat sediment still reaches the channel, but mineral particles occur as well and the water is less brown. Because the land is less flat, flow is swifter, though the force of water after rain is still low. (Rainfall does not affect the nature of this river community, as streams of this type can be found where there is an annual rainfall of anything between 87.5 cm (35") and 200 cm (80") per year.) In these stream types sedimentation leads to a decrease, not an increase, in trophic status, because the sediment here includes particles of solid peat (the substrate of lowest nutrient status among those with fine particles). The vegetation (Table 13.1) contains oligotrophic, though not bog species (except in streams intermediate between these and bog streams). For example:

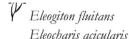 *Eleogiton fluitans*
Eleocharis acicularis

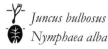 *Juncus bulbosus*
Nymphaea alba

The ubiquitous *Sparganium erectum* is found also. Two species are also present (*Nuphar lutea* and *Sparganium emersum*), which on soft rocks are eutrophic in distribution.

Species diversity is a high as on chalk and clay, some sites containing 10–12 species, and 2–5 species being common. Species diversity in British streams is therefore not influenced by trophic status. (The bog streams are not species-rich, but as they are too shallow for most aquatics their lack of species cannot be attributed to nutrient supply.) Almost half the sites recorded were full of plants, a proportion nearly equal to that for chalk streams and greater than that for all other channel types with flowing water. The smallest tributaries tend to contain fewer species, and submerged species avoid streams liable to dry in summer. The width–slope patterns (Figure 13.3) show wide distributions for *Callitriche*, *Sparganium erectum* and mosses. The fringing herbs avoid the sites of greatest water force (i.e. the steeper, wider streams) and the other species have even more restricted habitat ranges.

As is typical of hard rocks, the banks have frequent

Juncus effusus

and, compared to the soft rocks, much less

Epilobium hirsutum   *Urtica dioica*

 Sparganium erectum

This particular hard rock habitat also has frequent

Phragmites australis

The moorland plains streams seldom extend far downstream, as topography usually changes and the river plants change to those species characteristic of upland or mountain streams (e.g. Chapter 11, Figure 11.4). They occur chiefly in south-west England and south-west Scotland.

In the more truly lowland country, gentle hills mean somewhat swifter water flow and, more importantly, no acid peat. The sediment, therefore, is inorganic, and, as on soft rocks, silt increases trophic status. The streams usually occur as small tributaries in or near the flood plain of a larger river and resemble soft rock streams of a similar size, though they are more likely to be kept clear of plants by water flow.

With little water: *Phalaris arundinacea*, *Urtica dioica*, and other tall herbs

With some scour: Sparse fringing herbs, with perhaps *Callitriche* or *Sparganium erectum* entering lower

With much scour: No plants

271

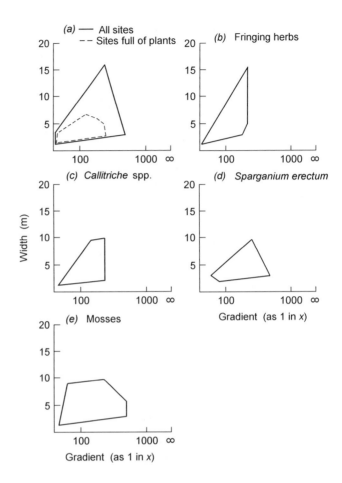

Figure 13.3
Width–slope patterns of moorland plains streams on resistant rocks. For details see Figure 12.3.

Streams in the uplands and mountains

The streams on resistant rocks form a continuous series from the bog tributaries to the very mountainous streams. It is, however, convenient to divide them into those with and without frequent destructive spates. The hill streams, from upland to very mountainous, show decreasing vegetation and increasing water force. Some examples are shown in Figure 13.4 and Figures 11.2 and 11.3, which also demonstrate downstream variation. The typical species are shown in Table 13.1.

In the upper reaches of very mountainous streams the water force is excessive, even boulders being moved in spates, so these reaches are usually without angiosperms, mosses or prominent algae. In small streams of lower force, but in otherwise mountain habitats, *Juncus articulatus* is often present towards the sides, and mosses on the larger stones.

Table 13.1   Resistant rock species[a]

---

1 Moor and plains streams
(mainly south-west England, south-west Scotland)
(a) Channel species
Occurring in at least 40 % of sites recorded

 Callitriche spp.　　　　　　Mosses

Occurring in at least 20 % of sites recorded

Eleocharis acicularis　　　　*Potamogeton natans*

Eleogiton fluitans　　　　　　*Ranunculus omiophyllus*

Juncus bulbosus　　　　　　*Sparganium erectum*

Occurring in at least 10 % of sites recorded

Myosotis scorpioides　　　　*Oenanthe crocata*

Other species which, though sparser, are characteristic

Myriophyllum alterniflorum　　*Phragmites australis*

Nuphar lutea　　　　　　　*Sparganium emersum*

Nymphaea alba

(b) Bank species
Occurring in at least 40% of sites recorded

Juncus effusus

Occurring in at least 10% of sites recorded

Eupatorium cannabinum　　　　*Phragmites australis*

Filipendula ulmaria　　　　　　*Urtica dioica*

2 Streams of the north of Scotland (rare elsewhere)
(a) Channel species
Occurring in at least 40% of sites recorded

Mosses

Occurring in at least 10% of sites recorded

Juncus articulatus

Occurring in at least 5% of sites recorded

Eleocharis palustris

Other species which, though sparser, are characteristic of some part of the range

 Callitriche spp.　　　　　　　*Myriophyllum alterniflorum*

Eleocharis acicularis　　　　　　*Potamogeton polygonifolius*

273

Table 13.1   Continued

Littorella uniflora   Ranunculus flammula

Menyanthes trifoliata

(b) Bank species

Occurring in at least 40% of the sites recorded

Juncus effusus

Occurring in at least 5% of the sites recorded

Juncus articulatus   Urtica dioica

3 Farmland streams
(a) Channel species

Occurring in at least 40% of sites

Mosses

Occurring in at least 10% of sites

Callitriche spp.   Veronica beccabunga

Occurring in at least 5% of sites

Myosotis scorpioides   Ranunculus spp.

Myriophyllum alterniflorum   Sparganium erectum

Phalaris arundinacea

Other species which, though sparser, are characteristic of some part of the range

Apium nodiflorum   Polygonum amphibium

Elodea canadensis   Potamogeton crispus

Mentha aquatica   Potamogeton perfoliatus

Mimulus guttatus agg.   Rorippa nasturtium-aquaticum agg.

Myriophyllum spicatum   Sparganium emersum

(b) Bank species

Occurring in at least 20% of sites recorded

Filipendula ulmaria   Phalaris arundinacea

Juncus effusus   Urtica dioica

---

a   See notes to Table 12.1

Further downstream on very mountainous rivers, where bog peat may enter the channel, there may sometimes be oligotrophic species present. For example:

Eleocharis acicularis	*Littorella uniflora*
-|- *Juncus articulatus*	*Ranunculus flammula*

The upper reaches of mountainous streams usually have sparse mosses (though these may be dense in the occasional stream with less water force, and in groves where trees can stabilise the channel) and very sparse fringing herbs. The upper reaches of upland streams, and the somewhat lower reaches of mountain ones, have more diverse species, and more frequent plants (Table 13.1). Mosses as a group are usually common in such habitats, often more so than angiosperms.

Callitriche spp. (including *Callitriche hamulata*) are fairly frequent, but most populations, and most well-grown stands, are in the smaller streams with shallower water and more stable substrates.

Mimulus guttatus agg. is a fringing herb important on hard rocks, though infrequent on soft ones.

Myriophyllum alterniflorum is an oligotrophic species which is locally frequent, though less common in Wales.

Phalaris arundinacea tends to be on stone or gravel banks flooded in high discharges, dry in low ones.

Veronica beccabunga is much the most frequent fringing herb on hard rocks, except that in south-west England it is replaced by *Apium nodiflorum* (the most frequent fringing herb species on soft rocks).

Downstream, water force is less, and water volume greater. Short-leaved species of *Ranunculus* may enter here and may even cover the channel.

Sparganium erectum and *Elodea canadensis* also enter here.

Further downstream, species of the penultimate group (i.e. mosses, *Callitriche*, *Mimulus guttatus* agg., *Myriophyllum alterniflorum*, *Phalaris arundinacea* and *Veronica beccabunga* tend to decrease, and the incoming species are those requiring a larger water volume, less water force, or a higher nutrient status. For example:

Myriophyllum spicatum	*Ranunculus fluitans*
Potamogeton perfoliatus	*Sparganium emersum*

Further eutrophication brings in more eutrophic species.

Species diversity is low. A few sites have 5–7 species, but most sites with angiosperms have only 1–2 species of these. With increased water force, fewer plants occur. The number of species present in over 5% of sites recorded varies from 12 (on the andesites of northern England and southern Scotland), to none in the very mountainous streams. The proportions of sites full of plants, and of those effectively empty, vary in the same way. The width–slope patterns in Figure 13.5 show larger habitat ranges than might have been expected and wider ranges than on soft rocks. This is because local conditions may decrease water force and permit plants to grow.

275

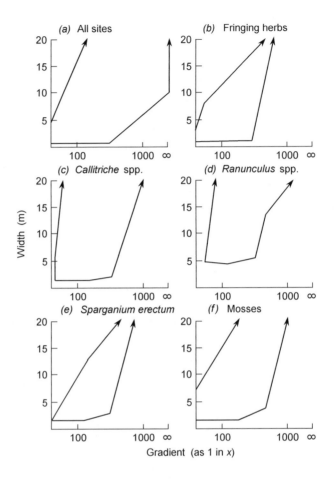

Figure 13.5
Width–slope patterns of hill
streams on resistant rocks.
For details see Figure 12.3.

Mosses have a large width–slope pattern, their habitat of large stones being common throughout upland and mountainous streams. *Callitriche* has a quite large pattern, as it grows both on stable medium-grained substrates and temporary silt or sand banks. *Myriophyllum alterniflorum* is an upstream species. Fringing herbs vary somewhat with rock type or topography.

On the banks of mountain streams, the most important plants are:

Filipendula ulmaria   *Phalaris arundinacea*
Juncus effusus   *Urtica dioica*

Locally important in the west of England are:

Apium nodiflorum   *Eupatorium cannabinum*

(*Epilobium hirsutum*, which is so frequent on soft rocks, is unimportant in the hills.)

Some controlling factors of plant distribution are illustrated well in the River Tweed (Figures 11.17 and 11.18). Megget Water, Yarrow Water and the River Tweed rise in hills over 600 m (2000'). The first two have falls from hill to stream of over 300 m (1000') in the upper reaches. Because of this great fall, water force is great, and angiosperms are almost absent and mosses sparse. A few tributaries without spate flow can bear dense fringing herbs and *Callitriche* on silt. The River Tweed has a lesser fall (nearer 250 m; 800'), and most sites recorded were on a channel slope flatter than 1:100. The force of water is thus less and fringing herbs and *Myriophyllum alterniflorum* are present, though sparse. (See also Holmes & Whitton, 1975a,b, and Haslam, 1982, for fuller and more detailed studies of the River Tweed.)

The Cheviot hills, lower in the catchment, are also over 600 m (2000'), but in contrast to those mentioned above their rainfall is less, 100–125 cm (40–50") instead of 125–150 cm (50–60"), and, more importantly, Oxnams Water, Kale Water, etc. have falls to the stream of only 60–120 m (200–400'). There is less moor than farther upstream, so perhaps a rather richer sediment. The main difference, however, is in the force of the water, which is less because the fall (and perhaps partly because the rainfall) is less. The streams bear a good vegetation of

Callitriche spp.	*Ranunculus* spp. (short-leaved)
Phalaris arundinacea	Fringing herbs

Resistant rocks outcrop over most of the Highland and Southern Uplands of Scotland, Wales, South-west England, the Lake District and part of the Pennines.

COAL MEASURES STREAMS

Coal Measures streams were usually polluted from the coal mines and associated industries. In the unpolluted areas the vegetation was sparse, and so is not easy to classify. Hill types range from lowland to nearly mountainous, though falls from hill to channel seldom exceed those of the upland category. Lowland tributaries could contain abundant vegetation:

With intermittent water: Tall emerged aquatics

With perennial flow: *Callitriche* spp.   *Lemna minor* agg.

 Potamogeton spp.   *Sparganium erectum*

In the hills, mosses were much less frequent than on resistant rocks (Table 13.2, Figure 13.6). *Callitriche* spp. were most frequent in smaller streams, as usual. *Sparganium erectum* is common. *Potamogeton pectinatus* was fairly frequent, except in streams with little water. This last species is characteristic of polluted sites, but it is not clear if it grows well in completely unpolluted parts of Coal Measures streams. The species

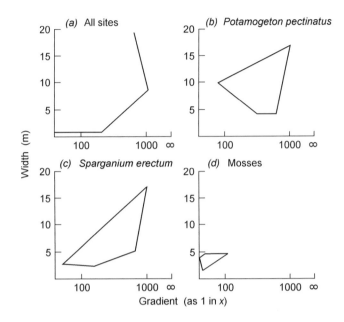

Figure 13.6
Width–slope patterns of Coal
Measures streams.
For details see Figure 12.3.

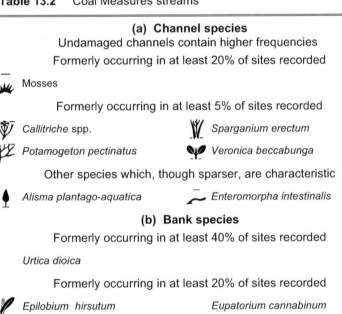

Table 13.2   Coal Measures streams[a]

(a) Channel species
Undamaged channels contain higher frequencies
Formerly occurring in at least 20% of sites recorded

Mosses

Formerly occurring in at least 5% of sites recorded

Callitriche spp.   *Sparganium erectum*

Potamogeton pectinatus   *Veronica beccabunga*

Other species which, though sparser, are characteristic

Alisma plantago-aquatica   *Enteromorpha intestinalis*

(b) Bank species

Formerly occurring in at least 40% of sites recorded

Urtica dioica

Formerly occurring in at least 20% of sites recorded

Epilobium hirsutum   *Eupatorium cannabinum*

a   See notes to Table 12.1

frequency was low. Over half the sites recorded were effectively empty, though about 10% of the sites were full of plants. Bank plants were infrequent also, but of this group *Epilobium hirsutum* and *Urtica dioica* are the most frequent, and *Juncus effusus* was not uncommon.

The main outcrops of Coal Measures are in the Pennines, South Wales and Southern Scotland.

Coal Measures streams were not re-surveyed for this study after the coal mines — therefore their pollution — were closed. A good deal of the heavy industry in the coal mine areas also closed. Other sources of pollution of course increased, but it is probable the vegetation is now of better quality.

LIMESTONE STREAMS

The most widespread hard limestone is Carboniferous limestone (Figure 13.7). It is a less pure limestone than chalk and most streams have a little non-limestone in the catchment (e.g. Millstone Grit, Boulder Clay). These streams have a somewhat higher trophic status for plants than does chalk and are closer to oolite streams (Chapter 12; Table 13.3). A lowland stream can be almost indistinguishable from a chalk one (compare Figures 11.7 and 11.14), and upland ones resemble those on upland sandstone (see below). In the upland streams fringing herbs are luxuriant, but because of the spates they are usually confined to the sides of the channel, growing in a carpet across the centre only where the water force is low. Several submergents may be frequent also.

Rorippa nasturtium-aquaticum agg. is the fringing herb which is the most likely to form carpets, to spread very rapidly and to be washed away in spates.

Callitriche spp. and *Ranunculus* spp. enter further downstream than in the lowlands, only where water volume increases and the flow is somewhat less fierce.

Figure 13.7
A hard limestone landscape (mountainous).

Table 13.3   Hard limestone species[a]

(a) Channel species
Upland channels have higher frequencies, mountain ones, lower

Occurring in at least 20% of sites recorded

Veronica beccabunga   Mosses

Occurring in at least 10% of sites recorded

Sparganium erectum

Occurring in at least 5% of sites recorded

Callitriche spp.   *Rorippa nasturtium-aquaticum* agg.

Ranunculus spp.

Other species which, though sparser, are characteristic

Apium nodiflorum   *Myriophyllum spicatum*

Groenlandia densa   *Zannichellia palustris*

Mimulus guttatus agg.

(b) Bank species
Occurring in at least 40% of sites recorded

Urtica dioica

Occurring in at least 20% of sites recorded

Filipendula ulmaria   *Phalaris arundinacea*

Occurring in at least 10% of sites recorded

Juncus effusus   *Rorippa nasturtium-aquaticum* agg.

---

a   See notes to Table 12.1

Groenlandia densa is characteristic, though infrequent. (It also occurs on limestone near Munich; Kohler *et al.*, 1971.) On soft rocks *Groenlandia densa* and *Potamogeton crispus* have a similar habitat range (see Chapter 12), but on hard rocks *Groenlandia densa* is found most on limestone while *Potamogeton crispus* is most frequent on sandstone and resistant rocks.

In the River Clyde system there are streams at *c.* 300 m (1000') with a low fall from hill to stream of only *c.* 60 m (200') so that flow is slow and thick silt may accumulate. The channels may be choked with, for example:

Potamogeton alpinus   *Sparganium emersum*

Potamogeton natans   *Sparganium erectum*

(*Ranunculus* enters where flow is swifter.)

Mountain-type vegetation occurs in lower hills here more than on any other rock type. In the North Yorkshire Moors it is found with hills only 300 m (1000') to 450 m (1500') high, but the more important determining factor is the fall from hill to stream, which at *c.* 250 m (800') is well into the mountainous category. Semi-mountainous streams can bear dense *Ranunculus* (including *Ranunculus penicillatus* ssp. *pseudofluitans*), some fringing herbs and some semi-eutrophic species (such as *Myriophyllum spicatum*) (Table 13.3). The same community, but with more fringing herbs, also develops in lower hills, where although storm flows are very deep their force is low (Figure 13.8). Mountain streams, in contrast, are almost barren, even more so than those on resistant rocks.

Downstream, trophic status increases, and in large rivers a semi-eutrophic vegetation may develop in flatter reaches where water force is lower, with, for example:

🅜 *Groenlandia densa*   🅟 *Zannichellia palustris*

🅜 *Myriophyllum spicatum*

A river with mountain limestone tributaries entering a flat alluvial plain was described in Chapter 11 (Figure 11.9). In the plain the streams, which are still small, have dominant *Ranunculus*, though the fluctuations in water level prevent fringing herbs from growing well.

Hard limestone streams are species-poor, rarely having more than 3–4 angiosperm species at the more spatey sites and most places with angiosperms having only one species. Half the sites recorded are effectively empty, and only 12% of them are full of plants. The width–slope pattern of all streams is large (Figure 13.8), and sites full of plants occupy a much larger area than usual (Figure 6.5). Some outcrops are in areas with low water force, and here the fertile rock and stable substrate encourage plant growth. The patterns for *Callitriche* and *Ranunculus* are fairly large. On the banks, *Juncus effusus* is less important than on the resistant rocks and *Urtica dioica* more important. This reflects the fact that limestone is much the more fertile rock.

The variation of vegetation with force of water is greater than on resistant rocks or Coal Measures. This is probably because limestone is a more fertile rock. Fierce flow, however, overrides any other factor, so the streams range from empty, through mesotrophic limestone, to a more nearly eutrophic habitat. The variation with geographical location is also considerable, but is mainly due to variations in water force and volume. For example, in the more southerly areas it so happens that water force is lower, and so vegetation is dense in both lowland and upland stream types, with *Ranunculus* being dominant. Most of the streams in north-east England, by contrast, are mountainous and empty, while those in north-west England have less

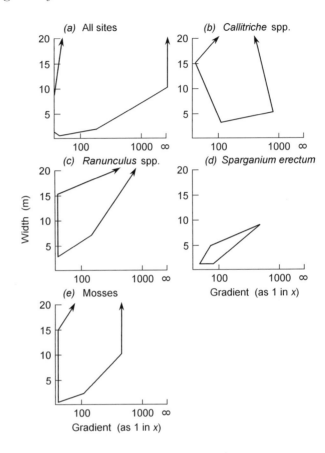

Figure 13.8
Width–slope patterns of hard
limestone streams.
For details see Figure 12.3.

water force and sparse vegetation including fringing herbs and
Groenlandia densa, as well as *Ranunculus*, etc. The Durness limestone
bears only small streams, the chief species being emergents which
include:

Caltha palustris	┼ *Juncus articulatus*
Filipendula ulmaria	🌱 *Mimulus guttatus* agg.

The main outcrops of hard limestone are the Carboniferous
limestone of the Pennines and northern England. The most southerly
region is the Mendip Hills, and the most northerly, the Durness
limestone, outcrops in the far north-west of Scotland.

SANDSTONE STREAMS

Old Red Sandstone is the most widespread hard sandstone, though
other types are locally important (Figure 13.9). There is more silt and
sand entering these streams than those on other hard rocks, and
consequently there is a greater quantity of sediment deposited in
sheltered areas and when flow slackens. Appreciable silting also

Figure 13.9
A hard sandstone landscape
(upland).

extends farther upstream, and in fact sandstone streams with a fall of 200 m (600') from hill to stream bed are likely to have an upland vegetation, though on other rock types they would have a mountain one. These streams are therefore more eutrophic. Because sandstone also tends to form lower hills, the rivers contain relatively more reaches where silting can occur than do those on other hard rock landscapes.

In relation to limestone, sandstone streams may either be more nutrient-poor (when there is swift flow and no silting) or more nutrient-rich (when there is slower flow and silting). Mosses are less common in sandstone than other hill streams (Table 13.4), presumably because sandstone beds are more easily eroded. Oligotrophic species are rare, if not absent.

Upland brooks typically have a rich fringing herb vegetation, and, if spates are low, these can grow across the bed. In contrast to chalk streams, however, these carpets are usually semi-emerged in shallow water. As on soft sandstone, *Callitriche* is more frequent than *Ranunculus*, though both are important. As water volume and trophic status increase downstream, *Ranunculus* increases and eutrophic species become prominent.

Myosotis scorpioides and *Veronica beccabunga* are the most important fringing herbs.

Callitriche spp. enter far upstream.

Ranunculus spp. enter below *Callitriche*, and usually occur only if other submergents are present. Short-leaved forms occur above long-leaved ones. This can dominate downstream.

Potamogeton spp., most often *Potamogeton crispus*, and *Sparganium emersum* enter downstream, and usually occur only if other submergents are present too.

Nuphar lutea, *Potamogeton pectinatus* and *Schoenoplectus lacustris* can grow well in lower reaches if flow is quiet and silting considerable.

Table 13.4   Hard sandstone species[a]

---

1 Except far north of Scotland
(a) Channel species
Upland channels have higher frequencies, mountain ones, lower

Occurring in at least 10% of sites recorded

Callitriche spp.   *Veronica beccabunga*

Sparganium erectum   Mosses

Occurring in at least 5% of sites recorded

Phalaris arundinacea   *Rorippa nasturtium-aquaticum* agg.

Ranunculus spp.

Other species which, though sparser, are characteristic of part of the range

Mimulus guttatus agg.   *Potamogeton crispus*

Myriophyllum alterniflorum   *Potamogeton natans*

Myriophyllum spicatum   *Sparganium emersum*

(b) Bank species
Occurring in at least 20% of sites recorded

Epilobium hirsutum   *Phalaris arundinacea*

Filipendula ulmaria   *Urtica dioica*

Occurring in at least to 10% of sites recorded

Juncus effusus

2 Caithness, etc.
(a) Channel species
Occurring in at least 20% of sites recorded

Juncus articulatus   Mosses

Sparganium erectum

Occurring in at least 10% of sites recorded

Callitriche spp.   *Mimulus guttatus* agg.

Equisetum spp.   *Myosotis scorpioides*

Mentha aquatica   *Potamogeton pectinatus*
                                 (larger channels. Dyke and North
                                 American habitat)

(b) Bank species
Occurring in at least 40% of sites recorded

Filipendula ulmaria   *Juncus effusus*

Table 13.4   Continued

Occurring in at least 20% of sites recorded

Caltha palustris		*Phalaris arundinacea*
Iris pseudacorus		*Urtica dioica*
Myosotis scorpioides		

Occurring in at least 10% of sites recorded

Ranunculus flammula   *Sparganium erectum*

a   See notes to Table 12.1

The effect of the fall from hill to stream is shown well by a comparison of the rivers Teme and Lugg, two adjoining rivers in the Welsh Marches. The River Teme has the larger catchment, and the fall in the lower reaches is *c.* 120 m (400'). *Ranunculus* is the dominant species. The River Lugg (Figure 11.18) has a quieter, more silty habitat in the lower reaches, with a fall of only *c.* 60 m (200'). Here eutrophic species are the most important, with *Ranunculus* only sparse and confined to the swifter parts (including ancient fords).

The River Tone (Figure 11.5) is a typical upland stream, except that there is an unusually large proportion of its length in the flood plain and, as it is sited in south-west England, *Apium nodiflorum* is the most frequent fringing herb.

The upland streams are slightly more species-rich than those on other hard rocks, with some sites having six or more species and the most frequent number (in sites where there are any plants) being two. Ten species are found in at least 5% of the sites recorded. The proportions of full and empty sites are similar to those on limestone. The width-slope patterns (Figure 13.10) include more of the flatter sites than those of other hard rocks.

Mosses have a wide habitat range, even though they are so sparse. *Callitriche* also has a large pattern, as on soft sandstone and chalk. *Sparganium erectum* is rather more restricted, presumably because of swifter flow. Fringing herbs decrease in sites liable to deep flooding. *Potamogeton crispus* and *Sparganium emersum* avoid the more extreme conditions. On the banks the more lowland plants (*Epilobium hirsutum*, *Urtica dioica*) are prominent, while the more mountainous species (*Juncus effusus*) is still frequent. Fringing herbs are frequent, as they are on chalk.

Where Old Red Sandstone forms a nearly lowland topography, slow flow and silting increase, and there are also increases in

Callitriche spp.		*Potamogeton natans*
Elodea canadensis		*Sparganium emersum*

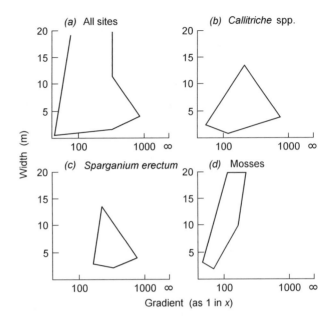

Figure 13.10
Width–slope patterns of hard
sandstone.
For details see Figure 12.3.

The low-lying parts of Caithness should be considered separately
from other areas. These have low water force but because the water is
stained very dark, plants cannot grow in deep water. Vegetation is
sparse, and in rivers plants are restricted almost entirely to the shallow
edges. The species present (Table 13.4) show that they are influenced
both by the sandstone and the effects associated with a combination of
very mountainous conditions (see above) and low scour. *Potamogeton
pectinatus* is not in its usual habit in British rivers, but in the shorter,
more delicate one of North American streams (see Plates 10, 11).

Mountain streams are few. Their substrate is somewhat erodible
and any sediment is unstable, so plants cannot anchor easily. No sites
recorded were full of plants and over 80% were empty. Mosses are
frequent where large stones can occur (in a small width-slope pattern,
Figure 13.9), but other plants are rare, though they do include
oligotrophic species, e.g. *Myriophyllum alterniflorum*). No typical site
bears submerged angiosperms.

The fall from hill to stream is again the most important factor
determining the plants of the mountain streams. For instance, one river
(River Rhee, Severn) has abnormally little vegetation considering that
its hills are only 520 m (1700') high and that the land is fertile grassland.
The fall, however, is *c.* 600 m (1000'), which is well into the mountainous
category.

Hard sandstones outcrop mainly in west England, the Welsh
Marches, northern England and much of central and eastern Scotland.

CALCAREOUS AND FELL SANDSTONE STREAMS

Compared with the other hard sandstones these streams contain more lime, and usually rise in lower hills. The vegetation is more eutrophic (Table 13.5) and is, of course, denser in streams not liable to spate.

Fringing herbs comprise nearly half of the more frequent species and *Rorippa nasturtium-aquaticum* agg. is particularly common.

Callitriche spp. are unusually low for sandstone.

Potamogeton natans is frequent, as is usual on sandstone.

Ranunculus spp. are frequent, but tend to be in flatter parts (Figure 13.8).

Sparganium emersum is the most frequent eutrophic species, as is usual on sandstone.

Sparganium erectum is frequent, but tends to be in flatter parts. Mosses are frequent, but tend to be in flatter parts.

On the banks, fringing herbs are much less common than on pure sandstone.

STREAMS ON MIXED CATCHMENTS

Many large rivers have more than one rock type in their catchment, and as is the case with soft rocks, mixed rock types lead to mixed vegetation types. However, as hard rocks have fewer species and less total vegetation than soft rocks, the effects on the plants are less, and are less easy to detect. In the hills, boulder clay is usually in scattered patches, too small, in comparison to the stream discharge, to affect the plants. Where, however, thick boulder clay covers most of the catchment, as in part of Anglesey, the vegetation is that of clay (see Chapter 12). The coarser drifts, e.g. moraines, have little effect on stream vegetation. When streams pass over different types of resistant rocks, topography may vary, and if so, plants vary also. Granite and basalt, for instance, form flatter country, and their streams contain more:

 *Callitriche* spp.   *Glyceria maxima*

Streams which have flowed over both sandstone and resistant rocks are necessarily usually large, and perhaps because of this have more *Ranunculus* and less fringing herbs than streams exclusively on one of these rock types.

Streams frequently rise on resistant rocks and later flow on to sandstone. When this happens, some species decrease with decreasing sandstone, for example:

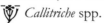 *Callitriche* spp.   *Sparganium erectum*

Potamogeton crispus

In mixed catchments, some species (excluding those whose distribution is related to stream size) are more frequent than they are on either rock type separately. Examples of such species are:

287

Table 13.5   Calcareous sandstone species[a]

(a) Channel species

Occurring in at least 40% of sites recorded

Mosses

Occurring in at least 20% of sites recorded

Veronica beccabunga

Occurring in at least 10% of sites recorded

Myosotis scorpioides   *Sparganium erectum*

Occurring in at least 5% of sites recorded

Potamogeton natans   *Rorippa nasturtium-aquaticum* agg.

Ranunculus spp.   *Sparganium emersum*

Other species which, though sparser, are characteristic

Callitriche spp.   *Polygonum amphibium*

Elodea canadensis   *Schoenoplectus lacustris*

Phalaris arundinacea   *Veronica anagallis-aquatica*

(b) Bank species

Occurring in at least 40% of sites recorded

Urtica dioica

Occurring in at least 20% of sites recorded

Epilobium hirsutum   *Juncus effusus*

Filipendula ulmaria   *Phalaris arundinacea*

Occurring in at least 10% of sites recorded

Sparganium erectum

---

a   See notes to Table 12.1

Elodea canadensis   *Sparganium emersum*

Potamogeton natans

On the banks, an increase in the proportion of resistant rocks produces an increase in

Juncus effusus   *Phalaris arundinacea*

and an increase in sandstone an increase in

Epilobium hirsutum   *Urtica dioica*

There are fewer streams which rise on sandstone and then cross on to resistant rocks. In these, with decreasing proportions of sandstone, *Rorippa nasturtium-aquaticum* agg. decreases. *Ranunculus* increases downstream, as it does on either rock type separately, but probably because of the increasing water volume and substrate stability rather than because of the mixed catchment. Sandstone and resistant rock streams may flow into each other, and the vegetation downstream of their confluence depends on the total proportion of the sandstone and on the flow regime, as described in Chapter 11. If over half the catchment is on sandstone then the vegetation is usually indistinguishable from that of sandstone streams. In small brooks on resistant rock with a short band of sandstone, little sediment is carried downstream, and sandstone vegetation can occur shortly after the boundary. Not many streams have catchments of both calcareous sandstone and resistant rocks, but those that do have a more diverse flora than streams entirely on calcareous sandstone, with more

Elodea canadensis   *Ranunculus* spp.

Enteromorpha intestinalis   *Sparganium erectum*

Myosotis scorpioides

and with less mosses. However, at least part of this difference is due to the larger size of the stream channels on mixed catchments. In streams on mixed limestone and resistant rock, mosses increase with the proportion of resistant rocks. The other differences observed (on mixed catchments there is less *Rorippa nasturtium-aquaticum* agg. and more *Ranunculus* and perhaps *Sparganium emersum*) may well be due solely to the increase in channel size.

The general effects of mixing rock types in different proportions are described more fully in Chapter 11.

STREAMS IN FLOOD PLAINS

Hill rivers have great fluctuations in depth in their flood plains. If silting is considerable then the substrate will be unstable, at least near the hills where water movement is greater, and so the plants present must be those species able to anchor securely to the bank. For example:

Phragmites australis   *Polygonum amphibium*

On deep stable silt the vegetation is likely to be lowland eutrophic in character (see Chapter 12). On a gravel bed with a swifter flow, likely species are:

Elodea canadensis   *Sparganium emersum*

Ranunculus fluitans

STREAM CLASSIFICATION

The topography of streams on hard rocks varies greatly, and so their vegetation is strongly influenced by flow regimes (Figure 13.1). For example, in many mountain streams the fierce flow keeps plants almost absent regardless of the type of rock in the catchment. As water force decreases, though, geological differences become increasingly important influences on vegetation.

One such influence that varies with rock type is silting. Silting increases trophic status. Consequently, as the water force decreases on each rock type and silt can be deposited, the streams become of higher trophic status (see Figure 13.1). There are two exceptions to this general pattern. The first arises because the flatter landscapes on resistant rock vary from acid bogs to fertile arable country, and as the sediment entering the stream from bogs is more oligotrophic than that from arable land, here it is the soil and land use that influence stream vegetation. The reasons for the other exception are less clear-cut. The Cheddar Gorge stream is on limestone with a lowland chalk vegetation, but, unlike the much longer upland limestone streams of north-west England, has no eutrophic species. However, this could well be simply because the Cheddar stream is too short to show downstream eutrophication. The colour of the water is also determined by land use and varies from clear to very dark brown (peat-stained). It is, however, only in northern Scotland that large streams are consistently sufficiently dark for this to have a regional effect on the plants.

14

Vegetation of channels with little flow

Dykes have little water movement, no scour and a fine substrate. Tall emerged monocotyledons dominate in shallow channels, and deeper or recently dredged ones can have a very diverse and variable vegetation dominated by submerged and floating plants. Undisturbed canals have a similar vegetation to dykes. Much management, whether by herbicides, boat traffic or other aspects of land or channel use, leads to species-poor watercourses.

Low-lying alluvial plains must have man-made drainage channels if the land is to bear good pasture or arable. These drainage channels have different names in different parts of Britain, but here we will adopt the names used in the Fenland, the largest such plain in the country. There the small channels between fields are called 'dykes', and the larger ones which collect dyke water and carry it to the rivers are 'drains'. (Channels used for navigation are called 'lodes', but their vegetation can be combined with that of drains.) Other common names are rhynes, in the west of England and South Wales (pronounced, and sometimes spelt, reens), and in the south of England, sewers. There is no effective scour from flow in these channels. Water may move freely by gravity, but in the larger plains there is usually a complex system of flood gates or pumps to ensure drainage. After heavy rain the water level may rise considerably but the water moves too slowly to do more than float off non-anchored plants.

The other main type of flat man-made channel is the canal, used for navigation. Canals usually lie above ground water level and so must have non-porous beds and sides, usually of clay, to prevent the water draining away. Their water levels vary less than those of drains, as they are not flood-relief systems. They receive little run-off, and excess water can drain from them. All these man-made channels have negligible flow, and require constant maintenance and management. Canals have low banks, because water level never fluctuates much, while dykes and drains may have high or low banks.

DYKES AND DRAINS

Dykes occur throughout Britain (Figure 14. 1; Table 14.1). The smaller and shallower ones often dry in summer. These typically bear tall emerged monocotyledons, either only one species or several, each dominating for short stretches. (Figure 14.2).

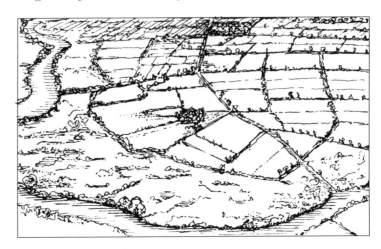

Figure 14.1
Alluvial plain with dykes, and marsh nearer the river.

Glyceria maxima is most frequent in dykes which are hardly more than shallow depressions, and mostly outside East England (except for the Silt Fens).

Phragmites australis is the commonest in the Fenland, Broadland and Romney Marsh, and in slightly deeper dykes than *Glyceria maxima*.

Phalaris arundinacea is rather less frequent than *Glyceria maxima* or *Phragmites australis* and is usually dominant only in dykes which are dry for most of the summer.

Epilobium hirsutum, *Urtica dioica* and other non-aquatics are found in dykes which are dry for most of the year.

Carex spp., *Scirpus* spp., *Sparganium erectum* and *Typha* spp. are infrequent and less likely to dominate long stretches of dyke.

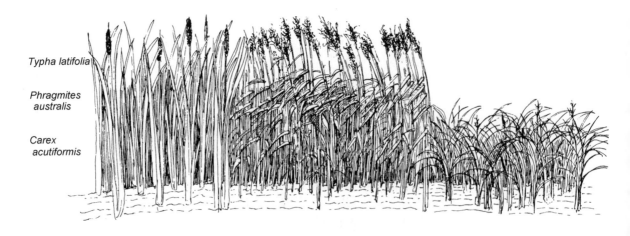

Typha latifolia

Phragmites australis

Carex acutiformis

Figure 14.2

292

Table 14.1   Dyke and drain species[a]

In the quarter century since these surveys, agriculture has become more intensive, and drainage is much more. Channels are deeper and drier. Vegetation is less and quite likely, different, especially in the most cultivated regions.

---

1 The Fenland
(mainly arable farmland)
Undamaged channels have higher frequencies
(i) Peat
(a) Channel species
Occurring in at least 20% of sites recorded

 Glyceria maxima   Phragmites australis

⊤ Lemna minor agg.   Sparganium erectum

Occurring in at least 10% of sites recorded

Alisma plantago-aquatica   Ceratophyllum demersum

Callitriche spp.   ∼ Enteromorpha intestinalis

 Carex acutiformis   Nuphar lutea

Other species which, though sparser, are characteristic

Elodea canadensis   Sagittaria sagittifolia

Myriophyllum spicatum   Sparganium emersum

Polygonum amphibium   Typha spp.

Potamogeton natans

and, in species-rich smaller dykes

Hottonia palustris   Potamogeton spp. (grass-leaved)

Myriophyllum verticillatum    Ranunculus spp. (short-leaved)

(b) Bank species
Occurring in at least 20% of sites recorded

 Glyceria maxima   Urtica dioica

 Phragmites australis

Occurring in at least 10% of sites recorded

Epilobium hirsutum   Juncus effusus

(ii) Silt
(a) Channel species
Occurring in at least 40% of sites recorded

 Phragmites australis

Occurring in at least 20% of sites recorded

Table 14.1 Continued

Agrostis stolonifera   Glyceria maxima

Callitriche spp.

Occurring in at least 10% of sites recorded

Enteromorpha intestinalis   Potamogeton pectinatus

Lemna minor agg.   Ranunculus spp.

Other species which, though sparser, are characteristic

Alisma plantago-aquatica   Potamogeton perfoliatus

Apium nodiflorum   Rorippa nasturtium-aquaticum agg.

Ceratophyllum demersum   Sagittaria sagittifolia

Myriophyllum spicatum   Sparganium emersum

Nuphar lutea

(b) Bank species
Occurring in at least 40% of sites recorded

Urtica dioica

Occurring in at least 20% of sites recorded

Phragmites australis

Occurring in at least 10% of sites recorded

Glyceria maxima   Phalaris arundinacea

(iii) Clay (at edge of plain)
(a) Channel species
Occurring in at least 20% of sites recorded

Apium nodiflorum   Phragmites australis

Callitriche spp.   Rorippa nasturtium-aquaticum agg.

Enteromorpha intestinalis   Sparganium erectum

Glyceria maxima   Veronica beccabunga

Phalaris arundinacea

Occurring in at least 10% of sites recorded

Agrostis stolonifera   Veronica anagallis-aquatica

Alisma plantago-aquatica

Other species which, though sparse, are characteristic

Myosotis scorpioides   Polygonum amphibium

Nuphar lutea

Figure 14.1 Continued

2 Somerset Levels
(when mainly pasture)
(i) Peat
(a) Channel species
Occurring in at least 40% of sites recorded

Lemna minor agg.

Occurring in at least 20% of sites recorded

Glyceria maxima   *Sparganium erectum*

Lemna trisculca

Occurring in at least 10% of sites recorded

Agrostis stolonifera   *Phalaris arundinacea*

Alisma plantago-aquatica   *Sagittaria sagittifolia*

Ceratophyllum demersum   *Spirodela polyrhiza*

Hydrocharis morsus-ranae (abundant stands)

(b) Bank species
Occurring in at least 20% of sites recorded

Glyceria maxima   *Urtica dioica*

Occurring in at least 10% of sites recorded

Phalaris arundinacea

(ii) Silt
(a) Channel species
Occurring in at least 40% of sites recorded

Lemna minor agg.

Occurring in at least 20% of sites recorded

Ceratophyllum demersum   *Potamogeton pectinatus*

Enteromorpha intestinalis   *Sagittaria sagittifolia*

Nuphar lutea   *Sparganium emersum*

Phalaris arundinacea   *Sparganium erectum*

Occurring in at least 10% of sites recorded

Callitriche spp.   *Potamogeton natans*

Elodea canadensis   *Spirodela polyrhiza*

Hydrocharis morsus-ranae (sparse stands)

Other species which, though sparser, are characteristic

 Alisma plantago-aquatica   *Schoenoplectus lacustris*

Table 14.1   Continued

Phragmites australis

(b) Bank species

Occurring in at least 40% of sites recorded

Phalaris arundinacea

Occurring in at least 20% of sites recorded

Phragmites australis

Occurring in at least 10% of sites recorded

Epilobium hirsutum   *Urtica dioica*

Glyceria maxima

3 Romney Marsh
(i) Silty, when mainly grassland
(a) Channel species

Occurring in at least 40% of sites recorded

Lemna minor agg.   *Phragmites australis*

Occurring in at least 20% of sites recorded

Agrostis stolonifera   *Enteromorpha intestinalis*

Alisma plantago-aquatica   *Glyceria maxima*

(10% level unsatisfactory)

Other species which, though sparse, are characteristic

Butomus umbellatus   *Lemna trisulca*

Callitriche spp.   *Nymphoides peltata*

Ceratophyllum demersum   *Potamogeton pectinatus*

Hydrocharis morsus-ranae   *Sparganium erectum*

(b) Bank species

Occurring in at least 40% of sites recorded

Phragmites australis   *Urtica dioica*

Occurring in at least 20% of sites recorded

Epilobium hirsutum

(10% level unsatisfactory)

(ii) Sandy, mainly arable, part brackish
(a) Channel species

Occurring in at least 40% of sites recorded

Enteromorpha intestinalis   *Lemna minor* agg.

Table 14.1   Continued

Phragmites australis

Occurring in at least 20% of sites recorded

Ceratophyllum demersum   *Potamogeton pectinatus*

Lemna trisculca   *Scirpus maritimus*

(10% level unsatisfactory)

Other species which, though sparse, are characteristic

Alisma plantago-aquatica

(b) Bank species

Occurring in at level 40% of sites recorded

Phragmites australis   *Urtica dioica*

(10% level unsatisfactory)

4 Pevensey Levels and nearby
(silty, when mainly grassland)
(a) Channel species

Occurring in at least 40% of sites recorded

Lemna minor agg.   *Phragmites australis*

Occurring in at least 20% of sites recorded

Glyceria maxima   *Sparganium erectum*

Hydrocharis morsus-ranae   *Spirodela polyrhiza*

Lemna minor agg.

Occurring in at least 10% of sites recorded

Agrostis stolonifera   *Polygonum amphibium*

Callitriche spp.   *Sagittaria sagittifolia*

Elodea canadensis

Species which, though sparser, are characteristic

Ceratophyllum demersum   *Potamogeton natans*

5 Norfolk, clay areas
(mainly grassland, some species locally very frequent — noted as local)
(a) Channel species

Occurring in at least 40% of sites recorded

Phragmites australis

Occurring in at least 20% of sites recorded

Callitriche spp.   *Myriophyllum spicatum*

Lemna minor agg.

Table 14.1   Continued

Occurring in at least in 10% of sites recorded

 Apium nodiflorum

 Enteromorpha intestinalis (local)

 Hippuris vulgaris (local)

Myriophyllum verticillatum (local)

 Phalaris arundinacea

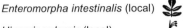 *Potamogeton pectinatus*

Rorippa nasturtium-aquaticum agg.

Scirpus maritimus (local)

 Sparganium erectum

6 Other areas

Prominent species in dykes of South Wales (silt, grassland)

Alisma plantago-aquatica, Callitriche spp., *Glyceria maxima, Hydrocharis morsus-ranae, Lemna minor* agg., *Potamogeton pectinatus, Sparganium erectum*

Prominent species in dykes of Essex marshes (clay, arable and grass)

Alisma plantago-aquatica, Apium nodiflorum, Callitriche spp., *Enteromorpha intestinalis, Lemna minor* agg., *Phalaris arundinacea, Phragmites australis, Rorippa nasturtium-aquaticum, Scirpus maritimus, Sparganium erectum*

Prominent species in dykes of Yorkshire plains (clay, silt, etc.)

Callitriche spp., *Epilobium hirsutum, Lemna minor* agg., *Rorippa nasturtium-aquaticum* agg., *Sparganium emersum, Veronica anagallis-aquatica, Veronica beccabunga*

Prominent species in dykes of Strine plain, Salop (silt)

Agrostis stolonifera, Glyceria maxima, Juncus effusus, Phalaris arundinacea

a   See notes to Table 12.1

Dykes which occasionally dry for short periods may bear a few submerged or floating plants, for example:

 Callitriche spp.

Lemna spp.

 Ranunculus spp. (short-leaved)

Dykes and drains which are normally flooded and are unpolluted show much variation in vegetation as a result of different habitat factors. These factors and their effects are described below.

Depth

In small channels up to 0.5 (–1) m deep, tall emerged monocotyledons are not confined to the sides by scour and flow as they are in flowing streams, and are able to dominate. Thus, if the channels are to be kept clear, human interference is necessary to restrict these plants to the side fringes. So when these channels bear submerged and floating plants, as most do, the occurrence of these different types of vegetation is

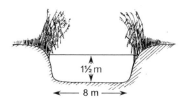

Figure 14.3

dependent on management. On steep banks of deep drains it is impossible for them to spread into the channel, so killing them with herbicides (as is often done) is quite unnecessary (Figure 14.3; also see Chapters 16 and 18).

The submerged and floating dyke species include both plants more frequent in shallow water (e.g. *Callitriche* spp.) and ones more frequent in deep water (e.g. *Nuphar lutea*). If the water level is stable, a species-rich flora of submerged plants can be present in only *c.* 25 cm of water. Usually, however, water level fluctuates, and species-rich communities occur in water normally at least 0.5 m deep. If a dyke does dry in summer, but conditions are otherwise suitable for a species-rich community, the plants present will be short emergents such as:

Alisma spp.   *Rumex* spp.

Juncus spp.   Short grasses

Ranunculus sceleratus

Width

Channel width as such has little effect on the plants, though a wide channel is also more likely to be deep. If fringing herbs are present they are more likely to become luxuriant in narrow channels. They are emerged, and so anchored only at the banks. Loosely anchored patches are blown away in strong winds and large patches are more likely to remain in place if anchored to both sides of the dyke (Figure 14.4). *Rorippa amphibia* and *Rorippa nasturtium-aquaticum* agg. are the most frequent species.

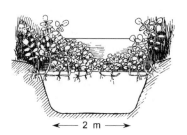

Figure 14.4

Turbidity

Turbid water decreases the light reaching the bed, and so prevents submerged plants from growing in deep channels. Turbidity is more important in drains than streams because drains are usually steep-sided and, unlike most streams, do not then have any shallow water at the sides of the channel where light can penetrate turbid water sufficiently for plants to be able to grow.

In dykes, lack of water movement means that upward growth of submergent plants is easy. Thus if a plant can become established on the bed, it can grow into brighter light and then do well. Turbidity, therefore, does not have any gradation of effect: either a submergent cannot grow on the bed, or it can potentially grow luxuriantly in the dyke (Figure 14.5). Species do, however, differ in the amount of light which they require (see Chapter 7). Those tolerating turbid water best usually have leaves above the water which can receive full light, e.g. emergents at the edges and, in the centre:

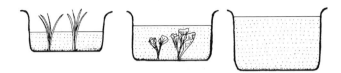

Figure 14.5

🍃 *Nuphar lutea*   ⌐ *Sparganium emersum*

🌱 *Sagittaria sagittifolia*

The species-richness of emerged and floating plants in turbid dykes is independent of the turbidity, provided toxic pollution is absent.

The water in dykes and drains may seep in through the soil of the alluvial plain, in which case it will usually be clear when it emerges into the channel, or it may come down in streams from the higher land around. One cause of the high turbidity in the Pevensey Levels, for example, is the very turbid water of the clay streams feeding them. Water in peat plains, such as part of the Fenland, is usually clear, but may, however, be stained brown, and if so has the same light-blocking effect on the plants as turbid water. In still water, especially when the larger plants are killed by herbicides, phytoplankton can grow well and these make the water turbid. Another effect of killing edge plants by herbicides is that it makes the banks less stable, and the fine particles washed into the channel as a result may also add to the turbidity. Boats often stir up silt on the channel bed, and thus create high turbidity. Turbid and clear-water dykes are sometimes found together. This can happen when turbid river water has access to part of a dyke system, or when herbicides have been used on just part of a dyke. The turbid dykes then usually have both less total vegetation and fewer species present than those with clear water (also see Chapter 19).

Substrate type and trophic status

Dykes and drains have fine-textured substrates, their beds being the subsoil of the alluvial plain together with any deposited sediment. The subsoil may be sand, mineral silt or organic matter, sand being the least frequent. The Fenland and the Somerset Levels, for instance, are partly on peat and partly on silt. The ground level of the channel is raised by sediment from the land being washed in during storms and lowered by intermittent dredging, but because scour is absent the substrate can be consolidated by root wefts in a way which is impossible in flowing waters (see Chapter 3).

In general peat dykes tend to be mesotrophic as do silt ones which do not receive eutrophic or polluted water (Figure 14.6). Mesotrophic dykes are characterised by:

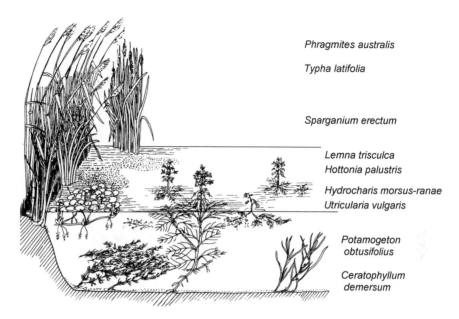

Figure 14.6
A mesotrophic peat dyke.

Lemna trisulca   *Hydrocharis morsus-ranae*

Both these however, may be absent, and Hydrocharis morsus-ranae is increased by dredging. Other typical species include:

Ceratophyllum demersum   *Spirodela polyrhiza*

Hottonia palustris   *Stratiotes aloides*

Potamogeton spp. (grass-leaved)   *Utricularia vulgaris*

The dykes of intermediate nutrient status, on e.g. clay, sand, slightly eutrophicated silt or eutrophicated peat, tend, if they are species-rich, to have (Figure 14.7), for example:

Callitriche spp.   *Myriophyllum verticillatum*

Ceratophyllum demersum   *Potamogeton natans*

Elodea canadensis (luxuriant growth)

Enteromorpha intestinalis   *Potamogeton pectinatus*

Lemna minor agg.   *Sagittaria sagittifolia*

Myriophyllum spicatum   *Spirodela polyrhiza*

The most eutrophic dykes and drains are on silt, often with some source of eutrophication (Figure 14.8). Typical species include:

Enteromorpha intestinalis   *Potamogeton perfoliatus*

Lemna minor agg.   *Sagittaria sagittifolia*

Nuphar lutea   *Sparganium emersum*

The larger species, however, prefer fairly deep channels.

301

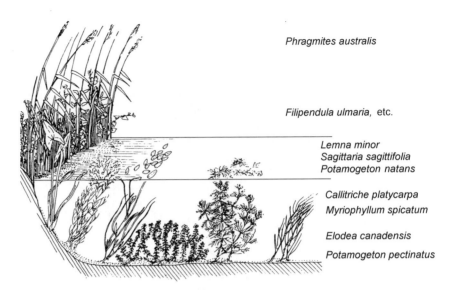

Phragmites australis

Filipendula ulmaria, etc.

Lemna minor
Sagittaria sagittifolia
Potamogeton natans

Callitriche platycarpa
Myriophyllum spicatum

Elodea canadensis

Potamogeton pectinatus

Figure 14.7
A semi-eutrophic dyke.

These groups are neither consistent nor exclusive, but they do illustrate the general trends as seen in, for example, the Somerset Levels dykes on peat, silt and eutrophicated silt.

Potamogeton pectinatus has a different distribution in dykes from that discussed in earlier chapters for streams. Here it is in a different form, with shorter leaves and shoots, and is usually very much finer and more delicate. Its occurrence is sporadic and is most frequent after dredging and in brackish water. In Romney Marsh, which still received sea water flooding early the twentieth century, the delicate form of *Potamogeton pectinatus* is frequent. In East Anglia, in dykes near the coast which receive sea water flooding every decade or two, *Potamogeton pectinatus* is often dominant, in a short but coarse form.

Geographical differences

Here, only the larger alluvial areas are being considered. More differences would arise if small flood plains with only one or two dykes were included in the comparison.

A few species are almost confined to one part of the country, for example:

Azolla filiculoides	South and Southwest England (spreading)
Nymphoides peltata	East England
Stratiotes aloides	East Anglia

Other species have habitat preferences, which affect their distribution within an alluvial plain. For example:

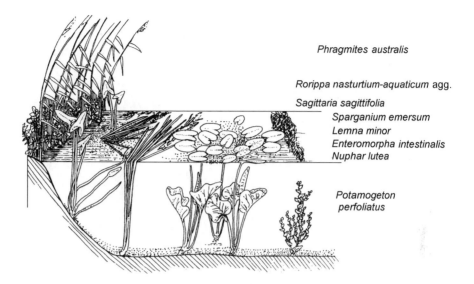

Phragmites australis

Rorippa nasturtium-aquaticum agg.

Sagittaria sagittifolia
Sparganium emersum
Lemna minor
Enteromorpha intestinalis
Nuphar lutea

Potamogeton
perfoliatus

Figure 14.8
A eutropic silt dyke.

Scirpus maritimus	Rare or absent far inland, frequent towards the coast, e.g. Essex, Norfolk. In Romney Marsh, perhaps commoner on sand than on clay.
Fringing herbs	Mainly at the edge of the plains, where dykes receive some water from the incoming streams. Sporadic occurrences elsewhere sometimes occur on locally higher ground.

Management

All dykes and drains are, or were, managed, and the frequency and depth of dredging, the frequency and season of cutting, and the type, season and frequency of herbicide application all affect the vegetation. The effects are discussed in Chapter 18.

Species-richness

Dykes may be choked with plants or empty, depending on the drainage pattern and management. Drains in use, however, must be kept clear as they are then able to carry more water. The plants are kept down partly by direct management and partly by making the channels deep and steep-sided so that the habitat is unsuitable for river plants. A variety of means have been used for direct management, both mechanical and chemical. It is generally observed that mechanical methods do not decrease species diversity, unless habitats unsuitable for plants are created (e.g. deep and turbid drains). Chemical methods, on the other hand, eliminate many species, and were used in some parts of the

303

country for a long time before modern herbicides were available. Pollution (agrochemicals, hard surface run-off, effluents, etc.) and turbidity, also eliminate many species (see also Chapter 19), and herbicides appear to be a common cause of species-poor dykes. There is a correlation between the proportion of these and the variation in herbicide use in different areas.

The plants most likely to be present in species-poor dykes are:

Agrostis stolonifera   *Enteromorpha intestinalis*

Callitriche spp. (less)   *Lemna minor* agg.

(Also, as described above, shallow dykes left unmanaged will become species-poor as a result of domination by tall monocotyledons such as *Phragmites australis*.)

The species-rich dykes are those which are kept fairly clear of tall plants by mechanical means, are not polluted or much eutrophicated, have a usual minimum water depth of at least 20 cm, and are not shaded from the banks. Such dykes are likely to contain many, often 10–12, submerged and floating species. Species characteristic of, but rare in, dykes tend to occur together, rather than to be scattered evenly throughout the dyke sites recorded. This is attributable to human interference making the species-poor dykes unsuitable for the less vigorous plants. It is the species-rich dykes which are described in the following section on patterns and communities.

Patterns and communities

In dykes, and to a lesser extent in the larger drains, the plant communities vary in both space and time. There are seasonal differences in the time at which species reach their maximum size, e.g.

Callitriche spp.	Maximum in spring
Hottonia palustris	Maximum in late spring
Myriophyllum spp.	Maximum in summer
Rorippa amphibia	Maximum in late summer

The differences in communities within the growing season are more prominent in dykes than in streams, as there are fewer other checks to growth in the dykes.

Because of the absence of flow, plants can occur at all levels within the water, and also above it (Figure 10.2; Figures 14.5–14.7). In a channel full of plants the upper layer will, therefore, shade the lower. The emergents are of course the tallest plants, and their effect depends on the intensity of the shade they cast (see Chapter 7). The effect of floating plants varies somewhat with the species, for example:

Enteromorpha spp. and *Lemna* spp. can be thick enough to prevent other plants growing below.

Callitriche spp. are submerged as well as floating. The floating leaves form an incomplete cover, but the submerged ones, mainly in the upper part of the water, add to the shade so that only shade-tolerant species grow below.

Potamogeton natans also forms an incomplete cover, but its submerged parts cast little shade.

There is also a characteristic group which grows in the upper part of the water. For example:

 Lemna trisulca   *Myriophyllum spicatum*

Hottonia palustris   *Ranunculus* spp.

(*Ranunculus* spp. belong in this group because they are usually delicate and unable to remain rooted because of dying from the base. Detached shoots therefore float to the surface and grow there. See Chapter 3.)

Finally there are the plants occupying mostly the bottom of the water. These are often shade-tolerant. They include, for example:

 Ceratophyllum spp.   *Potamogeton* spp. (grass-leaved)

 *Elodea canadensis*

In what appears to be the traditional conditions for such communities, many species grow well but none becomes the sole and dominant species — except in shallow dykes with tall emerged monocotyledons. The most prominent species may vary from year to year at the same place. This may be from several causes. For example, one species may find the weather unsuitable and be replaced by more tolerant plants (e.g. *Myriophyllum verticillatum* killed in a hot summer and replaced for a few years by *Elodea canadensis* and *Fontinalis antipyretica*); there may be changes after cutting (e.g. *Lemna* spp. replacing *Callitriche* spp.); and there are usually changes after dredging (described in Chapter 18), for example:

Hottonia palustris replacing *Callitriche* spp.

Ceratophyllum demersum replacing *Myriophyllum verticillatum*

Potamogeton natans replacing *Myriophyllum spicatum*

In streams, plant patterns within a reach are usually repetitive and are composed of the same few species, both the patterns and the species usually being controlled by simple habitat factors. In a short stretch of dyke, however, there can be a series of dominants within an apparently uniform habitat. For example, within 75 m were found (Figure 14.9):

 Callitriche spp.   *Myriophyllum verticillatum*

Hottonia palustris   *Phragmites australis*

 Lemna spp.   *Filamentous algae*

305

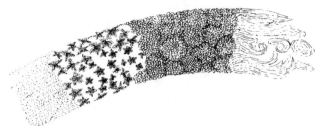

Blanket weed
Callitriche sp.
Hottonia palustris
Lemna minor

Figure 14.9

This variation of community is an important feature of dykes. In dykes, also, species occur together which in streams have different habitat preferences. For example:

Alternative habitat:

	Lemna trisulca	Chalk brooks
	Nuphar lutea	Slow-flowing silted eutrophic rivers, e.g. on clay
	Potamogeton natans	Particularly in sandstone streams
	Ranunculus aquatilis	Most frequent in sandstone or swift hill streams

CANALS

Canals are similar in size to drains, but can be allowed to bear more vegetation as they are not needed for the drainage of flood water (Figure 10.2; Table 14.2). If boat traffic is dense, however, plants are sparse or absent (see Chapter 18), and in some canals vegetation is reduced by serious pollution (see Chapter 19). Vegetation, as always, varies with depth. Ship canals are few, and are too deep and turbid to bear much vegetation, so they are not described here. Disused canals tend to silt up, and are commonly dominated by *Glyceria maxima*. The pleasure boat (once commercial) canals are *c.* (1–)1.5 m deep, and may have a varied and rich vegetation. As in dykes, water may become turbid from incoming particles, from pollution, or from boats whose movement stirs up silt on the bed. When bottom silt is disturbed, less light reaches the bed, poorly anchored plants are uprooted, and when the silt settles it tends to smother plants in the water. Under such disturbance, submerged plants are lost first and tall deep-rooted emergents remain the longest. Species which are more frequent in clearer water include:

Ceratophyllum demersum		*Myriophyllum spicatum*
Elodea canadensis		Mosses

Table 14.2 Canal species[a]

Navigation has much increased since these 1970s surveys, and vegetation has correspondingly decreased.
(Sites with severe pollution or dense boats are excluded.)

(a) Channel species
Occurring in at least 40% of sites recorded

Lemna minor agg.   *Sparganium erectum*

Occurring in at least 20% of sites recorded

Ceratophyllum demersum   *Rumex hydrolapathum*

Glyceria maxima   *Sparganium emersum*

Nuphar lutea

Potamogeton pectinatus (including mildly polluted sites)

Occurring in at least 10% of sites recorded

Carex acutiformis   *Enteromorpha intestinalis*

Elodea canadensis   *Sagittaria sagittifolia*

(b) Bank species
Occurring in at least 20% of sites recorded

Epilobium hirsutum   *Glyceria maxima*

Filipendula ulmaria   *Urtica dioica*

Occurring in at least 10% of sites recorded

Phalaris arundinacea   *Sparganium erectum*

a   See notes to Table 12.1

There is usually a band of emergents at the sides of canals, generally wider than that found in drains since canals often have a small ledge of shallow water at their sides on which the plants can grow. Plants of shallow water are, however, restricted in that they cannot grow beyond this ledge (Figure 10.2). A fringe of tall plants adds to the amenity value of a canal, improves the stability of the banks, and does not hinder navigation because boats usually keep to the middle, except for passing and mooring. Floating and submerged plants are also mainly at the sides, both because of the boats (their propellers damage the plants) and because of the shallower water there.

The more mesotrophic canals are those which are neither on clay nor comprise part of a river system. The most mesotrophic are on peat, and their characteristic species include:

Ceratophyllum demersum   *Potamogeton natans*

Hydrocharis morsus-ranae   *Spirodela polyrhiza*

Lemna trisulca   *Stratiotes aloides*

These canals have more species-rich sites than the other groups. The most northerly lowland canals, (Forth–Clyde and Union) have a rather different flora.

The eutrophic canals are those on clay. The vegetation is like that of clay streams of equivalent size, though more still-water species may be present. The characteristic species include:

Enteromorpha intestinalis   *Sagittaria sagittifolia*

Nuphar lutea   *Sparganium emersum*

 Potamogeton pectinatus

In canalised rivers the ground level changes and there are intermittent locks, beside each of which is a swifter stretch with a weir. As the boats pass through the lock surplus water flows over the weir. The swifter reach has vegetation like that of a clay stream of equivalent size, and usually has more *Schoenoplectus lacustris* and less *Sagittaria sagittifolia* than the slow reach by the lock.

In the third type of canal, plants are almost or completely absent. The Caledonian Canal in the Scottish Highlands has a stone and gravel bed, deep water, and negligible vegetation.

15

Uses and benefits of river plants

River plants, like other native vegetation, are natural heritage of the country. They add biodiversity. They are part of the natural ecosystem of the river, and if the one is to be preserved, the other must be also. Briefly, the reasons why plants may be unwanted are if they hinder the passage of water for drainage purposes, or hinder boats, anglers, etc. The benefits of river plants are that they anchor in, and stabilise, channel banks; provide shelter, a substrate, and sometimes food, for invertebrate animals; and their clumps purify pollution; shelter fish, can protect some fish while they are spawning, and can provide invertebrates as food. Some plant species can be used as food for man, birds or other animals, or as medicines for man.

The amounts of vegetation which do not cause flood hazard are described for different stream types.

Plants also have considerable aesthetic value, adding to the beauty and amenity of the riverscape with their varying textures, patterns and colours.

SOIL STABILISATION

Plant roots and rhizomes stabilise the substrate on the banks and on the channel bed. On the banks particularly they are most important for preventing erosion, and their loss often means major expenditure on bank maintenance. The tall monocotyledons or trees are the most effective group of plants for preventing erosion, followed probably by the shorter grasses. Silt banks, e.g. on silt alluvial plains, are perhaps the least stable of the common types of banks and so most care is needed to stabilise these.

During storm flows large bushy plants with poor anchorage are liable to be torn from the banks and the gaps left can start an erosion cycle. Where banks are deliberately cleared of plants, for example by the use of herbicides on dyke banks, then the risk of erosion may be serious. In narrow channels the stabilising effect of tall plants or bushes on the banks may be outweighed by the flood hazards they create, so the best protection from erosion then is trees and grass swards (see Chapter 14), which are able to stabilise the banks well while offering little resistance to flow. Though plants may also stabilise channel beds, their effect here is less than it is on the banks and they are not such an important factor in the maintenance of the watercourse. An exceptional situation is where boat traffic is dense over a silt bed. Here the silt is protected from disturbance while plants are present but if the plants are lost the disturbance prevents any recolonisation.

WATER PURIFICATION

When plants die they decompose. The dead organic matter is also a necessary part of the ecosystem, and dissolved substances are released from this into the soil and water.

Because water plants take nutrients from the soil and water, it is possible to use them for lowering the nutrient status of the water body where eutrophication has been great. This is done simply by allowing the plants to take up the nutrients during growth and then cutting and removing them from the water. The method is effective if the plants concerned grow very quickly, so as to fill the water body before their season for rapid growth comes to an end, and they are then removed as soon as the water is full. The plants are then allowed to grow again, both nutrients and other unwanted dissolved substances (such as compounds more toxic to animals than plants) having been removed from the habitat. This has proved successful in countries with hot summers, using submerged plants (e.g., McNabb & Tierney, 1972, in ponds).

River plants often oxygenate the water, and influence the concentration of dissolved carbon dioxide and the pH (Westlake 1960, 1965). The oxygen released by the plants is used by animals and by bacteria on decaying organic matter. If the oxygen demands of the water are great, as when organic effluents enter the stream, plants are most important for increasing oxygen.

The more complex cleaning by water and wetland plants was first noticed and demonstrated in rivers (Seidel, e.g., 1956–7). In those days, much German sewage was still discharged raw (untreated) into rivers, and Seidel noticed and recognised that thick beds of *Scirpus lacustris* were cleaning this pollution quicker than river reaches without plants. This important research was followed: and now created wetlands are used world-wide for water purification, where space is adequate and money is not (Standard Treatment Works are more expensive but need smaller areas).

Most of the later evidence and proof has been on wetland plants with a little, in warmer climates, on floating ones (e.g., Athie & Corrie, 1987; Cooper & Findlater, 1990; Hammer, 1989; Haslam, 1987, 1990, 2003; Mitsch, 1994; Moshiri, 1993; Neori, 2000; Reddy & Smith, 1987; Rubec & Overend, 1987; Vymazal, 2001; Vymazal *et al.*, 1998). River plants are both those emergents on which work has been done (e.g. *Phragmites australis, Typha* spp.) and the water-supported species which have had little research — though observation in the rivers shows they are effective. All species tested demonstrate cleaning, with different species differing somewhat in the cleaning of different substances.

So, how do plants clean, that is, remove pollutants from the water reaching them? Pollutants are filtered, transformed, adsorbed and stored, in various degrees. This happens:

1. by the micro-organisms living on the plants.

   They live on shoots and, much denser, on roots — but flowing river water passes more by the shoots than by the roots. The microbial population varies with (a) the plant species: chemistry of surface and exudates and (b) the pollutants passing by. (When pollution type changes in the effluent of chemical factory, it takes about three weeks for the microbial population to change to be that one most capable of feeding on, and so altering, the incoming pollution.)

   These microbes are widely distributed, and, generally speaking, will quickly occur in quantity once their food base arrives. Alternative microbes may be available to do the same process in different conditions, e.g., *Azotobacter* fixes nitrogen well at over pH6 and with abundant organic matter, and *Clostridium* fixes it at low pH.

   What can the microbes do? Nitrogen compounds, particularly simple ones like nitrate and ammonia, are broken down and the nitrogen leaves as the gas. Many complex chemicals, including toluene, chloroform, benzene, are broken down and the products are simpler and (usually, not always) less toxic. Chemicals like heavy metals may be bound, and effectively removed from circulation (while conditions are stable). All these clean water.

2. by the periphyton, the algae growing on surfaces in the water, both inorganic (silt, boulders) and organic (plants).

   If vegetation is present, obviously the greater part of the surface is plant. The algae remove and store many nutrients and heavy metals, etc. When stored chemicals return to the system on the death of the plant, they are often in more acceptable forms.

3. by the plants themselves, which may take up complex chemicals.

   This process has been studied for pesticides and heavy metals in land plants (e.g., DDT, Asulam), and may be assumed for others. If these chemicals are broken down, or if the plants are cut and removed, the toxicity may leave the system.

   Plants have gas exchange round their green parts. Oxygen reaches their roots and the zone outside them. This all aids transformations and cleaning.

4. by the soil.

   This also receives pollution, through the depositing of larger, pollutant-bearing particles (on silt, and pollutant particles themselves), and by adsorption from the water. Indeed in a normal polluted river most pollution is in the silt, from which it reaches the substrate below and so the plant roots, and the periphyton and microorganisms in the soil surface. Denser microorganisms mean cleaning is faster per unit area (see Haslam, 2003, for a further discussion).

River habitat also influences the amount and type of purification. Soil texture determines how much chemical is held in the river (see Chapter 8). Soil composition (nutrients, calcium) influence chemical processes, as do the type and amount of organic matter in the bed and held in the vegetation. Flow and, to a lesser extent, depth do so also.

The power of river plants to purify is easily demonstrated by walking downstream from effluent discharges, and seeing the change in vegetation, its improvement in diversity and change in species, and finally, in suitable conditions, its return to the community present upstream of the effluent (see Chapter 19). Sites can be compared using different amounts and types of vegetation.

Unfortunately (see Chapter 19), so much pollution enters rivers, not just as effluents but also as agricultural and hard surface run-off, that it is very difficult for the self-purifying ability of a river to completely clean it: long stretches with no contamination are needed, and in settled and agricultural areas these are rare indeed. Wetlands with water flowing through the soil are far more effective at purifying, because the soil is so rich in both microorganisms (roots, surfaces, soil (less)), and variable chemical habitats (aerobic/anaerobic, etc.). That done in rivers, though, is very important to the health of the ecosystem. It is the only purification most diffuse-source pollution receives. Animals, plants and public health all depend on it. It is free — and so generally unnoticed and ignored. When removed, however, it becomes noticeable.

Slowish flow through many beds of vegetation, and over a long distance (meanders, not straight channels) give a longer residence time of the pollutants near the plants, and so better cleaning. Factors increasing vegetation aid purification.

Highland areas with little vegetation and swift flow are well-oxygenated from that flow, and considerable cleaning takes place.

Water cleaning, self-purification, is perhaps the most important, and least regarded use and benefit of river plants for people.

PLANTS AND ANIMALS

The small invertebrate animals found in streams usually live on the surfaces of plants and stones in the watercourse and in the soil. Thus the more plants there are, the greater the surface area available and, generally, the more invertebrates there will be. Some invertebrates actually feed on the plants, though there are others that eat particles in the water, or other animals. Plants may also act as protection for a particular phase in the life cycle (e.g. eggs, larvae) of some species, where these would otherwise be eaten by other animals or (as in the case of mosquito eggs) washed away. Other species, such as dragonflies, use emerged plants to crawl up out of the water on when they change from their aquatic larval stage to the winged adult stage. In chalk streams it has been shown that the species of invertebrates present are not directly related to the species of plants, although their distributions are correlated because both are related to the flow type. In a chalk stream the plants — whatever their species — have more mayflies (Ephemeroptera) and blackflies (*Simulium*) in flow, while plants in sheltered places have more freshwater shrimps (*Gammarus*). However, in some still-water dykes some invertebrates may be associated with specific plants, and here animal conservation implies plant conservation.

Plants are a great benefit to some fisheries, increasing the food supply of the fish by increasing the invertebrates. In highly eutrophic water that already contains large quantities of detritus and algae, however, they are less necessary. They also provide shelter from storm flows, protection from predators for small fish, and for some species a sheltered environment for spawning. Some fish feed directly on the plants. Anglers tend to prefer fine-leaved species (e.g. *Myriophyllum* spp., *Ranunculus* spp.). This is partly through a misapprehension that these contain more food organisms (while, as explained above, it is in fact the flow type that primarily controls the distribution of both plants and invertebrates) and partly because if plants are dense the fine-leaved species are less hindrance to angling than, for example, the large floating leaves of *Nuphar lutea*.

Birds often feed on the fruits and shoots of river plants (Table 15.1) and emergent plants provide shelter both for the birds themselves and for their nests (also see Haslam, 1973a,b, and the section on recommended vegetation below).

FOOD FOR PEOPLE

Some plants can be used as food or medicine for man (Table 15.2). In Britain, however, watercress (*Rorippa nasturtium-aquaticum* agg.) is the only plant widely used now.

FERTILISER

Submerged and floating plants are soft and soon decompose when removed from the water, so they can be used as compost and fertiliser for fields near the streams. Unfortunately rubbish (tins, bottles, polythene, etc.) is often too abundant for this to be feasible, as the rubbish cannot be removed cheaply from the plant mass and the weight

Table 15.1   River plants eaten by birds

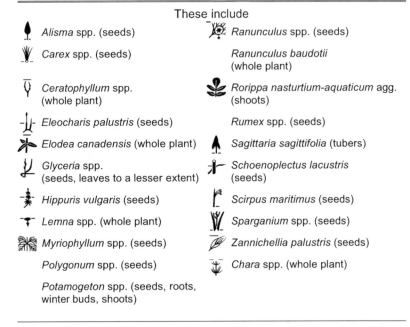

These include

Alisma spp. (seeds)	*Ranunculus* spp. (seeds)
Carex spp. (seeds)	*Ranunculus baudotii* (whole plant)
Ceratophyllum spp. (whole plant)	*Rorippa nasturtium-aquaticum* agg. (shoots)
Eleocharis palustris (seeds)	*Rumex* spp. (seeds)
Elodea canadensis (whole plant)	*Sagittaria sagittifolia* (tubers)
Glyceria spp. (seeds, leaves to a lesser extent)	*Schoenoplectus lacustris* (seeds)
Hippuris vulgaris (seeds)	*Scirpus maritimus* (seeds)
Lemna spp. (whole plant)	*Sparganium* spp. (seeds)
Myriophyllum spp. (seeds)	*Zannichellia palustris* (seeds)
Polygonum spp. (seeds)	*Chara* spp. (whole plant)
Potamogeton spp. (seeds, roots, winter buds, shoots)	

Swans, etc. eat shoots of many superficial plants.

Table 15.2   River plants eaten by man

These include:

Species	Part(s) used	Use
Acorus calamus	Underground parts	Medicinal
Butomus umbellatus	Underground parts	Medicinal
Glyceria fluitans	Seeds	
Phragmites australis	Underground parts	
Rorippa nasturtium-aquaticum agg.	Shoots	Food
Sagittaria sagittifolia	Underground parts	
Typha spp.	Pollen, underground parts	

These are British plants but their use is not necessarily British.

of the plants makes it impractical to move cut plants far from the river. It is also possible to process the plants to varying extents in order to produce, for example, poultry food supplements, mulch or commercial fertiliser (e.g. Lange 1965; Little 1968), but these attempts have met with only limited success.

CRAFT

The tall emerged monocotyledons have many possible uses if they are available in sufficiently large quantities. In Britain the chief use of *Phragmites australis* is for thatching, next for screening, while baskets and chair seats can be made from *Schoenoplectus lacustris*. Other crafts can produce many items from boards and mats to bird cages and all species can be used for animal bedding, packing material, insulation for horticulture, etc.

AESTHETIC VALUE

River plants add to the beauty of the landscape and are ornamental when transplanted to newly cleared areas or used as cut plants. The pleasure of a canal holiday is enhanced by water-lilies and reedswamp fringing the waterway. Unfortunately, dense boat traffic destroys vegetation in canals, rivers and lakes, though some protection can be given by baffles, etc. The plants also add to the pleasure of other activities in or beside the water, such as fishing, picnicking or walking, and may provide the habitat necessary for the birds wanted by bird-watchers. The variety and colour provided by river plants are usually much appreciated and it is unfortunate that the extent of this appreciation is usually not recognised until the plants are nearly lost, when it may be difficult and expensive to restore them.

VEGETATION SATISFACTORY FOR DIFFERENT STREAM TYPES

The main reason plants are sometimes considered undesirable in watercourses is the obstruction they can cause to water movement, boats, anglers and river gauges, sluices etc. The ways in which they can improve the watercourse are by stabilising banks and channels; providing food, substrates and protection for animals; oxygenating and purifying the water; adding to the aesthetic value; conserving rare species and biodiversity; and occasionally providing plants for practical use such as food, crafts, etc. The optimum vegetation is therefore that which produces as many of the desirable effects and as few of the undesirable effects as possible. The relative importance of each factor varies in different watercourses, and other influences may be important — for instance, swift rocky streams oxygenate water and so the function of plants in oxygenation is less important.

Mountain and upland streams

In the hills, the upper reaches are usually fairly swift, and natural oxygenation is good. Spate flows have sufficient force to sweep away thick vegetation before damaging floods occur and angling can take place unless plant cover is very thick. It is therefore quite satisfactory to have channels with the normal natural maximum vegetation. If, however, flow is regulated, and spates are decreased in force or frequency, vegetation may become too dense. If rainfall, and consequently spates, are low for a decade or so (as in the 1960s), then again vegetation may come too thick for angling, and river gauges. In the flood plains downstream, the river banks are alluvial, and tall fringing monocotyledons are advantageous for stabilising the soil. If spate flows have little force then thick vegetation may intensify the effect of floods.

As the flow decreases, oxygen in the water comes increasingly from plants. Passing down from the hills the particle size of the substrate decreases, so that as the boulders and stones disappear, animals requiring shelter rely more and more on plants. On the other hand, as flows get less there is some decrease in the need for shelter from flow, though the need for protection from other animals remains.

Chalk streams

Their vegetation, particularly *Ranunculus*, can grow very dense and create serious flood hazards. From the angler's point of view *Ranunculus* is, almost, necessary, but also can grow too dense and need to be controlled. The plants which occur naturally are those best suited to providing good food for fish, though after severe damage it may be advisable to import plants for recolonisation (see Chapter 1). In ordinary circumstances, if chalk streams have too few plants to support good fish populations, the remedy is to improve the physical characteristics and chemical quality of the river, and the plants will then invade and spread within a few years. In lower reaches the banks are on stable soil and subsoil, and though a fringe of tall plants is desirable, it is less essential than on banks more prone to erosion.

Sandstone streams (lowland)

Depending on the stream, the recommendations vary between those for chalk and for clay, for the reasons given in those sections.

Clay streams

Clay covers much of lowland Britain, and so receives much of the country's organic and industrial effluents into its streams. Because the streams have slower flows than those on chalk, oxygenation from plants is important in ordinary conditions as well as for purifying effluents. However, thick plants in warm water can cause serious deoxygenation at night, when plants are taking up but not producing oxygen. Stream discharges are also less, and effluents often enter in brooks upstream; thus small, and even large streams may be composed mainly of effluents liable to cause deoxygenation. Plants are usually sparse in the upper reaches and confined to the shallower sides in lower reaches, so although *Nuphar lutea* may be a nuisance to anglers when abundant at the sides, the plants are seldom a flood hazard — except where slow silting flows lead to large stands of tall monocotyledons. Plants are needed to protect animals, and in some parts to increase the animal food supply, though again the slow silting stretches are an exception, for here there may be sufficient detritus for the food supply even without plants. Banks are often alluvial on lower reaches and so stabilisation by plant stands is advisable.

Canals

In the centre, plants, if present, must be submerged and short to allow the passage of boats. On the other hand, boating on the canals means boats will usually do all the weed control necessary. Indeed, the destruction of canal plants by boat traffic may lead to bank erosion, and the need for more piling, etc. There is negligible water movement, and some inflow of effluent, so plants are important for cleaning (provided they are not too thick) and, as usual, for protection. As in the clay streams, the more eutrophic and detritus-rich channels have less need of plants to increase the food supply. Emerged or floating plants at the side can cause nuisance to anglers, but never constitute a flood hazard, as canals do not receive storm waters, and in general give much pleasure to those boating on, or walking by, the canals.

Dykes and drains

In primary channels, the need for drainage water to move freely takes precedence over all other considerations, so few plants are permissible. Minor channels lying outside the main drainage system may bear high-quality vegetation and fauna. However, banks are usually alluvial and unstable, and stabilisation by plants is particularly important. Tall plants in narrow channels create obstructions to flow, but a narrow band in wide, deep channels should be encouraged. Trees and grasses are the best plants for stabilising the banks. The considerations for fishing and for oxygenation and cleaning of the water are the same as those for canals.

16

Flood hazards created by river plants

Watercourses can be choked by vegetation, and then cause damage to low-lying surrounding land through ponding and flooding. The amount of vegetation which is safe from this point of view depends on the flow regime. Dykes and drains need to be kept clear if much water must move through them; lowland streams are generally safe if they are not more than a quarter full of plants; and in the mountains, spates can normally remove any amount of vegetation, so channels away from habitation can safely be choked with plants during low flows.

Plants can obstruct the flow of water and create flood hazards in various way: channels may be choked by emerged plants, or by floating and submerged ones; banks and edges may be covered by tall plants; cut river plants, land plants, branches, etc. may be washed downstream and become lodged to cause obstructions; or shoals may be deposited because plants are present. Plants that have become a nuisance can be removed or decreased by dredging, cutting, use of herbicides, shading by trees (see Chapter 18), having water too turbid or deep for river plants to grow in the channel. It is easy to increase catchment run-off by more intensive agriculture, more hard surface, and straightening, and less floodable land for storm water storage; and then to wreak vengeance on the wicked rivers and vegetation which flood house or crop. It is important to know exactly when plants do or do not constitute a hazard and need to be controlled. For example, many stretches of streams are prevented from developing choking vegetation because the flow, substrate or some other habitat factor prevents this, and yet often the plants along such stretches are routinely cut. Thus time and money could be saved by a greater botanical understanding of the river plants. Again, in many reaches, a distinction can be made between potentially explosive populations, which may create a hazard, and non-invasive sparse plants which are not hazardous. Channels which have been much altered by recent management have unstable plant populations, and the vegetation may be expected to change.

Once rivers have had their beds deepened and channellised, water level is lower in the ground, and consequently can rise much higher without causing a hazard — and this deepening is now common. Pollution has become more widespread in the past three decades, so this also, by lessening vegetation, has lessened flood hazard.

HAZARDS FROM PLANTS 'IN SITU'

Surplus water can occur as a result of either ponding or flooding. Ponding occurs when, although flow may be small, choking vegetation causes a rise in water level. This is commonly of the order of 30–50 cm, though 2 m has been reported (Figure 16.1). It is harmful when land becomes waterlogged and under-drainage systems are destroyed, and farm production is reduced. Flooding results from run-off being unable to move freely along the channel after heavy rain. In contrast to ponding, the effect may be quite independent of the plants, may be increased by the plants, or it may be due only to the plants, as happens when the weight of water eventually forces its way through plants after land near by has been flooded for a while (Figure 16.2). The damage caused by both ponding and flooding varies according to the type of land affected, being least if the land is unused, usually little if it is pasture and most if it is built over. Thus planning for flood prevention means taking land use as well as water levels into account. For example, in some built-up areas it may be an advantage to have water held up by plants if this means that storm water floods farming land upstream rather than the built-up area.

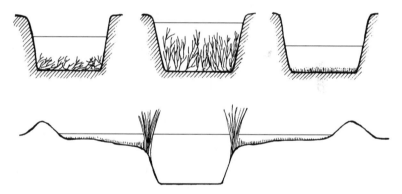

Figure 16.1

Figure 16.2

    The levels of land and water affect the height to which water may rise with safety. In a little-drained chalk river where there may be less than a 50 cm difference in level between the surrounding land and the water level before cutting plants, a pile-up of only 30 cm of water would create a flood hazard in a severe storm, whereas 30 cm is a negligible variation in level on the flood plain of a large hill-river with banks several metres high.

    Before removing plants that are flood hazards the effect of the removal and the most desirable vegetation for the watercourse should be considered. Without management, vegetation is usually thickest between June and September, but cutting can itself lead to greater weed growth and so the cutting of plants which are not flood hazards at the

319

time of the cut may actually create a flood hazard later. Also, if one type of river plant is removed, another often takes its place, e.g. emergents are replaced by submergents which are then replaced by algae. (Also see Chapters 5–8 and 20.)

WATER MOVEMENT THROUGH VEGETATION

Any obstruction in a channel decrease its ability to transport water. Even sparse plants increase the roughness of a channel, and the greater the roughness the less the discharge which can pass through it (Figure 16.3). If the plants are thick then although the water can flow freely above the plants it percolates only slowly through the plants themselves. This means that the effective size of the channel, upon which the discharge depends, is that of the part without plants (Figure 16.4).

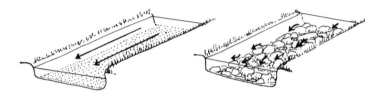

Figure 16.3

If plants in a channel are to be cut, this can be done in various ways. (See Chapter 20 for conservation cutting.) They can be cut almost at ground level, or part way down, or narrow deep channels may be cut in the centre of the bed (Figure 16.4). Because narrow deep channels carry more water than wide shallow ones of the same cross-sectional area of free water, this type of cutting is preferable, other things being equal. When narrow deep swathes are cut by weed-cutting launches, a double swathe carries more than twice the water of a single swathe. Again, uncut channels with plants only at the sides carry more water than equivalent channels where the plants are spread evenly over the floor (Figure 16.4).

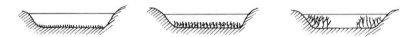

Figure 16.4

The degree to which plants obstruct water movement depends on the type of plant, as well as on its position and its bulk. Resistance to flow increases the greater the perimeter of the plant parts in the water, and thus a fine-leaved species like *Ranunculus* is a greater obstruction to flow than the same weight of a large-leaved species like *Nuphar lutea* (Figure 16.5). Hindrance to flow can also vary with season, being greatest in mid-summer when the plant parts are most rigid. Note that there is an important distinction, when considering resistance offered to flow, between the effect on the stream, as described here, and the effect on the individual plant, as described in Chapter 3. It was explained above that a certain weight of *Ranunculus* causes more ponding than the same weight of *Nuphar lutea*, but the streamlined shoots of *Ranunculus* are much less liable to damage from velocity pull than the bushy ones of *Nuphar lutea*.

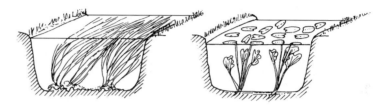

Figure 16.5

OTHER FLOOD HAZARDS FROM PLANTS

Material being washed downstream can create obstructions, particularly where the channel is constricted, and may cause flooding. Some of this material is vegetation, such as filamentous algae, floating plants (e.g. *Lemna* spp.), cut river plants left in the channel, and crop debris, straw bales, branches and other plants washed in from the land. There is also rubbish of various kinds — even including caravans! It is the large and firm objects like trees and bales of straw — and not the river plants — that cause the worst flooding. Material in the channel can also cause blockages in sluices, etc., which can, particularly in flash floods, cause flooding by decreasing the amount of water that can pass through the sluice. Gauging stations can be blocked in this way.

Plants accumulate silt, and this can also cause a flood hazard if accumulated in large quantity. The amount depends on the flow type, the amount of sediment passing through the habitat and the type of plant. Emergents accumulate the most, particularly if their above-ground parts are still present in winter.

DYKES AND DRAINS

The gradient along dykes and drains is very small, values between 1:10 000 and 1:40 000 being common, so gravity is often inadequate to move enough water for drainage and pumps or flood gates are needed. The habitat can he considered as a long narrow pond, and because water moves so little under gravity, ponding is likely when there is extra water for some reason. (Because of the lack of slope, the difference between ponding and flooding is less than in other types of watercourse.)

321

For drainage purposes, all hindrances to water movement must be minimised, and this includes keeping plants sparse or absent. The only important exception is that dykes at the head of a drainage system, which receive little or no water from outside and merely pass their water to a lower dyke, can be choked with plants. Also, in the west and north where most plains are small, dykes are liable to some scour during storm flows from the hills, and if these can wash away plants then the dykes can, between storms, be more nearly choked with plants without causing flood hazards.

All types of river plants are much more of a flood hazard in dykes than they are in streams, but as the emergents accumulate most silt, and obstruct flow even when the water level has risen, they usually hinder water transport most. Tall plants on the bank create the greatest flood hazard in narrow dykes, because the banks occupy more of the cross-sectional area of the watercourse as the water level rises (Figure 16.6). They hinder flow and are dragged by flood water, and if pulled out into the channel impede water movement there. Short plants, in contrast, can serve the same function in preventing bank erosion without creating this hazard. In wider drains the banks occupy less of the cross-sectional area (Figure 16.7) and larger channels are likely to be too deep for emergents anyway, except in a narrow band by the bank, so both tall (e.g. *Phragmites australis*) and short (e.g. *Alisma* spp.) emergents can grow at the sides without impeding water transport, provided they are non-invasive in the drain concerned. Sparse non-invasive plants can also be permitted in the channel. The main drains which collect water from a wide area, however, must be able to transport it quickly and so must be kept almost empty of plants.

A cover of free-floating plants (e.g. *Lemna* spp.) hardly decreases the capacity of the channel to move water and can be useful because its shading effect prevents submerged plants from growing below. In wider dykes and drains, though, particularly in exposed places or where the plant cover is thin, wind may blow the cover so that parts of the water surface are left clear and plants are able to grow below. Such a cover is only a nuisance where water has to pass through pumps, flood gates, or other constrictions which could be blocked by the plants.

CANALS

Canals receive little run-off and have stabilising channels which prevent much alteration in the water level. Because they do not normally have the function of moving water, they can safely contain more vegetation than drains. Floods are prevented by the general management procedures rather than by the absence of plants.

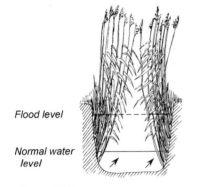

Flood level

Normal water level

Figure 16.6

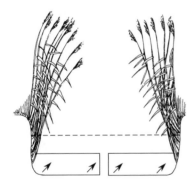

Figure 16.7

LOWLAND STREAMS

Lowland streams have a continuous flow of water under gravity, even though some stretches may be tide-locked or have water retained by gates, and because of the force and flow of the water, much more vegetation is permissible than in dykes. However, although storm flows may damage plants, enough vegetation may be left behind to represent a flood hazard. More damage to the surrounding land can usually be expected from ponding than from flooding, and ponding is frequent in areas liable to choking plants if streams are not managed. Streams which can potentially have choking vegetation occur in a definable width-slope pattern (Figure 6.5). If other factors are suitable, flatter streams up to *c.* 20–30 m wide and under *c.* 2 m deep may be choked, but outside this range management for flood control would seem unnecessary. The non-permissible amount of vegetation is that bulk which could, during a spell of warm weather, grow to a dangerous level. In general the vegetation is considered safe if the stream is 25% full (i.e. when looking at the stream it appears that 25% of the water volume is occupied by plants). This level provides enough plant material for the conservation of the plants themselves, and the invertebrates, fish and other animals dependent on them.

There are several patterns of plants which constitute a safe level of vegetation (Figure 16.8):

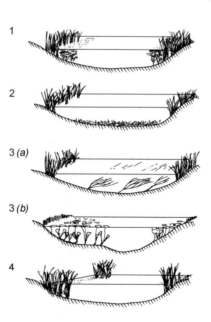

Figure 16.8

1.   Floating and submerged plants at the sides, as in many clay streams.
2.   A continuous layer of submerged plants, as in many chalk streams in winter.
3.   Sparse plants growing throughout the water.
4.   Emergents at the side.

The first is the arrangement most efficient for water transport. It is, however, characteristic of clay streams, and chalk streams often have the advantage over clay streams in terms of a steeper slope to the channel and therefore a faster flow. If the surrounding land is such that moderate ponding or flooding does no harm, choking plants are safe. Tall herbs on banks of narrow brooks cover a good deal of the channel cross-section when water level rises (Figure 16.6), but it is usually sufficient for the banks to be cut in late summer or autumn, before the winter storm flows begin, and summer growth causes trouble only when the bank is steep, storm flows are deep and shading is little.

Chalk streams usually have a good flow throughout their length. Typically the substrate is stable, the water clear and its depth not great, so submerged plants occur right across the channel (Figure 10.2). Growth is potentially very rapid, and backing up of water by the plants is common, usually leading to rises of 30–50 cm. Tall emerged monocotyledons are seldom troublesome. Brooks usually have coarse substrates, little silting and fast flow, which confines luxuriant emergents to local silted areas, and rivers often have steep non-silty banks, which confine the tall emergents to narrow non-invasive bands (Figure 10.2). Emergents tolerating the coarse substrate (particularly *Schoenoplectus lacustris*) may occur in the channel, but as long as the shoots are sparse enough to be beaten down by the storm water (and do not exceed the permitted bulk of vegetation) they do not create a flood hazard. Temporary flooding can be caused by *Rorippa nasturtium-aquaticum* agg., but even the low force of storm flows in chalk streams can wash away carpets of this species. In chalk streams, flood hazards are most likely to be created by submerged plants.

Clay streams typically have less fall and slower flow, a more fluctuating flow regime and more water retention, more suspended and deposited sediment, and a less stable substrate. The emerged plants are more troublesome than on chalk. Small brooks with little slope and soft beds can be completely choked and downstream the emergents at the sides accumulate silt and spread to form large stands. Dense stands are not flattened by ordinary storm flows and may cover most of the channel width, thus creating a flood hazard. Brooks with steeper slopes generally bear little or no vegetation, though fringing herbs are locally luxuriant and may impede flow, particularly in winter. Usually, however, dense vegetation is found only in the silting downstream stretches. Clay species are typically coarse-leaved, causing less resistance to flow than the fine-leaved species typical of chalk streams. They also tend to be shorter (1–2 m long, compared to 3–5 m for the usual length of *Ranunculus* choking chalk streams), which means less choking occurs on clay and so less management is usually required. Plants normally grow right across the channel only if the water is *c.* 75 cm deep, the low light and unstable substrate in the deeper areas confining plants to the sides, so the floating and submerged plants often keep within the safe quarter-full limit without any management. In at least some parts of Britain, removal of *Nuphar lutea* is discouraged. With its large leaves and long flexible stalks it is a plant that causes little resistance to flow, and its removal, by dredging or herbicides, would probably result in its being replaced by species that impeded water flow more. In general, flood hazards in clay streams are most likely to be created by things washed in from the land, though emergents are locally troublesome.

Sandstone streams tend to resemble chalk ones in plant type, but to have fewer species and less bulk of vegetation (see Chapter 12). Emergents are often intermediate in amount between those of chalk and of clay.

Lowland streams on resistant rocks are more likely to have flood hazards created by oddments washed in from the land than by plants in the streams.

UPLAND AND MOUNTAIN STREAMS

The force of water in these streams during severe spates can wash away any vegetation, and so flooding is usually caused by blockages of branches, fallen trees, crop debris and other rubbish being carried downstream rather than by rooted plants. In some upland streams, though, vegetation can become very dense between spates in the slower stretches, and ponding is a possible hazard. And even in the hills (usually upland rather than mountain) there may be some brooks which do not receive scour and become choked with emergents that cause local nuisances and may need management. In the flood plains below, flooding is frequent unless the channel is embanked, but this is not much affected by plant growth.

The width–slope patterns (Figure 6.5) show that the wider flatter channels do not become choked, their substrates being unstable. Sandstone and limestone streams can, however, be full in rather flatter sites than can streams on resistant rocks. Fine-leaved submergents are common in the channel, but tall emerged monocotyledons are usually restricted to the banks of slower stretches and the sides of some slower brooks.

17

Changes in flow patterns

Flow regimes can alter as the result of abstraction, the construction or removal of weirs, sluices, reservoirs, etc., changes in land use and catchment management, drainage, channellisation, etc., the regulation of flow, the transfer of water from one river to another, or annual variations in rainfall. The effect of altering the discharge varies with the type of channel. Variations in silting alter nutrient status and the type of substrate available for roots to anchor in, while variations in flow type alter the velocity pull, battering and scour which influence the plants.

The effects of these changes on the vegetation can often be predicted.

STRUCTURES IMPEDING FLOW

A water mill is an ancient way of controlling the flow of a stream, when a weir with gates crosses the river. In the mill stream the water may be allowed to build up above the mill so that the maximum water force is available to turn the wheel when the gates are opened. Consequently flow is slower above, and faster below the mill, and there may also be a deep mill pool below, or, less often, above. Three habitats are thus created by the mill which differ in flow, substrate and trophic status from the original stream (see Chapters 2, 3, 4 and 9 for effect of these factors on plants) and consequently differ in their vegetation. For example, *Potamogeton pectinatus* was able to grow in a silted stretch of stream above a mill when the original stream — a near-clean chalk brook — was a mesotrophic habitat unsuitable for its growth. Where a mill stream is separated and narrower than the main river, resembling a minor tributary, its soil quality is the same as that of the main channel so it may bear vegetation unduly eutrophic for its size. Other sidestreams may be created for irrigation, navigation supply, etc. and for ornament and they are influenced similarly, though the last may also have foreign species planted in them for ornamental purposes.

Weirs, sluices and other flood gates are other impediments to flow. Their chief uses are for irrigation, drainage, flood control, navigation, ornament, fish pools and abstraction. Their main effect on the stream is that flow is slower above and faster below them (Plate 7). In hill streams species are frequently able to colonise the stretches of slower flow above small weirs in sites lying outside their width–slope pattern. For example:

Potamogeton alpinus   *Sparganium emersum*
Potamogeton polygonifolius

Lowland streams have at least intermittent slow stretches, and the vegetation above the weir is the same as this. Some rivers, particularly lower stretches of clay streams, have structures at close enough intervals to retain deep slow water between them. The vegetation is that of deep slow silted rivers.

Flow may be varied from year to year when the gates controlling flow in a single channel are opened differently or when those controlling a stream with several channels (e.g. braided rivers, mill streams) alter the proportion of the water entering each channel. Such variations cause changes in the vegetation. Examples of this are:

a) Braided stream — the relative proportions of *Elodea canadensis* and *Ranunculus penicillatus* ssp. *pseudofluitans* in the minor channel varied with flow type and silting.

b) Mill stream — the minor channel had, in different summers:
    (i) *Ceratophyllum demersum* dominant in a slow silted flow;
    (ii) *Zannichellia palustris* abundant in water that was shallow with a moderate flow and sandy substrate (the silt having been washed away);
    (iii) *Myriophyllum spicatum* and *Ranunculus fluitans* colonising the sand; and
    (iv) in a flow that was again slow and silted these species becoming very unhealthy, particularly *Ranunculus fluitans*.

c) Single channel — with *Myriophyllum spicatum*, *Potamogeton pectinatus* and *Ranunculus penicillatus* ssp. *penicillatus*. In summers with shallow swift water *Ranunculus penicillatus* ssp. *penicillatus* dominated, while *Myriophyllum spicatum* increased when the water was almost still.

d) Single channel — with a carpet of *Berula erecta* in water less than 50 cm deep above a sluice. When the water depth was increased to *c.* 75 cm for over a year, *Berula erecta* grew much more slowly, and since erosion is easy in older patches (see Chapter 3), the carpet was almost destroyed through the lack of new shoots.

If minor changes in flow regime fall inside the tolerance limits of a plant then there is little overall effect on the vegetation, but if changes are more drastic, or if they move a site outside the tolerance limits of a species, then the vegetation alters markedly. The effect is greatest if the change is between a turbulent eroding flow and a slow silting one. A turbulent flow can be created both by increasing the discharge and by lowering the water level (which increases the influence of stones, etc. on the bed). In several chalk-clay streams it was found that in summers when there were shallower more turbulent waters *Ranunculus* and other chalky species increased and when there were deeper silting flows clay species increased.

Reservoirs are usually sited upstream and the water flowing from them is controlled. This means that both drought and storm flows are usually decreased and thus the substrate is stabilised also. This allows vegetation characteristic of a slower flow type to develop. In hill streams, plants increase. For example:

🌱 *Callitriche* spp. ✿ *Ranunculus* spp.

🌿 *Myriophyllum* spp. 𝌆 *Sparganium emersum*

And in a lowland stream a reservoir altered:

Ranunculus –Zannichellia palustris to *Enteromorpha – Sparganium emersum*

Reservoirs sometimes substantially alter the general quality of the stream water, and this may affect plants also. Dark-stained water decreases plant growth in deeper places (see Chapters 7 and 13). Alterations in temperature and dissolved gases are unlikely to be sufficient to alter the vegetation. The extent of the effect of a reservoir on a river depends on the proportion of the total river discharge which comes from the reservoir. The effect is greatest and persists the farthest downstream if the other tributaries are few and small, but if there are many large tributaries joining the river below the reservoir then the regulatory effect of the reservoir will decrease as each enters. This may mean that plants can grow well in the stable substrate just below a reservoir, but then disappear as soon as a stream of comparable size joins the river. If much water is let out of a reservoir very rapidly, the effect is that of a damaging spate flow, and recovery could take some years (see Chapter 5).

The vegetation changes expected when flow is regulated can be predicted from the information in Chapters 2–6 and 12–13.

LOWERING OF THE WATER LEVEL

The ground water table in lowland Britain has fallen substantially during the past century as the result of man's activities, and this has affected the stream vegetation. Years of low rainfall have a similar effect. In the hills, man's use of the water is less and the rainfall is higher than it is in the lowlands, so the effect on the plants is also less than in the lowlands.

The lower discharges and spate flows which the lower water level causes in the hills lead to denser vegetation, both over a single summer (e.g. Ayrshire River Purification Board, 1968) and over a decade or so (e.g. several northern rivers such as the River Eden, Cumbria, in the mid-1970s). The damage done to a single chalk stream by the lowering of the water level is charted in Figure 17.1 for the River Darent (Thames Water Authority). Figure 17.2 illustrates the situation diagrammatically. Plates 8a, b show the early stages of this effect in another chalk stream.

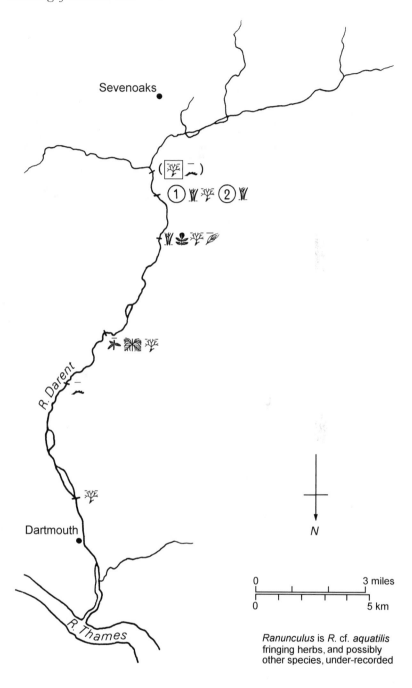

Figure 17.1a
Lowland chalk river.
River Darent (Thames); 1969.

Ranunculus is *R.* cf. *aquatilis*
fringing herbs, and possibly
other species, under-recorded

329

Figure 17.1b
Lowland chalk river.
River Darent (Thames); 1972.

Ranunculus is *R.* cf. *aquatilis*

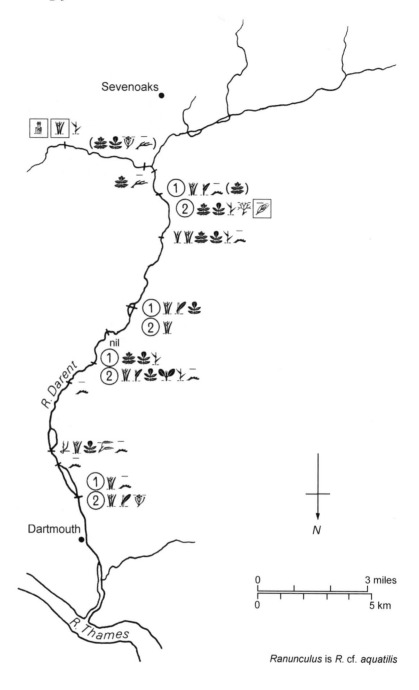

Figure 17.1c
Lowland chalk river.
River Darent (Thames); 1974.

Ranunculus is *R*. cf. *aquatilis*

331

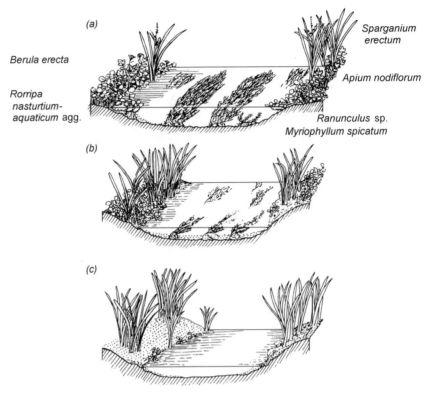

(a)

Berula erecta

Rorripa nasturtium-aquaticum agg.

Sparganium erectum

Apium nodiflorum

Ranunculus sp.
Myriophyllum spicatum

(b)

(c)

Figure 17.2
Changes in a chalk stream due to a fall in water level.
(a) Original state.
(b) First stage after the fall in water level.
(c) Second and stable stage after the fall in water level.

River Darent

a) 1969 — Survey unfortunately scanty and done during storm flow, but *Ranunculus* was frequent.

b) 1972 — Flow had decreased, the water was slower, and the substrate silty. *Ranunculus* had decreased (though at one site this was due to children paddling) and the few *Ranunculus* shoots seen were small, as is usual in slow flow. These small shoots cannot form a dense root weft, and are likely to become at least partly rooted in the silt above the gravel bed (see Chapter 3). *Myriophyllum spicatum* was frequent. This roots in silt more than in gravel and does not form a stabilising root weft, which, together with the bushiness of the shoots, means that plants are easily swept away by velocity pull (see Chapter 3). (The good growth of *Myriophyllum spicatum* in this chalk stream was attributable to the unusual amount of silt on the bed.) Thus by the end of 1972 the plants of the channel were potentially easy to wash away. In addition to this, submerged trailing plants usually grow poorly or die in shallow water (see Chapter 4). The damage, therefore, was due to a combination of flow, silting and depth factor.

c) 1974 — The water was shallow enough to cause turbulence and much of the silt in the centre had been removed. Most submerged plants were lost with the silt, and the water was too shallow for submergents to grow (except those of upper chalk brooks (Chapter 12), and these were absent anyway). This same decrease in *Ranunculus* was seen in other streams between 1971 and 1974, and it could he attributed only to the change in water depth, as in these other streams flow and substrate types did not alter. The gravel bed was exposed over most of the channel. The fringing herbs had altered less since 1972 than the plants in the channel, for although silting and storms must have moved individual patches, the general habitat of shallow water at the edge of a chalk stream had remained. *Sparganium erectum*, however, increased substantially and some bands were considerably larger than those expected in a chalk stream. This species grows well on silt banks, and even in the turbulent shallow flow of 1974 could both stabilise and accumulate silt.

d) 1977 — Motorway run-off had reached the river, bringing much pollution as well as more (rain) water. The middle of the river was the most affected. Even downstream, *Ranunculus* was rare: the 1976 drought as well as pollution had intervened. Fringing herbs and tall monocotyledons were adequate, the water-supported species were not.

e) 1979 — Motorway pollution was unchanged, but recovery was shown from the 1976 drought. After three years with more water there was some *Ranunculus* at top and bottom, though water was mostly still inadequate for dense, let alone dominant, populations. Diversity had increased further and, away from the worst-polluted or shaded sites, was satisfactory (five to nine species in 25 m). However, where there 'should' be a chalk community downstream, the pollution had in fact brought in more nutrient-rich species (e.g., *Butomus umbellatus*, *Potamogeton perfoliatus*): more appropriate for downstream on a long chalk river, or on a fertile sandstone one (with some abundant *Callitriche* sp., *Elodea canadensis*, *Enteromorpha intestinalis*). Regulation and more run-off had stabilised the water level, at a lower level than earlier, but better than in 1972–4 and 1976. Road run-off is very polluting, and the river was not long enough (10 km before becoming urban), or otherwise clean enough, for proper self-purification.

In Hertfordshire, lowering of the water level has damaged fisheries and plants in chalk streams, and the River Mimram is cited as a particularly bad early case (Parkin, 1973). Its vegetation resembles that of the River Darent in 1974, with fringing herbs but few submerged plants in the shallow water except the abundant Blanket weed upsteam also indicates pollution there (Haslam, 1982). It is reasonable to conclude the vegetation has been damaged in the same way as that of the River Darent. Silted parts of the River Mimram bear dense stands of *Sparganium erectum*, attributable partly to the lowering of water level, as in the River Darent, though partly also to the presence of some clay in the catchment.

Major changes in river plants due to a lack of water have been documented for chalk streams and been deduced for clay and sandstone streams from the dryness of the upper tributaries (see Chapter 1) and subsequently documented for these, e.g. Plate 2, Haslam (1982, 1987). The status of river communities was unsatisfactory, and has deteriorated further. The cause of the fall in water level is irrelevant to its effects. This makes predictions difficult, because while abstractions can be forecast, droughts cannot, and when the discharge after abstraction should be tolerable for the vegetation, droughts may further lower the water level and kill the plants. As described above, silting is an important short-term cause of the damage from lowering of the water level.

There was an unusually severe drought in 1976, and the short-term effects of this were probably similar to those of a long-term equivalent lowering of water table by man's activities or a change in the climate. From changes in streams surveyed in both 1976 and an earlier, normal, year, Table 17.1 was constructed, showing the minimum safe water level for different groups of plants, the minimum level which is tolerable for most populations for fairly short periods, and the level which can be expected to cause substantial damage (see Plate 3).

Table 17.1 can be used for predictions and planning. If a certain plant group is required in a stream (e.g. *Ranunculus* in chalk streams for fish), then the planned water level should not be less than the 'safe' level given in Table 17.1. The rare occasions when the water drops below this, as it did in summer 1976, are then likely to do little or no harm.

Although depth is the easiest factor to use in predictions, it is, of course, not the only one, as substrate and flow type are also important. These are summarised in the width-slope diagrams, and their use in predictions is discussed below. Briefly, if the water is too shallow for a species (as noted in Table 17.1) it will, eventually, die, and if originally absent it will not colonise the habitat. If, however, the water is deep enough, the species can only survive if the flow and substrate are suitable also.

WATER TRANSFERS

The effects of a water transfer depend on the amount of water transferred, the duration and season of the transfer, and the quality of the water. At one extreme, the stream discharge could be vastly increased on a

Table 17.1   Crucial water depths for different groups of river plants
(1976)

(a) Streams
The figures are the normal summer depths of the centre of the stream
(as described in Chapter 4)

	Damaging[a] (cm)	Critical[b] (cm)	Safe[c] (cm)
Fringing herbs	0	10	20
Tall emerged monocotyledons (excluding *Phalaris arundinacea*)	10	20	30
Water-supported plants[d]			
(a) Shallow-preference[e]	10	20	30
(b) Medium-preference[f]	30	40	50
(c) Deep-preference[g]	40	50	60

(b) Dykes, etc.
(Fringing herbs are unimportant)

Tall monocotyledons tolerate summer drying

Water-supported plants have the same depth ranges as in streams

a   Damaging means some loss in species presence, usually between two and five out of ten occurrences.
b   Critical means satisfactory for one summer, but leading to damage if continued for long periods.
c   Safe means recommended for the preservation of the species.
d   The water-supported plants comprise submerged species and floating ones rooted to the ground.
e   Shallow-preference species include: *Callitriche* spp., (*Elodea canadensis* to some extent), *Ranunculus aquatilis* (short-leaved), *Ranunculus peltatus* (short-leaved).
f   Medium-preference species include: *Ceratophyllum demersum*, *Elodea canadensis*, *Hottonia palustris*, *Myriophyllum spicatum*, *Myriophyllum verticillatum*, *Ranunculus penicillatus* ssp. *pseudofluitans*, *Ranunculus penicillatus* ssp. *penicillatus* and other medium-leaved species, *Schoenoplectus lacustris*, *Sparganium emersum*, *Zannichellia palustris* (except in chalk streams where shallower water is tolerated).
g   Deep-preference species include: *Nuphar lutea*, *Ranunculus fluitans*, *Sagittaria sagittifolia*.

permanent basis, which would completely change both the recipient and the donor stream below the point of transfer. At the other extreme, small amounts of water could be added to a stream solely during drought flows, and this would have a negligible effect on the plants. Large changes in discharge will influence the size, flow type and substrate of the river, and if these change sufficiently to alter the habitat for plants then new species will invade (providing the new habitat permits plant growth) and some time may elapse before the vegetation becomes stable. If the colonising species are present near-by and the new substrate is as stable as the original one (see

Chapter 18), then a new stable vegetation can be expected in 1–3 years, but otherwise the process of stabilisation will take longer.

Below the point of transfer, the donor stream contains less water than before, and the recipient stream more. Regulation decreases spate force, and irregular rapid discharges from reservoirs increase spate force. Thus in the transfer system the river may alter its topographical flow type either towards a more or a less spatey flow regime. The new width–slope pattern for vegetation can be predicted according to the width–slope patterns in Chapter 6 showing what range of plants can grow in different flow types. If the transfer means that the water depth changes so that, for example, a plant able to grow in a certain width and slope in a depth less than 75 cm is subjected to water over 1 m deep, then this species will be lost. If, on the other hand, the change of depth is from 35 to 70 cm then this same species would be able to survive.

A discontinuous and irregular transfer may have other effects. The worst possible flow regime for plants is one alternating frequently (at less than 2-year intervals) between a turbulent eroding flow and a slow silting one (i.e. between the flows shown above and below a bridge), for as soon as, or even before, one community is established it is destroyed by the change in flow type. If the changes in flow stay within the width–slope–depth tolerance for the species (see above and Chapter 6), however, then discontinuous transfers, if made gradually, do no harm.

The movement of water and at least some suspended sediment from the donor to the recipient stream during a transfer has the same effect on the plants as would the addition to the river of a tributary with that discharge (see Chapters 11–13) if nutrient-poor water is transferred to nutrient-rich rivers, unless the discharge of the transfer is approaching that of the recipient stream the plants are not likely to be altered. If the donor is more nutrient-rich than the recipient stream, however, then the effects may be greater. Because trophic status increases downstream, then if a transfer is from the lower reaches of one river to the upper reaches of another, the trophic status of the recipient is likely to increase even if the two rivers are of equal trophic status (see Chapter 11). If the transfer leads to more silting, in either donor or recipient stream, a more eutrophic vegetation is likely to develop, and vice versa. Any alteration to the amount of silting will more than counteract any changes in the nutrient content of the water (or suspended sediment), and predictions of vegetation changes must take this into account.

Water toxic to plants should not, of course, be transferred. However, since water is often assessed by just a few chemicals and an invertebrate index, major crop damage has occurred when irrigation water suddenly contains unexpected toxins.

18

Maintenance and mechanical use of watercourses

Dredging, plant cutting, herbicides and shading are techniques used to maintain watercourses. Dredging is primarily done to keep a suitable depth and width in the channels, but of course it decreases vegetation too. The vegetation normally recovers in 2–3 years. Cutting is the traditional, and often the present way, of removing plants which constitute flood hazards. Streams with fast-growing Ranunculus *may be cut up to five times each summer, but one or two cuts are more usual in streams with potentially choking vegetation, and too early or too much cutting may be counterproductive. Herbicides are effective for weed control, but must be used with caution to prevent toxicity and bank erosion, etc. Shading by trees is a cheap and, in many circumstances, effective method of decreasing plants.*

This chapter describes the effects of channel maintenance on river plants, but not the practical aspects of maintenance. The equipment used for mechanical clearance of channels and banks is described in Robson (1974). Herbicides should be used only in accordance with the Department for Environment Food and Rural Affairs (DEFRA) *Code of practice for the use of herbicides on weeds in watercourses and lakes* (latest edition).

DREDGING

Watercourses are dredged mainly for channel maintenance, and only secondarily to decrease vegetation. Dredging may be done to form a new channel, to deepen an existing one, or to remove accumulated sediment (Plates 17–19). All or only part of the channel may be dredged.

In alluvial plains the subsoil is soft, so that after dredging a soft substrate is left which is stable only because there is no scour. In streams, if the hard bed is untouched by the dredging then plants recover quickly. If the hard bed is broken but the stream is silting, silt quickly accumulates and plants invade. If, however, the hard bed is broken, and this is left unstable, in a habitat without deposition of sediment, the vegetation returns very slowly: e.g. a chalk brook, dredged 50 cm deep, was not stable enough for plants even at the sides for 4 years. Recovery is also slow if the final water depth is too great for plants or when a coarse firm bed is left in a stretch with slow flow. In this last case neither the plants of swift flow nor those of soft soils can grow well and such places may remain bare until enough silt has accumulated to allow silt-rooting species to colonise.

Frequency of dredging required in different stream types

1. Mountain streams — Any accumulated silt is removed by spates so dredging is unnecessary.
2. Upland streams — A few short stretches need dredging at fairly long intervals.
3. Chalk streams — Those with little silting and swift flow need no dredging. Where sedimentation is rather more (e.g. because of intensive agriculture or because some sandstone or clay occurs in the catchment), some stretches need occasional dredging. Most chalk streams have valuable fisheries, which means that the vegetation is important. Dredging is therefore kept shallow so as not to break the hard bed and disturb plant rhizomes, allowing vegetation to recover quickly.
4. Sandstone streams; and
5. Chalk–clay streams — These have more sedimentation and are likely to need dredging at 10+ year intervals.
6. Clay streams — These have much silting unless restoration methods have been used (Chapter 20), and low-lying rivers are typically dredged every 5–10 years.
7. Dykes and drains — In those in the middle of alluvial plains there is little silting but no scour to move any silt that does accumulate. They are usually dredged every 5–12 years. In those at the edge of higher ground silting is greater, and dredging may be necessary as often as every 2–3 years.

Generally species return to a site within 2 years after dredging, and the amount of vegetation is back to normal within 3 years. Simple dredging usually restores the habitat to its earlier state, though occasionally a slow silting reach is changed to a swift gravel one, or vice versa. If this happens then naturally the potential species present will also change (e.g. *Ranunculus* will invade a newly formed gravel habitat). (Interestingly, *Nuphar lutea* has survived in 20–30 cm of swift water over gravel for over 3 years, though in a small form.) In many plants, particularly those of slow eutrophic habitats, the rooting level remains fairly constant while silt accumulates above (see Chapter 3). When the deposited silt is very deep (e.g. 1 m) the plants may grow badly and dredging improves the vegetation.

Channellisation dredging, however, creates a new bed, lowered below and perhaps beside the old one. This will not be a naturally-created hard bed, and it may take time to stabilise. Propagules and fragments will initially be few.

Tall emerged monocotyledons recover relatively slowly after simple dredging because most have complex rhizome systems which they need to rebuild before they can dominate again. Other plants are likely to invade first, and then be shaded out by the regrowth of the tall species. For example, small silting clay brooks, regularly dredged, which have tall monocotyledons (e.g. *Sparganium erectum*) dominant for most of the time may have short species (e.g. *Potamogeton pectinatus, Sagittaria sagittifolia*) dominating for 2 years after simple dredging. The short species have parts buried in the undredged soil and can remain dormant with little above-ground vegetation during several years of heavy shading, and growing quickly when light is restored.

The speed of recovery of submerged and floating plants depends on what proportion of the propagules (fruits, stems, rhizomes, fragments, etc.) has been removed. Recovery can be within one growing season after shallow dredging, but if the plants are completely removed then recovery may take several years. However, in silting clay streams in Sussex, dredging 15 cm or *c*. 125 cm deep has little effect on the rate of recovery of the vegetation, for silt quickly accumulates and plants soon grow well in this. Dredging is also usually done in short stretches, so propagules are able to invade freely from upstream. If a watercourse is isolated, invasion may be very slow. In the first few years after simple dredging, plants change least when little vegetation is present and most where tall emergents dominate.

Undamaged plant communities in shallow waters without scour are dominated by tall monocotyledons and are species-poor. In order to conserve the diverse and species-rich communities of dykes, etc. (see Chapter 14), dredging is a much better way of keeping the channels clear than spraying with herbicides, for dredging, unlike herbicides, provides a new substrate, does not introduce toxins, and does not harm invading propagules. The dredging should not, however, be so deep as to prevent submerged plants colonising: e.g. one dyke dredged to 1.5 m deep, with steep sides and water too turbid for light to reach the bed, bore no channel plants for at least 10 years. Deep drains bear good vegetation only if there are shallow ledges at the sides, and when large channels are dredged the final shape should include such ledges. (If dredging is used for weed control, rather than conservation, the reverse applies and the channels should have straight steep sides and be too deep for channel plants to grow.) In dykes on the Pevensey Levels and some clay streams in Sussex, there was a management cycle of a shallow dredge (15–30 cm), followed by herbicide in the second year, and spraying of potentially choking plants in the third year. For 2 (–4) years thereafter no management is needed and this cycle is very satisfactory.

The changes in plants brought about by dredging in clay and part-clay streams of the rivers Great Ouse and Lee are shown in Table 18.1. In most sites the streams will never become choked with plants and vegetation is too sparse to constitute a flood hazard, so dredging is to remove sediment. Plants regenerating quickly from small fragments (e.g. *Callitriche* spp., *Elodea canadensis*) are likely to increase soon after dredging,

339

Table 18.1   Recovery after dredging

(a) River Great Ouse
Approximately 30 sites with rather shallow dredging in 1971/2;
recorded in 1972, 1973,1974

(1) Species growing better, or occurring only, in the first or second season

Apium nodiflorum   *Myosotis scorpioides*

Callitriche spp. (from fragments)   *Potamogeton perfoliatus*

Elodea canadensis   *Rorippa nasturtium-aquaticum* agg.

Glyceria maxima   *Veronica beccabunga*

Lemna minor agg.

(2) Species increasing to stable populations in the second or third season

Agrostis stolonifera   *Phragmites australis*

Callitriche spp. (long-term plants) *Potamogeton pectinatus*

Enteromorpha intestinalis   *Sagittaria sagittifolia*

Mentha aquatica   *Sparganium emersum*

Nuphar lutea   *Sparganium erectum*

(3) Sixteen sites had more vegetation in the second than the first season;
five sites more in the third than the second.
Eleven sites had a similar amount of vegetation in the second and first years;
17 sites in the third and second.

(b) River Lee
Approximately 20 sites of varying dredging depth; dredged in 1971/2;
recorded in 1972, 1973, 1974.

(1) Species growing better, or occurring only in the first or second season:

Agrostis stolonifera   *Mentha aquatica*

Apium nodiflorum   *Ranunculus* spp.

 Callitriche spp.   *Rorippa nasturtium-aquaticum* agg.

 Elodea canadensis

(2) Species increasing to stable populations in the second or third season.

Enteromorpha intestinalis   *Potamogeton natans*

Epilobium hirsutum   *Schoenoplectus lacustris*

 Glyceria maxima   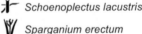 *Sparganium erectum*

(3) Five sites had more vegetation in the second than the first season;
three sites had more in the third than the second.

Seven sites had a similar amount of vegetation in the second and
first years; 17 sites had similar amounts in the third and second.

and fringing herbs may also increase, though as silt builds up later anchorage becomes more difficult and they are washed away (see Chapter 3). Recovery is usually complete within 3 years. Sites choked with plants may not be choked again for *c.* 5 years after dredging or they may be full of plants in the first season. For example, one shallow dyke was choked in the first year by a fringing herb (*Apium nodiflorum*) and after that by a tall monocotyledon (*Glyceria maxima*). This pattern of choking fringing herbs in shallow channels soon after dredging (usually *Apium nodiflorum* or *Rorippa nasturtium-aquaticum* agg.) is found in many parts of Britain. Later, the plants are washed away by flow or are replaced by taller species.

Less detailed records from the Essex and Bristol Avon areas confirm that plants recover quickly after dredging, except that the development of choking vegetation may take several years.

The Pevensey Levels in Sussex were sprayed with herbicide as well as being dredged (see above). Tall monocotyledons are usually sparse, partly because the banks are steep and the dykes are deep, and partly because of the spraying. However they do, as is usual, dominate shallow dykes without recent management (see Chapter 14). In the first year after dredging there are slightly fewer angiosperms and rather more algae. In the second year *Hydrocharis morsus-ranae* and *Sagittaria sagittifolia* reappear, the former being characteristic of recently dredged sites. The regular management and turbid water (from the clay) mean that few dykes bear much vegetation.

In the Fens, species more frequent after dredging include:

 *Callitriche* spp.   *Potamogeton pectinatus*

Lemna minor agg.

Large deep-rooted plants of the channel re-appear later, for example:

 Nuphar lutea   *Sagittaria sagittifolia*

Disused canals are deep dredged when they are restored, and canals in use occasionally have a simple dredge when silt has built up. In the first year after dredging the firm clay bottom is exposed and few plants are able to colonise. By the second year some silt has accumulated and quick-growing species (e.g. *Elodea canadensis*) invade. The vegetation recovers in 2–3 years. Even after restoration of a largely-silted canal, species are able to appear quickly (e.g. eight species in 2 years). Much vegetation in canals that are in use is on shallow-water ledges at the sides, so to preserve their amenity value canals should be dredged in such a way as to leave this shallow ledge in place.

Less detailed records for other habitats and regions confirm the time-scale of recolonisation stated above.

CUTTING (Also see Chapter 20 — Restoration methods)

Cutting is the traditional way, often still used, of removing plants which constitute flood hazards (but can itself cause flood hazards if the cut material is not removed but left to float downstream) (Plates 17, 18). A very important character of cutting is that its effects are predictable (Robson, 1974). Spraying, on the other hand, is less predictable as its effects depend on, for example, the weather after the spray, and side effects may be unexpected. Dredging theoretically has predictable results if the type of dredging is known, but in practice its effects are variable. Removing plant growth by cutting means dredging is needed less often, and water movement is improved (Robinson, 1971; see also Chapter 16). In flowing water, removing plants slows the development of shoals, or even erodes them, and in still water, removal prevents the continued accumulation of organic matter and humus.

Where tall plants are used as shelter by birds or mammals, cutting should not be done during critical stages of their cycles, e.g. nesting, and the cutting should be in short stretches so that the animals can always find cover nearby. Unfortunately, plants that are non-invasive in their habitat are often cut or sprayed unnecessarily. This is harmful to the environment because cutting removes not only the plants but also the animals and algae associated with them. It likewise removes the shelter, protection, food and silt that the plants provided. It is also harmful if cut plants are not removed from the water because decaying plants require much oxygen for decomposition, and the resulting shortage of oxygen can kill fish and other animals. The general effects of cutting on the oxygen and carbon dioxide of river waters are described in Westlake (1960).

Tall plants on the bank

These are cut to remove flood hazards in narrow channels, to keep paths clear for walking, to prevent bushes growing, or to improve the general look of the landscape (nettle beds are generally rather ugly). Tall bank plants die in winter but their shoots usually remain standing, so banks where they are a flood hazard should be cut at least in late summer or autumn before the winter storms. Paths may need cutting twice in summer if their plants are potentially tall and there is little trampling to help keep plants down. The denser the cutting, the greater the proportion of short plants.

Cutting dead shoots in winter has little effect on next summers' vegetation, but cutting in summer may have a long-term effect, depending on the species and its stage of growth.

Some examples are:

Urtica dioica — regrows quickly during the growing season and there is no long term effect of cutting.

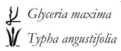 *Glyceria maxima* } regrow quickly during the growing season but next year's crop is reduced by 30% (Robson, 1974).
Typha angustifolia }

Phragmites australis — has a strong internal rhythm of growing and dormant periods. Regrowth is quick after cutting during the period of rapid growth (in spring and early summer), and there are no long-term effects. Cutting in late summer means little regrowth and a substantially lower crop the following year.

Tall emergents in the channel

These decrease water flow and increase silting. If their shoots are sparse and easily flattened in storm flows then they are no more hindrance than short emergents (e.g. *Schoenoplectus lacustris* when sparse in chalk rivers), which have a similar effect but are less troublesome. When emergents are cut, soil is exposed and loose sediment is washed away. This may increase deposition somewhere else. Erosion-sedimentation patterns can, therefore, be altered by cutting. If the cut stubble of emerged plants is flooded, the rhizomes get inadequate oxygen and re-growth is decreased. This can be used as a technique to decrease growth (Robson, 1974). In dykes and slow clay brooks, choking tall monocotyledons hinder flow at normal water levels, and do so even more after storms (see Chapter 16). Cutting prevents this, but must be done frequently, so a more satisfactory control measure is to dredge the main drains too deep for these plants. Dykes which carry little water can be cut in autumn, while those carrying more water need to be cut perhaps twice in summer, or be dredged approximately every 5 years with possibly one cut between dredges.

Submerged and floating plants

These accumulate less silt, partly because of their shape and partly because in the channel centres, where they grow, the current is swifter than at the sides. Deposited silt is eroded quickly after cutting in streams with swift flow (e.g. *Ranunculus* communities) and all plants rooted in this are lost also (e.g. *Elodea canadensis*, *Groenlandia densa*). Cutting is not needed in winter as these plants die-back either partially or completely, but may be required any time between late spring and early autumn when the plants grow thickly. Early-growing species in Southern England may need cutting in April (e.g. *Ranunculus penicillatus* ssp. *pseudofluitans*) while late-growing ones may not become thick, before early July (e.g. *Sagittaria sagittifolia*). Most streams in fact are not cut at all. Some lowland streams are cut sporadically, when equipment happens to be available, or plant growth is unusually thick. The general pattern, though, in streams where there is a hazard is:

0–1 cuts per year in clay streams,
0–3 cuts per year in soft sandstone streams,
1–5 cuts per year in soft limestone streams.

The warmer the weather the greater the plant growth, so a stream normally cut once a year may need cutting three times in hot summers. However, if there are frequent summer storms these prevent plants from becoming choking and so decrease the need for cutting. In long droughts the water may become too shallow for submerged plants to grow well (e.g. Chapters 4 and 17), and when a change of depth alters flow type, vegetation may be lost (e.g. the erosion of soft-soil plants by a turbulent flow) and cutting rendered unnecessary. Another possibility, reported from several parts of Britain, is that increased plant growth may occur after storms in May, and this is attributed to fertilisers washed out of the land.

In the best trout streams on chalk, cutting is for the benefit of the fishing, and only secondarily for flood prevention. The small-scale cutting patterns in summer are done according to local traditions. In autumn a general cut removes enough of the winter-green plants to allow the safe passage of the winter storm flows. In the rest of the country cutting is usually either right across the channel, or in the form of swathes in the centre made by weed-cutting launches.

Seasonal changes in the plant's growth cycle can be important. One reason why dyke vegetation can be particularly troublesome is that several potentially choking species with different periods of maximum development can replace each other during the summer (e.g. *Callitriche* spp., spring; *Elodea canadensis*, early summer; *Ceratophyllum demersum*, late summer), and after a cut more than one can spread very quickly again.

The main dominant of chalk streams is *Ranunculus*, (though *Rorippa nasturtium-aquaticum* agg. may be choking in brooks in later summer) and in this genus growth is greatest in early summer, after which it decreases. If *Ranunculus* is cut at this time, however, the new growth is quick and dense and choking vegetation is more likely to recur. This has been reported from various parts of England and has also been proved quantitatively (Dawson, 1976). Thus if the early summer growth does not present a flood hazard it should not be cut, or the regrowth may constitute a flood hazard later in the year.

A different type of growth cycle is shown by *Potamogeton pectinatus*. This too grows rapidly in early summer, but later in the year even cutting will not stimulate further growth. (This is a comparable cycle to *Phragmites australis* among the emergents.) Its clumps are smaller too, seldom exceeding 2 m long while those of *Ranunculus* are often 3–5 m. In circumstances particularly favourable for growth *Potamogeton pectinatus* may need cutting three times a year, but once is usual, even in choking stands.

Yet another growth type is shown by *Callitriche* spp. and *Elodea canadensis*. If undisturbed, *Callitriche* spp. reach their maximum size in spring, and *Elodea canadensis* in early summer. After cutting, luxuriant growth can occur any time between spring and autumn.

Cutting is the traditional form of management, and so the vegetation of rivers that are cut regularly consists of species with developmental patterns that can tolerate this. There is much similarity between the vegetation of frequently-cut chalk streams, and those spate-damaged hill streams with:

Fringing herbs  *Myriophyllum* spp.

Callitriche spp. *Ranunculus* spp.

HERBICIDES

Herbicide use became widespread in the 1960s and 1970s. The choice, and concentrations etc., are now controlled by EU Directives as well as DEFRA.

Different herbicides have somewhat different effects, but in general delicate plants are killed easily while tough large ones are more resilient, though this varies with physiological, anatomical and phenological factors. More care and judgement are needed in the treatment of submerged than of emerged plants, since careless use of aquatic herbicides can lead to empty dykes. An empty dyke, or a dyke containing much phytoplankton (which are unaffected or developed afterwards in the absence of larger plants) is bad for bank stability, water turbidity, conservation, aesthetic value and (perhaps) future use of water for irrigation or cattle.

Many of the comments made about cutting in the previous section apply equally well to spraying: for example, non-invasive plants need not be treated, and, for conservation, only short stretches should be treated at one time so that animals able to move can find alternative habitats. In contrast to cutting, where the cut parts of the plants remain alive in the water for several days or weeks and can be removed from the water at leisure, herbicides kill aquatic plants very quickly, and serious deoxygenation of the water can easily follow. Whenever possible, therefore, submerged and floating plants should be sprayed early in the year to prevent plants growing thickly, rather than later in the year, when they are already choking. Indiscriminate use of herbicides leads to a quite unnecessary loss of species and communities. Cutting with care conserves the habitat much better. Herbicides, however, are a cheaper way of controlling plants.

Emergents can be killed easily by herbicides, but unless the habitat is left barren and unstable the space left by them will be colonised by other plants. Before spraying, therefore, the preferred vegetation should be decided upon and any management directed towards this end. For instance, if in a dyke used for water supply, replacement of emergents by submerged plants would be more troublesome than the original emergents, then the dyke should be deeply dredged so as to prevent any plant growth in the channel. Short grasses bind the soil but offer little hydraulic resistance to flow.

Tall non-bushy plants at the sides are a nuisance only if they cover much of the width of the channel. If they are confined to narrow bands, treatment is unnecessary for flood control, and harmful as regards bank stability and conservation. These bands may be above, at or below water level, the crucial point being whether, in the prevailing environment, they can spread. Invasive plants must be controlled, non-invasive ones should be left alone. In clay streams, tall emergents sometimes choke brooks and cover large parts of the channels downstream.

TREES

Trees are the most old-fashioned, cheapest, and often most useful means of decreasing river plants and stabilising river banks. They are more used on the continent than in Britain, as a deliberate control tool (e.g., Hermens, 1975; Lohmeyer & Krause, 1975). If law prevents riverside trees, only very tall ones can shade the channel from, say, 10 m away. The difficulty with planting trees is that while the trees are small they cannot fully maintain the channel, and their presence makes it difficult to use large maintenance equipment. However, if the saplings are as large as possible when planted, it will only be a few (?4) years before they cast sufficient shade to prevent choking river plants growing in the near channel or on the (near) bank. Trees and hedges are now often deliberately preserved in order to prevent plants blocking the channel. Where recent schemes have removed shading, hazards have sometimes been created both by choking river plants, and by increasing, even doubling, the width of the river. At present many channels have trees and bushes too far apart to be useful for weed control, and too close together to be convenient for use of large machines in channel maintenance. Pollards, however, are a centuries-old resource, and should be maintained as valuable heritage; and for their biodiversity.

The reduction in light required to keep plants from being a flood hazard varies with the potential dominant of the stream (see Chapter 7).

A continuous light canopy of tree tops meets or exceeds these requirements. Bank plants may be more shade-tolerant than channel ones. In particular, *Urtica dioica* can still grow tall when the channel is almost empty (though it is shorter and sparser than when it is in full light). In less eutrophic and more heavily shaded areas, bank plants are less bulky. With tree trunks to break the force of the water, tall plants are much less likely to be pulled from the bank.

The shading effects can be provided by any tree species capable of growing close to the water, though deciduous trees are preferable because these allow growth of river plants in early spring before the leaf canopy is complete. An advantage of, e.g., alders, is in the second function of the trees: bank stability. Alders, unlike some other trees capable of growing in damp conditions, have long deep roots going down below water level and perhaps even under the channel bottom. Willows are the commonest riverside tree, and are normally satisfactory. Trees can be planted in the 0.5 m above the water level. They will become established even on the steepest slopes, and so can be planted close to the water or on the bank above. Trees at the waterside take up less space and are less likely to shade crops, though trees farther away allow easy access to the channel. It is natural for some of their roots to lie outside the soil and this does not mean that the bank is falling down. Using trees for channel maintenance means that machines do not need to pass on the banks, which is an advantage because long-term use of such machines is liable to damage the banks. Brooks in the recommended stable low-maintenance state provided by alders are shown in Plate 6. This has remained unchanged for 10 years.

Plants can live in small breaks in tree canopy and in very light shade (see Chapter 1) and in shade neither the plants on the bank nor those in the channel can grow thickly, while the tree trunks are sparse enough to cause little obstruction to flow. Trees live for many decades or even centuries, so replacement management is minimal. Coppicing (or pollarding) can be done at *c.* 15-year intervals if the trees are shading crops, but it is not necessary for stream maintenance in these circumstances. Sometimes more frequent lopping may be required.

Maintenance by trees is not possible where man-made banks are unsuitable for trees or in the rare situations where they are serious obstructions to flash floods, and life or property are at risk.

GRAZING

Channels can also be managed by grazing. Sheep are the most effective animals for keeping down vegetation on sloping banks, as they graze close to the ground and are small enough to do little damage by trampling. Grazed areas develop into short grassland which stabilises the soil without impeding water flow (Plate 5). In many hill streams (where bank plants are in fact irrelevant to channel maintenance) tall plants are few because the land is grazed by livestock. Grazing is also very effective in flatter country where sheep are allowed on to the banks, e.g. in parts of Romney Marsh. In the channels themselves, sheep grazing is effective only at the edges, or on dry, firm beds, and cannot be used where the weight of the animals can damage the banks. Grazing was a standard, indeed an unnoticed management method, but increased riverside arable has removed much of the habitat, in both lowlands and uplands.

Some fish eat large quantities of water plants, and are useful for controlling these. Care is needed, however, because if introduced fish can grow well and breed (as did various carp species introduced into North America), they not only eliminate all plants, but, by stirring up the bottom silt, keep the water almost as liquid mud, which is very unsatisfactory. Native fish are usually kept in check by predators, habitat, etc.

Among birds, swans — because of their large food requirement — are particularly successful at controlling vegetation.

BOATS

Canals are principally used for navigation (Plate 14). The largest canals are the ship canals, and these are too deep and turbid to have much vegetation. The (now) pleasure boat canals are used mainly by motor boats. These travel fast enough to stir up silt from the bed; their propellers cut plants, and, in thick vegetation, can become entangled in plants; and if boat traffic is dense, their wash is sufficient to sweep away bank plants.

The different types of canal have different types of vegetation:

a) Disused canals which are silted up. These are species-poor and commonly dominated by *Glyceria maxima*, with *Phragmites australis* and *Urtica dioica* on the banks.

b) Disused canals over 1 m deep. These are species-rich both in the bed and at the sides (often 10+ species present per site). The channel is usually choked with submerged and floating plants.

c) Canals which are little-used, up to two boats per mile on the spot counts. These are side arms of other canals, or are remote from the main centres of navigation, or are in process of being restored. They are species-rich in the bed and at the edges (often eight or more species per site) and the channel may be choked. It is in this group that plants may impede navigation and need controlling.

d) Three groups of canals which have heavier boat traffic:
   (i) Spot counts 3–11 boats per mile, averaging 7. These are unpolluted or little-polluted canals and they may have a rather short boating season. There is little or no bed vegetation, but in shallow water at the sides vegetation is luxuriant and species-rich (often five and more species per 25 m site).
   (ii) Spot counts 9–30 boats per mile, averaging 12. These canals may have a longer boating season and some receive industrial pollution. Bed vegetation is again negligible, but here the edge vegetation is species-poor and only intermittent.
   (iii) Spot counts 3–45 boats per mile, averaging 8. These are the canals which have heavy use, considerable pollution, or both. Plants are almost absent.

Boats and pollution thus both affect the plants in canals. Canals without plants on the edges must have their banks protected from scour in some other way and are usually piled.

Many rivers and drains are navigable for part or all of their length. The effects of boat traffic appear similar to those in canals, except that shorter or swifter stretches tend to have rowing craft only. Rowing boats and canoes damage plants less than motor boats, and river plants hamper their movement more.

TRAMPLING

Trampling is another common, though localised, form of mechanical disturbance. Cattle watering at a stream usually keep their watering place clear of plants and depending on the substrate, trampling may lead to a compacted firm substrate or a loose disturbed silt. Children (and indeed adults too) have a similar effect, though mostly at bridges on chalk streams and 'beauty spots' in the hills. These places have a combination of easy access, pleasant surroundings, bright sparkling water, a firm bed and, on various stream types, an attractive edge of fringing herbs (until the plants are destroyed).

19

Pollution

The most important types of pollution for British river plants are the sewage and industrial effluent from sewage works (improving), and run-off from hard surfaces (roads and settlements) and intensively-farmed land (which are deteriorating). Plants can be used to assess and monitor this pollution, as different species have different sensitivity thresholds. Potamogeton pectinatus *and Blanket weed (long filamentous algae) are the most tolerant species of polluted British rivers: indeed, are favoured by some pollutants.*

Inorganic eutrophication (the raising of nutrient status), from fertilisers or sewage effluents of suitable quality, alters the vegetation to that of a clean stream of a higher nutrient status, and is easily diagnosed in principle, though in practice other pollutants are usually present and mask the nutrients.

In most British rivers, heavy metal pollution from mines, industry or ore-bearing rocks, is not important to vegetation. Pollution from sediments is damaging where the water is turbid or the substrate unstable. Paper mill, coal mine, etc., effluents have local but decreasing effects. Boats lead to substrate disturbance, turbidity and chemical pollution, and thus harm the vegetation.

Harmful pollution eliminates or decreases sensitive species, thus decreasing species diversity, and it increases any species actually favoured by the pollutant concerned. Because different species vary in their sensitivity to different pollutants, vegetation patterns differ and are diagnostic of the different contaminants.

The term 'pollution' is used here to describe chemical effects of substances or factors introduced into the watercourse by human impact (which are not for restoring water or sediment quality to its original composition). The effects of flow regulation and watercourse management are described in Chapters 17 and 18.

Pollution can consist of:

1. Dissolved substances, such as sewage and industrial effluents, fertiliser, herbicides, road and other hard surface run-off, and farm silage liquor. These alter the chemical status of the soil and water and may result in increased, decreased or unaltered plant growth.
2. Sediments (sometimes with dissolved substances also) such as silt from farmland, run-off from hard surfaces, and effluents from farm, sewage treatment, factories, etc., (e.g., paper mill factories). Disturbances caused by boats, cattle, paddling, etc., alter sedimentation and cause turbidity.
3. Heat.
4. Radioactivity.

Under natural conditions many substances enter watercourses. For example, nutrients are washed out of soils; some chemicals are found locally in high concentrations (e.g. salt near Droitwich); and sediments are washed in from the land, fall in from banks, and are created by erosion of the channel bed and decomposition of organic matter. As rock type, topography and general ecology vary from place to place, the quantity and chemical composition of substances entering streams vary similarly (Chapter 8). Because of this large natural variation, human interference may create conditions which, although new to that site, occur naturally in other places. High chloride, for instance, is found in coastal channels receiving occasional sea flooding and in inland saltpan areas, as well as being a constituent of town effluents. This last is pollution, but the first two situations are not, even if the effects on the plants are similar in each case (other habitat factors being equal).

When human interference alters the incoming substances, the effects vary because natural streams vary. Adding a given concentration of a chemical may affect plants in a stream with a low natural level of that substance while having no effect on a stream containing more of the chemical. Thus a nutrient inflow which alters the trophic status of an oligotrophic stream may not change a eutrophic one. The dilution of the inflow, which depends on the discharge (on channel size and water movement), is also important, and effluents which seriously pollute small brooks may have little effect on large and swift rivers (Haslam, 1990).

SEVERITY OF POLLUTION

Any natural river chemical may harm plants if it is present in excess, and many substances are damaging even in low concentrations. Levels of pollution vary from river to river, and from day to day. For convenience they can be grouped into three categories, although these are arbitrary and all intermediate levels occur.

1. Streams with continuous very severe pollution — and either with no plants at all, or with very sparse *Potamogeton pectinatus*, e.g. parts of: River Douglas (Lancashire), River Roch (Mersey and Weaver), Rhymney River (Glamorgan), River Tame (Trent) in the 1970s (Plate 10). The water is visibly polluted, and the gross pollution prevents vegetation development.

2. Streams with accidental very poisonous spillages — usually lasting only a few hours. These spillages may be due, for example, to temporary faults in sewage works, to dumping of waste (e.g. road washings from overturned tankers), or to toxic trade effluents reaching sewage works by mistake. The effects depend on the type

of poison, its concentration, and the time it stays in any one part of the river. Damage varies from a few frail leaves being lost to a total kill of the entire vegetation. Short-term pollutions are unlikely to harm the soil or the underground plant parts, though, and the vegetation can regrow. The maximum effect of a temporary poison cannot be greater than that of thorough dredging, and is usually much less since it leaves below-ground parts and some tough above-ground parts alive. Vegetation recovers from dredging quickly, usually in not more than 3 years (see Chapter 18), so these accidental pollutions seldom have an important effect on vegetation, unless they recur frequently in the same stream. Their influence on fisheries is greater, both because a temporary loss of fish is economically undesirable, and because fish populations, though not much harmed by dredging, recover only slowly after a kill.

Toxic pollutions may, however, have a long-term effect if the plants are already under stress from another cause. In one river studied, mild pollution had been causing some decline in vegetation for over a decade and when the plants were then killed by an accidental poisonous pollution their recovery was very slow, being far from complete 3 years later.

3. Streams with continuous mild pollution — Here the chemical composition has been altered in such a way that, while plants still grow, the vegetation differs in species presence or abundance from that characteristic of a clean site in the same habitat. This is much the commonest type of pollution in Britain and over the years the vegetation has come to be in equilibrium with the pollution. Its effects are unfortunately often unrecognised, since observers merely note vegetation is present and do not realise that this vegetation is not that of a clean stream.

INORGANIC EUTROPHIC POLLUTION

Different species, and different groups of species, are characteristic of different chemical regimes, and this is one cause of the different vegetation in the upper and lower reaches of the same stream, and in streams on different rock types (see Chapter 8). Eutrophication is the increasing of the nutrients available to the plants and tends to change the nutrient regime to that of a clean stream of a higher trophic status. It can occur when fertilisers are added to the water. In a small chalk brook, fertilised effluent from a watercress bed led to:

Groenlandia densa   *Zannichellia palustris*

(see Chapter 12 for the little-polluted vegetation). Some sewage works effluents produce the same result, when this is not masked by the toxic effects described below, as when these same species were brought into a near-mesotrophic brook (see Figure 19.4; River Witham, the site somewhat below the upstream effluent source).

The most eutrophic clean streams are the lower reaches of silted clay rivers. Eutrophication here cannot lead to the appearance of species characteristic of a higher nutrient status since the most eutrophic British species are already present. However, when such reaches are clean they normally also contain a few species typical of less eutrophic habitats (see Chapters 1, 8 and 12). The most eutrophic species, when occurring as a group, are:

Enteromorpha intestinalis		*Sagittaria sagittifolia*
Nuphar lutea		*Schoenoplectus lacustris*
Rorippa amphibia		*Sparganium emersum*

There are other species which, if present, do not alter this diagnosis of nutrient status:

Lemna minor agg.		*Sparganium erectum*
Potamogeton pectinatus		

The presence of the following, however, indicates the habitat is less eutrophic, or, possibly, cleaner:

Alisma plantago-aquatica		*Potamogeton lucens*
Elodea canadensis		*Potamogeton perfoliatus*
Phalaris arundinacea		*Ranunculus* spp.
Polygonum amphibium		Fringing herbs

List of symbols

Acorus calamus		*Nuphar lutea*
Agrostis stolonifera and other small grasses		*Oenanthe crocata*
Alisma plantago-aquatica		*Oenanthe fluviatilis*
Apium nodiflorum		*Phalaris arundinacea*
Berula erecta		*Phragmites australis*
Butomus umbellatus		*Polygonum amphibium*
Callitriche spp.		*Potamogeton crispus*
Carex acutiformis/riparia		*Potamogeton lucens*
Carex spp.		*Potamogeton pectinatus*
(*Catabrosa aquatica*, see *Agrostis*)		*Potamogeton perfoliatus*
Ceratophyllum demersum		*Ranunculus aquatilis*
Elodea canadensis		*Ranunculus fluitans*

Eleocharis acicularis			*Ranunculus peltatus*
Eleocharis palustris			*Ranunculus* spp.
Eleogiton fluitans			*Rorippa amphibia*
Epilobium hirsutum			*Rorippa nasturtium-aquaticum* agg.
Equisetum palustre			*Rumex hydrolapathum*
Eriophorum angustifolium			*Sagittaria sagittifolia*
(*Glyceria fluitans*, see *Agrostis*)			*Schoenoplectus lacustris*
Glyceria maxima			*Scirpus* spp.
Groenlandia densa			*Sparganium emersum*
Hippuris vulgaris			*Sparganium erectum*
Iris pseudacorus			*Spirodela polyrhiza*
Juncus articulatus			*Symphytum officinale*
Juncus bulbosus			*Typha latifolia*
Juncus effusus (and other spp.)			*Utricularia vulgaris*
Lemna minor agg.			*Veronica anagallis-aquatica* agg.
Lemna trisulca			*Veronica beccabunga*
Mentha aquatica			*Zannichellia palustris*
Menyanthes trifoliata			Mosses
Mimulus guttatus agg.			Benthic algae
Myosotis scorpioides			Blanket weed (trailing algae)
Myriophyllum alterniflorum			*Enteromorpha intestinalis*
Myriophyllum spicatum			Other species
Ranunculus omiophyllus			

Species-richness usually indicates a habitat is both unpolluted and favourable for river plants in other factors also. In fairly clean clay rivers, sites on the lower reaches usually contain five to eight species from all three of the above groups (e.g. River Chelmer, Figure 11.12). Exceptionally clean rivers may have 10–18 species per site (e.g. River Blythe, Figure 19.1b). In order to diagnose inorganic eutrophication there must be marked changes in the vegetation, such as the appearance of species which could not occur in a similar clean site, or the loss of a whole group of species (not of just one or two plants from that group).

Fertiliser run-off from agricultural land is a source of eutrophication. Also, fertilisers, pesticides and other agrochemicals percolate down to

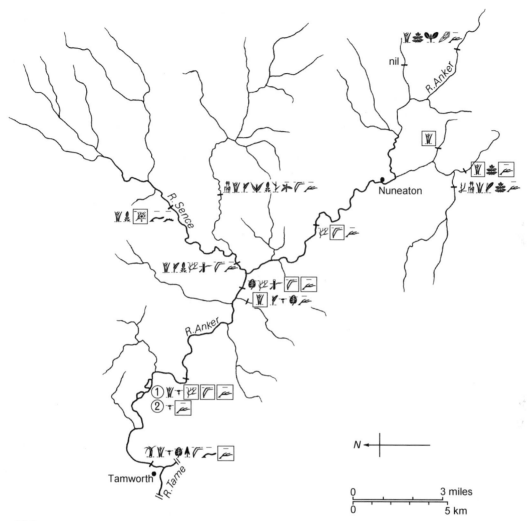

Figure 19.1a
Clean, fairly polluted and very polluted tributaries of the River Tame (Trent). Mainly clay. River Anker; most records 1974. (For general notes on whole river diagram see Chapter 11 — Explanation of Figures 11.2–11.8.)

the aquifers, contaminating the ground water and, in course of time, the streams. Agrochemicals are potentially a worse hazard than effluents, for effluents come from point sources and so can, at least in theory, be cleaned before their water enters the rivers, while agrochemicals affect the whole length of the river and so no cleaning-up is possible. Agrochemicals have been added to agricultural land in large quantities for only a few decades. To detect differences in plants correlated with the amount of fertiliser added near the river (arable with mixed fertilisers, grassland with nitrogen, grassland without

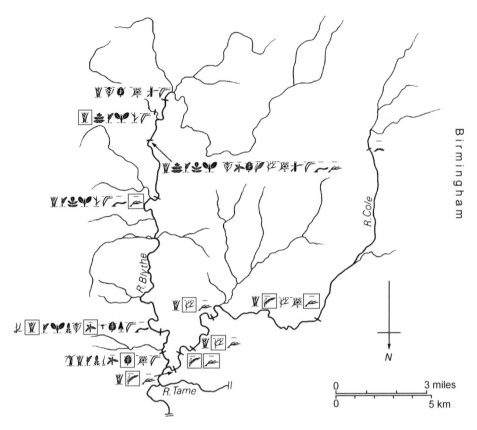

Figure 19.1b
Clean, fairly polluted and very polluted tributaries of the River Tame (Trent). Mainly clay. Rivers Blyth and Cole; most records 1974. (For general notes on whole river diagram see Chapter 11 — Explanation of Figures 11.2–11.8.)

fertilisers), requires clean, or at least cleaner, but similar sites to establish the basic differences; or, clean riversides to help clean the river.

SEWAGE AND INDUSTRIAL EFFLUENTS

Effluents from towns and cities have increasingly less effects as treatment technology increases. Hard surface and farmland run-off pollution continue to increase.

Their effects are:

a) to cause the decrease and loss of the species most sensitive to such pollution;

b) to decrease the species diversity at each site (this is the common and usual response to toxic pollution; (Kulberg, 1974; Lachavanne & Wattenhofer, 1975; Volker & Smith, 1965);

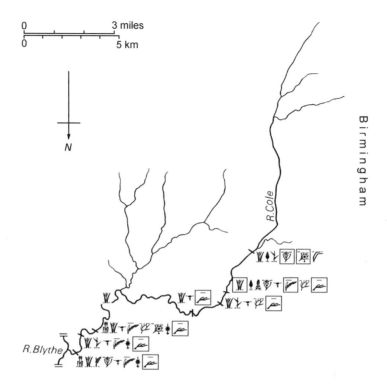

‡ Elodea callitrichoides

Figure 19.1c
Clean, fairly polluted and very polluted tributaries of the River Tame (Trent). Mainly clay. River Cole 1976.
(For general notes on whole river diagram see Chapter 11 — Explanation of Figures 11.2–11.8.)

c)   to increase any species actually favoured by this pollution
     (except where the pollution is too severe)

     The widespread species of British river plants which are most
tolerant to sewage and industrial pollution are described below.

1.   Very tolerant — *Potamogeton pectinatus*
     This is the only species which is actually brought into a habitat, and
     made more luxuriant there, by suitable levels of pollution. In
     moderately-polluted habitats it occurs most often in the middle
     reaches of chalk-clay streams (where it can become luxuriant), and
     in the lower reaches of hill rivers with some hard sandstone in the
     catchment. *Potamogeton pectinatus* cannot, however, occur in all
     polluted streams, since some are too shallow or too swift, etc. for
     this species (see Chapters 2–4 and 6). The most polluted rivers to
     bear plants usually have sparse *Potamogeton pectinatus*; e.g. parts of

the River Dearne (Yorkshire), River Stour (Severn) and River Tame (Trent) (in the 1970s).

Potamogeton pectinatus is also encouraged by sea salt (see Chapter 14), a coarse short form being commonly luxuriant in coastal dykes which have occasional sea flooding. It is also characteristic of saltpan areas (Hynes, 1960) and may be abundant in salt- (and minor town-) polluted streams; e.g. River Salwharpe (Severn). Elsewhere, the salt levels in ordinary sewage effluents do not appear to have an effect independent of that of the other elements in the pollution. Infrequently, luxuriant *Potamogeton pectinatus* can occur in a species-rich polluted site, suggesting more than one chemical factor may be involved.

Blanket weed (usually *Cladophora* sp.) is also pollution-favoured. Those filamentous algae are always present, but are only noticeable when conditions allow them to grow from the bed, and are termed 'Blanket weed' only when large enough to blanket part or all of the bed. Disturbance, by releasing nutrients, also favours Blanket weed, but its abundance most commonly indicates pollution. As an ephemeral, it can occur in near-clean spatey rivers where competitive larger plants are unable to develop — but if it is itself large, the river is polluted.

2. Tolerant

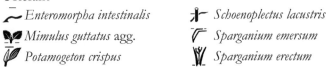

Enteromorpha intestinalis   *Schoenoplectus lacustris*
Mimulus guttatus agg.   *Sparganium emersum*
Potamogeton crispus   *Sparganium erectum*

These are all common in both clean and polluted stream, *Sparganium erectum* being the most widespread species in Britain. The other species occur in polluted places within their ordinary habitat range, but — unlike *Potamogeton pectinatus* — they are rarely, of ever, brought into other habitats merely because there is pollution. In South Wales coal streams *Mimulus guttatus* agg. is often the first species to appear when pollution decreases.

3. Fairly tolerant

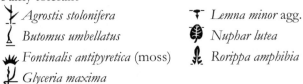

Agrostis stolonifera   *Lemna minor* agg.
Butomus umbellatus   *Nuphar lutea*
Fontinalis antipyretica (moss)   *Rorippa amphibia*
Glyceria maxima

These all tolerate some pollution but, like the last group, are not brought in to habitats outside their normal range by pollution.

These groups are of the plants most commonly found in polluted areas. With some types of pollution, and in some types of stream, other species may occur with *Potamogeton pectinatus*. Most of the tolerant species are excluded from small brooks anyway (see Chapters 2–4 and 6), and in these, semi-emergent species, such as *Apium nodiflorum*, can occur where there is considerable pollution. *Potamogeton pectinatus* is unusually tolerant to pollution in North America, as well as in Britain (Kulberg, 1974). Species are considered to be most sensitive to pollution when at the extremes of their geographic range (Haslam, 1987; Stuckey, 1971; Stuckey & Wentz, 1969). In such regions plants are under stress from an unsuitable climate, and so the additional stress of pollution is the more easily lethal. (Also see Chapter 3, for interacting stresses.)

The loss of species diversity in polluted streams is due to the small number of species able to tolerate pollution (Groups 1–3 above). The effect of the pollution is that where, in a clean site, there would be perhaps 5–10 species present covering a good deal of the bed, in a typical polluted site half or more of these species are absent, and some of the remainder may be growing less luxuriantly.

Figure 11.12 of the River Chelmer shows two similar and adjacent tributaries: River Can, which is clean, and River Wid, which receives industrial and town pollution. Taking into account the fact that upper reaches of clay brooks are generally species-poor (see Chapter 12), it is clear that the River Can is relatively species-rich and the River Wid species-poor, with the main part of the River Wid having only pollution-tolerant species (see above). Other tributaries of the River Chelmer are also fairly species-rich and fairly clean. Its lower reaches are only mildly polluted and the vegetation consists of both the eutrophic and the less eutrophic species listed above. Diversity is high throughout, and *Potamogeton pectinatus* is absent from the sites recorded.

Figures 19.1a–c show three tributaries of the River Tame (Trent): River Blythe, River Anker and River Cole, which are comparable except for pollution. The River Tame has been mentioned above as one of the most polluted British rivers, bearing either no plants or sparse *Potamogeton pectinatus*. The River Blythe is clean enough to be used for water supply, and the main river is very species-rich. The River Anker is polluted from near the source and species-richness and pollution-sensitive species occur only in clean, rather small tributaries. The main river is species-poor, with few sensitive species and considerable *Potamogeton pectinatus*, though near the mouth the vegetation is recovering further from the source of pollution, and species diversity is increasing. The River Sence, the main tributary of the River Anker, is cleaner and more species-rich. The River Cole used to be seriously polluted. It was cleaned up in 1971/2 but in 1974 still had very few, mostly pollution-tolerant species. *Potamogeton pectinatus* was luxuriant, as was *Potamogeton crispus*. (It is rare to find luxuriant growth of *Potamogeton crispus* associated with pollution.) Pollution, of course, remains in the soil longer than in water, and because silt moves downstream, the upper reaches become clean quicker than the lower ones. The lowest site here remained unchanged from the clean-up until 1975, when 2 less tolerant species appeared, showing recovery was in progress. The *Ranunculus* at one middle site in 1974 was an early sign of recovery. The change in 1976 (Figure 19.1c) is dramatic. Species diversity is greatly increased, and the pollution-tolerant *Potamogeton pectinatus* and *Potamogeton crispus*, though still present, are hardly luxuriant. The river, except for the upper site recorded, is not yet clean for plants, but in 1976 could no longer be classed as seriously polluted.

The River Strine (Severn) showed a similar period between clean-up and recovery, though here the pattern was complicated by drought and dredging. In 1972 (around the time of the clean-up) *Potamogeton pectinatus* was the most important species, and the tolerant *Sparganium emersum* the only other abundant one. Lowering of the water level probably eliminated *Potamogeton pectinatus* from the upper reaches. By 1975 *Potamogeton pectinatus* was no longer luxuriant, and was nearly absent in stretches where the polluted soil had been removed by dredging. *Sparganium emersum* was still growing well and it seemed likely that a clean vegetation pattern would develop.

Figure 19.2 shows the effect of Stoke-on-Trent and Newcastle-under-Lyme on the River Trent. The river has exceptionally low species diversity, with *Potamogeton pectinatus* luxuriant and other species effectively absent. When this polluted stream is diluted by the entry of the clean rivers Penk and Sowe, species diversity improves, though the plants present are pollution-tolerant.

Figures 19.3 and 19.4 are of rivers with many effluent sources, the largest of which are marked. Most affect the vegetation, though considerable recovery is shown between sources. The River Avon (Severn), shown in Figure 19.3, takes sewage from the large towns of Rugby and Coventry. Rugby sewage brings dominant *Potamogeton pectinatus* into the River Avon, and greatly decreases species diversity. There is some recovery downstream, though diversity remains fairly low, and sensitive plants remain rare or absent. Coventry sewage has a similar effect in the River Sowe, except that downstream recovery is less, so that when the River Sowe enters the River Avon, the River Avon becomes more polluted, more species-poor and has more *Potamogeton pectinatus*. Even though smaller amounts of sewage enter farther down, there is a recovery in that species diversity increases somewhat, and *Potamogeton pectinatus* decreases. However, comparing the lower River Avon with the lower River Chelmer (Figure 11. 12), the cleaner river is more species-rich and has species which are pollution-sensitive and typical of less eutrophic areas. (The contrast

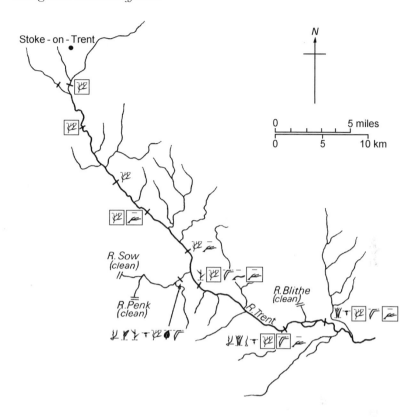

Figure 19.2
Very polluted River Trent
downstream of Stoke-on-Trent.
Mainly clay; 1974.

with the River Blythe in Figure 19.1, is even greater.) The River Soar, described above, is intermediate between the rivers Avon and Chelmer. Two tributaries of the River Avon, rivers Alne and Arrow, are inadequately recorded on Figure 19.3, but the clean River Alne bears dense vegetation while the polluted River Arrow contains much less (Hynes, 1960). Below the confluence of these two rivers, the sites recorded bear only tolerant species, and diversity is not high.

The upper River Witham (Lincolnshire) in Figure 19.4 shows loss of species diversity below most of the major effluent inflows. Most pollution-tolerant species do not grow in small brooks, and the most polluted brook sites here contain only algae. The sewage from Grantham has the greatest effect on the vegetation, with species diversity low for a considerable distance and *Potamogeton pectinatus* luxuriant. The effluents entering farther downstream on the rivers Witham and Brant have similar but shorter effects. The upper effluent on the River Brant has little effect on the sites recorded. A solely eutrophic effluent in a clay brook is not easy to detect because of the naturally high trophic status of the site. In contrast, the more mesotrophic habitat of the upper River Witham shows eutrophication

Figure 19.3
Intermittently polluted River Avon (Severn). Mainly clay; most records 1975. Main effluent sources starred.

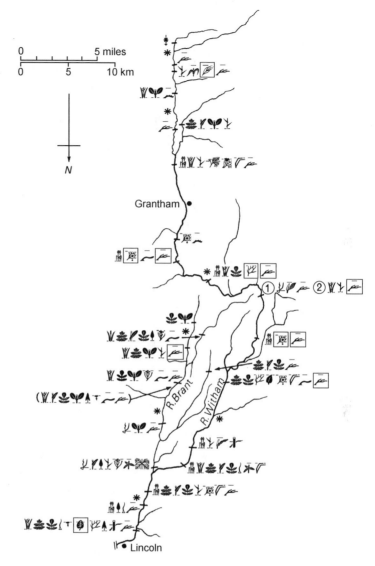

Figure 19.4
Intermittently polluted River Witham (Lincolnshire). Mostly clay, but upper River Witham on soft limestone; most records 1974 and 1975. Main effluent sources starred.

✳ Land species in brook

(see above). There is less *Potamogeton pectinatus* here than in the River Avon: River Avon receives sewage from larger towns.

The examples described so far have been lowland, usually clay rivers. The same effects, however, occur on other rock types, provided the flow in hill streams is not too strong for plant growth (see Chapters 2, 5, 6 and 13). The Rivers Don and Dearne (Yorkshire) on Coal Measures and resistant rocks have species-rich sites only on clean tributaries without fierce spates. The main rivers are polluted, species-poor, and with *Potamogeton pectinatus* as the most frequent species. The River Ribble

363

(Lancashire, 1973) on mountainous resistant rock has a clean tributary, the River Hodder, which has little but pollution-sensitive vegetation; a seriously polluted one, the River Calder, with widespread *Potamogeton pectinatus* and little else (in fact the flow in the River Calder appears too fierce for *Potamogeton pectinatus* in its ordinary habitat range. Here it must grow fast, fast enough for new growth to replace wash-out.); and the River Ribble itself, which is clean above but becomes slightly polluted and eutrophicated (upstream of the confluence with the River Calder), with a species-rich flora including *Potamogeton pectinatus*.

Pollution cannot, however, be assessed solely by species lists. The River Leadon (Figure 11.6) receives harmful organic pollution from Ledbury, though recovery is shown farther downstream and the vegetation of Figure 11.6 fits this pattern. However, this river has a very fluctuating water level, much silting and considerable shading, all of which decrease vegetation, and even some fairly large tributaries are species-poor. The main river may indeed have its vegetation damaged by pollution, but this cannot be proved by the species found there because of the other unfavourable factors involved.

Species diversity may vary with large fluctuations in weather. For instance, fringing herbs increase when there are few storms, as do submerged plants in hill streams. This must be considered when interpreting vegetation records.

HEAVY METAL POLLUTION

Many metals, such as iron, zinc and lead, may enter rivers in trade effluents, in streams draining from mines, and in general run-off from ore-bearing rocks. Plant occurrence (for size, see below) seem to be little affected by the usual metal concentrations in most British streams, and a country-wide survey (see Chapter 8) showed no detectable correlation of plant patterns with the variability shown by any or all of ten heavy metals (beryllium, cadmium, chromium, cobalt, copper, iron, lead, manganese, nickel, tin and zinc in acid solution). This is so even in sites generally considered to be polluted. For example:

    River Dee (Dee and Clyde), trade effluent from chemical factory
    River Hayle (Cornwall), copper, etc. effluent from mines
    River Lydney (Wye), iron effluent from mine
    Canal, Coventry, metal trade effluent

Of course, effects of trade effluents from towns can be masked by the other effects of sewage effluents (see above) and by the unusual nature of the effect. Heavy metal poisoning (when non-lethal) leads to fewer shoots in the clump. As colour and size are hardly affected, it is very difficult to say a clump of 10 shoots would have 15 if there was no heavy metal pollution. (Plant vigour, wash-out, substrate, grazing, etc., also influence size.) In tiny brooks in mining areas, damage may occur. The very severely polluted rivers, e.g., River Tame (Trent) contain so many toxic pollutants that it is not now possible to say which of these pollutants harm plants the most.

POLLUTIONS IN WHICH SUSPENDED OR DEPOSITED SEDIMENTS ARE IMPORTANT

Coal mine pollution produces turbidity and deposited sediment, and was still frequent in the 1970s. Turbidity decreases light penetration, confining plants to shallower water, decreasing both the total amount of vegetation present and (selectively) the most light-sensitive species (see Chapter 7). Sedimentation causes unstable substrates and extra sediment moving during faster flows (see Chapter 3). In the lowlands, plants can grow well with extra coal dust sediment in brooks where there is little storm flow. In the hills, however, the swifter normal flow and the spate flows make the habitat very unstable, and therefore the plants sparse. Coal rivers usually have sewage and industrial pollution also, and *Potamogeton pectinatus* is the most tolerant species (in Greater Manchester, however, *Sparganium emersum* is the more common). This plant can anchor in and partly stabilise fine sediment, and as it grows afresh each season from winter buds it is not affected by the wash-out in winter which would be very damaging to plants with winter rhizomes. (Winter buds are scattered by wash-out but enough remain in suitable sites for regrowth.) The next most tolerant species in coal streams are emergents at the edges, and these are naturally less affected by the coal dust. *Ranunculus*, which is light-sensitive and has winter rhizomes, can recolonise and increase rapidly in suitable streams if coal pollution is removed (Whitton & Buckmaster, 1970).

Lead mining can cause much deposition of sludge, and any smothering sediment causes at least temporary damage (see Chapter 3).

Paper mill effluents are lighter and do not accumulate on the channel bed. Light penetration is decreased of course, but when particles are pale, plants can grow well below the depth of water visible when looking down on the stream. In the River Don (Aberdeen), the following grow satisfactorily:

Potamogeton × sparganifolium   *Sparganium emersum*
Ranunculus cf. *aquatilis*

Sewage and industrial effluents of poor quality may be turbid, but their chemical effects (see above) are the more important to river plants.

Boats stir up silt on channel beds causing turbidity and unstable substrates, and dredging off the loose sediment may improve vegetation. Boat propellers also cause mechanical damage, and the chemical pollution from rubbish, sewage waste, etc. can be considerable, although theoretically non-existent. Canals are sometimes polluted by industrial effluents as well as by boats. The most tolerant canal species are:

𝕵	*Glyceria maxima*	𝕲	*Sparganium emersum*
𝕿	*Lemna minor* agg.	𝖂	*Sparganium erectum*
𝖄	*Potamogeton pectinatus*		

Silt is always washed out from the land, but the amount is much increased by deep ploughing, intensive agriculture and generally by the conditions causing rapid run-off and flash floods (Green, 1975). This extra silt (see Chapter 3):

1. increases nutrient status;
2. favours deep-rooted (silt) species, and discouraged shallow-rooted (gravel) ones;
3. decreases substrate stability by increasing the amount of loose sediment;
4. increases turbidity;
5. increases abrasion (but not significantly).

The effects are most noticeable in clay catchments, where silt is most abundant. The increase in sediment is less than the amount occurring in coal streams, however, and so the plants are affected less. (Also see Chapter 17 — Lowering of the water level.)

Sediments washed out from clay, sand or gravel works increase the amount of sediment of these in streams. The effects on vegetation are similar to those from agricultural silting, except that sand and gravel hardly affect nutrient status and affect rooting differently to silt (see Chapter 3). Such sediments enhance the natural sedimentation–erosion patterns (e.g. River Don, Aberdeen), except that in swift streams with little deposition the extra sediment may not affect plants (e.g. River Wheeler, River Clwyd).

Cattle trampling, swimming, etc., also cause disturbance, and with sufficient disturbance plants are damaged and, later, killed. The tall monocotyledons are the most resistant, as they are large and receive least trampling.

HERBICIDES AND PESTICIDES

Herbicides sprayed onto crops may drift onto, or be accidentally sprayed on, watercourses and cause damage to plants (e.g. herbicides containing 2,4-D harm emerged dicotyledons). Intentional spraying of watercourse emergents is described in Chapter 18.

Chemicals entering the water may come from:

1. Aquatic herbicides applied to dykes, drains and, to a lesser extent, canals (see Chapter 18).

2. Land herbicides washed out from the land or falling in from above.
3. Herbicides and pesticides dumped into watercourses as the easiest method of disposing of them, or being washed in from accidental spillages.

The effects on the plants are greatest in dykes and drains, both because herbicides are deliberately applied in these and because they have very little water movement, so the chemicals remain in the habitat instead of being quickly washed out to sea. Unfortunately for plant growth, herbicides do drift with water movement within the dyke system, and so affect areas far from those that are actually sprayed. The dyke species most tolerant to management and pollution (not necessarily only herbicides; see Chapter 18) are:

Agrostis stolonifera   *Enteromorpha intestinalis*

Callitriche spp.   *Lemna minor* agg.

With the exception of *Callitriche* spp. these are among the plants most tolerant to sewage pollution. Most of the pollution-tolerant stream species, however, do not grow well in dykes anyway (see Chapters 3, 12, 13 and 14).

HEAT

Vallisneria spiralis is not native to Britain, but it occurs where heated effluents enter rivers in some lowland regions (Hynes, 1960). For the distinctive patterns of other types of pollution, see e.g. Haslam (1987) and the works of Kohler *et al.*, listed in the Bibliography.

RECENT CHANGES IN POLLUTION

Some examples of recovery after rivers have been cleaned up have been described above and in Chapter 20. In the River Tees (Yorkshire), in *c.* 30 years (Whitton & Dalpra, 1968) there has been a decrease in *Elodea canadensis*, an increase in *Ranunculus fluitans*, and the appearance of *Enteromorpha intestinalis* in freshwater parts. In the habitat there has been a decrease in coal dust and an increase in organic pollution in the tributary River Skerne, which increased eutrophication and pollution in the lower River Tees. Subsequently, pollution has been improved, but was still considerable in the River Skerne near Darlington in 2000.

Unfortunately, there is reliable evidence concerning vegetation in the nineteenth and early twentieth century for only a few watercourses, and most of the surveys are of streams which were, and remain, fairly clean (e.g. Butcher, 1927, 1933; records of rare *Potamogeton* spp.). It is, however, generally agreed that the vegetation of Fenland dykes has seriously declined in both quality and quantity since around 1950, coinciding with the increased use of herbicides. *Chara* was reportedly widespread and abundant in dykes, but is now almost absent from both dykes and streams. In general, British rivers with the worst industrial pollution have been cleaned, particularly with the coming of EU Directives.

As indicated above, however, hard surface run-off is increasing fast, and is perhaps the main current danger. This comes because:

1. General increase in wealth and mobility means far more vehicles on the roads.
2. This increase is not confined to the major roads, but affects the minor roads as well with the spread of out-of-town (a) housing estates, (b) business and industrial estates, and (c) road instead of rail freight transport.

By the 1970s, both fertiliser and 'killing' agrochemicals were being used freely, though their effects varied over the country.

The main change in river pollutions from the 1970s to the 2000s has therefore been:

•   Lessening the gross pollutions from heavy industry and mines (closing these down as much as improving their treatment) and from towns with then-unsatisfactory treatment works. But:
•   Increasing the mild to moderate pollution from the other causes, which has now spread far too nearly throughout the country.

That is, from having much localised gross pollution and widespread low pollution, three decades have brought moderate pollution country-wide. Obviously pockets of gross pollution remain, there is much variation within 'moderate pollution', and some streams are remote enough to remain clean. (Though it is depressing how even Highland streams may be polluted by cattle units and peat drainage!)

In theory, hard surface — and indeed farmland — run-off could be cleaned by well designed buffer zones and sewer drainage, but the expense would be considerable. And those who have never seen a clean river are likely to consider a moderately-polluted one 'wild' and acceptable.

CASE STUDY: THE (ABERDEEN) RIVER DON, 1969–1991

This river rises in resistant rock mountains, where by bog peat leaches (and erodes) into the mountain tributaries, giving nutrient-poor vegetation. Downstream it flows through hills and agricultural lowlands before reaching its mouth at Aberdeen. The urban area by and near Aberdeen is increasingly developed. The tale of the different chemical influences on the river plants, and their response is illuminating.

Chemical impacts

1. Peat (bog peat) influence

   This traditionally affects the streams on and from the mountain bogs. By the early 1980s, the upper peat was being drained (drainage channels were cut deep, so erosion followed). Therefore more peat was, temporarily, entering the river, the water became browner and nutrient-poor species (e.g. *Callitriche hamulata*, *Myriophyllum alterniflorum*) became more frequent in the middle river.

2. Channelling influence upstream

   This also was a 1980s phenomenon. In the mountain region, far too much of the typical streams was dredged (presumably also for drainage). The storm-swept gravel bars at the gentle edges of streams were replaced by steep, more stable slopes of disturbed (so more nutrient-rich) soil. Consequently fringe species such as *Juncus articulatus* and *Petasites hybridus* were replaced by fringing herbs such as *Mentha aquatica*, *Mimulus guttatus* agg. and *Myosotis scorpioides* (more nutrient-rich than their predecessors).

3. Paper mill effluent

   There were two long-standing factories in the lower reaches. In 1969, their effluent looked like Instant Milk, white, turbid and streaky. Sewage fungus was abundant, and the downstream community very poor (being assessed at *e* on the Haslam & Wolseley index, Haslam, 1987, 1997). With growing awareness of the damage done by river pollution, clean-up started, and by the mid-1980s there was no effect on the plants of the lower mill and, by 1991, not even a short-term effect from the effluent of the upper mill. Effluent from a nearby sewage treatment works also had no detectable effect. These, all still discharging effluent, show how possible it is (with money and goodwill) to improve effluents until they are apparently harmless. 'Apparently', because (a) the lower river has other contaminations, so small effects could be masked, and (b) the amount of pollution which is acceptable in a large river may yet destroy the chemical environment of a small stream, particularly one with a low general chemical content (Haslam, 1990).

   Improvements showed in:

   - increase of water-supported species by an average of two per site between 1981 and 1987 (more, if starting from 1969 and 1978). Species included: *Ranunculus* spp., *Callitriche* spp., *Elodea canadensis*, *Potamogeton sparganifolius*, *Sparganium emersum*, and mosses.
   - arrival of fringing herbs downstream of the effluents. Obviously fragments had been passing from upstream all the time, but established populations developed only with the clean-up (e.g.

Mentha aquatica, Mimulus guttatus agg., *Myosotis scorpioides, Veronica beccabunga*). Polluted fringing herbs have poor root systems and are easily washed out, and slow to recover.

- increase of other short emergents, better-rooting and rather less sensitive to pollution than the fringing herbs (e.g. *Caltha palustris, Equisetum palustre, Polygonum amphibium*).
- arrival of mosses downstream of the three effluents (factories, and sewage treatment works). Despite many bouldery reaches, which if clean would undoubtedly bear mosses, these were sparse or absent, except for the cleanest year of 1987 (see below).
- arrival of the nutrient-poor and pollution-sensitive *Callitriche hamulata* and *Myriophyllum alterniflorum*.
- complete loss of sewage fungus directly associated with the mills, which used to near-blanket the river.
- Other effluents in the river were also improved, but their vegetation was studied less closely.

4. Improper use of herbicide

Midstream (diquat alginate) was mis-applied to the lower river in 1990, causing massive kills of vegetation, including of the (probably best British population of the) rare *Potamogeton sparganifolius*. This was done for anglers: and should have been properly applied on the bed only, early in the year, to lessen future plant growth in salmon pools. Fortunately, in 1991 the vegetation had much recovered.

In 1990, there was also over-use of herbicide on tall monocotyledon fringes. Such fringes, although sometimes annoying to anglers, protect banks from eroding in spate flows. It is expensive to mend banks! Spate flows wash away such bands that extend into the river, away from the anchoring bank (see, e.g., Chapter 3), and this comes free.

5. Increase of urbanisation with no corresponding increase in anti-pollution measures

On the outskirts of Aberdeen, and in nearby settlements, there was much development: housing, airport, supermarkets, industry. This was spread over a 'large' area, the catchments of many small burns (streams). By 1990 the local river authority had noted 18 polluted incoming tributaries in this lower stretch, and these did not include the smallest, five of which were present and polluted by 1991 in the most-studied part. Sewage fungus and algae were again frequent, but not due to the factories. One was polluted for the first time in 1991. Those investigated were linked to development. Even a supermarket car park, when built above the river, had enough dirty run-off to be noticeable by the flourishing Blanket weed and lowered diversity in a swift, rocky (so well-oxygenated) part of the main river.

That is, the pollution effects are first noticed in the river plants, and exploration finds the (even only 0.5 m wide) dirty tributary and follows it upstream to locate the source of the contamination.

Glyceria maxima is one of the species whose shoots in the water become pale with (particularly organic) pollution (and usually on silt). In 1981, this yellowing occurred on the entry of tributaries polluted by both the airport and the factory effluents. From 1981 to 1985 the frequency of such yellowed sites decreased, but in 1986 it began to rise, being found in about half the recorded burns in 1989. Up to 1988, yellowed sites were at and downstream of the airport tributaries only. Thereafter they extended some miles upstream also.

6. Self-purification

The river cleans itself, transforms and removes contaminants, from source to mouth. The pollutants needing cleaning are:
- agrochemicals from the farmed land covering most of the catchment (roughly stable);
- run-off from hard surfaces (getting worse rapidly);
- effluents from the occasional farm, industrial or house settlement, which have not yet been brought to modern standards;
- treated effluents (improving).

Throughout, the river plants and the stream both clean (also see Haslam, 1990, 2003). Like a sewage treatment works, the plants can be overloaded, or receive contamination they cannot deal with. But they clean greatly, though less now so many minor streams are dried. The total area of such streams (area of purifying) is considerable.

Purification is most when no contaminants enter from the land beside, such as in the moors upstream, or a wood or wetland downstream, and is of course least when much pollution is entering.

7. Change of rock type

Most of the Don catchment is on resistant rock and, at the level of investigation reported here, its variations have no direct effect on the river vegetation (which is altered by topography, flow, downstream variation, and human impact). However, in the upper catchments occasional outcrops of sandstone make vegetation changes visible at a glance. Where the sandstone starts, banks and hard substrate are immediately sandstone. A little further down unstable sediment and water become influenced by sandstone, and these continue to influence the plants for a short distance downstream of the return to resistant rock. So the upstream marking of sandstone is immediate, the downstream marking, a little fuzzy.

On the sandstone:

- the water-supported species (*Callitriche* spp., *Ranunculus* spp., etc.) increase in cover, e.g. from *c.* 15% to *c.* 80%. Both anchorage and nutrients are better for these species on the sandstone.
- the fringing herbs become more frequent, forming more of, or indeed fully, a fringe. Roots grow better, and can anchor better.
- because of the fringing herbs, cover and diversity (two of the standard measures) both increase. In short sandstone reaches there may be no new species, but the increased frequency of each of the resistant rock species increases site diversity on the sandstone.
- because of the increase in fringing herbs (a generally mesotrophic group) the floral analyses show a skewing to mesotrophic, even when the sandstone is in an upstream generally moorland area.

And indeed, most sandstones are of higher nutrient status than resistant rocks (see Chapter 8), partly as the sandstone rock, partly as the nutrient-rich silt it gives rise to in the river bed. As usual, the vegetation change draws attention to itself and its potential causes, and observation — and the use of a geological map — show the cause is rock type.

Non-chemical changes

1. Drought and high-flow summers

   In drought summers the water level is lower on the banks, leaving more exposed 'edge' ground, and additionally there are (probably) fewer storm flows. This allows:

   - fringing herbs, small grasses and other short emergents colonise more, and have longer to grow between wash-outs. (This is separable from the effects of pollution, because drought affects the whole river; pollution, only downstream of its entry.)
   - tall monocotyledon bands, if composed of suitable species, can grow out further into the river. *Sparganium erectum*, a river more than a bank species, can grow particularly far in the river, though *Glyceria maxima* can come out some way. (*G. maxima* is firmly anchored only to the bank.) Sometimes this band extends 3 m or more into the river channel. The next spate flow will find resistance from these clumps, resistance increases

because the plants are so far into the flow channel. The spates will wash them away. Because of this added resistance, and the interlocking of the mosaic of rhizomes, more of the band is likely to be removed than if it was narrower. Therefore, in some places all the tall monocots are taken away, leaving bare areas which can be quickly colonised by fringing herbs — until the slower-growing tall monocotyledons shade them out.

- *Lemna minor*, washed into the river, can grow well and form good populations in indentations in the bank and such-like sheltered places — and get caught and grow in dense water-supported plants reaching the water surface.

- silt is deposited on sides, shoals and islands which provide habitat and (see Chapter 8) nutrients, especially for species upstream that cannot grow unless they have this extra source.

In high flow summers the reverse occurs. There is less habitat for fringing herbs, tall monocotyledon bands remain narrow, and there is little or no *Lemna minor* and silting. With this decrease in diversity, it is important to understand the habitat, and not attribute the loss to increased pollution!

2. Drying: drainage and abstraction

As always, the farmer's wish for drier farmland means drainage and the drying of smaller streams. In the hilly middle reaches in the 1970s, streams formerly bearing only water-supported plants, instead bore more easily scoured emerged plants, such as *Mimulus guttatus* agg. These were previously restricted to the banks. By 1990, many more were dry and grassed over, or at any rate too dry for a good river plant community.

Abstraction is partly by factories, which return the water to the river some tens of metres downstream (and, in the most-studied part, do not take enough water to harm the main river). But abstraction is also for mains supplies, and this water is lost to the river. If, once depth and discharge are lowered, they still fall within the optimum range for the species (or improve them to the optimum) this will not damage the habitat.

Where the river becomes too shallow for the water-supported species which were there before, though, these decrease in frequency and cover, and so in site diversity also. At the same time the shallow-water habitat at the river edges becomes wider, and emergents can invade and colonise the new habitat (subject, of course, to spate flows). The characteristic way of recognising severely abstracted sites — and indeed sites equally severely affected by drought — is that, compared with a reference site (see above), the diversity and cover of water-supported species is too low. If that of emergents is too high, that is supporting evidence for the diagnosis.

Other evidence is required (e.g. knowing the rainfall) to distinguish between sites dried by abstraction (which will be long-term, and the vegetation may, but often does not, adjust) or by drought (which is usually for 1–2 years only).

3. General habitat

As in all rivers, separate factors also make habitats suitable or less suitable for vegetation. The River Don ranges from mountain to lowland, from moor to urban, and there are, for example, mills on tributaries, places where livestock drink — all the ordinary hindrances to good vegetation. In the lower river there are, as usual, parts too deep (or unstable) for macrophytes, and vegetation at the shallow sides has to be used for interpretation. There are shaded reaches, where vegetation is reduced or even removed through lack of light. There are bridges, with piers and lined banks, which shade and alter substrates both directly and indirectly (either by piers or by a small weir associated with the bridge) causing alterations in flow, depth and substrate around the bridge: and so, alterations in vegetation. There are constructed channels, there are weirs. All alter habitat, and so, potentially, vegetation.

The year 1987

1987 had the highest quality of vegetation in the lower river, in the years between 1969 and 1991. By 1987, the effluents entering the river were reasonably clean. And although the number of polluted tributaries was increasing, their effects were not yet serious.

In 1988, vegetation quality was down, which was puzzling. Effluents, weather, disturbance, herbicide: none of these accounted for the deterioration. Just one of those things? No: by 1989 the reason became clear. It is very sad when so much trouble has been put into a clean-up and new pollutions arrive to undo most of the good. The calculated damage ratings downstream of the factories and sewage treatment effluents were similar in the early 1980s and early 1990s.

And the River Don is no more complex than other rivers of its size! Its complexities may be different, habitat variations are many, but to interpret whole rivers, plant behaviour must be understood.

CONCLUSION

No streams are now truly free of chemical alteration by human impact. With pollution, species lists become shorter, and skewed in ways varying with the type of pollution. Frequency and cover of species sensitive to particular pollutants decrease, leaving the species which are more tolerant, or actually favour it. These later succumb, and eventually, in gross pollution, no macrophytes remain.

The first and greatest effect of common pollution is to reduce root systems. This, plus the increased shoot growth found with some mild types of contamination increase wash-out, and so vegetation loss. As pollution increases further, both shoots and roots become very weak and unhealthy, and easily washed out, and eventually plants cannot grow.

Pollution tolerance varies both with the effect on the species, and with the suitability of the site for anchorage of the available species. With good anchorage (e.g. firm gravel for *Ranunculus*) a species can grow in pollutions it would not be able to with poor anchorage (e.g. deep silt for *Ranunculus*). There is an important difference here to still waters, lakes, ponds, dykes, etc. Generally speaking their substrate is not disturbed (apart from, e.g. wave-swept headlands), so plants can remain in place even with very poor root systems: and indeed if there is plenty of vegetation and enough nutrients, floating shoots of formerly-rooted plants may remain. Pollution-tolerance of species in still waters is thus related only to the general effect on the plant's welfare. In running waters, the effect on the development of the root system is of at least equal importance.

Chemical ranges of different species differ greatly: from those of blanket bog streams to those of large clay rivers, with all the variants between. Therefore a nutrient-rich pollution (enough to destroy the calcium-dominated community of an upper chalk stream, e.g., Haslam, 1990) could have little effect on a clay river in a rich alluvial plain. Species of nutrient-rich habitats are more tolerant to nutrient-rich pollutions; species extending into brackish-water habitats are more tolerant to salt pollution, and so on. It is therefore necessary to know the behaviour and range of species before using them to detect and assess pollution. Geographic range must also be considered. A species in its centre of distribution is more tolerant to a given pollution than one at the extreme end of its range (see Haslam, 1987). In the former instance, climate is optimum, so also the potential habitat factors associated with that climate. In the later instance, the plant is barely able to survive even when other factors are optimal for the region. Adding another stress, a chemical one, can be just too much.

Physical and chemical, organic and inorganic habitat factors all influence river plants, as has been described in earlier chapters. Once each is understood for its effect on each species, their integration to produce a given community also becomes understandable. It is like having an onion: first, the brown outer covering — say, the flow — is seen, studied and understood, then this becomes transparent, and the next habitat layer — say, the substrate — is seen, studied and understood. The chemical layers, of the natural and the impact chemicals, are usually one of the last. They are so complex, and indeed so not understood, that it is best to be able to interpret the physical habitat before considering them. It is not generally known, but no water has been completely analysed chemically. Several tens of thousands of chemicals are known to occur in fresh water. How many are not known of? And how many of the known ones occur in any given water? Tap, clean river, or polluted river? No one knows. And how few of the known ones have been tested for their effects on water plants! Therefore doubt must remain on effects. When river waters have their nitrate, phosphate, pesticides, etc., measured, these add up to (roughly) 10% of the Total Dissolved Solids in the water! What is the effect of the other 90%?

Chemicals enter rivers from:

- the rock below;
- the subsoil, which may be entirely derived from the rock, or may much differ (e.g., glacial deposits);
- the soil, which may or may not be from the subsoil and rock (not, when the soil is shallow peat, for instance);
- the land use;
- impacts (which include land use, and usually also include soil). These vary greatly as described above.

Once plant behaviours are known, it becomes as simple to interpret the vegetation of a polluted stream (provided there is enough of it!) as of one less damaged. Although pollution patterns, and tolerant etc. species are characteristic, for accurate assessments it is necessary to know what the vegetation would be if all chemical impact, all pollution, was removed. This is the importance of reference communities, communities of streams known to have low damage, so that all other communities can be measured against them. It is then possible to say how great the loss of species and cover is, and how great the skewing (the loss of pollution-sensitive species). And so to assess the damage, chemical (pollution) and otherwise.

Shallowing (drying), shading, disturbance, etc., also give characteristic communities (see Haslam, 1987, 1990, 1997).

As long as the researcher really knows plant behaviour, all indices and assessment methods using plants will be correct: within their parameters. There are plenty of different ways of assessment available in 2005, and the one chosen should be the one best suited to the purpose of the investigation, chosen by first knowing the plant behaviour and habitat for this purpose.

Despite the work of, e.g. Butcher (1927, 1933), by 1960 it was generally considered in Britain that river plants were 'weed', pests that needed removing, and were of no use for interpreting river habitats. Further study has, generally speaking, reversed this opinion (e.g. Caffrey *et al.*, 2002; Gonzales *et al.*, 2002; Haslam, 1981, 1987, 1990, 1997; Haury *et al.*, 2002; Holmes, 1983, 1985; Sabbatini *et al.*, 2002; Triest, 2002. See Bibliography for a fuller list.). It can now be said that river plants are excellent bioindicators. They are of suitable size to be seen from bank, boat or bridge, there is no need (usually) for trawling, magnifying glass or microscope. They are of suitable number to be easily learnt. Using just 70 species the common British habitats can all be identified and assessed. Using 120 species refines the process and identifies all. It is relatively easy to learn 100! River plants also have the advantage of being stationary. (They do not swim or run away from the investigation.) Their extreme sensitivity to the habitats in which they live, which has been demonstrated throughout this book, means their presence, pattern, amount and behaviour can interpret those conditions. (See Chapter 8: as site species number, or repetition increase, so does the accuracy of the diagnosis, the habitat range in which all the site species can occur becoming increasingly specific.)

20

Restoration

Restoration is the term commonly used for the removal of the worse excesses of human impact on rivers, both directly, as giving a more natural channel shape, and indirectly, as reducing pollution from hard surfaces. It has become desirable partly on ethical grounds and partly to improve water quality, decrease flooding of housing and crops, decrease maintenance costs and decrease land erosion. Difficulties include the pressure on farmers for non-sustainable land management, including (not intentionally) erosion, flood, water pollution, and the cultivation of riverside land (so no space is allowed for meandering of channels and local floods); the wish of planners and developers to build on flood plains, which then need major defences from flood; and the general wish to dispose of waste free by putting it in the river.

The cost of restoration methods varies greatly: from inserting meanders and returning riverside land to flood grassland, to leaving channel shape alone, to become, over time, more natural.

This chapter describes the larger picture, from upstream land management to the effect of fencing off livestock. These all act on river plants through channel depth, flow, substrate, disturbance, pollution, etc.: the factors described in other chapters of this book.

For several decades (roughly the late 1960s to the 1990s) the ideal planners' and river engineers' river was close to Figure 20.1: this example is in fact in Hertfordshire, but can be easily found in other lowland counties. This is as far as possible from the high-quality rivers shown in, especially, Chapters 10–13. The channel is straight, to remove (evil!) water from the land as quickly as possible, and to allow maximum cultivation. No land is 'wasted' in meanders.

The bed has been deepened, so water level is well below ground level. This means the risk of flooding is reduced (as water level can rise so much without flooding) and that the land is drained. Water from the soil and subsoil is drawn down into the stream, removed from the land, which is now dry. (So it needs irrigation in summer, wasting water

Figure 20.1
Hard engineering for drainage and rapid disposal of water.
(Y. Bower, in Haslam, 1991.)

378

twice, firstly by removing to the sea that needed on the land, secondly by removing loss on land, to be that water which is needed in the river.)

The channel shape is trapezoid, the standard slope being 1.5:1, becoming steeper below water level. The slopes are thus unsuitably steep for good edge vegetation. The channel is uniform in shape, with few niches. It is uniform in texture, and without the seedbed and faunal resting stages found in a more natural bed.

With minimum length and vegetation, and relatively swift through flow, the water has minimum purifying ability (see Chapters 8 and 19). It also has minimum fauna — though for some groups, e.g. some coarse fish, these channels can be satisfactory. This was all done for the laudable purpose of increasing crop production and lessening flood damage. Unfortunately, wider aspects were not included.

In such channels the hydrological coupling of run-off, flood plain and river has been broken, with serious consequences for all aspects of water regime (discharge, storage, sources, ground water, drying ditches and streams, so irrigation and drainage; and so also water quality. See, e.g., Haslam 2003, In preparation). Drying leads to the loss of small streams and wet ditches and so to the loss of much of the total river length. Planners easily forget that the 0.25–1 m wide wet channels, though low in discharge, are great in length: Let them go!

Biodiversity, habitat types and communities are lost from and beside channels. Trees are removed (they obstruct machinery, and, should they fall, perhaps obstruct flow). Local niches are lost where, e.g. *Potamogeton crispus* could grow where silt was deposited in a low-nutrient meandering stream.

The riverscape value, beauty, diversity, interest and consequent wish of the public to visit and enjoy streams, is lost. Purseglove (1989) records talking to an engineer sending in bulldozers to create a Figure 20.1 river, who had, in his caravan, one of the more famous Essex river pictures of John Constable, *The Haywain*. To turn England's green and pleasant land into Figure 20.1 is a destruction of heritage, history, culture — and of the more important uses the river has for people.

As the ugliness and destruction spread, so did the movement for reform. In Britain, Purseglove (1989) produced early warning. Denmark took action sooner with a 1982 Watercourse Act. The British Water Acts 1989–91 direct most aspects of water resources and disposal, but have much less environmental content. And the European Union started taking notice. The 1978 Directive on the quality of fresh waters needing protection or improvement in order to support fish life showed the old and naive outlook, rivers have a use: but only for fish to be caught by people. The 1992 Habitats Directive, and the 2000 Water Framework Directive value rivers. The 1992 Rio [de Janeiro] Biodiversity Convention caused a radical re-think by authorities, large and small. Quite quickly, to have more plant and animal species became Good (for public relations, even if for nothing else!) and barren land, barren waters were no longer to be admired.

The environmental part of the EU Commission has a tradition of employing forward-looking scientists, and their efforts in Directives are very well intended. They give effect to many justified concerns raised in their own countries by field ecologists.

What should be the proper name for what these endeavour to do? 'Restoration' is that usually used, and so is the title of this chapter. However, 'restoration' really means turning something made bad by people into what it was before: almost possible with a garden, a cultivated field or a wall, but not possible with a river.

British rivers have been changed by human impact. Direct changes (for flood protection, transport) go back certainly over 2000 years, and indirect ones (resulting from forest removal, increased grazing, and cultivation) for much longer. There is little evidence of the natural state of rivers, and indeed with the invasion of Man following soon after the retreat of the glaciers (the latter some 10 000 years ago) there was no long period of temperate climate for 'natural rivers', untouched by Man, to become established and stable.

Restoring is therefore aimed at a much more recent state — pre-1950 is satisfactory, 1850–1940 (from after the first to before the second main round of drainage) even more so. The channels can be located (e.g. by digging) and restored. Channel shape could perhaps be restored, too. The least satisfactory method of restoration, and so — not surprisingly — that most used, is to plan in an office. Natural rivers have meanders. Therefore the restored river will, too, nice rounded ones. Natural rivers have stones on the bed in riffles. Therefore get some lorry loads dumped: and this is such a Good thing to do, that there is no need to check the stones are of the same rock type as the bed, or whether the arrangements increases oxygenation. Natural rivers have trees. So plant some: and fail to realise some tree species, and indeed many strains of native species sold in nursery gardens are in fact alien, and form a different and non-British riverscape. And so on. The snags are becoming more widely known (though non-native, e.g. willows, will spoil riverscapes for even centuries to come).

Although such riverscapes have, technically, been created rather than restored, restoration is now the normal term for the process.

THE WATER FRAMEWORK DIRECTIVE

The implications of this directive had yet to be worked out when this chapter was written. The Directive has the potential to be the most beneficial legislation for rivers ever enacted in Britain, but could also end in token works and many words.

(The following is based partly on the Directive, Everard 2004; Everard *et al.,* 2002, 2004; Kohler & Veit, 2003a,b.)

'Water is not a commercial product like any other but, rather, **a heritage** which must be **protected, defended** and treated as such.' (author's bold). The water, when treated like that, bears a characteristic and diverse plant community, related to this water and its environs. The Directive requires Integrated River Basin Management, managing all waters (watercourses, water bodies, ground waters, affected lands) as dynamic systems, land–water systems. This means integrated, cross-discipline planning. There are five purposes:

1. The prevention of further deterioration and the protection and enhancement of the status of aquatic ecosystems.
2. The promotion of sustainable water use.
3. The enhanced protection and improvement of the aquatic environment.
4. The progressive reduction of pollution of groundwater.
5. The mitigation of the effects of floods and droughts.

The first, third and fourth of these purposes affect river plants directly (polluted groundwater means polluted spring water), and the second and fifth purposes, indirectly (no further surface water loss, no excesses of discharge).

Catchments, river basins, have to be described in such a way that impacts as well as features are identified, and impacts and their effects can be compared from time to time. Descriptions like this have, before, been only of those rivers and catchments which were selected for study by researchers (from authorities, universities or elsewhere). Provided human impact is properly identified and assessed, these characterisations make an enormous contribution to understanding and interpretation and the potential improvement of unsustainable uses.

From the characterisations, Programmes of Measures are to be established which will lead to Good Ecological Status (via Measures, divided into Basic, Legal, Supplementary, code and voluntary). Unlike so many other organisations and procedures, assessment of High Ecological Status includes aquatic flora! So the value of river plants has been established in Community Law! Of course, until the later twentieth century, good vegetation could be taken for granted in areas of low population and industry (e.g., Haslam, 1990), so it was unnecessary for law to take cognisance of anything other than the hazards they created — plants are weeds, liable to be pests. It is only when destruction is extreme that law is needed for protection. The change in thinking, in mindset, is, however, sharp. During the research for the first edition of this book, in conferences on rivers, to comment that river vegetation was a subject of study was to make colleagues depart to the far end of the room.

High Ecological Status is what would be present in the absence of human impact. As mentioned above, this is not a practical concept in a highly-impacted land like Britain, so has to be defined in relation to a particular era and management. Good Ecological Status is the best which can now be found (see Haslam, 1987, 1997), and it should not differ greatly from the High Ecological Status. Since the High has to be deduced from the present Good, this in practice means all river vegetation should reach the standard of the best found: and so have all habitat factors suitable for this.

Good vegetation requires suitable channel shape, discharge, diversity of niches and low impact of pollution and disturbance (see earlier chapters). To ensure rivers remain in a good state, assessments every three years are required, and experience in Britain and Germany confirms this interval should be sufficient: periods that, without impact assessments, (1) engineers may not do, e.g. channelling, (2) planners and industry may not create new pollution from fresh areas of hard surface or new effluents; (3) neither farmers nor developers may increase run-off by creating hard or firm surfaces; and (4) no more water may be abstracted, above and below ground. Without these four, which can all have sudden, dramatic effects, tri-annual assessments are quite satisfactory.

Before the days of motor traffic, and of agrochemicals, severe pollution was mainly from the point sources of sewage and industrial effluent discharge. These, therefore are what Britain has been identifying and improving for over a century. Indeed, it is hard to detect, in an already moderately polluted river, the effects of the best-quality effluents entering rivers. Diffuse source pollution has crept up in the past half century: fertilisers then pesticides over cultivated land, and the enormous increase of traffic pollution (increases in roads, housing estates, supermarket car parks, etc., and vast increases of the polluting vehicles). Britain is beginning to tackle the former, but measures to combat the latter are still in their infancy. Regular monitoring of river plants has made the deterioration all too clear.

For the first time the impacts on rivers can be considered as a whole. It is a principle of Common Law (e.g., Haslam, 1990) that each riparian owner must pass on downstream water in the same condition it entered upstream. This has been used for mills, boats, etc., but could now, as well as the Directive, be used for pollution.

Buffer zones (see Chapter 19) are used to help clean middle and lower streams. However, when streams rise in cultivated land, the water is little, but the leaching of agrochemicals is as great, per length, as downstream, and so the pollution is far greater. This polluted water is then passed to the next downstream owner, and so on. Eventually, downstream owners may be unfairly blamed for the agrochemical and indeed vehicle pollution they received from upstream: and which is, quite properly, monitored (and it may be, monitored partly by the river plants). If *Cryptosporidium* gets from upstream to downstream and abstractable water, for instance, the consequences can be great, and at present fall on the downstream owner.

Similarly, if upstream land is altered to increase flash run-off, either by hardening the surface, or by removing wetlands (tiny as well as large!) beside the stream, the effect of unstable discharge may be most felt downstream.

Community water policy should be, according to the Directive, based on a combined approach using control of pollution at source ('at source', not just at 'point' source), through the setting of emission limit values and of environmental quality standards. To honour the spirit and vision of the Directive, a new relationship with the water environment is required and, necessarily, with the lands as well (Everard *et al.,* 2002). Thinking sustainably means acknowledging that human use and impact is fully integrated with ecosystem functions. Catchment integrity is not just one natural flow of water, energy, organisms and sediment, but also the impact of flows of cultivation, transport, settlements and other economic driving forces. This concept is easy to put on paper, but to describe and interpret in each and every catchment requires a sophistication of survey and interpretation which is not, at the time of writing, available. With such characterisations much can be done.

Where implemented, the earlier EU Habitat Directive is already giving environmental benefits. Special Areas for Conservation (SACs) can greatly improve pollutions, etc. However, there is a danger in paying out too much for conservation to farmers. Where possible, improvements should pay for themselves. For instance, it is expensive to clean abstracted river water to drinking water standards, and the more so the more polluted the water. If upstream improvements lower such costs, the savings can fund the improvements. Where effluents are unlawfully discharged, the polluter should pay.

There is a tendency to think that as long as drinking water is clean, the contamination of the river is irrelevant. It is 'quite all right' to damage and destroy flora and fauna, particularly if, to the non-expert, the river looks all right: has mallard, minnows and 'weed'. The Water Framework Directive, fully implemented, will give far more awareness and (even if initially reluctant) understanding of rivers and their plants.

HUMAN IMPACT

It is the destruction caused by excessive human impact which in turn requires restoration, the need being felt by, e.g., ecologists, anglers, flood managers, boaters, hydrologists and mains water suppliers. Each has different needs: that for quality fauna and flora; easy and good fishing; no flash or deep floods; water of suitable depth and flow; no obstructions to flow; groundwater and all water linked; clean when abstracted, whether from river or from aquifer. The Water Framework Directive is intended to integrate all of these, and more. And also to show those with river uses irrelevant to Good Ecological Status that this does have practical advantages. Given the great change in outlook that came with the Rio Biodiversity Convention, this new hope is not unreasonable.

Table 20.1 summarises the main types of human impact. All alter vegetation, via the habitat alterations described in other chapters.

Restoration is the removing of alterations which are damaging to the river, and which are neither of heritage value in themselves (e.g., old town wharfs, old water mills) nor essential for human life (and no alternative means, such as Whole Catchment Management and avoiding building on flood plains, are practical).

Conferences on restoration tend to be, and properly, congratulatory on what has been achieved by the — pitifully few — researchers and engineers involved. Funding tends to run out soon after the works are complete. In one instance an official was only able to visit his restoration area a year later because he had leave to show it to a visiting scientist.

To ensure restoration:
1. Projects needs to be monitored for ten years or until stable (if longer).
2. When stable, the river should resemble the best, hardly damaged, similar river in the region.
   And, to be satisfied with the policy:
3. The length of river restored each year should far exceed that further destroyed. (At the time of writing, this is not so.) Restoration works vary from the very costly, e.g. re-instating a meandering course and changing land use to permit riverside flooding, to the relatively cheap, e.g. fencing a stream from livestock to prevent trampling and disturbance of the channel and destruction of the bank.

Economics unfortunately often keeps land use unfriendly to rivers. Ninety-four per cent of the subsidies under the EU's Common Agricultural Policy are intended to increase yields, environmental impacts being considered irrelevant. The major British food retailers

Table 20.1   Main types of human impact

1 Drying

Land drainage, abstraction of groundwater and river water, flood defence. Leading to loss of smaller streams, and breaking the functional connection between river and flood plain.

2 Moving courses (including straightening)

For: irrigation, navigation, drainage, supply, flood defence. Property and field boundaries difficulties. Islands, etc., moved, removed. Leading to uniform, usually over-straight channels.

3 Altering bank and channel shape

Lowering water level, lowering bed level; changing shape, slope and smoothness; embanking, etc. That is, creating new channels verging towards that of Figure 20.1.

4 Altering width

From channelling, drying, constructions, altering trees, etc.

5 Changing substrate

Amount of sedimentation and erosion. Particle size, consolidation, pattern.

6 Regulation and flood control

More stable discharge. Catchment management for drought run-off and peak flows, and floodwater storage.

7 Inserting constructions

Bridges, locks, weirs, sluices, mills, roads, docks, pipes, fords, etc. Lining banks and sometimes beds, by stones, piles, biofibre, willow spilling, reeds. etc.

8 Pollution

Effluents of domestic, farm and industrial wastes (including mines and fish farms). Run-off from hard surfaces (settlements, roads, out-of-town car parks, etc.). Agrochemicals from cultivated land.

9 Disturbance

Creating and maintaining channel changes for the above. More local from livestock, recreation, wildlife, etc.

10 Putting underground

Small streams may be culverted in the country. In towns, larger ones may be also.

11 Altering vegetation

River vegetation now exists and flourishes only in relation to human impact, which can leave it, remove it or skew it. Direct impact is by altering habitat, is by: cutting, grazing, herbicide, removing (or planting) riverside trees; and, for restoration, importing channel or bank species (far too often non-local and even non-British). Indirect impact is by altering habitat (see above).

are continually trying to buy cheaper from farms, so the farmer's profit margin is minimal for leaving beetle banks and buffer strips, and for paying for time spent maintaining riverside woods and hedges. As Everard *et al.* (2004) point out, if upstream, and particularly hill farmers protect the environment, it is the downstream users, particularly for abstraction (but see above), angling and recreation activities, which benefit. For instance, keeping hill streams clear of eroded silt (from intensive agriculture) allows trout to spawn on clean gravel, but the tiny trout are no (angling) benefit to the landowners without the larger downstream reaches in which catchable fish live. A hill farm is described where the (particularly 1980s) intensification of agriculture and over-use of agrochemicals, led to over-stocking and reduction of bird and floral biodiversity, and the loss of small wetlands. Improving the farming practices improved all these, and, more important economically, led to the re-opening of an abstraction point, which had been closed due to the pollution from over-farming. The commercial value of this water was over six times the rental value of the farm. This is highly significant, and emphasises what was learnt from the 2001 Foot and Mouth disease outbreak: that farming, while the activity covering by far the greatest part of the lands, is not the most important, economically, to the countryside. Full and holistic appraisals should take place before encouraging or indeed allowing farming practices destructive to natural heritage: including rivers. (Farmers are the guardians of the land, and, down the centuries have, though altering it, preserved and protected it sustainably. It is only recently that government and EU policies have required them to destroy instead, and if these can be reversed, new guardianship will surely return.)

PLACE AND TIME

Most Restoration Schemes are from a few tens of metres to 2–3 km long. To be worth considering for restoration by the Environment Agency, or a research group, etc., a stream is usually 30–300+ km long. Necessarily, any small reach depends on the habitat conditions and management upstream. So the small Restoration Schemes start with the potential disadvantage of receiving upstream severe damage, such as flash floods, or unrecognised or unimproved pollution. Contamination of hard surfaces is perhaps the worst current pollution: and is too often unrecognised, or considered (incorrectly) as impossible to improve.

Piecemeal restoration can be locally successful, but only if (a) upstream damage is low and (b) it recognises and includes heterogeneity. It is far too easy to plan a river in the office, or to take the nearest reach as a template and copy it all along. The river has diversity and biodiversity, and it is the earlier diversity (not the planners' idea of diversity) which should be discovered and restored (Harper *et al.*, 1997).

Whole catchment management is therefore what should be aimed at, and the principles of this have been available for some years (by, e.g., Gardiner, 1992; Harper & Ferguson, 1995). Harper *et al.* (1997) recognise five principles:

1. That there is a hierarchy of river systems, i.e. that big rivers have smaller tributaries and tiny tributaries, and each is a catchment and ecosystem in its own right, but each also interacts with the whole, so must be planned and managed as part of that whole. And the small ones must not be further lost.

2. That discharge is related to channel dimensions. When a stream dries, it no longer occupies the whole of the channel it used to flow in. If the restraints to expansion of a watercourse are removed, as when riverside trees, supporting the bank, are taken away, the river can become much wider, even double the width (and see other chapters).

3. That the river is a continuous system, and the importance of both the physical and the biological continuities is of vital importance. Killing the normal flora and fauna over many kilometres makes a barrier to movement as great as the (unimproved) weirs of hydropower stations, for instance. Vegetation changes downstream (Chapter 11), but all reaches should be in integrated contact with those upstream.

4. That the river exists in four dimensions. It has length horizontally, it has width, it has vertical height, and it exists in time. Whatever the innate stability of the first three, time constantly changes them. In the long term, natural weathering lowers hills and alters flow and flooding, in the medium term major floods alter courses, in the short term, new dredging (not in the management plan of a decade ago) may drastically change water level, river shape and channel position.

5. That heterogeneity is needed to maintain biodiversity, and that disturbance is important in maintaining heterogeneity. Heterogeneity of course exists on all scales. The importance of large-scale heterogeneity has been stressed above, that with topography, with downstream change, and the incoming of tributaries. On a smaller scale is the diversity with meanders, with small-scale topographical changes (including riverside wetlands, however small), with riverside woods and tree-bands sufficient to shade and with riffles-and-pools. Smaller-scale again are the islands and berms in the river, the irregular bank edges formed by livestock or wash-out, the variations in depth and substrate and consequently

flow, etc. These change the most rapidly (excluding major human interference!), changing the habitat for different species often from year to year. Major floods and droughts cause larger changes. Human impact superimposes on all — and directs the major floods, not necessarily intentionally. To remove the natural processes of change, to impose uniformity, decreases biodiversity as well as naturalness.

How long does it take to restore vegetation after restoration? The answer varies with the circumstances, and in relation to plant species is described in Chapter 18. Clearing up factory effluents and dredging away the polluted silt can bring back reasonable vegetation in a couple of years. But in a German river it took 15 years after improving the water before the vegetation improved (Veit & Kohler, 2003). Restoring the meanders to a couple of kilometres of the Wiltshire Cole brought a good quantity of standard mildly polluted vegetation quickly, but after a decade the rare species of high-quality chalk streams were still absent. Unfortunately, these often require (a) good physical structure and diversity of it, (b) nearly clean water and (c) populations near enough to travel to the site. Restoring only (a) may not be enough, at least in the short term.

Case studies emphasise the importance of time, time to alter and to stabilise, and so the importance of funding so that these effects can be assessed, understood and used in future planning.

RESTORATION METHODS

Before turning down restoration as too expensive, a full cost-benefit account should be prepared, including not only the cost of taking land out of (heavily subsidised) use, or of re-inserting meanders, but also the benefits of cleaner water downstream and in the ground, better fishing and other forms of recreation, and of keeping the spirit of the Water Framework Directive and respecting habitats and forms of life other than those of the crop and the garden, see, for actual examples, e.g., Everard (2004) and Everard *et al.* (2004), which stresses the importance of reward and recognition for those working for the environment: for ecosystem service.

Ecosystem functions are vital and central to sustainable social and economic progress. Protecting or restoring ecosystem functions may be the only sustainable type of investment in catchments. Valuation of ecosystem functions is particularly relevant to sustainable development, indicating the benefits. Economic analyses may well show benefits exceed costs of using these methods, though current policies still tend to degrade (Everard, 2004). Major river alterations said

Table 20.2 Maintenance principles, Vejen, Denmark
(after Madsen, 1995)

Category I
Site of special scientific interest

1. The stream should be checked annually to remove obstructions to flow (fallen branches, etc.). If possible, no other maintenance.

Category II
High quality fish waters

1. Vegetation is cut close to the bed in the current channel to ensure the stipulated discharge capacity is met.

   As far as possible, the cut channel meanders, and does not reach the banks.

2. Vegetation outside the flow channel is left unless it hinders water entry from pipes, ditches, etc.

3. Cut vegetation is removed unless it would do no harm.

4. Bank vegetation is cut only if it significantly reduces stipulated discharge capacity.

5. Vegetation is cut only between 15 May and 31 October, and is only done if the stipulated discharge capacity is reduced. (N.B. Denmark's climate differs slightly to that of Britain. Early cutting often increases plant growth. Eels burrow and trout spawn after mid-October.)

6. Deposited sediment and irregular banks should be left, as far as possible, and if cleared, not before late summer. Minor depositional obstructions may, though, be removed at any time. During dredging, stone and gravel beds must not be disturbed (if possible), and overhanging banks must not be damaged.

7. Maintenance is to be done manually.

Category III
Streams intended primarily for drainage or not yet improvable from pollution or abstraction

1. The stream is to be maintained to its stipulated dimensions.

2. Where the actual dimensions and so discharge capacity exceed this, the vegetation is to be cut only in a flow channel of the dimensions stipulated.

3. Bank vegetation is to be cut only to keep the channel to its stipulated dimensions. It may, though, be done by machine.

4. Maintenance is to be done once a year, before 1 November.

5. Dredging of the bed and smoothing of banks may be done by machine at any season.

---

to be justified by increased crops or lessened flooding always need wider cost-benefit calculations first. These may well show the river schemes waste money as well as destroy habitat, and much simpler and cheaper schemes are better for both (e.g., allowing flood meadows).

389

The natural capital of catchments is a basic and principal resource for social and economic progress (Everard, 2004).

The Danes, having passed a Watercourse Act requiring a high environmental impact in 1982, and followed it, in 1992 with an Act requiring 2 m of buffer zone (i.e., unpoisoned, undisturbed land where native plants can grow) on both sides of all flowing streams, have more experience of Restoration than most countries, and much of Section I below is based on Madsen (1995). These techniques are unnecessary in some habitats (a wetland present does not need re-inserting, a narrow gorge stream has never had meanders), and impossible in others (London must be protected from flood, which means hard engineering, a town on a hill cannot be demolished to remove hard surface run-off). However, the list gives an idea of what should be considered when plans are first proposed.

The term 'hard engineering' means channelling, stoning (bricking, piling, concreting, etc.), straightening, and generally wrenching the river from its natural state. 'Soft' or, better, 'gentle' engineering is maintaining or restoring a river to a more natural state, using trees, plants, gentle slopes, meanders, etc. Soft is the more usual term, but carries the disadvantage that, in other subjects, 'hard' may mean true, 'soft', doubtful. 'Gentle' (as translated from the Danish) has the correct resonance.

The following are possible measures applying to some, but not all, rivers, except for I (1), which is essential.

I   Within the River

1. To stipulate discharge. The most important of all. Without water, there is no river. Abstraction and drainage kill rivers. Restoration must keep the streams, and, where possible, bring back lost ones.

2. Discover, by depressions, maps, or digging, where the original course lay, and re-dig it, so the water flows as it always used to. Flowing slowly, the water has:
   - time for much better purification;
   - good and diverse physical structure, and therefore diverse habitat for vegetation and animals. Flow, depth, banks, shelter, erosion and sedimentation all vary;
   - more interaction with flood plains, ground water, etc.;
   - raising bed level and water level where the riverside land can flood, so the natural water processes are improved;
   - more stable channels. The widening or deepening following on straightening and increased flash floods is less where water is stabilised by meanders. Faster flow erodes the

bottoms of the banks of trapezoid channels, particularly if there is no protective vegetation;

- return of riffles and pools. These follow, more or less, the meander pattern, and give variation in substrate texture (and therefore nutrient status, see Chapter 8) as well as in depth, flow and shelter, and they oxygenate water.

3. Make substrate and flow variations, such as artificial riffles and pools, if these do not return naturally, and meanders cannot be inserted. These are secondary measures, likely to be used where water and bed level remain well below ground level, and flooding does not occur. They should be planned to maintain discharge, and not to permit flooding.

- Gravel/stone banks can be laid in the watercourse at what would be the natural distance (five to seven times the river width). The current is then likely to erode pools between the stone banks, and a pseudo-natural riffle-and-pool system be developed. Clean gravel, of course, allows good trout spawning.
- More 'artificial' constructions are:
  - current deflectors, stone banks jutting out, which concentrate the current, deepen the water, and so give the habitat diversity required;
  - artificial shelters, for otters, fish, etc. These can be pipes, piles of stones, planted tall monocotyledons, etc.;
  - establishing artificial overhanging banks;
  - inserting logs and similar (eventually degradable) objects on the bed, to provide habitat variation (and organic carbon).
- Allowing gentle slopes at the water's edge, so emergent plants can form bands, giving good biodiversity and conservation for plants, and so habitats for animals. Storm flows change and alter, so may provide recolonisable habitats.
- Wherever possible, allowing the river to move and make its own course so that dredging is reduced. Normal dredging leaves the watercourse uniform, smooth, with no habitat diversity and therefore little biodiversity.

4. Cutting 'weed' in a path, which may be half the width of the river, allows free flow, increased current, and so more transport and less deposition of upstream sediment. Complete cutting is not always necessary! By a cheaper maintenance — cutting only half the channel — dredging is reduced, so saving money, and habitat is greatly improved. Indeed, with *Sparganium erectum* in

Denmark, even a quarter of the channel cut will allow free flow. The flow channel should be over the deepest part, as here the current will increase most (to prevent flooding and excess sediment).

Cutting depends on the species of plant and the danger of flooding. Where a flooding plain is re-inserted, or where the water level is so far below ground level that flooding is virtually impossible, cutting is not needed for direct flood control. If, though, over-much sediment is washed down from upstream, and silting up of channels is not desirable, then sufficient cutting to give free and swift flow is advisable. In a natural channel the flow is in a meandering pattern, which reflects (and creates) the meanders of the river.

As the depth and speed of flow change, so does the resistance given by different species (see other chapters). When water can pass over the vegetation layer without flooding adjoining land, the vegetation is irrelevant and need not be cut. Strap-shaped plants are hazardous when slow water is pushing through them and its level rises to flood or even ponding levels. Once flood water is sweeping through, the straps are kept flat near the ground and water can pass through freely (discharge capacity increases).

Restoration and costs can both be improved by watching the plants before destroying habitat by cutting or dredging.

Where a steep-sided channel is wider and shallower than is necessary for the discharge, a flow channel can be dredged or made by cutting (as above). This deposits sediment on its edges, while maintaining the discharge in the centre. Gradually, therefore, gentle slopes and banks build up at the side, allowing fringe vegetation — and all the animals it harbours — to develop. The flow channel may become deeper, with more gravelly and stony substrate, and the rest becoming more silty, with slower and shallower water. Thus diversity is created. Management costs per cut are saved. In some streams the flow channel, once cut, maintains itself, so total costs decrease. In others, though, the vegetation regrows quickly and extra partial cuts are required. It is possible for the flow channel to become too bare, and if this occurs, a new flow channel should be cut in the vegetation.

To ensure cutting occurs only when needed, it is both possible and simple to measure the water level and observe the vegetation and discharge.

5. To stipulate discharge capacity of each stream requires some planning first, but saves much money on dredging and cutting later. And by limiting maintenance, it is a restoration technique.

   Flexibility in maintenance requires more ecological thought and knowledge, and less work from machines, etc.

6. As a result of these techniques, less stocking of trout is needed to maintain the same population. Spawning grounds, and shelter, food and hiding places are all increased. In any stream with native genotypes, to prevent re-stocking with alien ones preserves biodiversity.

   Danish good spawning grounds are 10–20(–30) cm deep, with 50–70(30–110) cm/sec flow, swirling over the beds. Their gradient is 2%–17%. The gravel beds are (10–)25(–50) cm deep, and the grain size is mostly (70%) (2–)10–20(–63) mm wide, mostly irregular (irregular particles have more and larger spaces than rounded ones). The distance between spawning grounds is like that between natural riffles, about seven to five times watercourse width: which, therefore, should be copied when inserting gravel for restoration.

   Where trout are used as a measure of success, gentle maintenance greatly increases fish numbers, e.g., from two to three per 100 m² to 20–35 (Madsen, 1995). Using gentle cutting rather than brutal total weed-cutting is of vital importance, because this both leaves and creates habitats.

7. Obstructions to flow, like weirs and dams, do not allow salmon, sea trout and indeed eels to pass (though eels can travel on wet grass). Other fish, invertebrates and even plants may not need to migrate for survival, but may need to move for survival, to move above or well downstream of a dam, bad pollution, or dredging or other disturbance. And general movement to colonise the whole of a stream is obviously desirable. Animals colonise newly-unculverted streams within a few months — duck, small fish, many invertebrates, etc. So restoration involves putting in bypass channels as other ways round. A new departure for fairly low weirs is to replace them with riffles. This both allows transport, and creates a new habitat (heterogeneity).

   This also includes looking at pipes. Often, pipes under bridges are so placed that the bottom of the pipe downstream is above the substrate level, so there is a little 'fall' downstream. A little stream, why not? Well, because for small fish this is as much of a barrier as a hydropower dam is for salmon. Such falls also apply with longer pipes, culverts, etc., but these also have the problem of length. Resting places in this uniform smooth habitat are needed. These also make flow more variable. Much better, of course, is to open up underground streams, and make real stream habitat, for biodiversity and conservation, and also for water purification. Without light and vegetation, self-cleaning is very much reduced, and agrochemical run-off comes most into these small streams.

The amount of money spent should be related to (a) the length of watercourse that will become available as habitat, and (b) the value of that habitat for biodiversity or indeed recreation. (It is more important to open access to a trout spawning reach if there are only two in the catchment than if there are a hundred.)

8. Using meanders to reduce pollution from the subsoil can be very effective. Salt or metals (in Denmark, ochre) can leach out and contaminate the stream. The deeper the bed, the swifter is the flow and the less the vegetation and the residence time of the water in that vegetation. So more contamination leaches out, and less is cleaned. New meanders and a higher water level produce much cleaner water.

9. Even a box-shape lined channel in a town can be much improved, as long as the alterations do not reduce its discharge capacity below acceptable levels.

Cobbles can be placed on the beds. If conditions are such that they would be swept away, they can be cemented down. Even this gives habitat diversity, shelter and oxygenation, and small amounts of silt, etc., are able to lodge. On the sides, concrete boxes or (better) wooden piles or stones can form planters and be given soil and plants (those appropriate to the river type but also tolerant to the difficult conditions of such a stream, see Chapters 3, 6, 12, 13, 19).

II *By-river management*

1. Use buffer zones whenever possible. The 2 m required by law in Denmark is surprisingly effective. Wider ones are more so — 50 m being recommended for efficient cleaning of all nitrate, etc., in heavy soils (e.g., Haslam, 2003). Even narrow zones:
   - filter sediment and other particles;
   - remove or decrease many contaminants;
   - lessen the chance of agrochemical sprays reaching the watercourse;
   - provide habitat for animals and waterside plants, including water voles, otters, birds and numerous invertebrates;

- provide stalks for dragonfly, mosquito, etc., to climb out of the water and pupate before turning into their aerial phase;
- protect banks from erosion (particularly vegetation that is strong (e.g., trees) and smooth (e.g., grasses, tall monocots) (see Table 20.3).

2. Trees on the bank:
   - pollards (mainly willows now) provide cultural heritage and are habitat for many plants as well as very many animals;
   - other trees are also good habitat (see Table 20.3);
   - roots bind and stabilise banks, and keep streams narrow;
   - shade decreases vegetation in the river, so giving cheap 'weed control' for flood hazard, as well as diversity of habitat;
   - overhanging leaves add valuable organic carbon to the stream when they drop, and invertebrates, etc., on them also provide food for larger animals;
   - shaded water — if the shade extends far enough — is cooler, and suits some organisms better (habitat diversity);
   - roots provide holes for animals — and may catch plant fragments;
   - roots also allow animals to climb into the air (see above);
   - debris dams, of branches across the stream, plus the organic carbon and mixed-texture particles collected on them, create diversity and provide many niches. Indeed dead trees can form diversity 'islands' for decades. Fallen wood is excellent habitat, and should be allowed, except where it could cause floods;
   - self-purification from pollution is aided by trees, by their roots (particularly the micro-organisms on them, by their organic carbon adding to the 'chemical factory', and, when close to the bank, by preventing agrochemical sprays reaching the river.

3. Fencing:
   - fencing riversides prevents damage by livestock. Particularly when over-stocked, these animals may destroy banks and their habitat, and disturb or destroy channel vegetation. Waterers can be put in for the use of the herds;
   - with low stocking, e.g., traditional mountain and moorland, streams should be left unfenced to give heterogeneity.

III Land use and management (affecting the river)

1. Allow rain to sink into the land surface.
   - Soft buffer zones beside the stream.
   - Re-insert or insert wetlands, even if only 2 m wide.

- Under-drainage feeding the buffer zones or wetlands, not going straight to the river.
- Re-arranging gutters, ditches and other drainage channels, to give open water moving slowly.
- On surfaces such as car parks, inserting plenty of grids through which water can sink and be filtered.

2. Consider whether firm-soil farming, particularly in upstream areas (upstream of tributaries as well as of the principal river!), is necessary, and whether downstream costs outweigh upstream benefits.

3. Reduce agrochemical run-off to the river. Buffer zones, thought and planning of run-off, and responsible use of the chemicals lessen this with existing crop patterns. But adding 'reduced agrochemical loss' to the considerations used when choosing crops may reduce this far more.

4. Reduce hard surface run-off reaching the river. This is less recognised and has less researched techniques. It is also impossible at present to decrease the number of vehicles, the pollution they cause and the position of the hard surfaces. River pollution is decreased by having run-off going to created wetlands or sewage treatment works, through meshes in the road surface to the soil and, though effective only for minor pollutions, to settling lagoons and buffer zones. (A settling lagoon may still contaminate and ruin river vegetation, e.g. Haslam, 1990.)

5. Use trees, hedges, walls to decrease and manage erosion and sedimentation, particularly with open-soil and firm-soil (much run-off) farming, to prevent sediment reaching the river. Insert buffer zones to catch sediment coming down to the stream.

6. When changing land use in a way that changes the chemistry of the run-off, first consider the impact (and, as usual, the total impact downstream). For instance, draining (bog) peat first acidifies the river, altering its status. For great human benefit? But is it? Or is it being done just to obtain a subsidy?

7. Restore flood meadows to being flooded in storm flows (it is, after all, free fertiliser from the silt!). If the water is clean enough not to damage (which most downstream lowland waters are not) also allow flooding on wetlands and wet woodlands. Restore the coupling between groundwater, flood alluvial plains and rivers.

   Restore small wetlands along the length, and those where seepage or flowing waters surface near rivers. The more wetlands, the cleaner and the more stable the stream, and the better the ecosystem.

Table 20.3 Species that, when necessary, can be planted on banks (Newbold *et al.*, 1989)

Seeds and plants used for planting must be strains obtained from near the river in question. Buying foreign strains of native species is not restoration but destroying the native biodiversity and genotypes. (Many plant nurseries use foreign strains, or ones from distant parts of Britain.)

(a) Grasses

Species	Qualities
Cynosurus cristatus (Crested dog's-tail)	Short, tufted, likes poor conditions, low productivity
Agrostis capillaris, synonym: *A. tenuis* (Common bent-grass)	Likes poor conditions, rhizomes, good binding quality
Agrostis castellana (Highland bent-grass)	Is cheaper and is usually sold instead of *A. capillaris* in mixes. It is relatively productive and hence very invasive, with vigorous rhizomes and stolons. In contrast with the native species, it is taller, more productive, has poor summer colour but is very green in winter
Poa compressa (Flattened meadow-grass)	Good binding quality, low productivity
Trisetum flavesecens (Golden hair-grass)	Stress tolerant, tufted, low productivity, attractive
Festuca rubra (Ordinary red fescue)	Good binding ability but will swamp herbs if sown in any quantity
Festuca rubra ssp. *rubra* (Slender creeping red fescue)	Good binding quality, low productivity
Festuca rubra ssp. *commutata* (Chewings fescue)	Stress tolerant, tufted, low productivity
Festuca ovina (Sheep's-fescue)	Tufted, drought resistant, low productivity, wide adaptability to pH
Anthoxanthum odoratum (Sweet vernal-grass)	Short, tufted, likes poor conditions. Low productivity, attractive to livestock

(b) Herbs

Species	Qualities	Flowering
Lotus corniculatus (Bird's-foot-trefoil)	Food plant of common blue butterfly and six-spot burnet; a tufted legume; it has little enriching effect, unlike white and suckling clovers, which should be avoided	May–September
Hypochaeris radicata (Common cat's-ear)	Good nectar/pollen source, bright yellow flowers, rosette	June–September

Table 20.3   Continued

(*Leontodon autumnalis* (Autumn hawkbit) and *Leontodon hispidus* (*Rough* hawkbit) are good alternatives when seed is in short supply.)

Primula veris (Cowslip)	Early pollen source, spreads readily once established, rosette	April–May
Prunella vulgaris (Selfheal)	Generally short, pollen and nectar source	June–September
Leucanthemum vulgare (Oxeye daisy)	Nectar source, aesthetically pleasing, readily established on neutral to basic soils	June–August
Torilis japonica (Upright hedge-parsley)	Annual, but seeds readily. Medium height, attractive	June–August
Daucus carota (Wild carrot)	Does well on neutral to basic soils; good nectar/pollen source, biennial, deep rooted, medium height	June–August
Achillea millefolium (Yarrow)	Medium height, nectar source, deep rooted	June–August

(c) Woody plants

Species	Type of soil			Number of associated invertebrate species
	Acid	Neutral	Alkaline	
Less than 5 metres in height				
Alnus glutinosa (Alder) [1]		★	★	141
Betula spp. (Birch)	★		★	334
Prunus spinosa (Blackthorn)		★	★	151
Malus sylvestris (Crab apple)		★	★	116
Cornus sanguinea (Dogwood)		★	★	
Acer campestre (Field marple)		★	★	51
Viburnum opulus (Guelder rose)		★	★	205
Crataegus monogyna (Hawthorn)	★	★	★	106
Corylus avellana (Hazel)		★	★	96
Ilex aquifolium (Holly)	★	★	★	58
Sorbus aucuparia (Rowan)	★	★		
Over 5 metres				
Fraxinus excelsior (Ash)		★	★	68
Querus spp. (Oak)	★	★	★	423
Salix spp. (Willow)	★	★	★	

[1] *Phytophthera* disease is killing riverside alders patchily but increasingly.

Table 20.3   Continued

(d) Plants for encouraging butterflies and moths

By encouraging the appropriate food plants for caterpillars, nectar plants for adults and in some cases scrub for sheltered flight, conditions for the following can be created

(i) Butterflies

Plant	*Gonepteryx rhamni* Brimstone	*Polyommatus icarus* Common blue	*Pyronia tithonus* Gatekeeper	*Ochlodes venatus* Large skipper	*Maniola jurtina* Meadow brown	*Anthocharis cardamines* Orange-tip	*Lasiommata megera* Wall brown
Wild grasses			★	★	★		★
Lotus corniculatus (Bird's-foot-trefoil)							
Medicago lupulina/Vicia spp. (Black medick/vetches)		★					
Cardamine pratensis (Lady's smock)						★	
Rorippa nasturtium-aquaticum (Watercress)						★	
Sisymbrium officinale (Hedge mustard)						★	
Rhamnus spp. (Buckthorn) *Alnus glutinosa* and *Rhamnus cathartica* (Alder and purging buckthorn)	★						
Scrub for shelter	★		★	★			

(ii) Moths

Plant	*Nonagria typhae* Bulrush Wainscot	*Smerinthus ocellata* Eyed hawkmoth	*Scoliopteryx libatrix* Herald moth	*Athetis pallustris* Marsh moth[1]	*Ceruva vinula* Puss moth	*Xanthia icteritia* Sallow moth	*Furcular furcular* Sallow kitten	*Zygaena filipendulae* Six-spot burnet moth
Lotus corniculatus (Bird's-foot-trefoil)								★
Thalictrum spp. (Meadow rue)				★				
Typha spp. (Bulrush)	★							

Salix caprea (Sallow)	★	★		★	★	★
Other *Salix* spp. (Willow)	★	★		★	★	★

[1] Unlike the other moths listed, this moth is very local in its occurrence. It is found with its food plant on drain banks on the Nottinghamshire/Lincolnshire border. Its continued survival is largely dependent on the sympathetic management of these banks.

8. If (7) is insufficient or impractical, plan flood storage areas (floodable meadow or fields, lagoons, reservoirs) so storm run-off is diverted from the river and does not flood town or country. This is part of whole catchment planning.

It is primarily the natural forces at work in the streams that must be harnessed to enable streams to return to or near their natural form (Madsen, 1995). Their natural form is the best for water purification. Good and diverse physical structure is a pre-requisite for good and diverse vegetation. This vegetation then gives the best purification. The residence time of the water in the vegetation is important: the longer, the better the cleaning. So to obtain the best quality water, physical and vegetation structure must also be good. To have high water quality in the stream is of commercial and public health importance. That consideration may appeal when that of biodiversity and conservation does not?

There is no single restoration technique to be applied to all brooks and rivers. There is the principle of good structure, and the possibly opposing principle of stipulated discharge capacity of a stream, to avoid it causing flood damage. These two can be worked in harmony, to the advantage of all interests (see above, Table 20.2). It takes much more time at the level of planning and creative thought, but less, with machines on the ground. And it gives much more pleasure, aesthetic and amenity value (as well as the conservation and practical values) to streams. Contributing to human happiness is something to aim at, not to despise!

There is restoration danger, too often unrecognised. In nature, in our country, there are many different kinds of stream, depending on rock type and topography (see Chapters 11–14), and within each type, each stream has its own individual characteristics of, among others, vegetation. It is vital to keep this biodiversity, this heterogeneity. The thought and planning recommended above must take into account the natural differences between an upstream sandstone and a downstream clay river, a downstream alluvial plain stream and a hilly hard clay one, and indeed between the chalk streams of Dorset and of Yorkshire. No one plan fits all! Restoration principles should be applied to re-create each river as it was, not to produce ones which are as near clones as can be done. There is no stream so awful that, with goodwill and money it cannot be enhanced, even if not restored. Money — whether from Authority or polluter — is usually needed to remove sources of pollution. After all, rivers are used for waste disposal because they are the cheapest way to dispose of waste! Further restoration, depending on circumstances, may be left to time alone (in rivers, as in human affairs, time is a great healer), or may need interventions of the kinds described in this chapter, some cheap and done 'at the bottom of the garden', others, expensive. But all conducing to making Britain's fresh water and its contents nearer to those of the highest quality.

LAW RELATING TO RIVERS (mostly from Carty & Payne, 1998)

Various local authorities and organisations may also have by-laws or Codes of Practice, affecting their areas. These may not be aimed at restoration and may indeed be brutal in their effects on rivers.

European Commission

Dangerous Substances Directive, 1976
Freshwater Fish Directive, 1978
Birds Directive, 1979
Shellfish Directive, 1979
Drinking Water Directive, 1980
Nitrates Directive, 1991
Habitats Directive, 1992
Water Framework Directive, 2000.

English and Welsh

Town and Country Planning Orders 1995, Regulations 1988
Surface Waters (Shellfish) Regulations, 1997
Surface Waters (Dangerous Substances) Regulations, 1989
Surface Waters (River Ecosystems) Regulations, 1994
Surface Waters (Fish life) Regulations, 1997
Statutory Nuisance Regulations, 1995
Registration of Fish Farming and Shellfisheries Order, 1985
Protection of Water Against Nitrate Pollution (England and Wales) Regulations, 1996
Prohibition of Keeping of Live Fish (Crayfish) Order, 1996
Nitrate Sensitive Areas Order, 1990
Land Drainage Improvement Works Regulations, 1988
Fish Health Regulations, 1992
Environmental Information Regulation, 1992 (EC Directive, 1990)

401

Diseases of Fish Regulations, 1994
Control of Pollution Regulations 1991, 1962(2), Order, 1936
Wildlife and Countryside Act, 1981
Water Industry Act, 1991
Water Act, 1989
Water Consolidation Act, 1991
Environment Act, 1995
Countryside Act, 1968
Diseases of Fish Act, 1983, 1937
Environment Protection Act, 1990
Fisheries Act, 1981
Land Drainage Act, 1994, 1991, 1930
Freshwater Fisheries Act, 1878
Magna Carta, 1225
Prevention of Oil Pollution Act, 1971
Rivers Act, 1951
Salmon Act, 1986, 1961
Salmon and Freshwater Fisheries Act, 1971, 1923, 1907
Salmon and Fishery Act 1865, 1861
Thames Conservancy Act, 1932, 1857
Tweed Fisheries Act, 1859
Statutory Instrument 1217, 1988 (under Land Drainage Improvement)
Ministry of Agriculture, Fisheries and Food Habitat Scheme, Water
  Fringe Areas, 1994
(Scottish law is basically similar or the same, but, because of the greater
  area of Highlands and lesser population density, less attention has
  been needed for, e.g., drainage and water resources, but more for
  fisheries.)
(Rio) Biodiversity Convention, 1991.

Reading this list shows the wide range of human uses that have been and are demanded from rivers. The earliest concerned with environment are in fact dealing with the land, rivers are incidental (and the policies are overridden by those, like drainage, involving river deterioration (drainage, etc.). After 1991, 5% or even 10% of the budget for major river works could be used for enhancement. This is not enough to compensate for the damage done. The sad thing is, of course, as can be seen in the Water Framework Directive, that it is possible to reconcile most uses provided the centre of thinking is that the river and its environs are of extreme value, and that alterations can both keep that value and, e.g., allow boating and drainage. Using the river for disposal of waste and for non-sustainable abstraction (of river or groundwater) are, however, not compatible.

Glossary

Some of these terms are explained more fully in the text. Some are terms in general use, which are, in this book, used in a more limited sense, and are defined here.

Abrasion Rubbing off or away.

Abstraction Drawing off water (e.g. from below the ground, usually soft limestone or sandstone, from springs or from a river or lake).

Accretion Deposition of material on the bed of a stream either generally over the bed, or in the form of shoals (see Sedimentation).

Acid Poor in nutrients, of low pH (see Alkaline, Basic, Dystrophic, Oligotrophic, Mesotrophic and Eutrophic).

Agg. (aggregate) Used after a plant name to denote an aggregate of species which are difficult to identify separately, e.g. *Rorippa nasturtium-aquaticum* agg. for *Rorippa nasturtium-aquaticum*, *Rorippa microphylla*, and the hybrid between them.

Algae Small green plants, not composed of stems, roots and leaves. Strictly, chlorophyll-containing thallophytes, which usually grow immersed in water (fresh or marine). *Chara* and *Enteromorpha* are unusually large, and are the algae named in this book.

Alkaline With relatively high amounts of bases, such as lime; with pH above 7 (see Acid, Basic, Dystrophic, Oligotrophic, Mesotrophic and Eutrophic).

Alluvial plain Flat tract of country composed of alluvium.

Alluvium Deposits of silt, sand, etc. left by water flowing over land which is not permanently submerged; especially those left in river valleys and deltas.

Anatomical Of the study of plant structure, especially at the microscopic level (see Biological, Morphology, Physiological).

Angiosperm Higher plants; seed plants with their seeds enclosed in an ovary; including all plants described in this book except for algae, mosses, *Equisetum* and *Azolla* (see Macrophyte, Dicotyledon, Monocotyledon).

Anion Electronegative substance such as nitrate, phosphate, sulphate and chloride (see Cation).

Aquatic (1) Living or growing in or near water. (2) An aquatic plant or animal.

Aquifer Rock which yields water.

Arable Land fit for ploughing and tillage; not grassland, woodland, or built-up land; bearing crops.

Arithmetic scale Scale on which the terms differ by a constant difference, as in 1, 3, 5, 7, 9 (see Geometric scale).

Bank Sloping margin of a watercourse, in this book normally used for that part above normal water level.

Basic Rich in lime or similar alkaline mineral, and probably in other nutrients also (see Acid, Alkaline, Dystrophic, Oligotrophic, Mesotrophic and Eutrophic).

Bed (of river) Bottom or floor of watercourse.

Bed (of watercress etc.) Flat open channel or space in which plants are cultivated; also the plants which grow in it.

403

Biological Of the structure and functioning of animals (see Anatomical, Morphology, Physiological).

Biomass Total weight of living things present at any one time (see Production, Productivity).

Biotic Of plants or animals (see Organic, Chemical and Physical factors, and Mechanical management).

Bog Wet spongy ground, consisting chiefly of decayed moss (normally *Sphagnum*) and other plants; nutrient-poor and acid (see Fen, Peat, Swamp).

Boulder Large particle of stone which is too large to be picked up, or to be picked up easily, by hand (see Rock, Stone, Gravel, Sand, Silt, Mud).

Brackish Of water, intermediate between fresh and sea.

Braided Of a stream divided into two or more (more or less) parallel channels.

Brook Small stream (see Stream, River, Creek).

Calcareous Chalky; composed of, or containing, lime or limestone (see Alkaline, Basic).

Canal Artificial watercourse uniting rivers, lakes or seas for the purpose of inland navigation.

Carbon Essential element in organic compounds and hence life.

Carbon dioxide (CO_2) A gas; the main source of carbon for photosynthesis (see Gases).

Carpet Covering of plants resembling a carpet in spread and (more or less) in uniformity (see Clump).

Catchment Natural drainage area or basin, wherein rainfall is caught and channelled to a single exit point (see Watershed).

Cation Electropositive substance, such as calcium, sodium, copper or manganese (see Anion).

Chalk Soft, white, comparatively pure limestone, consisting of calcium carbonate (see Clay, Sandstone, Oolite, Resistant rock, Lime, Limestone, Calcareous).

Channel Bed and sides of a watercourse.

Chemical factors Those of a chemical nature; variations in concentration of, for example, nitrate, calcium or pollution (see Biotic and Physical factors, and Physiological).

Chemical management (of watercourses) Herbicides, pesticides and their application (see Biotic and Mechanical factors).

Clay Soft rock, or stiff earth, consisting mainly of aluminium silicate and derived mostly from the decomposition of felspathic rocks (see Chalk, Limestone, Resistant rock, Sandstone).

Clump Tuft, cluster; in separate patches, not forming a smooth carpet (see Carpet).

Coliform bacteria A type of bacteria potentially harmful to man; in the effluent from sewage works (as *Escherichia coli*), and of faecal origin.

Community plant The plants present in a site and their social ordering (see Population, Stand).

Competition Striving (rivalry) of two or more for the same objective.

Consolidated Made solid, firm or compact.

Correlate To have or establish a mutual relation of association between different structures, characteristics, etc.

Cover Extend over, occupy, e.g. 25% cover, occupying 25% of the horizontal area.

Creek In Britain, a narrow inlet in the coastline of the sea, tidal estuary, etc.

Critical velocity Water speed at which particles of a specified size will move on the channel bed.

Culvert Conduit or drain of brick or timber, etc. to convey water beneath, for example, a road.

Cumec Measure of discharge: a cubic metre of water per second (see Discharge).

Current Portion of a body of water moving in a definite direction; that which runs or flows (see Discharge, Flow, Velocity).

Cusec Measure of discharge: a cubic foot of water per second (see Discharge).

Cuticle Outer skin of leaves, stems, etc. composed of a fatty substance not easily permeable by water. Often little or negligible on submerged plant parts.

Debris Remains of plants, etc. broken down or destroyed (see Humus, Detritus, Peat).

Deoxygenation Deprivation of free oxygen, leading to death of animals and plants requiring this for survival.

Detritus Debris and other broken-down material (e.g. from river beds), usually broken down more than that referred to as debris (see Humus, Peat).

Dicotyledon One of the two main groups of angiosperms, having two seed-leaves. Typically with leaves relatively wide and shoots bushy (see Angiosperm, Monocotyledon).

Discharge Total volume of water per unit time flowing through the channel (see Flow, Cumec).

Disperse To spread about, to distribute from a source.

Dissolved gases See Gases.

Ditch (1) A long narrow hollow dug to receive or conduct water. Usually 0.5-2 m wide. Found throughout the country, particularly on poorly drained soils now normally dry. In this book termed 'dyke' when occurring in wetlands and frequently flooded. (2) In much of Europe (when translated) and North America used synonymously with dyke, drain, rhyne etc. in Britain.

Dolomite Rock consisting of both calcium carbonate, as limestone, and magnesium carbonate (see Limestone).

Dominant Of a plant species occupying the most space in, and controlling the character of, a plant community (see Luxuriant, Performance).

Drain Drainage channel, the larger channels of the Fenland drainage system, receiving water from dykes, usually by gravity, and passing it to the rivers, etc., usually through pumping systems. Usually 6–20 m wide.

Drainage order Analyses of the pattern of tributaries of a river.

Drift, glacial Material deposited during the glaciations of the Quaternary era (as opposed to the solid rock of more ancient origin).

Dyke An artificial watercourse for draining marshy land and moving surface water. Usually 2–4 m wide, found beside roads and between fields, draining into larger drains, sewers, rivers or the sea. Found in East Anglia and Fenland, and, by extension, elsewhere. Originally of a moat-and-bank defensive system. The bank part of a drain was also, in East England, known as dyke until recently. In Scotland, dyke by derivation, is a wall. Dijk in The Netherlands is a bank, as is dike in eastern North America. Dike may be used for dyke, in translations from Europe.

Dystrophic Of negligible nutrient content; acid and usually containing, or stained with, bog peat. By extension, used to describe species characteristic of such a habitat: strictly, dystraphent (see Oligotrophic, Mesotrophic, Eutrophic and Peat).

Ecology Study of plants and animals in their homes; mutual relations between plants and animals and their environment (see Ecosystem, Environment, Habitat).

Ecosystem The land and water, the plants and animals in these, the climate, and the functioning of all these together (see Ecology, Environment, Habitat).

Effluent Outflow from sewage works, factories, farms, etc.

Emerged (of plant parts) Above water (see Submerged, Floating, Free floating).

Emergent A plant mainly or entirely above water (see Submergent).

Energy Capacity to do work; radiant energy (light energy) is used in photosynthesis (see Photosynthesis).

Environment Conditions or influences under which a plant (or animal) lives or develops; its surroundings (see Ecology, Ecosystem, Habitat).

Ephemeral Short-lived, transitory (see Perennial).

Epidermis Outer layer of tissue (of cells) on plant parts.

Epiphyte Plant living on another plant; usually of algae living on larger plants.

Erode Wear away.

Erosion Scour; the removal of material from the channel of a stream (see Abrasion).

Established Securely or permanently settled.

Eutrophic Of high nutrient regime, with ample or even excess nutrients for plant growth present. By extension, used to describe species characteristic of very nutrient-rich habitats: strictly, eutraphent (see Dystrophic, Oligotrophic, Mesotrophic).

Eutrophication Raising of nutrient status.

Fen Low land, now or formerly covered with shallow water, or intermittently so covered. Any peat developed is alkaline (contrast bog peat) because of the high base status of the waters, derived from the land around. Fen silt is alluvial and nutrient-rich. Particularly the Fenland of East England, and by extension, other regions (see Bog, Peat, Swamp).

Fertiliser That which fertilises land; especially describing nutrients added as powders or sprays.

Flash flood Storm flow in which discharge rises very rapidly, due to a combination of heavy rainfall and quick run-off from the catchment (see Flood, Spate, Storm flow).

Floating Lying flat on and in the plane of the water surface, or occasionally just below it (see Emerged, Free floating, Submerged).

Flood (1) An overflowing of water over land. (2) A storm flow (see Flash flood, Storm flow).

Flood gate Contrivance for stopping or regulating the passage of water (see Lock, Sluice, Weir).

Flood hazard That which, by obstructing water movement, may or will cause flooding.

Flood meadow Grassland intermittently flooded by a stream (see Alluvial plain, Flood plain, Water meadow).

Flood plain Flat land beside the lower reaches of a river which, at least in the past, was flooded during high discharges (see Alluvial plain).

Flora List or descriptive catalogue of the plants of an area, etc. (see Vegetation).

Flow Water movement; quantity of water moving (see Discharge).

Free floating (of a plant) Floating and not anchored to the substrate (see Emerged, Submerged).

Fringing herbs Group of semi-emergent, somewhat bushy short dicotyledons, commonly fringing the edge of certain stream types, and occurring more sparsely in a wider range of types.

Gases Used here for the two gases, oxygen and carbon dioxide, which are required for plant life, and which reach emerged and floating plant parts through the air, and submerged ones through the water in which they dissolve (and, where relevant, by transport from aerial parts).

Gauging station Structure to measure water discharge, normally with a small weir.

Geology Geological features (rock types, etc.) of a district.

Geometric scale Scale on which the ratio between the successive quantities is constant, as in 1,3,9,27, 81 (see Arithmetic scale).

Glacial drift Material deposited during the glaciations of the Quaternary era (as opposed to the solid rock of more ancient origin).

Gradient (1) Of slope: amount of inclination to the horizontal. (2) Of temperature, etc.: rising or descending by regular degrees.

Gravel Strictly, particles over 2 mm wide. Here used for particles large enough to be easily picked up separately, and under *c.*2 cm wide (see Boulder, Stone, Sand, Silt, Mud).

Ground water level Plane below which the rock or soil is saturated with water (see Water table).

Gypsum Calcium sulphate (the material from which plaster of Paris is made).

Habit Characteristic mode of growth and appearance of a plant or animal (see Morphology, Ecology).

Habitat Kind of locality in which a plant or animal naturally lives and grows, as, the fast-flow habitat (see Ecosystem, Environment, Site).

Hard rock Here used to describe those very hard types of rock which do not erode easily and so can potentially, and often actually, form hilly and mountainous country. They include Carboniferous limestone, Coal Measures, resistant rocks and Old Red Sandstone. etc. (see Soft rock).

Headwater Stream near the source of a river.

Heavy metal Metallic element of high specific gravity, such as cadmium, copper, lead. Often toxic in high quantities.

Herb Plant of which the aerial stem does not become woody or persistent. Herbicide Chemical which kills plants; used for weed control (see Pesticide).

Highland High or elevated land. Used here in a general sense for hilly ground, or, with the capital H. for the Highlands of North Scotland (and perhaps elsewhere) (see Lowland, Hill, Upland, Mountain).

Hill Natural elevation of the earth's surface. Used here in a general sense (see Highland, Upland, Mountain).

Histogram Chart in which the relative frequency of different items is indicated by the height of a bar (strictly the area of the bar, but here bars are of equal width in each chart).

Hummock Protuberance arising above the general level of a surface.

Humus Vegetable mould; dark-brown or black substance resulting from the slow decomposition of organic matter (see Debris, Detritus, Peat).

Hybrid Offspring of two plants of different species.

Hydraulic Pertaining to water as conveyed through channels.

Impoundment A pond caused by a dam across a stream, used for water supply, water power, etc. (commoner n North America).

Inorganic Not formed from plant or animal parts (except when completely broken down); mineral (see Mineral, Organic).

Invertebrate animals Animals without backbones. comprising insects, spiders. snails, worms, etc.

Laminar flow Flow where water particles appear to move in smooth paths, and one layer of water slides over another. Viscous forces are strong compared to inertial forces (see Turbulent flow).

Lime Calcium carbonate (see Chalk, Oolite, Calcareous).

Limestone Rock consisting chiefly of carbonate of lime (calcium) (see Chalk, Oolite, Clay, Sandstone, Resistant rock).

Glossary

Lock (of canal, etc.) Portion of the channel shut off above and below by gates and provided with sluices to let the water out and in; used to raise or lower boats from one level to another. (Strictly, a lock with two gates is a pound lock. An – usually earlier — one with a single gate, is a lock, or after pound locks were used, a flash-lock (see Canals, Sluice).

Lode Navigable watercourse in the Fenland, usually developed from a stream. Commonly 3–10 m wide (see Drain, Dyke, Stream).

Lowland Low-lying land. Used here in a specialised sense see Chapter 13 (see Upland, Mountain).

Luxuriant Growing profusely. Used of stands which cover a considerable proportion of the ground and/or occupy a considerable proportion of the water (see Dominant, Performance).

Macrophyte Large plant; the plants discussed in this book, the higher plants (angiosperms), horsetails, water fern, mosses and the large algae *Chara* and *Enteromorpha*.

Mechanical management Maintaining a watercourse by dredging, cutting, etc. (see Biotic, Chemical).

Mesotrophic Of moderate nutrient regime. By extension, used to describe species characteristic of these habitats: strictly mesotraphent (see Dystrophic, Oligotrophic, Eutrophic).

Mesozoic Geological name for the period, and hence describing the rocks formed, between *c.* 180 million and *c.* 50 million years ago (see Pre-Cambrian, Palaeozoic, Tertiary, Quaternary).

Metabolism The process by which nutritive material is built up into living matter, or by which the complex substances of protoplasm are broken down to perform special functions (see Photosynthesis, Respiration).

Microhabitat Subdivision of a habitat, in which one or more environmental influences differ somewhat to those of other parts of the same habitat, as, stony and silty patches on a stream bed (see Habitat).

Mill (water mill) Building fitted with machinery (for grinding, e.g. corn, or hammering, cutting, polishing, fulling, etc.) in which the power is provided by a wheel on a stream. Most British mill wheels are disused, but structures for water regulation may be present.

Mill pool Pool or pond often found in a mill stream downstream of the mill wheel; or upstream to give a head of water.

Mill stream Stream turning a mill wheel, usually of a stream diverted from the main river for this purpose.

Mineral Natural substance of neither animal nor vegetable origin; inorganic (see Organic).

Monocotyledon One of the two main groups of angiosperms (seed plants), having one seed-leaf. Typically with narrow leaves (some wide), with parallel veins (see Angiosperms, Dicotyledon).

Moraine Glacial drift deposited around the side or end of a glacier.

Morphology Study of the form of plants and animals, and the structures etc. which influence that form (see Anatomical, Habit, Physiological).

Mountain Large hill. A mountain stream is here defined in a specialised sense in Chapter 13 (see Lowland, Upland).

Mud Strictly, particles below 0.002 mm diameter. Here included within 'silt' (see Boulder, Stone, Gravel, Sand, Silt, Mud)

Mulch Partly decayed vegetation, perhaps mixed with earth, used as a manure, etc. (see Humus, Detritus).

Niche, ecological Place or position suited to a particular plant species or community (see Habitat).

Nutrient Serving as nourishment; normally used of inorganic substances necessary for plant growth, such as calcium, phosphate, etc. (see Dystrophic, Oligotrophic, Mesotrophic, Eutrophic).

Oligotrophic Low in nutrients. By extension, used to describe species characteristic of this habitat: strictly, oligotraphent (see Dystrophic, Mesotrophic, Eutrophic).

Oolite Pale soft limestone, composed of small rounded granules, with a lower proportion of calcium carbonate than chalk (see Limestone, Clay, Sandstone, Resistant rock).

Organic Of, pertaining to, or composing plants or animals (see Biotic, Inorganic).

Outcrop The cropping out or exposure of a rock type at the surface (see Rock).

Oxygen (O_2) A gas used in respiration by plants and animals (see Gases).

Oxygenate To supply with oxygen (see Deoxygenate).

Palaeozoic Geological name for the period, and hence describing the rocks formed, between *c*. 500 million and *c*. 180 million years ago (see Pre-Cambrian, Mesozoic, Tertiary, Quaternary).

Particle Portion of matter.

Peat Plant material stored and partly decomposed under water. Found in fens (alkaline peat), bogs (acid peat) and swamps (see Debris, Detritus, Humus).

Perennial flow Of a stream flowing throughout the year.

Perennial plant Plant which remains alive through a number of years.

Performance, good or **high** Growing profusely. Used of stands which cover a considerable proportion of the ground and/or occupy a considerable proportion of the water (see Dominant, Luxuriant).

Perimeter Outer boundary of an area or surface.

Pesticide Chemical which kills pests, usually used for those killing small animals which are dangerous for crop production or human health. Often used in a general sense to include herbicides (see Herbicide).

pH Measure of acidity in terms of hydrogen ion concentration $[H^+]$, ranging from 0 or less at the acid end through 7 (neutral) to 14 or more at the alkaline end. Most British rivers have a pH between 6.8 and 8.5.

Phenology Study of the periodic phenomena of plants, such as leafing or flowering.

Photosynthesis Conversion in plants of carbon dioxide and water into carbohydrates in the presence of light (see Respiration).

Physical factors Those factors of a material nature (e.g. flow, substrate textures, water turbidity), as opposed to chemical and biotic factors.

Physiological Of the functions of plants or animals (see Anatomical, Biotic, Chemical factors, Physical factors).

Phytoplankton Floating microscopic plants, including desmids and diatoms.

Piled banks Those with piles (pointed stakes) driven into the bed of a river or canal for the support of a wall, bridge, steep-sided bank, etc.

Plant community See Community.

Plateau Elevated tract of comparatively flat or level land. When dissected, gullies or valleys are cut into this table-land.

Pollutant Substance causing pollution.

Pollution The alteration of the chemical status of a watercourse by human interference. By extension, any chemical alteration by man which is not restoring the original water quality (see Effluent).

Ponding Rising of water level, even though flow may be small, because a channel is choked with plants.

Population Group of plants at a site (see Community, Stand).

Porous Having minute interstices through which water, air, etc. may pass.

Pre-Cambrian Geological name for the period, and hence describing rocks formed, earlier than *c.* 500 million years ago (see Palaeozoic, Mesozoic, Tertiary and Quaternary).

Production Weight of new organic matter made by plants (or animals) over a period (see Biomass).

Productivity Rate at which new organic matter is formed (see Biomass).

Propagule Plant part used for propagation, such as fruit, seed, corm, bulb, rhizome fragment, winter bud, etc.

Quaternary Geological name for the period, and hence describing the materials deposited, during the last 1 million years. Glacial deposits are termed 'drift' (see Pre-Cambrian, Palaeozoic, Mesozoic and Tertiary).

Reach Portion of a river etc. which can be seen in one view. Hence 'lower reaches' for the lower or downstream end of a river and 'upper reaches' for the part nearer the sources (see Stretch).

Reen See Rhyne.

Reservoir Receptacle specially constructed to contain and store a large supply of water for ordinary uses (see Impoundment).

Resistant rock Very hard rock resistant to both erosion and solution; including andesite, basalt, gneiss, granite, Millstone Grit, schist, shale and slate (see Limestone, Clay, Sandstone).

Respiration Conversion of carbohydrates to carbon dioxide and water, using oxygen and releasing energy for growth etc. (see Photosynthesis).

Rhizome Perennial, horizontal, root-like stem, usually underground but sometimes floating (see Stolon, Propagule).

Rhyne A system of dykes and drains. South Wales, South West England (see Ditch, Dyke, Drain, Sewer).

River A large stream of water flowing in a channel towards the sea, a lake, or another stream (see Stream, Brook, Creek).

Rock (bedrock) Material composing the hard surface of the earth (see Clay, Limestone, Sandstone, Resistant rock).

Rock (of particle size) Bedrock exposed in the channel, or large particles of the size of boulders.

Root weft Layer of closely interwoven roots.

Saltation Particle movement by leaping or bounding along the bed of a river.

Sand Strictly, cohesionless material between 0.06 and 2 mm wide. Here used for particles large enough to be easily seen as separate particles when held in the hand, but too small to be easily picked up separately (see Boulder, Stone, Gravel, Silt, Mud).

Sandstone Rock composed of consolidated sand (see Clay, Limestone, Resistant rock).

Sediment Particles which fall by gravity in water; mud, silt, sand, gravel, stones and boulders.

Sedimentation Deposition of material on the bed of a stream, either generally over the bed or in the form of shoals (see Accretion, Silting).

Semi- Half, partly, to some extent.

Sewer In Southern England, an artificial watercourse for draining marshy land and moving surface water into a river or the sea. Often 2–6 m wide (see Ditch, Dyke, Drain, Rhyne). (Ordinarily used for the underground pipes of the foul drainage system, leading — or should be leading — to Sewage Treatment Works.)

Shoal Place where the water is of little depth; a submerged bank or bar.

Shoot Stem together with its leaves.

Silt Strictly, cohesionless material between 0.002 and 0.06 mm diameter. Here used to include mud, and those particles too fine to be seen individually from a little distance (see Boulder, Stone, Gravel, Sand and Mud).

Silting Depositing silt (see Accretion, Sedimentation).

Site Place, position, situation; place occupied by some specified plant or object (see Habitat).

Sluice Structure for impounding the water of a river, canal etc., provided with an adjustable gate or gates by which the volume of water is regulated or controlled (see Flood gate, Weir, Lock).

Soft rock Here used to describe the softer types of rock which erode easily and always form lowland landscapes. They include chalk, oolite, clay, Tertiary sandstones, etc. (see Hard rock).

Soil Earth, substrate.

Solid rock All rock types except Glacial Drift and recent alluvial deposits (see Rock).

Spate Large discharge or storm flow caused by heavy rains, etc. in hill streams where the water force is great (see Storm flow, Flood).

Species Group of plants (or animals) having certain common and permanent characteristics distinguishing it from other groups.

Specific gravity Relative heaviness of any kind of matter (the ratio of the weight of a given volume to that of an equal volume of some substance, usually water, taken as a standard).

Spring Flow of water rising or issuing naturally out of the ground.

Stable Able to maintain its place or position. A stable river is one which over a long period of time does not progressively scour or accrete, though it may both scour and accrete at various times.

Stand Group of plants at a site, normally of a single species (see Community, Population).

Stolon Annual, horizontal, leafy stem, borne above or below ground (see Rhizome).

Stone Strictly, a particle over 2 cm wide. Here used for particles larger than gravel which can be easily picked up by hand (see Boulder, Gravel, Sand, Silt, Mud).

Storm flow The large water discharge following heavy rain (see Spate, Flood).

Stream Course of water flowing continuously along a bed on the earth, forming a river or brook.

Streamlined The shape of a moving body, e.g. a fish, which gives the smallest amount of resistance as it passes through its medium, e.g. water; the similar shape of some stationary objects in moving water.

Stretch (of river) A continuous length or distance; an expanse of water (see Reach).

Submerged (of plant parts) Within the water (see Emerged, Floating, Free-floating).

Submergent A plant within the water (see Emergent).

Subsoil Stratum of soil lying immediately under the surface soil.

Substrate Material near the surface of the bed of the watercourse; the rooting medium; the soil.

Suspended Of particles diffused through the water.

Suspension The condition of being suspended, as particles in water.

Swamp In North America and, by derivation, Britain. A piece of wet spongy ground, a marsh, fen or bog.

Swathe Space covered by a sweep of a mower's scythe or the scythes of a weed-cutting launch.

411

Tall monocotyledons Group of tall emergent aquatics with long narrow leaves, forming dense stands which shade out all shorter plants.

Terrestrial Of or pertaining to the land as distinct from the water.

Tertiary Geological name for the period, and hence describing the rocks formed, between *c.* 180 million and *c.* 1 million years ago (see Pre-Cambrian, Palaeozoic, Mesozoic, Quaternary).

Texture (of a soil) The character of a substrate as to its being fine, coarse, etc.; the structure of its constituents.

Topography Features of a region or locality collectively.

Toxic Poisonous.

Transpiration Evaporation of water from plant leaves etc. into the air.

Tributary A stream or river which flows into another.

Trophic Of or pertaining to nutrition (see Nutrient, Dystrophic, Oligotrophic, Mesotrophic, Eutrophic).

Turbid Thick or opaque with suspended matter; not clear; cloudy.

Turbulence Agitation, disturbance, commotion of the water; movement within a limited space rather than along a single direction. Strictly, turbulent flow occurs when the viscous forces are weak compared to the inertial forces (see Laminar flow).

Unstable Apt to change or alter.

Upland Hilly country. An upland stream is here defined in a specialised sense, see Chapter 13. Formerly and strictly, land just inland and above that flooded by river or sea. In geography used for tracts of high-lying land (see also Lowland, Mountain, Hill).

Vegetation Plants in general; the plant life at a site (see Flora).

Vegetative Of all parts of a plant other than its flowers and fruits and their stems.

Velocity Speed of motion, normally along the length of the stream (see Current, Flow, Discharge).

Watercourse A stream of water, a river or brook; an artificial channel for the movement of water. The general term for water channels, including all the other types defined here.

Water meadow Grassland beside chalk streams, kept intermittently wet under a particular form of management. Now mainly disused.

Watershed Tract of ground between two drainage areas.

Water table Plane below which the rock or soil is saturated with water (see Ground water level).

Weathering Disintegration resulting from the action of the atmosphere (including rainfall, and river action) on substances exposed to this.

Weft See Root weft.

Weir Barrier or dam to restrain water (see Flood gate, Sluice).

Winterbourne Brook on soft limestone which has water flowing in a well defined channel in winter, but dries in summer.

Bibliography

A — PUBLICATIONS UP TO 1976

Publications giving the earlier work on rivers, whether or not referred to in the text. These were the references used in the first edition.

Agami M. 1973. Effects of water pollution on the flora and vegetation of the Alexander and Yarkon rivers. Abstract of MSc Thesis, Tel-Aviv University.

Aiken S. & Gillet J.M. 1974. The distribution of aquatic plants in selected lakes in Gatineau Park, Quebec. *Can. Field Nat.* **88:** 437–448.

Alabaster J.S., Garland J.H.N., Hart I.C. & Solbé J.F. de L.G. 1972. An approach to the problem of pollution and fisheries. *Symp. Zool. Soc. Lond.* **29:** 87–114.

Allenby K.G. 1966. The manganese and calcium contents of some aquatic plants and the water in which they grow. *Hydrobiol.* **27:** 498–500.

Allenby K.G. 1968. Some analyses of aquatic plants and water. *Hydrobiol.* **32:** 486–490.

Almestrand A. 1951. Studies on the vegetation and hydrochemistry of Scanian Lakes. II. Ion determination in lake waters. *Botan. Notis. Suppl.* **2:** 142–174.

Anderson R.R., Brown R.G. & Rappleye R.D. 1966. The mineral content of *Myriophyllum spicatum* L. in relation to its aquatic environment. *Ecology* **47:** 844–846.

Andrews F.W. 1945. Water plants in the Gezira canals. A study of aquatic plants and their control in the canals of the Gezira cotton area (Anglo-Egyptian Sudan). *Ann. Appl. Biol.* **32:** 1–14.

Anon. 1946. *The University Atlas.* London: George Philip & Son.

Anon. 1960. The control of aquatic and marginal weeds. In: *Abstr. Meet. Weed Soc. Amer., 1960.* pp. 62–68.

Arber A. 1920. *Water plants.* London: Cambridge University Press.

Auerbach S., Prufer P. & Weise G. 1972. CO_2-Stoffwechsel submerser Wasserpflanzen vom Typ *Fontinalis antipyretica* L. bei intermittierender Beleuchtung. *Biol. Zentrlbl.* **91:** 463–475.

Ayrshire River Purification Board. *Fifteenth annual report, to 31 December 1968.*

Barrett P.R.F. & Robson T.O. 1974. Further studies on the seasonal changes in the susceptibility of some emergent plants to dalapon. In: *Proc. 12th Brit. Weed Control Conf.* pp. 249–253.

Berrie A.D. 1972. Productivity of the River Thames at Reading. *Symp. Zool. Soc. Lond.* **29:** 69–86.

Bombówna M. 1971. Sklad chemiczy wody potoków Polskich Tatr Wysokick ze szczególnym uwzgledneiniem Suchej Wody. (The chemical composition of the water of streams of the Polish High Tatra Mts, particularly with regard to the Stream Sucha Woda.) *Acta Hydrobiol.* **13:** 379–391.

Bovey R.W., Burnett E., Richardson C., Merkle M.G., Baur J.R. & Knisel W.G. 1974. Occurrence of 2,4,5-T and picloram in surface runoff water in the blacklands of Texas. *J. Environ. Qual.* **6:** 1–4.

Brink N. & Widell N. 1967. Eutrophication in a small stream in Central Sweden. *Schweiz. Z. Hydrol.* **29:** 336–360.

Bristow J.M. & Whitcombe M. 1971. The role of roots in the nutrition of aquatic vascular plants. *Amer. J. Bot.* **58:** 8–13.

Bristow J.M. 1909. The effects of carbon dioxide on the growth and development of amphibious plants. *Can. J. Bot.* **47:** 1803–1807.

Bristow J.M. 1975. The structure and function of roots in aquatic vascular plants. In: Torrey J.G. & Clarkson D.T., eds. *The development and function of roots.* London & New York: Academic Press.

Brooker M.P. & Edwards R.W. 1973. Effects of the herbicide paraquat on the ecology of a reservoir. I. Botanical and chemical aspects. *Freshwater Biol.* **3:** 157–175.

Butcher R.W., Pentelow F.T.K. & Woodley J.W.A. 1930. Variations in composition of river waters. *Int. Revue Ges. Hydrobiol. Hydrogr.* **24:** 47–80.

Butcher R.W. 1927. A preliminary account of the vegetation of the river Itchen. *J. Ecol.* **15:** 55–65.

Butcher R.W. 1933. Studies on the ecology of rivers. I. On the distribution of macrophytic vegetation in the rivers of Britain. *Journal of Ecology* **21:** 58–91.

Carpenter K.E. 1926. The lead mine as an active agent in river pollution. *Ann. Appl. Biol.* **13:** 395–401.

Carr J. 1969a. The primary productivity and physiology of *Ceratophyllum demersum*. I. Gross macroprimary productivity. *Aust. J. Mar. Freshwater Res.* **20:** 115–126.

Carr J. 1969b. The primary productivity and physiology of *Ceratophyllum demersum*. II. Microprimary productivity, pH and P/R ratio. *Aust. J. Mar. Freshwater Res.* **20:** 127–142.

Casey H. & Downing A. 1976. Levels of inorganic nutrients in *Ranunculus penicillatus* var. *calcareous* in relation to water chemistry. *Aquat. Bot.* **2:** 75–79.

Casey H. & Newton P.V.R. 1973. The chemical composition and flow of the River Frome and its main tributaries. *Freshwater Biol.* **3:** 337–353.

Casey H. & Westlake D.F. 1974. Growth and nutrient relationships of macrophytes in Sydling Water, a small unpolluted chalkstream. In: *Proc. Eur. Weed Res. Coun. 4th Int. Symp. Aquatic Weeds 1974.* pp. 69–76.

Chancellor A.P. 1958. *The control of aquatic weeds and algae.* London: HMSO.

Chancellor R.J. 1962. *The identification of common water weeds.* Bull. Minist. Agric. Fish. Food, London, no. 183.

Clapham A.R., Tutin T.G. & Warburg E.F. 1962. *Flora of the British Isles.* London: Cambridge University Press.

Cook C.D.K. 1961. *Sparganium* in Britain. *Watsonia* **5:** 1–10.

Cook C.D.K. 1966. A monographic study of *Ranunculus* subgenus *Batrachium* (DC) A. Gray. *Mitt. Bot. München* **6:** 47–237.

Cope O.B. 1966. Contamination of the freshwater system by pesticides. In: Moore N.W., ed. *Pesticides in the environment and their effects on wildlife. J. Appl. Ecol.* **3 (suppl.):** 33–44.

Countryman W.D. 1968. *Alisma gramineum* in Vermont. *Rhodora* **70:** 577–579.

Cowles R.P. & Schwitalla A.M. 1923. The hydrogen-ion concentration of a creek, its waterfall, swamp and ponds. *Ecology* **4:** 402–415.

Crisp D.J. 1970. Input and output of minerals from a small watercress bed fed by chalk water. *J. Appl. Ecol.* **7:** 117–140.

Denny P. 1972. Sites of nutrient absorption in aquatic macrophytes. *J. Ecol.* **60:** 819–829.

Department of the Environment. 1971. *Report of a river pollution survey of England and Wales.* Vol. 1. London: HMSO.

Devon River Authority. 1968. *Annual report for the year ended 31 March 1968.*

Dijkshoorn W., Sujitno J.S.A. & Ismunadji M. 1974. Potassium uptake by rice plants and interaction with other cations. *Plant Soil* **40:** 525–534.

Donselaar van J. 1961. On the vegetation of former river beds in The Netherlands. *Wentia* **5:** 1–85.

Dore W.G. & Gillett J.M. 1955. *Botanical survey of the St Lawrence Seaway area in Ontario.* Botany and Plant Pathology Division, Science Survey, Canada. Ottawa, Ontario: Department of Agriculture.

Edwards A.M.C. 1975. Long term changes in the water quality of agricultural catchments. In: Hey R.D. & Davies T.D., eds. *Science, technology and environmental management.* Lexington: Saxon House.

Edwards D. 1969. Some effects of siltation upon aquatic macrophyte vegetation in rivers. *Hydrobiol.* **34:** 29–36.

Edwards R.W. 1968. Plants as oxygenators in rivers. *Water Res.* **2:** 243–248.

Edwards R.W. & Owens M. 1960. The effects of plants on river conditions. I. Summer crops and estimates of net productivity of macrophytes in a chalk stream. *J. Ecol.* **48:** 151–180.

Edwards R.W. & Owens M. 1962. The effects of plants on river conditions IV. The oxygen balance of a chalk stream. *J. Ecol.* **50:** 207–220.

Edwards R.W. & Owens M. 1965. The oxygen balance of streams. *Symp. Brit. Ecol. Soc.* **5:** 149–172.

Ericksen Jones J.R. 1940. A study of the zinc-polluted river Ystwyth in North Cardiganshire, Wales. *Ann. Appl. Biol.* **27:** 368–378.

Farrar C.F. 1921. *Ouse's silent tide.* Bedford: Sidney Press.

Fassett N.C. 1957. *A manual of aquatic plants.* (With Revision Appendix by Eugene C. Ogden.) Madison: University of Wisconsin Press.

Forsberg C. 1964. The vegetation changes in Lake Takern. *Svensk Bot Tidskr.* **58:** 44–55.

Fryer A. & Bennet A. 1900. *The* Potamogetons *of the British Isles.* London: L. Reeve.

Gaevskaya N.S. 1966; translated 1969. *The role of higher aquatic plants in the nutrition of the animals of freshwater basins.* Moscow: Nauka. (National Lending Library for Science and Technology, Boston Spa, Yorks.)

Gehu J.M. 1961. Les groupements végétaux du Bassin de la Sambre Française. I. **10:** 69–148.

Gorham E. & Gordon A. 1963. Some effects of smelter pollution upon aquatic vegetation near Sudbury, Ontario. *Can. J. Bot.* **41:** 371–378.

Goulder R. & Boatman D.J. 1971. Evidence that nitrogen supply influences the distribution of freshwater macrophyte, *Ceratophyllum demersum. J. Ecol.* **59:** 783–791.

Grahn O., Hultberg H. & Landner L. 1974. Oligotrophication — a self-accelerating process in lakes subjected to excessive supply of acid substances. *Ambio* **3:** 93–94.

Green F.H.W. 1975. The effect of climatic and other environmental changes in water quality in rural areas. In: Hey R.D. & Davies T.D., eds. *Science, technology and environmental management.* Lexington: Saxon House. pp. 123–136.

Grizzell R.A. & Neely W.W. 1962. Biological controls for waterweeds. In: *Trans 27th N. Amer. Wildl. Nat. Resour. Conf.* pp. 107–113.

Haller W.T., Sutton D.L. & Barlow W.C. 1974. Effects of salinity on growth of several aquatic macrophytes. *Ecology* **55:** 891–894.

Haslam H.W. 1975. Geochemical survey of stream waters and stream sediments from the Cheviot area. *Rep. Inst. Geol. Sci.* **75/6.**

Haslam S.M. 1968. The biology of reed (*Phragmites communis*) in relation to its control. In: *Proc. 9th Brit. Weed Control Conf. 1968.* pp. 392–397.

Haslam S.M. 1971. Physical factors and some river weeds. In: *Proc. Eur. Weed Res. Coun., 3rd Int. Symp. Aquatic Weeds 1971.* pp. 29–39.

Haslam S.M. 1973a. The management of British wetlands. I. Economic and amenity use. *J. Eviron. Manage.* **1:** 303–320.

Haslam S.M. 1973b. The management of British wetlands. II. Conservation. *J. Eviron. Manage.* **1:** 345–361.

Haslam S.M. 1973c. Some aspects of the life history and autecology of *Phragmites communis* Trin. *Pol. Arch. Hydrobiol.* **20:** 79–100.

Haslam S.M. 1975. River vegetation and pollution. In: Hey R.D. & Davies T.D., eds. *Science, technology and environmental management.* Lexington: Saxon House. pp. 123–186.

Haslam S.M., Klotzli F., Sukopp H. & Szczepanski A. 1979. Management. In: Kvet J., Szczepanski A. & Westlake D.F., eds. *Ecology of wetlands.* London: Cambridge University Press.

Haslam S.M., Sinker C.S. & Wolseley P.A. 1975. *British water plants.* London: Field Studies Council.

Hayes S.A. 1967. The herbicidal activity of various organic acids on the growth of *Elodea canadensis.* In: *Proc. 20th Sth Weed Control Conf.* pp. 294–297.

Haynes R.R. 1974. A revision of North American *Potamogeton* subsection *Pusilli* (Potamogetonaceae). *Rhodora* **76:** 564–649.

Hermens L.C.M. 1975. Levend groen. II. Groene beken in Limburg. *Tijdschrift* **86:** 473–481.

Heslop-Harrison Y. 1955. *Nuphar* Sm. *Biol. Fl. Brit. Isles. J. Ecol.* **43:** 342–364.

Holmes N.T.H. & Whitton B.A. 1975a. Macrophytes of the River Tweed. *Trans. Bot. Soc. Edinb.* **42:** 369–381.

Holmes N.T.H. & Whitton B.A. 1975b. Submerged bryophytes and angiosperms of the River Tweed and its tributaries. *Trans. Bot. Soc. Edinb.* **42:** 383–395.

Holmes N.T.H., Lloyd E.J.H., Potts M. & Whitton B.A. 1972. Plants of the River Tyne and future water transfer scheme. *Vasculum* **57:** 56–78.

Houghton G.V. 1964. The River Stour (Essex and Suffolk) — hardness, chloride and nitrate content. *Proc. Soc. Water Treat. Exam.* **13:** 145–152.

Houghton G.V. 1972. Long-term increases in planktonic growth in the Essex Stour. *Proc. Soc. Water Treat. Exam.* **21:** 299–308.

Howard H.W. & Lyon A.G. 1950. The identification and distribution of the British watercress species. *Watsonia* **1:** 228–233.

Howard H.W. & Lyon A.G. 1952. *Nasturtium* R. Br. *Nasturtium officinale* R. Br. (*Rorippa nasturtium-aquaticum* (L.) Hayet). Biol. Fl. Brit. Isles. *J. Ecol.* **40:** 228–245.

Hutchinson E.L. 1975. *Treatise on Limnology. III. Limnological Botany.* New York & London: Wiley-Interscience.

Hutchinson G.E. 1970. The chemical ecology of three species of *Myriophyllum* (Angiospermae, Haloragaceae). *Limnol Oceanogr.* **15:** 1–5.

Hynes H.B.N. 1960. *The biology of polluted waters.* Liverpool University Press.

Hynes H.B.N. 1965. A survey of water pollution problems. *Symp. Brit. Ecol. Soc.* **5:** 49–63.

Hynes H.B.N. 1970. *The ecology of running waters.* Liverpool University Press.

Hynes H.B.N. & Roberts F.W. 1962. The biological effects of synthetic detergents in the River Lee, Hertfordshire. *Ann. Appl. Biol.* **50:** 779–790.

Jones E.N. 1931. The morphology and biology of *Ceratophyllum demersum. Stud. Nat. Hist. Iowa Univ.* **13:** 11–33.

Jones H. 1955. Studies on the ecology of the river Rheidol. I. Plant colonisation and permanent quadrat records in the main stream of the lower Rheidol. *J. Ecol.* **43:** 462–476.

Jones H. 1956. Studies on the ecology of the river Rheidol. II. An ox-bow of the lower Rheidol. *J. Ecol.* **44:** 12–27.

Jones H.R. & Peters J.C. 1976. Physical and biological typing of unpolluted rivers. In: *EIFAC Symposium, Helsinki.*

Jones H.R. & Peters J.C. 1977. In: *Water Research Centre Technical Report.*

Keble Martin W. 1965. *The concise British flora in colour.* London: Ebony Press/Michael Joseph.

Klausner S.D., Zwerman P.J. & Ellis D.F. 1974. Surface runoff losses of soluble nitrogen and phosphorus under two systems of soil management. *J. Environ. Qual.* **3:** 42–46.

Kohler A., Vollrath H. & Beisl E. 1971. Zur Verbreitung, Vergesellschaftung und Ökologie der Gefässmakrophyten im Fliesswassersystem Moosach (Münchener Ebene). (The distribution, the phytosociological composition and the ecology of the vascular macrophytes in the Moosach river system near Munich.) *Arch. Hydrobiol.* **69:** 333–365.

Kohler A., Wonneberger R. & Zeltner G. 1973. Die Bedeutung chemischer und pflanzlicher 'Verschmutzungsindikatoren' im Fliessgewässersystem Moosach (Münchener Ebene. (Chemical data and aquatic vascular plants as indicators for pollution in the Mossach river system near Munich.) *Arch. Hydrobiol.* **72:** 533–549.

Krause A. 1972. Einfluss der Eutrophierung auf die Makrophytenvegetation der Oberflächengewässer. *Ber. Landwirtsch.* **50:** 140–146.

Krull J.N. 1970. Aquatic plant-macroinvertebrate associations and water fowl. *J. Wildlife Manage.* **34:** 707–718.

Kulberg R.K. 1974. Distribution of aquatic macrophytes related to paper mill effluents in a southern Michigan stream. *Amer. Midl. Nat.* **91:** 271–281.

Lachavenne J-B. & Wattenhofer R. 1975. *Contribution a l'étude des macrophytes du Léman. Commission Internationale pour la protection des Eaux du Léman contre la pollution.* Conservatoire Botanique du Geneva.

Ladle M. & Casey H. 1971. Growth and nutrient relationships of *Ranunculus penicillatus* var. *calcareous* in a small chalk stream. In: *Proc. Eur. Weed Res. Count. 3rd Int. Symp. Aquatic Weeds.* pp. 53–64.

Laing H.E. 1941. Effect of concentration of oxygen and pressure of water upon growth of rhizomes of semi-submerged water plants. *Bot. Gaz.* **102:** 712–724.

Lange S.R. 1965. The control of aquatic plants by commercial harvesting, processing and marketing. In: *Proc. 18th Sth Weed Control Conf.* pp. 536–542.

Laurie E.M.O. 1942. The dissolved oxygen of an upland pond and its inflowing stream at Ystumtuen, North Cardiganshire, Wales. *J. Ecol.* **30:** 357–381.

Lewis K. 1973. The effect of suspended coal particles on the life forms of the aquatic moss *Eurhynchium riparioides* (Hedw.). I. The gametophyte plant. *Freshwater Biol.* **3:** 251–257.

Lindsay A.A., Petty R.O., Sterling D.K. & Van Adall W.V. 1961. Vegetation and environment along the Wabash and Tippecanoe rivers. *Ecol. Monogr.* **31:** 105–156.

Lindstrom H.V. & Sandstrom W.M. 1939. Nutritive value and chemical composition of certain freshwater plants of Minnesota. III. The nature of the carbohydrates of species of *Elodea, Myriophyllum, Ceratophyllum, Ruppia* and *Ranunculus. Min. Agric. Exp. Stn. Techn. Bull.* **136:** 43–47.

Litar M. & Agami M. 1976. Relationship between water pollution and the glaa of two coastal rivers of Israel. *Aquat. Bot.* **2:** 23–41.

Little E.C.S. 1968. Handbook of utilisation of aquatic plants. *A compilation of the world's publications.* Rome: FAO.

Lohmeyer W. & Krause A. 1975. Über die Auswirkungen des Gewölbewuchses an kleinen Wasserläufen des Münsterlandes auf die Vegetation im Wasser und an den Böschungen im Hinblick auf die Unterhaltung der Gewässer. *Schweiz. Reihe Veg.* **9:** 105 pp.

Macan T.T. & Worthington E.B. 1951. *Life in lakes and rivers.* London: Collins.

Macan T.T. 1974. Running water. *Mitt. Int. Verein. Limnol.* **20:** 301–321.

Malmer N. 1960. Some ecologic studies on lakes and brooks in the south Swedish uplands. *Botan. Notis.* **113:** 87–116.

Mann K.H., Britton R.H., Kowalczewski A., Lack T.J., Mathews C.P. & McDonald I. 1972. Productivity and energy float at all trophic levels in the River Thames, England. In: Kajak Z. & Hillbricht-Ilkowska A., eds. *Productivity problems of freshwaters.* Poland: IBP-UNESCO, Kazimierz Dolny. pp. 579–596.

Mathews C.P. & Kowalczewski A. 1960. The disappearance of leaf litter and its contribution to production in the river Thames. *J. Ecol.* **57:** 543–552.

McNabb Jr C.D. & Tierney D.P. 1972. *Growth and mineral accumulation of submerged vascular hydrophytes in pleioeutrophic environs.* Institute of Water Resources, Michigan State University, Technical Report 26.

Meyer B.S. & Heritage A.C. 1941. Effect of turbidity and depth of immersion on apparent photosynthesis in *Ceratophyllum demersum. Ecology* **22:** 17–22.

Meyer B.S., Bell F.H., Thompson L.C. & Clay E.I. 1943. Effect of depth of immersion on apparent photosynthesis in submerged vascular aquatics. *Ecology* **24:** 393–399.

Ministry of Agriculture, Fisheries and Food. 1975. *Code of Practice for the use of herbicides on weeds in watercourses and lakes.*

Mitchell R.S. Unpublished Data. Effects of Radford army ammunition plant wastes on aquatic vegetation in the New River, Virginia.

Morgan N.C. 1970. Changes in the fauna and flora of nutrient-enriched lake. *Hydrobiol.* **35:** 545–553.

Moss B. 1976. The effects of fertilization and fish on community structure and biomass of aquatic macrophytes and epiphytic algal populations: an ecosystem experiment. *J. Ecol.* **64:** 313–342.

Moyle J.B. 1945. Some chemical factors influencing the distribution of aquatic plants in Minnesota. *Amer. Midl. Nat.* **34:** 402–420.

Newton L. 1944. Pollution of the rivers of West Wales by lead and zinc mine effluent. *Ann. Appl. Biol.* **31:** 1–72.

Nicholls K.H. 1974. Nutrients in subsurface and runoff waters of the Holland Marsh, Ontario. *J. Environ. Qual.* **3:** 31–35.

Nicholson S.A., Levey R.A. & Clute P.R. 1975. Macrophyte-sediment relationships in relationships in Chautanqua Lake. *Verh. Int. Verein. Limnol.* **19:** 2758–2764.

Nuttall P.M. 1972. The effects of sand deposition upon the macroinvertebrate fauna of the river Camel, Cornwall. *Freshwater Biol.* **2:** 181–186.

Ogg A.G., Bruns V.F. & Kelly A.D. 1969. Response of Sago Pondweed to periodic removal of top growth. *Weed Sci.* **17:** 139–141.

Oglesby R.T., Carlson C.A. & McCann J.A. 1972. *River ecology and man.* New York & London: Academic Press.

Olsen S. 1964. Vegetations aendringer i Lyngby Sø Bidragtilanalyse af kulturpåvirkninger på vand- og sumpplantevegetationem. *Bot. Tidsskr.* **59:** 273–300.

Owens M. & Edwards R.W. 1961. The effects of plants on river conditions. II. Further crop studies and estimates of net productivity of macrophytes in a chalk stream. *J. Ecol.* **49:** 119–126.

Owens M. & Edwards R.W. 1962. The effects of plants on river conditions. III. Crop studies estimates of net productivity of macrophytes in four streams in southern England. *J. Ecol.* **50:** 157–162.

Owens M. & Edwards R.W. 1963. Some oxygen studies in the River Lark. *Proc. Soc. Water Treat. Exam.* **12:** 126–144.

Owens M. & Whitton B.A., eds. 1975. *River ecology.* Oxford: Blackwells.

Owens M. & Wood G. 1968. Some aspects of the eutrophication of water. *Water Res.* **2:** 151–159.

Owens M., Garland J.H.N., Hart I.C. & Wood G. 1972. Nutrient budgets in rivers. *Symp. Zool. Soc. Lond.* **29:** 21–40.

Parkin L. 1973. Last throw on the Mimram. In: *Association of River Authorities Year Book and Directory 1973.* London: National Water Council. pp. 199–205.

Pasternak K. 1973. Pozprzestrzonienie metali ciezkich w wodach plynach w rejionie wystepowania naturalnych zlóz oraz przemysly cynku I olowiu. (The spreading of heavy metals in flowing water in the region of occurrence of natural deposits and of the zinc and lead industry.) *Acta Hydrobiol.* **15:** 145–166.

Pekkari S. 1965. The north east corner: notes on aquatic vegetation. *Acta Phytogeog. Suec.* **50:** 209–214.

Peltier W.H. & Welch E.B. 1969. Factors affecting growth of rooted aquatics in a river. *Weed Sci.* **17:** 412–416.

Proctor H.G. 1971. Aquatic macrophytes in the Wheel of the Tees. *Vasculum* **56:** 59–66.

Quennerstedt N. 1958. Effect of water level fluctuation on lake vegetation. *Verh. Int. Verein. Limnol.* **13:** 901–906.

Quennerstedt N. 1965. The major rivers of Northern Sweden. *Acta Phytogeogr. Suec.* **50:** 198–294.

Royal Meteorological Society. 1926. *Rainfall Atlas of the British Isles.* London: Royal Meteorological Society.

Robbins W.W., Crofts A.S. & Raynor R.N. 1942. *Weed control.* New York & London: McGraw Hill.

Robinson G.W. 1971. Practical aspects of chemical control of weeds in land drainage channels in England and Wales. In: *Proc. Eur. Weed. Res. Coun., 3rd Int. Symp. Aquatic Weeds 1971.* pp. 297–302.

Robinson G.W. & Leeming J.B. 1969. The experimental treatment of some waters in Kent with diuron to control aquatic weed growth. In: *Association of River Authorities Year Book 1969.* pp. 58–63.

Robson T.O. 1972. Recommendations for the control of aquatic weeds. In: Fryer J. & Makepeace R., eds. *Weed control handbook,* 7th edn. Oxford: Blackwell.

Robson T.O. 1973a. Recent trends in weed control in freshwater. *OEPP/EPPO* **3:** 5–17.

Robson T.O. 1973b. *The control of aquatic weeds.* Ministry of Agriculture, Fisheries and Food, Bulletin 194.

Robson T.O. 1974. Mechanical control. In: Mitchell D.S., ed. *Aquatic vegetation and its use and control.* Paris: UNESCO.

Robson T.O. & Fearon J.H. 1976. *Aquatic herbicides.* London: British Crop Protection Council.

Römkens M.J.M. & Nelson D.W. 1974. Phosphorus relationships in runoff from fertilised soils. *J. Environ. Qual.* **3:** 10–31.

Rudescu L., Niculescu C. & Chivu. 1965. *Monografia stufului den delta Dunarii.* Bucharest: Editura Academiei Republicii Socialiste Romania.

Sansom C.H. 1947. *Cultivation of watercress.* Bull. Minist. Agric. Fish., no. 136.

Sawyer F. 1952. *Keeper of the stream.* London: A. & C. Black.

Schneider von S., Dewes E., Krause A., Kroesch U., Lorenz D. & Miosaga G. 1974. *Gewässerüberwachung durch Fernerkundung der mittleren Saar.* Bonn-Bad Godesberg: Selbstverlag der Bundesforschungsanstalt für Landeskunde und Raumordnung. pp. 49–70.

Sculthorpe C.D. 1967. *The biology of aquatic vascular plants.* London: Edward Arnold.

Seddon B. 1967. The lacustrine environment in relation to macrophytic vegetation. In: Cushing E.J. & Wright H.E., eds. *Quaternary Palaeoecology.* New Haven & London: Yale University Press. pp. 205–215.

Seddon B. 1972. Aquatic macrophytes as limnological indicators. *Freshwater Biol.* **2:** 107–130.

Smith S.G. 1973. *Ecological studies of the surface waters of the Whitewater Creek watershed, Walworth, Rock and Jefferson Counties, Wisconsin.* Madison: University of Wisconsin Water Resources Centre.

Smith S.G. Unpublished Data. Aquatic macrophytes of the Pine and Popple river system, Florence and Forest Counties, Wisconsin.

Spence D.H.N. 1964. The macrophytic vegetation of freshwater lochs, swamps and associated fens. In: Burnett J.H., ed. *The vegetation of Scotland.* Edinburgh: Oliver & Boyd. pp. 306–425.

Spence D.H.N. 1972. Light on freshwater macrophytes. *Trans. Bot. Soc. Edinb.* **41:** 491–505.

Spence D.H.N. & Chrystal J. 1970a. Photosynthesis and zonation of freshwater macrophytes. I. Depth distribution and shade tolerance. *New Phytol.* **69:** 205–215.

Spence D.H.N. & Chrystal J. 1970a. Photosynthesis and zonation of freshwater macrophytes. II. Adaptability of species of deep and shallow water. *New Phytol.* **69:** 217–227.

Stake E. 1967. Higher vegetation and nitrogen in a rivulet. *Schweiz. Z. Hydrol.* **29:** 107–124.

Stake E. 1968. Higher vegetation in a small stream in Central Sweden. *Schweiz. Z. Hydrol.* **30:** 353–373.

Stott B. & Robson T.O. 1970. Efficiency of Grass Carp (*Ctenopharyngodon idella* Val) in controlling submerged water weeds. *Nature, Lond.* **226:** 870.

Stuckley R.L. & Wentz W.A. 1969, Effect of industrial pollution on the aquatic and shore angiosperm flora in the Ottawa River, Allen and Putnam Counties, Ohio. *Ohio J. Sci.* **69:** 226–242.

Stuckley R.L. 1971. Changes of vascular aquatic flowering plants during 70 years in Put-in-Bay harbor, Lake Erie, Ohio. *Ohio J. Sci.* **71:** 321–342.

Transley A.G. 1949. The British Islands and their vegetation. London: Cambridge University Press.

Thomas G.W. & Crutchfield J.D. 1974. Nitrate-nitrogen and phosphorus contents of streams draining small agricultural watersheds in Kentucky. *J. Environ. Qual.* **3:** 46–49.

Thomson Jr J.W. 1945. A survey of the larger aquatic plants and bank flora of the Brule River. *Trans. Wisc. Acad. Sci. Arts Lett.* **36:** 57–76.

Thompson T.W. 1972. Control of Water Milfoil in Wisconsin. In: *Meeting Weed Sci. Soc. America, St Louis.* pp. 61–62 (abstr.).

Thornton I., Watling H. & Darracott A. 1975. Geochemical studies in several rivers and estuaries used for oyster rearing. *Sci. Total Environ.* **4:** 325–345.

Usk River Authority. 1968. *Third Annual Report for the year ended 31 March 1968.*

Volker R. & Smith S.G. 1965. Changes in the aquatic vascular flora of Lake East Okobogi in historic times. *Iowa Acad. Sci.* **72:** 65–72.

Voo van der E.E. & Westhoff V. 1961. An autecological study of some limnophytes and halophytes in the area of the large rivers. *Wentia* **5:** 163–258.

Water Resources Data for Wisconsin. 1973. United States Department of the Interior, Geological Survey.

Weber-Oldecop D.W. 1970. Wasserpflanzengesellschaften im östlichen Niedersachsen. I. *Int. Revue Ges. Hydrobiol.* **55:** 913–967.

Weber-Oldecop D.W. 1971. Wasserpflanzengesellschaften im östlichen Niedersachsen. II. *Int. Revue Ges. Hydrobiol.* **56:** 79–122.

Westlake D.F. 1900. The weight of water-weed in the river Frome. In: *Association of River Authorities Year Book.* pp. 1–12.

Westlake D.F. 1959a. The effects of biological communities on conditions in polluted streams. *Symp. Inst. Biol.* **8:** 25–31.

Westlake D.F. 1959b. The effects of organisms on pollution. *Proc. Limnol. Soc. Lond.* **170:** 171–172.

Westlake D.F. 1960. Water weed and water management. *Inst. Publ. Health Eng. J.* **59:** 148–160.

Westlake D.F. 1961. Aquatic macrophytes and the oxygen balance of running water. *Int. Ver. Theor. Angew. Limnol. Verh.* **15:** 499–504.

Westlake D.F. 1964. Light extinction, standing crop and photosynthesis within weedbeds. *Verh. Int. Verein Limnol.* **15:** 415–425.

Westlake D.F. 1965. Some basic data for investigations of the productivity of aquatic macrophytes. *Mem. Ist. Ital. Idrobiol.* **18:** 229–248.

Westlake D.F. 1966a. A model for quantitative studies of photosynthesis by higher plants in streams. *Int. J. Air Water Pollut.* **10:** 883–896.

Westlake D.F. 1966b. The light climate for plants in rivers. *Symp. Brit. Ecol. Soc.* **6:** 99–119.

Westlake D.F. 1967. Some effects of low velocity currents on the metabolism of aquatic macrophytes. *Journal of Experimental Botany* **18:** 187–205.

Westlake D.F. 1968. The biology of aquatic weeds in relation to their management. In: *Proc. 9th Brit. Weed Control Conf.* pp. 372–379.

Westlake D.F. 1973. Aquatic macrophytes in rivers. *Pol. Arch. Hydrobiol.* **20:** 31–40.

Westlake D.F. 1975a. Macrophytes. In: Owens M. & Whitton B.A., eds. *River ecology.* Oxford: Blackwell. pp. 106–128.

Westlake D.F. 1975b. Primary production of freshwater macrophytes. In: Cooper J.P., ed. *Photosynthesis and productivity in different environments.* London: Cambridge University Press. pp. 189–206.

Westlake D.F. 1977. In: Le Cren E.D., ed. *Freshwater Ecosystems.* International Biological Programme Synthesis Volumes. London: Cambridge University Press.

Westlake D.F, Casey H., Dawson F.A., Ladle M., Mann R.H.K. & Marker F.H. 1972. The chalk-stream ecosystem. In: Kajak Z. & Hillbricht-Ilkowska A., eds. *Productivity problems of freshwaters.* Poland: IBP-UNESCO, Kazimierz Dolny. pp. 615–637.

Whitton B.A. & Buckmaster R.C. 1970. Macrophytes of the River Wear. *Naturalist* **914:** 97–116.

Whitton B.A. & Dalpra M. 1968. Floristic changes in the River Tees. *Hydrobiol.* **32:** 545–550.

Wium-Andersen S. 1971. Photosynthetic uptake of free CO_2 by the roots of *Lobelia dortmanna*. *Physiol. Plant.* **25:** 245–248.

Yoe R.R. 1965. Life history of Sago Pondweed. *Weeds 1965* **13:** 314–321.

B — PUBLICATIONS 1976 TO 2004

This is less complete than A, as the literature has greatly increased. Like A, it includes references not used in the text. It is intended to allow readers to enter the later and current literature, whether or not the publications have been incorporated in the revision of the second edition (also see Preface to the second edition). It covers countries and subjects not in the book.

Anon. 1996. *River Habitats in England and Wales.* A preliminary national overview. River Habitat Survey Report No. 1, National Rivers Authority, March 1996.

Anon. 1999. *The River Restoration Centre Information Sheets 1–7.* Silsoe: RRC.

Armitage P.D. & Pardo I. 1995. Impact assessment of regulation at the reach level using macroinvertebrate information from mesohabitats. *Regul. Rivers: Res. Mgmt.* **10:** 147–158.

Association Français de Normalisation AFNOR. 2003. Norme NF T90-395, Octobre 2003. *Qualité de l'eau. Détermination de l'indice biologique macrophytique en rivière (IGMR).* Association Française de Normalisation. 28 pp.

Athie D. & Corrie C.C., eds. 1987. *The use of macrophytes in water pollution control.* Oxford: Pergamon Press.

Badsen B.L. 1995. *A River Keeper's Field Book.* Copenhagen: Danish Environmental Protection Agency.

Bain M.B., Finn J.F. & Booke H.E. 1985. Quantifying stream substrate for habitat analysis studies. *North American Journal of Fisheries Management* **5:** 499–506.

Beardall C.H., Harding M., Holmes N. & Condor A. 1992. *Water for Wildlife.* A review of water resource management issues in the Anglian Region. RSNC Wildlife Trust Partnership, Water for Wildlife Campaign.

Bernez I., Coudreuse J., Daniel H., Haury J. & Le Cœur D. (In Press). Bioindication using vegetation of three regulated rivers under agro-industrial pressure in Western France. *Annali di Botanica di Napoli.*

Bernez I., Daniel H. & Haury J. 2000. Etude des variations des communautés végétales aquatiques sous l'effet des perturbations anthropiques en rivière régulée. *Bull. fr. Pêche Piscic.* **357/358:** 169–189.

Bernez I., Daniel H., Haury J. & Ferreira M.T. 2004. Combined effects of environmental factors and regulation on macrophyte vegetation along three rivers in Western France. *River Research and Applications (ex. Regulated Rivers: Research and Management)* **20:** 43–59.

Bernez I., Haury J. & Ferreira M.T. 2002. Downstream effects of a hydroelectric reservoir on aquatic plant assemblages. [Research Article, Proc. 2nd Symp. European Freshwater Systems.] *The Scientific World Journal* **2:** 740–750.

Berrie A.D. 1992. The chalk-stream environment. *Hydrobiologia* **248:** 3–9.

Biggs J., Corfield A., Gron P., Hansen H.O., Walker D., Whitfield M. & Williams P. 1998. Restoration of the rivers Brede, Cole and Skerne: a joint Danish and British EU-LIFE demonstration project. Short-term impacts on the conservation value of aquatic macroinvertebrate and macrophyte assemblages. *Aquat. Conserv.: Mar. Freshwater Ecosyst.* **8(1):** 241–255.

Bolton P. & Dawson F.H. 1992. The use of a check-list in assessing possible environmental impacts in planning watercourse improvements. *Proceedings of the International Symposium on Effects of Watercourse Improvements: Assessment, Methodology, Management Assistance, 10–12 September 1991, Wepion, Namure, Belgium. Department for non-navigable watercourses of the Walloon Region.* Final Proceedings. pp. 29–42.

Boon P.J. & Raven P.J. 1998. The application of classification and assessment methods to river management in the UK. *Aquatic Conservation* (Special issue) **8(4).**

Bornette G. & Amoros C. 1991. Aquatic vegetation and hydrology of a braided river flood plain. *Journal of Vegetation Science* **2:** 497–512.

Bornette G., Amoros C. & Collileux G. 1994. Role of seepage supply former river channels: prediction testing using a hydroelectric construction. *Environmental Management* **18:** 223–224.

Bornette G., Henry C., Barrat M.H. & Amoros C. 1993. Theoretical habitat template, species traits, and species richness: aquatic macrophytes in the Upper Rhône River and its flood plain. Thesis, Université Lyon 1.

Bornette G., Henry C., Barrat M.H. & Amoros C. 1994. Theoretical template, species traits, and species richness: aquatic macrophytes in the Upper Rhône River and its flood plain. *Freshwater Biology* **31:** 487–505.

Breugnot E., Dutartre A., Laplace-Treyture C. & Haury J. 2004. Variabilité des peuplements de macrophytes en grands cours d'eau — Premiers résultats sur l'hydrosstème Adour-Garonne. *Ingénieries* **37:** 37–50.

Brookes A., Gregory K.J. & Dawson F.H. 1983. An assessment of river channelization in England and Wales. *Science of the Total Environment* **27:** 97–111.

Caffrey J.M. 1991. Aquatic plant management in Irish rivers. In: Steer M.W., ed. *Irish rivers.* Dublin: Royal Irish Academy. pp. 85–93.

Caffrey J.M. & Beglin T. 1996. Bankside stabilisation and reed transplantation in a newly constructed Irish canal habitat. *Hydrobiologia* **340:** 349–357.

Caffrey J.M., Monahan C. & Tierney D. 2002. Factors influencing the distribution of aquatic plant communities in Irish canals. *Proceedings of the 11th EWRS International Symposium on Aquatic Weeds.* Moliêts et Maâ (France), September 2–6 2002. pp. 99–103.

Carbiener R., Trémolières M., Mercier J.L. & Ortscheit A. 1990. Aquatic macrophyte communities as bioindicators of eutrophication in calcareous oligosaprobe stream waters. Lower Rhine plain, Alsace). *Vegetation* **86:** 71–88.

Carty P. & Payne R. 1998. *Angling and the Law.* Ludlow: Merlin Unwin Books.

Chatenet P., Botineau M., Haury J. & Ghestem A. 2000. Typologie de la végétation des rivières et affluents de la Vienne et de la Gartempe (Limousin, France). *Acta Bot. Gallica* **147(2):** 151–164.

Chatenet P., Haury J., Botineau M. & Picaud F. 2002. Impact de pollutions ponctuelles sur les phytocénoses des rivières acides à neutres du Limousin (Massif Central, France). *Rev. Sci. Eau* **16(1):** 397–410.

Chatters C. 1996. Conserving rare plants in muddy places. *British Wildlife* **7:** 281–286.

Cook H.F. 1998. *The protection and conservation of water resources. A British perspective.* Chichester: John Wiley & Sons.

Cooper P.F. & Findlater B.C., eds. 1990. *Constructed wetlands in water pollution control.* Oxford: Pergamon Press.

Cowx I.G. & Welcomme R.L., eds. 1998. *Rehabilitation of rivers for fish.* Oxford: Fishing New Books.

Daniel H., Bernez I. & Haury J. 2002. Relations entre la morphologie des macrophytes et les charactéristiques physiques des habitats en rivière. In: Dutartre A. & Montel M.H.N., eds. *Gestion des plantes aquatiques (11th International Symposium on Aquatic Weeds — EWRS, CEMAGREF, Conseil Général des Landes, INRA, ENSAR), 2–6 Septembre 2002, Moliêts et Maâ, France.* pp. 115–118.

Daniel H., Bernez I., Haury J. & Le Cœur D. (In Press). The ability of macrophytes to assess. fish farm pollution in two salmonid rivers. *Hydrobiologia.*

Dawson F.H. 1976. The annual production of the aquatic macrophyte *Ranunculus penicillatus* var. *calcareus* (R.W. Butcher), C.D.K. Cook. *Aquatic Botany* **3:** 51–73.

Dawson F.H. 1988. Water flow and the vegetation of running waters. In: Symoens J.J., ed. *Handbook of Vegetation Sciences series, 15, Vegetation of Inland Waters*. The Hague: Junk. pp. 283–309.

Dawson F.H. 1989. Ecology and management of water plants in lowland streams. *Annual Report of the Freshwater Biological Association* **57:** 43–60.

Dawson F.H. 1994. The spread of *Crassula helmsii* (Kirk) Cockayne in Britain. In: de Waal L.C., Child P.M. & Brock J.H., eds. *Ecology & Management of Invasive Riverside Plants*. Proceedings of first international workshop on ecology and management of invasive riparian and aquatic plants, 22–23 April 1992, ICOLE, Loughborough University. Chichester: John Wiley & Sons. pp. 1–14.

Dawson F.H., Castellano E. & Ladle M. 1978. The concept of species succession in relation to river vegetation and management. *Verhandlung Internationale Vereinigung für Theoretische und Angewandte Limnologie* **20:** 1451–1456.

Dawson F.H. & Charlton F.G. 1988. A bibliography on the hydraulic resistance or roughness of vegetated watercourses. *Freshwater Biological Association Occasional Publication* **25:** 50 pp.

Dawson F.H., Clinton E.M.F. & Ladle M. 1991. Invertebrates on cut-weed removed during a weed-cut operation along an English river, the River Frome, Dorset. *Aquaculture & Fisheries Management* **22:** 113–121.

Dawson F.H. & Kern-Hansen U. 1978. Aquatic weed management in natural streams: the effect of shade by marginal vegetation. *Verhandlung Internationale Vereinigung für Theoretische und Angewandte Limnologie* **20:** 1429–1434.

Dawson F.H., Kern-Hansen U. & Westlake D.F. 1982. Water plants and the temperature and oxygen regimes of lowland streams. In: Symoens J.J., Hooper S.S. & Compere P., eds. *Studies on Aquatic Vascular Plants*. Proceedings International Colloquium on Aquatic Vascular Plants, Brussels, 23–25 January 1981. Brussels: Royal Botanical Society of Belgium. pp. 214–221.

Dawson F.H. & Newman J.R. 1998. Decline of *Ranunculus* in British rivers: true or false? *Proceedings of the 10th European Weed Research Symposium*, Lisbon, Portugal, September 1998. pp. 95–98.

Dawson F.H., Raven P.J. & Holmes N.T.H. 1998. The distribution of aquatic plants by morphological group for rivers in the UK. *Proceedings of the 10th European Weed Research Symposium*, Lisbon, Portugal, September 1998. pp. 183–186.

Dawson F.H. & Robinson W.N. 1984. Submerged macrophytes and the hydraulic roughness of a lowland chalkstream. *Verhandlung Internationale Vereinigung für Theoretische und Angewandte Limnologie* **22(3):** 1944–1948.

Dawson F.H. & Szoszkiewicz K. 1998. Ecological factors and the associations of aquatic vegetation in the British rivers. *Proceedings of the 10th European Weed Research Symposium*, Lisbon, Portugal, September 1998. pp. 179–182.

Dokulil M. & Janauer G.A. 2000. Alternative stable states of macrophytes versus phytoplankton in two interconnected impoundments of the New Danube (Vienna, Austria). *Large Rivers* **12/1:** 75–83.

Environment Agency. 1996. *River Wylye low flow study.* Environment Agency, Wessex Region.

Environment Agency. 1997. *'Middle and lower river Wylye': Fisheries Survey.* Draft Report by Fisheries Surveys. The Environment Agency, South West Region.

Everard M. 2004. Investing in sustainable catchments. *Science of the Total Environment* **324:** 1–24.

Everard M., James R.E., Carty P. & Powell A.M. 2002. Implementing the Water Framework Directive: opportunities and risks. *FBA News* **17:** 1–4.

Everard M., Kenmir B., Walters C. & Holt E. 2004. Upland hill farming for water, wildlife and food. *Freshwater Forum* **21**: 48–73.

Extence C.A., Balbi D.M. & Chadd R.P. 1999. River flow indexing using British benthic macro invertebrates: A framework for setting hydroecological objectives. *Regulated Rivers: Research & Management* **15**: 543–574.

Frake A. 1999. *Monitoring protocol for river rehabilitation projects.* F.E.R. 26.3.98. Blandford, Dorset: Environment Agency.

Fritz R., Tremp A. & Kohler A. 1998. Klassifizierung und Bewertung der südbadischen Rheinseitengewässer mit Wasserpflanzen. *Verhandlungen der Gesellschaft für Ökologie* **28**: 113–122.

Game Conservancy Trust. Undated. *Restoring the river Piddle.* Fordingbridge, Hampshire: The Game Conservancy Trust.

Gardiner J.L., ed. 1992. *River Projects and Conservation.* Chichester: John Wiley & Sons.

Giles N. 1997a. *Malmesbury Avon habitat improvement research project 1996/7.* First Annual Report. Verwood, Dorset: N. Giles & Associates.

Giles N. 1997b. *River Wylye habitat improvement research project 1996/7.* First Annual Report. Verwood, Dorset: N. Giles & Associates.

Giles N. 1999a. *Malmesbury Avon habitat improvement research project 1998/9.* Third Annual Report, January 1999. Verwood, Dorset: N. Giles & Associates.

Giles N. 1999b. *River Wylye habitat improvement research project 1998/9.* Third Annual Report, March 1999. Verwood, Dorset: N. Giles & Associates.

Giles N. & Summers D.W. 1999. *Lowland river habitat rehabilitation for sustainable game and coarse fish stocks.*

Gonzales P., Albuquerque A., Ferreira M.T. & Espìrito-Santo D. 2002. Assessing ecological integrity of river plants: indicator value of species composition and plant assemblages. *Proceedings of the 11th EWRS International Symposium on Aquatic Weeds.* Moliêts et Maâ (France), September 2–6 2002. pp. 235–239.

Hammer D.A., ed. 1989. *Constructed wetlands for wastewater treatment.* Chelsea, Michigan: Lewis Publishers.

Harper D., Smith C., Barham P. & Howell R. 1995. The Ecological basis for the management of the natural river environment. In: Harper D.M. & Ferguson A.J.D., eds. *The ecological basis for river management.* Chichester: John Wiley & Sons. pp. 219–238.

Harper D.M. & Ferguson A.J.D., eds. 1995. The *ecological basis for river management.* Chichester: John Wiley & Sons.

Haslam S.M. (In Preparation). *The riverscape and the river.* Cambridge: Cambridge University Press.

Haslam S.M. 1971a. Community regulation in *Phragmites communis* Trin.. I. Mixed stands. *Journal of Ecology* **59**: 65–73.

Haslam S.M. 1971b. Community regulation in *Phragmites communis* Trin.. II. Mixed stands. *Journal of Ecology* **59**: 75–88.

Haslam S.M. 1972. *Phragmites communis* Trin. Biological Flora of the British Isles 128. *Journal of Ecology* **60**: 585–610.

Haslam S.M. 1973. Some aspects of the life history and autecology of *Phragmites communis* Trin. *Polskie Archiwum Hydrobiologia* **20**: 79–100.

Haslam S.M. 1978. *River Plants.* Cambridge: Cambridge University Press. 396 pp.

Haslam S.M. 1981. Changing rivers and changing vegetation in the past half century. *Proceedings Aquatic Weeds and their Control, 1981.* pp. 49–57.

Haslam S.M. 1982a. Indices for dyke vegetation. *Nature in Cambridgeshire* **25**: 34–40.

Haslam S.M. 1982b. *Vegetation in British rivers.* Nature Conservancy Council. 2 Vols.

Haslam S.M. 1986. Causes of changes in river vegetation giving rise to complaints. *Proceedings EWRS/AAB 7th Symposium on Aquatic Weeds 1986.* pp. 151–156.

Haslam S.M. 1987. *River Plants of Western Europe.* Cambridge: Cambridge University Press.

Haslam S.M. 1990. *River Pollution: An Ecological Perspective.* London: Belhaven Press.

Haslam S.M. 1991. *The Historic River.* Cambridge: Cobden of Cambridge Press.

Haslam S.M. 1994. *Wetland habitat differentiation and sensitivity to chemical pollutants (non open water wetlands).* London: Her Majesty's Inspectorate of Pollution. 145 + 110 pp.

Haslam S.M. 1995. Cultural variation in river quality and macrophyte response. *Acta Botanica Gallica* **142:** 345–348.

Haslam S.M. 1996. Enhancing river vegetation: conservation, development and restoration. *Hydrobiologia* **340:** 345–348.

Haslam S.M. 1997a. Deterioration and fragmentation of rivers in Malta. *Freshwater Forum* **9:** 55–61.

Haslam S.M. 1997b. River habitat fragmentation in Malta: a danger needing investigation. *Fresenius Environmental Bulletin* **6:** 43–47.

Haslam S.M. 1997c. The precarious state of the rivers of Malta. *Fresenius Environmental Bulletin* **6:** 343–348.

Haslam S.M. 1997d. *The River Scene: ecology and cultural heritage.* Cambridge: Cambridge University Press. 344 pp.

Haslam S.M. 1998. The deterioration of water quality in Malta. *Fresenius Environmental Bulletin* **7:** 96–99.

Haslam S.M. 2000a. Impact of land use changes on rivers. *Aspects of Applied Biology* **58:** 197–204.

Haslam S.M. 2000b. The evaluation of river pollution in the Maltese Islands. *Fresenius Environmental Bulletin* **9:** 347–351.

Haslam S.M. 2001. Retaining the cultural heritage of rivers? In: Mander Ü., Rintsmann A. & Palang H., eds. *Development of European Landscapes*, Vol. 1. Tartu. pp. 206–209.

Haslam S.M. 2002. Stream community lists as bioindicators. *Proceedings of the 11th EWRS* (European Weed Research Society) *International Symposium on Aquatic Weeds*, September 2–6, 2002. Moliêts et Maâ, France. pp. 243–246.

Haslam S.M. 2003. *Understanding wetlands: fen, bog and marsh.* London: Taylor & Francis.

Haslam S.M. & Borg J. 1998. *The river valleys of the Maltese Islands.* Malta: Ciheam, Bari, and Islands and Small States Institute, Foundation of International Studies.

Haslam S.M., Borg J. & Psaila J.M. 2004. *River Kbir: the Hidden Wonder, Malta.* 192 pp.

Haslam S.M., Harding J.P.C. & Spence D.H.N. 1987. *Methods for the use of Aquatic Macrophytes for assessing water quality 1985. Methods for the examination of waters and associated materials.* London: Her Majesty's Stationery Office.

Haslam S.M., Klötzli F., Sukopp H. & Szczepanski A. 1998. The management of wetlands. In: Westlake D.F., Kvet J. & Szczepanski A., eds. *The production ecology of wetlands.* Cambridge: Cambridge University Press. pp. 405–464.

Haslam S.M., Sinker C.A. & Wolseley P.A. 1975. *British Water Plants.* Field Studies Council. (1982 — Reprint with corrections.) FSC Publication S10. 108 pp.

Haslam S.M. & Wolseley P.A. 1981. *River vegetation: its identification, assessment and management.* Cambridge: Cambridge University Press. 154 pp.

Haury J. 1989. Macrophytes du Trieux (Bretagne-Nord): II: Analyse des relations espèces-milieu physique par la méthode des profils écologiques. *Bull. Soc. Sc. Nat. Ouest de la France, Nouc. Sér.* **11 (4):** 193–207.

Haury J. 1996a. Assessing function typology involving water quality, physical features and macrophytes in a Normandy river. *Hydrobiologia* **340:** 43–49.

Haury J. 1996b. *Macrophytes des cours d'eau: bioindication et habitat piscicole.* Thèse d'Habilitation à Diriger des Recherches, Université de Rennes I. 3 vol. 99 pp.

Haury J. & Aidara L.G. 1999. Macrophyte cover and standing crop in the River Scorff and its tributaries (Brittany, northwestern France): scale, patterns and process. *Hydrobiologia* **415:** 109–115.

Haury J. & Bagliniere J.L. 1990. Relations entre la population de truites communes (*Salmo trutta* L.), les macrophytes et les paramètres du milieu sur un ruisseau. *Bull. fr. Pêche Piscic.* **318:** 118–131.

Haury J., Dutartre A., Binesse F., Codhant H. & Valkman G. 2001. Macrophyte biotypologies of rivers in Lozère, France. *Verhandlung Internationale Vereinigung für Theoretische und Angewandte Limnologie* Dublin, 1998 (Stuttgart, Sept. 2001) **27(6):** 3510–3517.

Haury J. & Gouesse Aidara L. 1999. Quantifying macrophyte cover and standing crops in a river and its tributaries (Brittany, Northwestern France). *Hydrobiologia* **415:** 109–115.

Haury J., Jaffre M., Dutartre A., Peltre M-C., Barbe J., Trémolières M., Guerlesquin M. & Muller S. 1998. Application de la méthode 'Milieu et végétaux aquatiques fixés' à 12 rivières françaises: topologie floristique préliminaire. *Annls Limnol.* **34(2):** 1–11.

Haury J., Merot P. & Riviere J.M. 1990. Under-utilization and intensification in two Brittany wetlands. *Bull. Ecol.* **21(3):** 61–64.

Haury J. & Muller S. 1991. Variations écologiques et chorologiques de la végétation macrophytique des rivières acides du Massif Armoricain et des Vosges du Nord (France). *Rev. Sci. Eau* **4(4):** 463–482.

Haury J. & Peltre M-C. 1993. Intérêts et limites des 'indices macrophytes' pour qualifier la mésologie et la physico-chimie des cours d'eau: exemples armoricaiins, picards et lorrains. *Annls Limnol.* **29(3–4):** 239–253.

Haury J., Peltre M-C., Muller S., Trémolières M., Barbe J., Dutartre A. & Guerlesquin M. 1996. Des indices macrophytiques pour estimer la qualité des cours d'eau français: premières propositions. *Ecologie* **27(4):** 79–90.

Haury J., Peltre M-C., Trémolières M., Barbe J., Thiebaut G., Bernez I., Daniel H., Chatenet P., Haan-Archipof G., Muller S., Dutartre A., Laplace-Treyture C., Cazaubon A. & Lambert-Servien E. (In Press). A new method to assess water trophy and organic pollution — the Macrophyte Biological Index for Rivers (IBMR): its application to different types of river and pollution. *Hydrobiologia.*

Haury J., Peltre M-C., Trémolières M., Barbe J., Thiebaut G., Bernez I., Daniel H., Chatenet P., Muller S., Dutartre A., Laplace-Treyture C., Cazaubon A. & Lambert-Servien E. 2002. A method involving macrophytes to assess water trophy and organic pollution: the Macrophyte Biological Index for Rivers (IBMR) — Application to different types of rivers and pollutions. In: Dutartre A. & Montel M.H.N., eds. *Gestion des plantes aquatiques* (11th International Symposium on Aquatic Weeds — EWRS, CEMAGREF, Conseil Général des Landes, INRA, ENSAR), 3–7 Septembre 2002. Moliêts et Maâ, France. pp. 247–250.

Hellsten S., Dieme C., Mbengue M., Janauer G.A., Hollander N. den & Pieterse A.H. 1999. *Typha* control efficiency of a weed-cutting boat in the Lac de Guiers in Senegal: a preliminary study on mowing speed and re-growth capacity. *Hydrobiologia* **415:** 249–255.

Holmes N.T.H. 1983a. *Focus on nature conservation. 3. Classification of British rivers according to the flora.* Peterborough: Nature Conservancy Council.

Holmes N.T.H. 1983b. *Focus on nature conservation. 4. Typing British rivers according to their macrophytic flora.* Peterborough: Nature Conservancy Council.

Holmes N.T.H. 1996. *Classification of Winterbournes.* Report to Environment Agency. Cambridge: Alconbury Environmental Consultants.

Holmes N.T.H. 1999a. Recovery of headwater stream flora following the 1989–92 groundwater drought. *Hydrological Processes* **13(3):** 341–354.

Holmes N.T.H. 1999b. British river macrophytes — perceptions and uses in the 20th Century. *Aquatic Conservation* **9(6):** 535–540.

Holmes N.T.H., Boon P. & Rowell T. 1999. *Vegetation communities of British rivers: a revised classification.* Joint Nature Conservation Committee. pp. 1–114.

Holmes N.T.H., Newman J.R., Chadd S., Rouen K.J., Saint L. & Dawson F.H. 1999. *Mean Trophic Rank: A User's Manual.* Environment Agency R & D Tech Rep E38. Bristol.

Janauer G.A. 1996. Macrophytes, hydrology, and aquatic ecotones: a GIS-supported ecological survey. *Aquatic Botany* **58:** 379–391.

Janauer G.A. 1999. Macrophytes of the River Danube: a diversity study of the Austrian stretch. *Arch. Hydrobiol. Suppl. Large Rivers* **11/3:** 399–412.

Janauer G.A. 2000. Ecohydrology: fusing concepts and scales. *Ecological Engineering* **16:** 9–16.

Janauer G.A. 2001a. Is what has been measured of any direct relevance to the success of the macrophyte in its particular environment? *Journal of Limnology* **60** *(Suppl. 1):* 33–38.

Janauer G.A. 2001b. The inventory of aquatic macrophytes in the Austrian stretch of the River Danube. *Verhandlung Internationale Vereinigung für Theoretische und Angewandte Limnologie* **27:** 3947–3949.

Janauer G.A. 2002. Establishing Ecohydrology in the Real World: The Lobau Biosphere Reserve and the integrated water scheme in Vienna. In: Zalewski M.& Harper D.M., eds. *Ecohydrology and Hydrobiology. The Application of Ecohydrology in Water Resources Development and Management.* Proceedings from the final Conference of the first phase of the IHP-V Project 2.3/2.4 on Ecohydrology, Venice, September 2001. pp. 120–125.

Janauer G.A. 2003a. Makrophyten der Augewässer. In: Janauer G.A. & Hary N., eds. *Ökotone-Donau-Marsch.* Veröff. Österr. MaB-Programm, Österr. Akad. Wiss. Innsbruck: Wagner. pp. 156–200.

Janauer G.A. 2003b. Overview and final remarks. *Large Rivers* **14:** 217–229.

Janauer G.A. & Exler N. 2003. Aquatic plants in the spotlight of international research. *Danube Watch* **02:** 26–28.

Janauer G.A. & Exler N. 2004. Distribution and habitat conditions of the six most frequent hydrophytes in the Danube River corridor: status 2002. *Proceedings 35 IAD Conf. Novi Sad (Montenegro).* pp. 407–412.

Janauer G.A. & Kum G. 1996. Macrophytes and floodplain water dynamics in the River Danube ecotone research region (Austria). *Hydrobiologia* **340:** 137–140.

Janauer G.A., Vukov D. & Igic R. 2003. Aquatic macrophytes of the Danube River near Novi Sad (Yugoslavia, river-km 1255–1260). *Arch. Hydrobiol. Suppl.* **147/1–2:** 195–204; *Large Rivers* 14/1–2.

Janauer G.A. & Wychera U. 2000. Biodiversity, succession and the functioning role of macrophytes in the New Danube. *Arch. Hydrobiol. Suppl. Large Rivers* **12/1:** 61–74.

Janes M.D. & Holmes N.T.H. 1998. *Audit of 20 rehabilitation projects.* Environmental Agency. Thames Region. River Restoration Centre, Silsoe, Beds.

Kern-Hansen U. & Dawson F.H. 1978. The standing crop of aquatic plants of lowland streams in Denmark and the inter-relationships of nutrients in plant, sediment and water. *Proceedings of the 5th European Weed Research Council Symposium on Aquatic Weeds.* pp. 143–150.

428

Klaason F.A., Newman T.R., Gravelle M.H., Rouen, K.J. 1999. *Assessment of the trophic status of rivers using macrophytes: evaluation of the mean trophic rank.* Bristol: Environment Agency.

Kohler A., Lange B. & Zeltner G-H. 1992. Veränderung von Flora und Vegetation in den Fließgewässern Pfreimd und Naab (Oberpfälzer Wald) 1972–1988. *Ber. Inst. Landeskultur und Pflanzenökologie* (Univ. Hohenheim) **1**: 72–138.

Kohler A. 1978. Methoden der Kartierung von Flora und Vegetation von Süßwasserbiotopen. *Landschaft und Stadt* **10**: 23–85.

Kohler A. 1982. Wasserpflanzen als Belastungsindikatoren. *Decheniana Beihefte* (Bonn) **26**: 31–42.

Kohler A. & Janauer G.A. 1995. Zur Methodik der Untersuchung von aquatischen Makrophyten in Fließgewässern. In: Steinberg Ch., Bernhardt H. & Klapper H., eds. *Handbuch Angewandte Limnologie.* Landsberg: Ecomed Verlag.

Kohler A. & Labus B.C. 1983. Eutrophication process and pollution of freshwater ecosystems including waste heat. *Encyclopedia of plant physiology. New series.* Volume 12 D. *Physiological plant ecology* **4**: 413–464.

Kohler A. & Schneider S. 2003. Macrophytes as bioindicators. *Large Rivers.* Vol. 14, No. 1–2. *Arch. Hydrobiol. Suppl.* **147/1–2**: 17–31.

Kohler A., Sipos V. & Björk S. 1996. Makrophytenvegetation und Standorte im humosen Bräkne Fluß (Südschweden). *Bot. Jahrb. Syst.* **118**: 451–503.

Kohler A., Sipos V., Sonntag E., Penksza K., Pozzi D. & Veit U. 2000. Makrophytenverbreitung und Standortqualität im Bjorka-Kävlinge Fluss (Skåne, Südschweden). *Hydrobiologia* **30**: 281–298.

Kohler A., Sipos V., Sonntag E, Penksza K., Pozzi D., Veit U. & Björk S. 2000. Makrophytenverbreitung und Standortqualität im eutrophen Björka Fluß (Skåne, Südschweden). *Limnologica* **30**: 281–298.

Kohler A., Sonntag E., Köhler M., Pall K., Veit U., Zeltner G-H. & Janauer G.A. 2003. Macrophyte distribution in the River Vils (Oberpfalz, Bavaria). *Large Rivers* **14**, No. 1–2; *Arch. Hydrobiol. Suppl.* **147/1–2**: 33–53.

Kohler A. & Veit U. 2003. Die EU-Wasserrahmenrichtlinie — Anmerkungen aus der Sicht der Makrophytenforschung in Fliessgewässern.

Kohler A. & Veit U. 2003. Makrophyten als biologische Qualitätskomponente bei den Fließgewässern. Bewertung — Anmerkungen zur EU Wasserrahmenrichtlinie. *Naturschutz und Landschaftsplanung* **35(12)**: 357–363.

Lange S.R. 1965. The control of aquatic plants by commercial harvesting, processing and marketing. In: *Proc. 18th South Weed Control Conference.* pp. 536–542.

Linløkken A. 1997. Effects of instream habitat enhancement on fish populations of a small Norwegian stream. *Nordic J. Fresw. Res.* **73**: 50–59.

Little E.C.S. 1968. *Handbook of utilisation of aquatic plants.* A compilation of the worlds' publication. Rome: FAO.

Maddock I. 1999. The importance of physical habitat assessment for evaluating river health. *Freshw. Biol.* **41**: 373–391.

Madsen B.L. 1995. *Danish Watercourses. Ten years with the new Watercourse Act.* Copenhagen: Danish Environment Protection Agency.

Mitsch W., ed. 1994. *Global wetlands: old and new.* Elsevier: Amsterdam.

Moshiri G.A., ed. 1993. *Constructed wetlands for water quality improvement.* Boca Raton, Florida: Lewis Publishers.

National Rivers Authority. 1996. *River habitats in England and Wales.* Bristol: National Rivers Authority.

Newbold C., Hannar I. & Buckley K. 1989. *Nature Conservation and the management of drainage channels.* Peterborough: Nature Conservancy Council.

Neori A., Reddy K.R., Cisková-Konclova H. & Agami M. 2000. Bioactive chemicals and biological-biochemical activities and their functions in rhizospheres of wetland plats. *The Botanical Review* **66**: 350–378.

Petti G. & Calow P. 1996. *River Restoration.* Oxford: Blackwell Science.

Purseglove I. 1989. Taming the flood. Oxford: University Press.

Pitlo R.H. & Dawson F.H. 1989. Flow resistance by aquatic vegetation. In: Pieterse A.H. & Murphy K.J., eds. *Aquatic Weeds.* Oxford: University Press. pp. 74–84.

Rath B., Janauer G.A., Pall K. & Berczik A. 2003. The aquatic macrophyte vegetation in the Old Danube/Hungarian Bank, and other water bodies of the Szigetköz wetlands. *Arch. Hydrobiol. Suppl.* **147/1–2:** 129–142; *Large Rivers* 14/1–2.

Raven P.J., Boon P.J., Dawson F.H. & Ferguson A.J.D. 1998. Towards an integrated approach to classifying and evaluating rivers in the UK. Special issue: The application of classification and assessment methods to river management in the UK. *Aquatic Conservation: Marine & Freshwater Ecosystems* **8(4):** 383–393.

Raven P.J., Fox P., Everard M., Holmes N.T.H. & Dawson F.H. 1997. *River Habitat Survey: a new system for classifying rivers according to their habitat quality.* London: HMSO.

Raven P.J., Holmes N.T.H., Naura M. & Dawson F.H. 1999. River habitat survey and its use in environmental assessment and integrated river basin management in the UK. *International Conference on assessing the ecological integrity of running waters.* Vienna, November, 1998.

Raven P.J., Holmes N.T.H, Dawson F.H. & Everard M. 1998. Quality assessment using River Habitat Survey data. Special issue: The application of classification and assessment methods to river management in the UK. *Aquatic Conservation: Marine & Freshwater Ecosystems* **8(4):** 477–499.

Reddy K.R. & Smith W.H., eds. 1987. *Aquatic plants for water treatment and resource recovery.* Orlando, Florida: Magnolia Publishers.

Robach F., Eglin I. & Carbiener R. 1991. Hydrosystems, Rhénan. *Bulletin Ecologique* **22:** 227–241.

Rubec C.D.A. & Overend R.P., eds. 1987. *Wetlands/Peatlands Proceedings of Symposium 1987. Edmonton, Alberta.*

Sabater F., Sabater S. & Armengol J. 1990. Chemical characteristics of a Mediterranean river as influenced by land uses in the watershed. *Land & Water Research* **24:** 143–155.

Sabbatini M.R., Sidorkewicz N.S., Murphy K.J., Marchena A., Irigoyen J.H. & Fernandez O.A. 2002. Macrophytes, bioseston and periphyton as water quality indicators in the Sauce Grande, river catchment, Argentina. *Proceedings of the 11th EWRS International Symposium on Aquatic Weeds.* Moliêts et Maâ (France), September 2–6 2002. pp. 251–256.

Satinet M. 1998. *The river Wylye: Otter and habitat report.* Wiltshire Wildlife Trust for Wessex Water.

Sear D., Armitage P.D. & Dawson F.H. 1999. Groundwater dominated rivers. *Hydrological Processes* **13:** 255–277.

Shaw P., Langford T.E. & Arbuthnott A. 2000. Chalk stream restoration and ecology: a spatial study of a restored reach. British Ecological Society Conference Poster, Leeds 2000.

Shrestha P. & Janauer G.A. 2000. Species diversity of aquatic macrophytes in Lake Phewa and Lake Rupa of Pokhara Valley, Nepal. *Int. J. Ecology and Environm. Science* **26:** 269–280.

Sipos A. & Shields F.D. 1996. *River Channel Restoration.* Chichester: John Wiley & Sons.

Sipos V., Kohler A. & Björk S. 2000. Makrophytenvegetation und Standorte im eutrophen Björka Fluß (Südschweden). *Botanisches Jahrbuch Systematische* **122:** 93–152.

Sipos V.K. 2001. *Makrophytenvegetation und Standorte in eutrophen und humosen Fliessgewässern.* Dissertation, Institut für Landschafts- und Pflanzenökologie Universität Hohenheim, Stuttgart-Hohenheim. 180 pp.

Sipos V.K., Kohler A., Köder M. & Janauer G.A. 2003. Macrophytic vegetation of Danube canals in Kiskunság (Hungary). *Arch. Hydrobiol. Suppl.* **147/1–2:** 143–166; *Large Rivers* 14/1–2.

Sipos V.K., Kohler A. & Veit U. 2001. Vergleichende Kennzeichnung der Makrophytenvegetation verschiedener Fliessgewässertypen anhand quantitativer Kenngrössen. *Berichte: Institut für Landschafts- und Pflanzenökologie Universität Hohenheim* **10:** 33–56.

Spink A.J., Murphy K.J. & Westlake D.F. 1997. Distribution and environmental regulation of species of *Ranunculus* sub-genus *Batrachium* in British rivers. *Archivum Hydrobiologica* **139:** 509–525.

Summers D.W., Giles N. & Willis D.J. 1996. *Restoration of riverine trout habitats: a guidance manual.* Fisheries Technical Manual 1. Bristol: The Environment Agency.

Summers D.W., Shields B., Phillips D. & Giles N. 1997. *River Piddle Trout Study.* Draft Progress Report April 1997. Fordingbridge, Hampshire: The Game Conservancy Trust.

Trémolières M., Carbiener D., Carbiener R., Eglin I., Robach J., Sanches-Pérez M., Schnitzler A. & Weis D. 1991. Zones inondabbe, végétation et qualité de l'eau en milieu alluvial Rhonen: e'lle de Rhinan, un site de recherches integrées. *Bulletin Ecologique* **22:** 317–336.

Trémolières M., Carbiener R., Urtscheit A. & Klein J.P. (No Date). Changes in aquatic vegetation in Rhine flood plain in Alsace in relation to disturbance. *Journal of Vegetation Science* **5,** 169–178.

Trémolières M., Eglin I., Roec U. & Carbiener R. 1993. The exchange process between river and groundwater on the Central flood plain (Eastern France). I. *Hydrobiologia* **254:** 133–148.

Trémolières M., Roeck U., Klein J.P. & Carbiener R. 1994. The exchange process between river and groundwater on the Central Alsace flood plain (Eastern France). II. The case of a river with functional flood plain. *Hydrobiologia* **273:** 19–36.

Tremp H. & Kohler A. 1993. *Wassermoose als Versäuerungsindikatoren. Praxisorientierte Bioindikationsverfahren mit Wassermoosen zur Überwachung des Säurezustandes von pufferschwachen Fließgewässern.* Veröff. PAÖ, Band 6. Landesanstalt für Umweltschutz, Karlsruhe. 126 pp.

Tremp H. & Kohler A. 1995. The usefulness of macrophyte monitoring-systems, exemplified on eutrophication and acidification of running waters. *Acta Bot. Gallica* **142:** 541–550.

Triest L. 2002. Macrophytes as biological indicators of Belgian rivers: a comparison of macrophyte indices with those of other organisms in high quality headwaters. *Proceedings of the 11th EWRS International Symposium on Aquatic Weeds.* Moliêts et Maâ (France), September 2–6 2002. pp. 263–266.

Veit U. & Kohler A. 2003. Long-term study of the macrophytic vegetation in the running waters of the Friedberger Au (near Augsburg, Germany). *Large Rivers* 14/1–2; *Arch. Hydrobiol. Suppl.* **147/1–2:** 65–86.

Veit U., Zeltner G-H. & Kohler A. 1997. Die Makrophytenvegetation des Fließgewässersystems der Friedberger Au (bei Augsburg) — Ihre Entwicklung von 1972 bis 1996. *Ber. Inst. Landschafts- Pflanzenökologie* (Univ. Hohenheim) **4:** 7–241.

Ventura M. & Harper D. 1996. The impacts of acid precipitation mediated by geology and forestry upland stream invertebrate communities. *Archivum Hydrobiologia* **138:** 161–173.

Vymazal I., ed. 2001. *Transformation of nutrients in natural and constructed wetlands.* Leiden: Backhuys.

Vymazal I., Brix H., Cooper P.F., Green M.B. & Haberl R., eds. 1998. *Constructed wetlands for wastewater treatment in Europe.* Leiden: Backhuys.

Walker A.M. 1998. Audit Survey in the Environment Agency.

Ward D. 1991. Riverbanks and their bird communities. In:Hall M. & Smith M.A. *River bank conservation.* Hatfield Polytechnic. pp. 9–20.

Westlake D.F. & Dawson F.H. 1988. The effects of autumnal weed cuts in a lowland stream on water levels and flooding in the following springs. *Verhandlung Internationale Vereinigung für Theoretische und Angewandte Limnologie* **23:** 1273–1277.

Westlake D.F., Casey H., Dawson F.H., Ladle M., Mann R.H.K. & Marker A.F.R. 1972. The chalk-stream ecosystem. In: Kajak Z. & Hillbricht-Ilkowska A., eds. *Productivity problems of freshwaters Warsaw-Kracov.* Proc. International Biological Programme/ UNESCO Symposium, Kazimierz Dolny, Poland 1970. pp. 615–635.

Westlake D.F. & Dawson F.H. 1982. Thirty years of weed cutting on a chalk stream. *Proceedings of the 6th European Weed Research Council Symposium Aquatic Weeds.* pp. 132–140.

Westlake D.F. & Dawson F.H. 1986. The management of *Ranunculus calcareus* by pre-emptive cutting in southern England. *European Weed Research Society, Association of Applied Biologists, 7th International Symposium on Aquatic Weeds, September 1986.* pp. 395–400.

Whitton B.A. & Lucas M.C. 1997. Biology of the Humber rivers. *The science of the total environment* **194/5:** 247–262.

Wierzback R., Zeltner G-H. & Kohler A. 1998. Die Makrophytenvegetation des Fliessgewässersystems der Moosach (Münchener Ebene). Krefeld: Deutsche Gesellschaft für Limnologie (DGL) 1998. pp. 437–441.

Index

Index